Horrors of War

Horrors of War

The Undead on the Battlefield

EDITED BY
CYNTHIA J. MILLER
A. BOWDOIN VAN RIPER

ROWMAN & LITTLEFIELD
Lanham • Boulder • New York • London

Published by Rowman & Littlefield
A wholly owned subsidiary of The Rowman & Littlefield Publishing Group, Inc.
4501 Forbes Boulevard, Suite 200, Lanham, Maryland 20706
www.rowman.com

Unit A, Whitacre Mews, 26-34 Stannary Street, London SE11 4AB

British Library Cataloguing in Publication Information Available

Library of Congress Cataloging-in-Publication Data

Horrors of war : the undead on the battlefield / edited by Cynthia J. Miller, A. Bowdoin
Van Riper.
    pages cm
  Includes bibliographical references and index.
  ISBN 978-1-4422-5111-3 (hardback : alk. paper) — ISBN 978-1-4422-5112-0
(ebook) 1. War films—History and criticism. 2. Horror films—History and criticism. 3.
Supernatural in literature. 4. Horror tales—History and criticism. 5. War in literature. I.
Miller, Cynthia J., 1958- editor. II. Van Riper, A. Bowdoin editor.
  PN1995.9.W3H68 2015
  791.43'6581—dc23

                                                                    2015003812

∞™ The paper used in this publication meets the minimum requirements of American
National Standard for Information Sciences—Permanence of Paper
for Printed Library Materials, ANSI/NISO Z39.48-1992.

Printed in the United States of America

For our fathers, whose war stories were larger than life . . .
but not supernatural

Alfred D. Lombardi, Technician Fifth Grade
747th Engineer Base Equipment Company
1940–1945

Anthony K. Van Riper, Private First Class
Headquarters Company, Third Battalion,
Thirty-First Infantry Regiment
1944–1946

When you see millions of the mouthless dead
Across your dreams in pale battalions go,
Say not soft things as other men have said,
That you'll remember. For you need not so.

—Charles Sorley;
Killed October 13, 1915, in the Battle of Loos

Contents

Acknowledgments

Like most other projects, this volume owes a great debt to the many scholars who have come before, and whose work has inspired and informed the essays that appear here. We would like to extend a special "thank you" to military historian Dave W. Tschanz, who first suggested that, given our fondness for tales of the undead, the battlefield would be a wonderful place to . . . unearth . . . a few more. Our deepest thanks also go to Stephen Ryan for his continued trust in our work and support of this project. For their incredible generosity of spirit, we would also like to thank Sara Borden and the Historical Society of Pennsylvania, Paul Wilson, Graham Masterson, the National Museum of Fine Art in Kiev, Michael Cushman and the Southern Nationalist Network, Eric Reynolds at Fantagraphics, DC Comics, Devijavi at Deviant Art, and Carter Reid at The Zombie Nation, as well as Meghan Tillett and the Hatchette Book Group. Finally, to each of the individuals whose work appears on the pages that follow, thank you, one and all.

Introduction

Cynthia J. Miller and A. Bowdoin Van Riper

War is hell, so the saying goes, and battlefields are places where the spirits of the dead linger. Bodies litter the landscapes of military conflicts, as the cowardly and the courageous alike become casualties of its devastation. As opposing forces battle for control, vast numbers of souls are lost, and the boundary between the living and the dead seems to erode, as those killed in war pass violently, quickly, and in great numbers from one world to the next. This proximity to death makes the battlefield a site of myth, lore, and superstition, and unseen forces are often blamed for misfortune, as well as credited for triumph. When the planes of Britain's Royal Air Force were plagued by unexplained mechanical problems, mysterious "gremlins" were blamed for wreaking havoc, and soon, the myth of the destructive supernatural beings had spread across all branches of the military among the Allied nations.[1]

Soldiers, pilots, and sailors throughout history have often created talismans to intercede with fate. "The more dangerous the job," reports Marine First Sergeant Vic Martin, "the more superstitious."[2] Silver dollars, mismatched socks and shoes, and other common personal items have all been used as conduits for good luck: Snipers stationed in Iraq wear amulets of 7.62 mm slugs around their necks as protection against the bullet that will bring about their own death; ground troops in both world wars often carried Bibles "tucked or pinned over the portion of a uniform covering the soldier's heart" to fend off bullets;[3] and contrary to their usual association, black cats were popular during World War I as symbols of good luck. In a particularly convincing case, pilot Edwin Parsons wired a stuffed black cat to the struts of his plane, and refused to fly without it. His belief in its protective power was borne out when he discovered it "bleeding" sawdust one day after taking a bullet that would have killed him.[4]

In a similar fashion, supernatural language and imagery—both sacred and secular—pervades modern depictions of warfare, but it is popular culture that

Diffy Dan, a wartime gremlin blamed for all manner of engine trouble, from fouling motor oil and filing down gear teeth to sabotaging transmissions and differentials (from which he gets his name). *Courtesy of the Historical Society of Pennsylvania's Propaganda Collection.*

routinely makes these metaphors concrete. Supernatural tales of war told in print, on screen, and in other media depict angels, demons, and legions of the undead fighting against—or alongside—human soldiers on the field of battle. Ghostly warships and phantom aircraft carry on their never-to-be-completed missions, and horrors deadlier than any bullet or bomb linger in the dark corners of abandoned fortifications. The spirits, and sometimes the corpses, of dead soldiers return to confront the enemies who killed them, the comrades who betrayed them, or the leaders who sacrificed them without reason. These tales endow the business of war with a mystery and foreboding unlike any other.

This volume explores the deeper significance of such stories: The ways in which they reflect, and often challenge, the popular memory of particular wars, and engage with cultural attitudes toward war in general, as well as with the tensions involved in wartime themes such as battlefield heroism, military ethics, and the politics of sacrifice. In each of these tales, the dead are invoked to both challenge and reinforce the belief systems of the living. The undead do not, however, challenge the morality of war itself, but rather, they illustrate that there are no "good" or "bad" wars—just the values, morals, and ethics of the men and women who fight them. In this way, the undead of war shine a spotlight on questions about the nature of humanity, both in wartime and beyond.

The Undead Battlefield before World War II

The lines that divide the living from the dead and the familiar from the uncanny—sharp and bright in peacetime—are blurred on the battlefield. Armor and helmets, war paint and battle cries, give ordinary men the appearance of monsters. Casualties of battle—armless, legless, blinded, insane—exist in a horrific no-man's-land, beyond saving but still capable of thought and feeling and speech. It is no surprise, then, that the fictional warriors of myth, legend, and story have, from time to time, encountered even greater horrors: monsters, witches, and the undead.

Battle as Homer described it in the *Iliad*—a collection of face-to-face duels between individual warriors—was already obsolete when the Greek and Persian armies clashed at Marathon in 490 BC. For the next two thousand years, however, tales of battlefield heroism continued to emphasize the feats of individual warriors, and established their larger-than-life qualities by describing their battles with undead or inhuman foes. Beowulf may be famous for defeating the Swedes, or King Arthur for holding back the Saxons, but their victories over monsters make them legends. It took the spread of firearms across European battlefields— begun in the mid-1400s and complete by the early 1700s—before the focus of war stories shifted from the individual warrior to the close-knit unit: *Henry V*'s "band of brothers" and its successors. Firearms also made battlefields larger and casualty lists longer. At Saratoga and Waterloo, Gettysburg and Verdun, thousands were cut down by enemies whose faces they never saw. A million men were killed and wounded, mostly by machine guns and long-range artillery, in the 141-day Battle of the Somme in 1916, a hundred-thousand on the first day alone.

The role of the undead in war stories evolved along with the battlefield. Monstrous opponents encountered in the midst of battle gave way to the restless ghosts of the dead, still roaming the battlefield days, months, or even years after their demise, searching for resolution to the unfinished business of their lives. Frequently, their mission is personal. The Headless Horseman of "The Legend of Sleepy Hollow" is the ghost of a Hessian mercenary, still searching for the head that he lost to a cannonball in "some nameless battle of the revolutionary war" more than a decade earlier.[5] The "Woman in White" glimpsed, at night, by visitors to the Civil War battlefield at Chickamauga is said to be seeking a dead loved one among the hundreds of soldiers who were buried, without markers, where they fell.[6] World War I, however, brought a flurry of stories about the undead deliberately reaching out to shape the affairs of those still living.

The earliest, "The Bowmen," written by Welsh fantasist Arthur Machen for the *London Evening News*, was a straightforward patriotic adventure story. In it, hard-pressed British soldiers facing overwhelming German attacks call on the spirit of St. George, and are saved by a contingent of ghostly archers who appear out of nowhere and rain destruction on the advancing enemy with their long-bows.[7] Later examples, however, have the dead return not to help the living, but to reproach them. In "Common Form," a couplet in Rudyard Kipling's poem-cycle "Epitaphs of the War," Britain's dead soldiers collectively reproach their fathers for the lies that led them, innocent and trusting, to their deaths. The next poem in the cycle imagines a newly dead politician, fearful that the glib tongue that served him in life will not appease the dead soldiers he calls "my angry and defrauded young."[8] Both Abel Gance's silent 1919 film *J'accuse* (remade as a sound film in 1938) and Irwin Shaw's 1936 play *Bury the Dead* imagine soldiers rising from their graves to call the living to account.

Kipling and Gance looked backward to the war that had just ended, Shaw (and Gance in his remake) forward to the next war, the coming of which seemed only a matter of time. War did come—to Asia in 1937, Europe in 1939, and America in 1941—and by the time peace returned in 1945, the role of the undead in war stories had, once again, been transformed. New weapons, new tactics, and new levels of savagery produced mass casualties on an unprecedented scale. The victims of earlier wars had died by the thousands, but the victims of World War II died by tens of thousands in concentration camps, bombed-out cities, and the irradiated wreckage of Hiroshima.[9] The war's technological legacy—atomic bombs and ballistic missiles, napalm and nerve gas—promised that wars-yet-to-come would be incalculably worse, and postwar revelations of experimentation on human subjects underscored the horrific lengths to which warring nations would go in pursuit of victory.[10]

The horrors of World War II and the simmering anxieties of the postwar era led, after 1945, to a new wave of war stories laced with elements of the fantastic, and populated by the undead. Figures familiar from older fictional battle-fields—singular, monstrous enemies and the ghosts of dead soldiers—mingled with undead legions enlisted by nations desperate for victory, the undead victims of horrific high-tech weapons, and no-longer-human soldiers transformed by wartime "mad science." Given sustained life by the fresh horrors emerging from the "small wars" of the post-1945 era, they continue to haunt the battlefields of our imagination.

Total War and Disillusionment

With the onset of World War II, military conflict became increasingly complex. The war, which, like World War I, had begun as a localized war between op-posing countries, spread to distant parts of the world, requiring vast amounts of resources. Entire national economies were directed toward war efforts, and civil-ians were both mobilized in war production and targeted by military strategies, introducing the notion of "total war." The scope of World War II, in particular, resulted in a level of destruction and devastation previously unknown. Civilians and military personnel died by the millions, as cities and towns were bombed, concentration camps were implemented, and disease and starvation ran rampant.

Changes in the structure, hardware, equipment, and strategic use of armed forces—unprecedented in both scope and significance—heightened the apoca-lyptic feel of the conflict. Mass-produced motor vehicles now made it possible to create fully motorized land units, and by the end of the 1930s, technical progress in the automotive industry enabled the production of a new generation of tanks that not only provided fire support for motorized infantry but also became a means of breaking through enemy defenses. Warfare at sea and in the air benefit-ted from similarly dramatic leaps forward in technologies and abilities: Aircraft carriers eclipsed battleships on the high seas, submarine blockades drove island nations to the brink of defeat, and long-range Air Force bombers obliterated industrial and civilian targets deep inside enemy territory.[11]

The beginning of World War II coincided with the appearance of early radar, which dramatically extended the horizon of combat. Meanwhile, the de-velopment of radio engineering led to the emergence of weapons that previously could only have been considered science fiction. Ballistic missiles (along with experimental samples of antiaircraft, anti-ship, and antitank missiles), guided torpedoes, and unmanned aircraft, as well as unmanned ground machines, ef-fectively the forerunners of modern robots, depersonalized killing and made possible the long-distance annihilation of the enemy. As the war ended, nuclear weapons introduced an apocalyptic dimension to "total war" that dramatically changed humankind's attitude to war and peace. Anxiety over military science gone awry in the hands of the military-industrial complex spilled over into popular culture narratives.[12] The word "blockbuster" had been coined, during the war, to describe a two-ton bomb said to be capable of wiping out an entire city block; the hydrogen bombs of the 1950s, designed to explode with the force of several *million* tons of TNT, were called, by analogy, "city-busters." Critics of the hydrogen bomb—including many of those who had worked on the Hiroshima and Nagasaki bombs—argued its use would be tantamount to genocide. Europe had been stunned, in 1916, when the Battle of the Somme had killed and wounded a million men over four months' time. Forty years later, a single weapon could do the same in the blink of an eye.

The multiple millions of casualties that the (implicitly nuclear) "next war" would generate were left discreetly offstage in the novels, films, and speculative articles about it that began to appear as early as 1946. The brutal details were readily available elsewhere, however: woven between the lines of civil defense literature, and stated openly in books like John Hersey's *Hiroshima* (1946). Those caught by a nuclear blast, but too far from "ground zero" to die instantly, would (like the survivors of Hiroshima and Nagasaki) find their bodies grotesquely transformed: faces lacerated by flying glass, exposed skin charred by the fireball, and eyes seared blind by a flash "brighter than a thousand suns." Many who survived the injuries inflicted by heat and blast would, in weeks or months or years, succumb to the insidious effects of radiation poisoning. The Bomb—as the science-fiction films of the Cold War obliquely hinted—would not simply kill: It would render the survivors grotesque, even monstrous. The dread created by that knowledge underlay Nikita Khrushchev's grim observation that, in the next war, the living would envy the dead.

Growing anxieties about technology were matched, in the post-1945 era, by growing disillusionment with war as an instrument of policy and the causes for which they were waged. Ever-expanding nuclear arsenals deterred the great powers from waging war directly with one another, but the superpowers engaged in a seemingly endless string of ideologically driven proxy wars in Asia, Africa, the Middle East, and Latin America, while Europe's fading colonial powers waded into protracted struggles with rebel groups seeking independence. Fought with brutally excessive force, in support of often corrupt regimes, and for politically suspect reasons, the "small wars" of the Cold War and post–Cold War eras lacked the moral clarity of the World Wars that preceded them. They generated deep political divisions and ferocious domestic opposition, tarnished national reputations, and provided a stage for acts that—to many onlookers—would have been labeled war crimes had they been committed by the losing side.

The blanket of idealism and nobility that had been draped over memories of earlier wars was also growing noticeably frayed and tattered as the twentieth century drew to a close. The genteel "consensus history" of the Civil War that had coalesced in the 1910s and remained dominant through the 1960s was challenged in the 1970s by a new generation of historians who argued that slavery—and thus race—was the war's defining theme. In the 1980s, American interventions in the Caribbean and the toppling of the Marcos regime in the Philippines brought new (and unflattering) attention to the "splendid little" Spanish-American War of 1898. Even World War II—styled "the Good War" in a best-selling collection of oral histories—lost some of its luster. New historical investigations, aided by the declassification of wartime records, revealed that ignorance, selfishness, prejudice, and brutality had been as much a part of World War II as they had been of wars before and since.

The ever-darker, ever-grimmer climate of opinion that surrounded the wars of the late twentieth century has continued to cling to the wars of the early twenty-first. It is perhaps no surprise, then, that the undead—who began to emerge in force on imaginary battlefields after 1950—have only grown in numbers, diversity, and tenacity as the new millennium has begun.

A Diversity of Horrors

The undead routinely appear, in folklore and legend, as enemies of the living, and the opening section of the volume, "Monstrous Enemies," looks at tales in which this conflict erupts into open warfare. The first two essays in the section focus on carefully crafted alternate histories, in which vampires are unseen agents of military devastation. In "'Blood-Thirsty Graybacks': The Monstrous Othering of the Confederacy in *Abraham Lincoln, Vampire Hunter*," Robert A. Saunders offers a geopolitical analysis of Seth Grahame-Smith's historical thriller, which turns on the notion that vampires not only plotted the demise of the Union, but also functioned as wartime spies, assassins, and combatants, nearly winning the Civil War for the Confederacy. Saunders contends that, by providing a supernatural overlay to what is arguably the most seminal and controversial event in American history, the Civil War, Grahame-Smith engages in the (literal) demonization of the Confederacy (1861–1865) and, by extension, the whole of the antebellum South.

Similarly, in "Cry 'Havoc!' and Let Slip the Vampires of War," Cynthia J. Miller examines Jasper Kent's novel *Twelve*, a sprawling epic that chronicles the supernatural forces responsible for turning the tide of battle during Napoleon's invasion of Russia in the Patriotic War of 1812. Drawing on figures from Russian history, such as Cossack marauders and Ivan the Terrible's Oprichniki, as well as the Slavic vampire tradition, Miller explores the ways in which Kent weaves together the monstrous of history, myth, and legend to create an undead menace in *Twelve* that draws on horrors and heroes that have persisted for centuries.

In the section's next essay, "Vampire Pilots and Industrialized War in *The Bloody Red Baron*," A. Bowdoin Van Riper looks at another form of alternate history, written into being by author Kim Newman, in which traditional warfare collides with the supernatural, resulting in an alliance between Dracula and German mad science that yields an almost invincible force of World War I fighter pilots led by Manfred von Richthofen, the legendary "Red Baron." Through a close analysis of Newman's work, Van Riper illustrates the ways in which the undead lend new meaning to the notion of "total warfare," as the novel's hellish vampire pilots demythologize the Great War's "knights of the air."

The association between Germany and the supernatural continues in James J. Ward's essay "Nazis on the Moon! Nazis under the Polar Ice Cap! And Other Recent Episodes in the Strange Cinematic Afterlife of the Third Reich." Ward's analysis illustrates that the theme of supernatural Nazi horror continues its cultural usefulness long after the end of World War II. His essay carefully examines the persistence of our cultural fascination with Nazi horror, considering the latest in a long trajectory of films that combine historical evidence of the Third Reich's involvement with the arcane and the occult, and staples of exploitation cinema such as zombies, robots, and hybrid beings.

The volume's next section, "The Dead Don't Rest," features essays focused on the continued presence of the wartime undead, as they haunt the living in search of retribution, reconciliation, and remembrance. In the section's opening essay, "The Wages of War: Spectral Children in *The Devil's Backbone*," Michael C. Reiff considers the ways in which Guillermo del Toro's film examines the history of the Spanish Civil War through its use of spectral characters and objects, as well as the ways in which the living both search for and deny violent and difficult truths during wartime. Reiff uses hauntological readings to explore the complexities of the characters' interactions with the specters in their midst, and considers how, by mixing the war and horror genres, the film sheds light on the historical and ontological issues that a seventy-five-year-old war continues to raise today.

The essay that follows, "Traversing the Afterlife Fantasy: The Haunted Soldier in *Jacob's Ladder*," Thomas Robert Argiro considers another sort of tortured haunting: that experienced by American servicemen in Vietnam who were the unwitting subjects of a covert US Army drug experiment. The drug—a powerful psychoactive agent known as "the Ladder"—leads to terrifying visions of demonic persecution that comment on not only the atrocities of chemical warfare during the Vietnam era, but also the horrors of war, more generally. Argiro argues that the film uses the supernatural to speak not only to the myths of war, but to the fact that we all inhabit a political reality in which the true nature of events is camouflaged by hidden forces without any ethical imperative.

The relationship of the undead to the myths and realities of war is also central to the next essay in the section, "The Haunted Tank," by Paul O'Connor.

O'Connor takes readers on a journey through three decades of DC Comics' series featuring a World War II tank guided by the spirit of a legendary Confederate cavalry general, who acts as a protector and mentor to its crew. O'Connor notes that here the war serves as a crucible where the spirit and courage of men are tested on the field of battle, and destinies are fulfilled with the help of supernatural agency. The tank, its crew, and their ghostly champion thus perpetuate the mid-century myth of the good soldier that is so sharply dispelled in later war narratives such as *Jacob's Ladder*.

In the essay that follows, "(Re)Remembering the Great War in *Deathwatch*," Marzena Sokołowska-Paryż considers Michael J. Bassett's film as a product of cultural memory, weaving together the themes, icons, and legends of World War I in a tale of undead horror. The film's labyrinthine trenches not only house the bodies of the dead, but their suffering and fears, as well—states that reach out from the earth to envelop the living—blurring the lines between absence and presence, life and death. In *Deathwatch*, Sokołowska-Paryż argues, it is the undead whose presence speaks of what it truly means to be a soldier.

The final essay of this section, "The U.N.dead: Cold War Ghosts in *Carol for Another Christmas*" by Christina M. Knopf, examines Rod Serling's apocalyptic twist on Charles Dickens's Christmas tale of supernatural visitation and transformation. *Carol for Another Christmas* presents a Victorian ghost story for the Atomic Age, placing themes of Cold War science fiction and atomic-bomb cinema into a Gothic package appropriate to post–World War II fantasy films and wrapping them in holiday trappings. Here, ghostly visitors to Daniel Grudge bring with them memories and projections of the horrors of war—past, present, and future—as impetus for reflection on dominant Cold War narratives.

Warring nations unleash monstrous weapons into the world, and—all too often—wars bring out the monstrous in those who wage them. The next group of essays, "Making Monsters," explores a diversity of such monsters, beginning with Christopher D. Stone's "Pall in the Family: *Deathdream*, *House*, and the Vietnam War." Both films in this paired reading use the presence of the undead among the living to explore the lingering effects of the Vietnam War on American society, but they form virtual mirror images of one another. *Deathdream* tells the story of a family haunted by the specter of the son they lost in Vietnam, while *House* focuses on a veteran forced to confront his war experiences when a long-dead comrade returns from the grave and kidnaps his young son. Despite their limited viewership and B-movie trappings, Stone argues, they were significant early steps in Hollywood's grappling with Vietnam.

Fernando Gabriel Pagnoni Berns's essay "Strategic Military Reconfiguration in Horror Fiction: The Case of F. Paul Wilson's *The Keep* and Graham Masterton's *The Devils of D-Day*" takes up a very different pair of mirror-image texts and a very different kind of monster. Both novels concern ancient beings of great power let loose amid the chaos of World War II. Noting the military habit of using language to impose order, and thus control, on their wartime surroundings, Pagnoni Berns considers how such efforts fare when armies confront forces beyond human understanding.

The monsters in Christina V. Cedillo's "Horror under the Radar: Memory, Revelation, and the Ghosts of *Below*" are all too human: submariners who turn a tragic error into an outright atrocity and resort to mutiny and murder in order to conceal it. Their descent into evil unfolds amid a series of uncanny, inexplicable events that may (or may not) be one of their victims, seeking justice from beyond the grave. Cedillo situates the film in the context of Americans' evolving historical memory of World War II, treating the film both as a modern ghost story and as a meditation on the ways that societies at war amplify the crimes of their enemies while systematically eliding their own.

Concluding the section, Steve Webley's "The Supernatural, Nazi Zombies, and the Play Instinct: The Gamification of War and the Reality of the Military Industrial Complex" examines the most popular of all war-spawned monsters. Weaving together the work of theorists from Carl von Clausewitz to Jacques Lacan, the reinvention (and politicization) of the zombie by George Romero, and the parallel rises of the military industrial complex and the computer gaming industry, Webley contends that our fascination with Nazi zombies is the most recent expression of an intertwining of war and play as old as human civilization. "Playing Nazi zombies" in immersive "first-person shooter" simulations like *Call of Duty* allows us to enter a space where multiple needs (not served by mainstream culture) can be met at once.

Wars do not end when the shooting stops; their effects—on individual lives and societies—persist for years, and memories linger for generations. The final group of essays, "Legacies and Memories," examines tales in which the echoes of war become entwined with the supernatural. It begins with "'Strange Things Happen in a War-Torn Land': Cat Demons, Samurai, Victims' Vengeance, and the Social Costs of War in Kaneto Shindo's *Kuroneko* (1968)," Thomas Prasch's exploration of a film about rape, murder, and demonic revenge set in medieval Japan and deeply rooted in Japanese culture. Prasch shows how Shindo interweaves the conventions of the cinema with those of Kabuki and Noh theater, and incorporates elements of both classical literary texts and traditional folktales. Consistent with its director's interest in the lives of ordinary people, the film takes a grim view of an era (and a war) usually wrapped in the warm glow of legend.

No such glow attaches itself to World War I, a conflict whose grim reputation—formed while it was still in progress—persists, undimmed, a century later. Jacques Tardi has, for two decades, depicted the war in a series of meticulously researched graphic novels, and *It Was the War of the Trenches*—among the most audacious—is the subject of Katherine Kelp-Stebbins's "Specters of Media:

Jacques Tardi's Graphic Reanimation of the *War of the Trenches*." Tardi's *War* combines the stories of twenty different soldiers into a complex narrative of shifting viewpoints and overlapping plots, and Kelp-Stebbins examines it using a similarly multilayered strategy, simultaneously employing diegetic, iconologic, and media-specific perspectives to show how Tardi conveys war's blurring of the line between life and death.

A wide gulf seems to separate Tardi's dense, complex work and the straight-forward adventure narratives of *Weird War Tales*, but—as Terence Check's essay shows—the latter was conceived by its creators as an attempt to bring a new sense of depth and seriousness to a storytelling medium (war comics) not known for either. In "Public Memory and Supernatural Presence: The Mystery and Madness of *Weird War Tales*," Check argues that the short-lived title failed to fulfill these ambitions. Its fables of ghostly intervention on the battlefields of (mostly) World War II reinforced, rather than challenged, the dominant narratives of American heroism and moral uprightness, even as the Vietnam War and its aftermath undermined them.

Rod Serling's television anthology series *The Twilight Zone* addressed war only occasionally in its five-year run, but the episodes that did so were shaped by his war experiences. Vincent Casaregola's essay "War in *The Twilight Zone*: Rod Serling's Haunted Visions of World War II" explores the unexpected ways in which Serling's deep awareness of the horrors of war—formed as a US Army paratrooper in the Philippines and as a Jewish American appalled by the institutionalized racism of the Nazis—shaped episodes set in wartime, but also those, such as "I Am the Night—Color Me Black," that attacked prejudice and intolerance in the postwar world.

Amanda Landa's "*R-Point* as Postcolonial Palimpsest: Generic Complexity and the Ghost in the War/Horror Film" rounds out the section, and the book, with a close reading of a Korean horror film about eight soldiers trapped in a haunted landscape bloodied by centuries of colonial and wartime violence. Peeling back *R-Point*'s layered meanings, the essay touches on multiple themes that range far beyond its Vietnam War setting: the bleeding of the wartime past into the present; spirits of the dead as agents of truth and justice; and the realization that not all wartime monsters unleashed by war are undead . . . or even un-human.

Notes

1. Hutto, "Ghosts in the Machines."
2. Phillips, "Superstitions Abound."
3. Watts, *Encyclopedia of American Folklore*, 419.

4. Wilkins, "Luck and Death."

5. Irving, *Rip Van Winkle and The Legend of Sleepy Hollow*, 111.

6. Nesbitt, *Civil War Ghost Trails*, 119–20.

7. McCreevy, "Irishman Who Was the 'Angel of Mons.'"

8. Kipling, "Common Form" and "A Dead Statesman."

9. On the convergence of these factors, see, for example: Dower, *War without Mercy* and Markusen, *Holocaust and Strategic Bombing*.

10. Spitz, *Doctors from Hell* is a harrowing firsthand account based on evidence from the Nuremberg war-crimes trials.

11. O'Connell, *Arms and Men*, 244–310.

12. See Boyer, *By the Bomb's Early Light* for the immediate postwar period, and Winkler, *Life under a Cloud* for the longer view.

Bibliography

Boyer, Paul. *By the Bomb's Early Light: American Thought and Culture at the Dawn of the Atomic Age.* New York: Pantheon, 1985.

Dower, John W. *War without Mercy: Race and Power in the Pacific War.* New York: Pantheon, 1986.

Hutto, Cary. "Ghosts in the Machines." *Fondly, Pennsylvania* [Pennsylvania Historical Society], June 24, 2011. https://hsp.org/blogs/fondly-pennsylvania/ghosts-in-the-machines.

Irving, Washington. *Rip Van Winkle and The Legend of Sleepy Hollow.* London: Macmillan, 1893.

Kipling, Rudyard. "Common Form" and "A Dead Statesman." In *Rudyard Kipling's Verse: Definitive Edition*, 384. Garden City, NY: Doubleday, 1940.

Markusen, Eric. *The Holocaust and Strategic Bombing: Genocide and Total War in the Twentieth Century.* Boulder, CO: Westview Press, 1995.

McCreevy, Ronan. "The Irishman Who Was the 'Angel of Mons.'" *Irish Times*, October 22, 2014. http://www.irishtimes.com/culture/heritage/irishman-who-was-angel-of-mons-1.1950837.

Nesbitt, Mark. *Civil War Ghost Trails: Stories from America's Most Haunted Battlefields.* Mechanicsburg, PA: Stackpole Books, 2004.

O'Connell, Robert L. *Of Arms and Men: A History of War, Weapons, and Aggression.* New York: Oxford University Press, 1990.

Phillips, Michael M. "Superstitions Abound at Camp as Soldiers Await War in Iraq." *Wall Street Journal*, March 3, 2003.

Spitz, Vivien. *Doctors from Hell: The Horrific Account of Nazi Experiments on Humans.* Boulder, CO: Sentient Publications, 2005.

Watts, Linda. *Encyclopedia of American Folklore.* New York: Facts On File, 2007.

Wilkins, Mark. "Luck and Death: WWI Pilots and their Superstitions." *Air & Space*, March 20, 2014. http://www.airspacemag.com/multimedia/luck-and-death-wwi-pilots-and-their-superstitions-180950158/.

Winkler, Allan M. *Life under a Cloud: American Anxiety about the Atom.* New York: Oxford University Press, 1993.

Part I

MONSTROUS ENEMIES

CHAPTER 1

"Blood-Thirsty Graybacks"

THE MONSTROUS OTHERING
OF THE CONFEDERACY IN
ABRAHAM LINCOLN, VAMPIRE HUNTER

Robert A. Saunders

In the opening passage of *This Republic of Suffering: Death and the American Civil War*, Drew Gilpin Faust writes, "Mortality defines the human condition. . . . Even though 'we all have our dead,' and though we all die, we do so differently from generation to generation and from place to place."[1] This historical truism is both reaffirmed and radically reimagined in Seth Grahame-Smith's "mashup" historical thriller *Abraham Lincoln, Vampire Hunter* (2010) and its 2012 film adaptation, *Abraham Lincoln: Vampire Hunter*, directed by Timur Bekmambetov.[2] In this narrative, not only do we have our Civil War *dead*, but we also have our *undead*. Grahame-Smith's fantastical retelling of the life of the United States' sixteenth president instructs us that a nefarious cabal of European vampires lurks in the shadows of our history, and that these blood-drinking wraiths were behind the secession of the Southern states. These monsters not only plotted the demise of the Union, but also functioned as wartime spies, assassins, and unearthly combatants on the battlefields of Manassas, Antietam, and Cold Harbor, nearly winning the Civil War for the Confederacy.

In keeping with the theme of this volume, the primary focus of this close reading of *Abraham Lincoln, Vampire Hunter* (hereafter *ALVH*) is on the depictions of Confederate soldiers as (or aided by) blood-sucking vampires; however, other "horrific" aspects of war will also be explored, including psychological operations, assassinations, and torture. My argument is that by providing a supernatural overlay to what is arguably the most seminal and controversial event in American history, the Civil War, Grahame-Smith (who also penned the screenplay of the film) engages in an "othering" of the American Confederacy (1861–1865)—and by extension, the whole of the antebellum South—as monstrous. My analysis is rooted in popular geopolitics,[3] drawing on certain lenses employed in international-relations approaches to popular culture (though these are, by necessity, retooled for use in a domestic framework). Through the spatial distancing of the Deep South and the social construction of the Rebels as willing (the elites) and witless (the masses) allies of iniquitous, "Old World" vampires bent on enslaving the entirety of the Americas, I contend that Grahame-Smith's revisionist narrative reiterates and extends key stereotypes about the American South, while simultaneously injecting the (radical) idea of demonic assistance to the "blood-thirsty graybacks."[4]

This chapter begins with a synopsis of *ALVH*, focusing on the vampire-Confederate alliance and the "horrors of war" mentioned above. In the subsequent section, I interrogate the jaundiced geographical depictions of the South and its citizenry in both narrative and visual forms, contextualizing Grahame-Smith and Bekmambetov's othering of the "Rebs" as monsters within the larger historical phenomenon of "hostile imagination" (i.e., dehumanization of the enemy[5]), and the construction of "essentialized geographical identities."[6] In the third part of the essay, I critically assess the contemporary political grounding and popular reception of this work of fiction in a country rived by a regionally sensitive "culture war," including the role of the movie in promoting the Lincoln-Obama parallel in popular culture and its denunciation by self-declared "Southern nationalists." The primary purpose of this essay is to investigate the role of horror as a tool for reframing historical events and providing "meaning"[7] in (monster) narratives associated with the national memory. Secondarily, I hope to shed light on the impact such historical "mashups" have on the cultural identity and political orientations of their readers/viewers.

Abraham Lincoln, Vampire Hunter: A Synopsis

Seemingly written in response to historian W. Scott Poole's claim that "secrets and lies" in American history create "dark places waiting to be explored,"[8] *Abraham Lincoln, Vampire Hunter* begins with a seemingly impossible fact: "For over 250 years, between 1607 and 1865, vampires thrived in the shadows of America. Few humans believed in them."[9] The ensuing narrative revolves around the "ridiculous genre conceit"[10] that the most popular president in American history secretly waged a war against these parasitic ghouls, who—not insignificantly—formed the bulwark of politico-economic support for the United States' "peculiar institution," slavery. Following a life spent in constant struggle with vampires, Lincoln finally purges their allies from the US government and defeats this undead scourge on the battlefield, thus making the American republic a nation safe for the living (white and black alike). Though in the final pages, he loses his life to an undead assassin, John Wilkes Booth, before being turned into a vampire himself.[11]

The novel begins in contemporary Rhinebeck, New York, where the author (a failed novelist who mans the local five-and-dime) meets a rather enigmatic customer, Henry, who we learn is a "good" vampire that trained a young Abraham Lincoln in the art of dispatching the undead. Henry passes on the president's secret diaries, which introduce the reader to an outlandish revisionist history of nineteenth-century America. As a number of reviews of the book have pointed out, the notion that Honest Abe was, in his spare time, a ruthless slayer of bloodsucking monsters lies in his iconic frontiersman status: "A giant among men—he was 6 ft. 4 in. tall—Lincoln adopts the ax, that most American of edged weapons, as the tool of his trade, hiding it inside his signature long black coat."[12] Going far beyond these idiosyncrasies, Grahame-Smith proves adept at folding elements of Lincoln's well-known hagiography into this tale of preternatural intrigue, thus reaffirming historian Eric Foner's claim that Lincoln remains "infinitely malleable" in the American national consciousness.[13] Building on Lincoln's already tragic biography, we discover that vampires took the lives of his grandfather, mother, fiancée Ann Rutledge, close friend Edgar Allan Poe, and finally his son Willy—the latter being a calculated act meant to distract the wartime president from his duties as commander in chief.

This chronological "hidden history of vampires in America," beginning with Abe's early life on the American frontier, is the frontline of an invisible war for the soul of the United States. Protected from scrutiny by the deadly nature of life at the edge of civilization, vampires prey on the living, easily covering their tracks under the guise of "Indian attacks" and "outbreaks of disease" (not insignificantly, the Old World vampires were simultaneously fleeing "persecution" in Europe following the disclosure of the vampirism of the "Blood Countess," Elizabeth Báthory [1560–1614]). Most importantly for the undead is America's territorial expanse, its lawlessness, and its slaves: "For here, unlike any other country fit for civilized men—here was a place they could feed on the intoxicating blood of man without the fear of reprisal."[14] Sensing the boon that a "free" republic in the New World would bring, vampires took to the battlefields of Lexington, Concord, and Fort Ticonderoga, while undead diplomats in the court of Louis XVI successfully lobbied for French support for the fledgling republic. Through a series of events, Lincoln learns just how tightly linked the institution of slavery and vampirism truly are in the New World, particularly when he witnesses a slave auction where the most enthusiastic bidders are seeking sustenance not labor. Once Lincoln grasps the enormity of the situation before him, he undertakes a campaign to "kill every vampire in America,"[15] though due to the logistical difficulties of travel at the time, he must content himself with slaughtering those residing in the Mississippi basin. At the urging of his tutor, Henry, Lincoln eventually realizes the shrewdness of his enemy, who has made common cause with the South, and he decides that to prevent the

Benjamin Walker as an ax-wielding Abe Lincoln. *Courtesy of Photofest/ Twentieth Century Fox.*

ultimate enslavement of every (living) man, woman, and child in the Americas, he must "put away the ax and pick up the pen" to defeat the undead who have "infiltrated" the American republic.[16]

The narrative quickly shifts to the political arena, specifically the storied debates between Lincoln and his Democratic rival Stephen A. Douglas (a shill for Southern vampires, though later in life he will repudiate his alliance with the undead). Working with living (future secretary of state William Seward) and undead (Henry and a trio of vampire bodyguards) allies, Lincoln mounts a successful run for the presidency in 1860, triggering the secession of the Southern states. But shortly before the election, Lincoln travels down to Mississippi on an errand: killing that most powerful of vampire allies, Jefferson Davis. Although the mission ultimately proves a failure, the sortie into "enemy territory" provides an opportunity for an interesting tête-à-tête between the two future heads of state and wartime adversaries. Davis extols the "natural order of things"[17]—superiority of the vampire over man (and the white race over the black)—while Lincoln tries to convince his fellow Kentuckian of the perils of (undead) tyranny. Unlike the gullible Douglas, we learn, the future president of the Confederacy is fully cognizant of the scale and scope of the European vampires' dark plans for the New World, and seeks to stay his own extinction by serving as their minion. (When Lincoln finally discloses the true nature of the Confederacy to his cabinet, he describes Jefferson Davis and his ilk as "pilot fish—cleaning the teeth of sharks to avoid being themselves bitten.")[18]

As president, Lincoln is forced to contend with a secessionist South and a camarilla of vampires who seek to destroy him at every turn, even making an attempt on his life before he can assume office. However, it is on the field of battle that vampires truly make their mark. The Confederate Army that arrives at Bull Run is peppered with the undead. In the words of one soldier:

> Even from a distance, I could see their strange, wild eyes. There was not a rifle, or a pistol, or a sword among them. . . . I mean to say that that these rebels—these thirty unarmed men—tore one hundred men to pieces with nothing more than their bare hands. I saw arms pulled off. Heads twisted backwards. I saw blood pour from the throats and bellies of men gutted by mere fingertips; a boy grasping at the holes where his eyes were a moment before.[19]

Eerily echoing Jefferson Davis's social Darwinist arguments, the defeated Union commander Irvin McDowell laments, "We brought the superior army, but it seems they brought the superior men."[20] As the war progresses, man's inhumanity toward man takes on a preternatural sheen. Intelligence reports delivered to Seward relate grisly scenes wherein Confederates hand over Union prisoners to Southern vampires for the purpose of torture and execution. These men are suspended upside down between trees as ghouls saw through their bodies and drink the blood before it hits the ground: "Because the prisoner's head is nearest the ground, his brain remains nourished, and he remains conscious until the blade tears slowly back and forth across his stomach, then chest. The other prisoners are made to watch this before being made to suffer it themselves."[21] Ultimately, Lincoln makes the fateful decision to "starve" out

Emancipated slaves turning on their vampire masters. *Courtesy of Grand Central Publishing/Abraham Lincoln: Vampire Hunter by Seth Grahame-Smith. Copyright © 2010 by Seth Grahame-Smith. All rights reserved.*

his undead nemeses by issuing the Emancipation Proclamation on New Year's Day, 1863. In declaring every slave south of the Mason-Dixon Line free, the backwoods lawyer turned chief executive and commander in chief denies his vampire enemies the fuel they need to sustain their existential threat to the American republic. In a purported woodcut from the period that appears in the text, former slaves take up arms against their "vampire captors," beheading their undead masters. In the wake of the announcement, the "ghost soldiers" of earlier battles grow scarce as they are forced to scavenge for the blood they once drew so easily from enslaved Negroes.

As the tide of the war turns in the union's favor, the parasitic vampires flee the republic heading for friendlier shores in "South America and the Orient," or back to Europe from whence they came, thus making America now—and forever—"a nation of living men."[22] The novel's coda, however, demonstrates that vampires, while down, are not yet out. The actor and Southern sympathizer John Wilkes Booth is, we learn, also a vampire. He takes the president's life in a bold assassination intended to revivify the morale of the undead in America, only to be shunned by his kin who have retreated into darkness. All is not lost, however, as Henry—banished from the White House for offering to turn young Willy into a vampire—does likewise with his father, believing that "some men are just too interesting to die,"[23] thus allowing an undead Lincoln to fight in the "Second Vampire Uprising" (World War II) and attend Martin Luther King's "I Have a Dream" speech on the steps of his own memorial.

John Wilkes Booth, vampire-assassin. *Courtesy of Grand Central Publishing/ Abraham Lincoln: Vampire Hunter by Seth Grahame-Smith. Copyright © 2010 by Seth Grahame-Smith. All rights reserved.*

In the 2012 film version, directed by Timur Bekmambetov and produced by Tim Burton, the relatively unknown actor Benjamin Walker plays Lincoln.[24] After seeing his mother murdered by a plantation owner, Lincoln seeks revenge, only to learn that his mother's killer, Jack Barts (Marton Csokas), is a vampire. He is saved by Henry Sturges (Dominic Cooper), who informs him about a network of vampire spawn across America and their master, the Louisiana slave-holder Adam (Rufus Sewell), and his leggy chief lieutenant, the lamia Vadoma (Erin Wasson).[25] Through intense training, the young frontiersman attains near superhuman skills, including the ability to fell a pine tree with a single swing of his ax, before embarking on a career as a vampire-slayer. Recognizing the bloody link between slavery and vampirism, Lincoln eventually launches a political campaign rooted in abolition. Following Lincoln's ascendency to the presidency, Jefferson Davis convinces Adam to deploy his hellish horde against the Union troops on the first day of fighting at Gettysburg, thus tipping the balance in favor of the South. Knowing vampires' vulnerability to silver, Lincoln confiscates all the lustrous metal in the Union, and using the Underground Railroad, ships it to Federals for use on the battlefield (while distracting Adam and his vampire minions from the real threat). Armed with weapons made from silver, the Union troops win the day, sending the undead to Hell. Within two years, the leaderless vampires quit the Republic; however, Lincoln, refusing Henry's offer of immortality, still dies at Ford's Theatre. The film ends with Henry seeking out another vampire hunter in contemporary Washington, D.C.

Othering the South on the Page and the Silver Screen

Triggered by an increasingly protean threat matrix following the end of the Cold War and strongly shaped by the attacks of 9/11, cultural theorists have suggested that monsters are more important than ever for representing the anxieties of our time, while historians have argued that "the monster reifies very real incidents, true horrors, true monsters."[26] In the words of Marina Levina and Diem-My T. Bui, "monstrosity has transcended its status as a metaphor and has indeed become a necessary condition of our existence in the twenty-first century."[27] Monsters loom large in our current cultural imagination; however, since 9/11, they have come to serve very particular purposes related to both the representation of danger and the purging of fear.[28] Zombies—and their cinematic cousins, the fast-moving "rage monsters" of *28 Days Later* (2002), *I Am Legend* (2007), and *World War Z* (2013)—represent the most popular post-9/11 threat; however, other monsters—familiar and novel—can be found lurking in our mediated consciousness, serving as "omens, warnings, and portents."[29] Some monsters are human—torturers like those in the *Saw* (2004–2010) and *Hostel* (2005–2011) franchises—while others are otherworldly beings: aliens (*Monsters* [2010], *Pacific Rim* [2013]), mutated humans (*The Descent* [2005], *Chernobyl Diaries* [2012]), demons (*Cabin in the Woods* [2012], *Evil Dead* [2013]), or ghosts (*Paranormal*

Activity [2007], *Mama* [2013]). However, besides the popular *Twilight* saga (2008–2012), the cinematic vampire has been rather rare in the new millennium. It is therefore even more striking when vampires appear in Bekmambetov's rendering of *ALVH*.

Known for his work on the Russian vampire films *Night Watch* (2004) and *Day Watch* (2006), the Kazakh director turned Grahame-Smith's historically rooted fantasy into a big-budget summer movie replete with exploding trains and an extended mixed-martial-arts melee in the midst of a stampede of horses, though one which garnered little praise from critics and performed poorly at the box office. Though Grahame-Smith cowrote the screenplay, Bekmambetov's film differs in a number of key ways from the original source material. Gone are the decidedly "European" vampires, with only a vague suggestion of Adam's "Old World" origins. Much of the detail of Lincoln's slow rise to prominence is also sacrificed. African Americans play a vital role in the film, not only as saviors of the Union forces at Gettysburg, but also as close friends of Lincoln throughout his life,[30] a cinematic legerdemain that does not fit well with Lincoln's view of racial difference revealed in his assertion that "there is a physical difference between the white and black races that will forever forbid the two races from living together on terms of social and political equality."[31]

Despite these incongruities, both the film and novel are in unison when it comes to the malevolence of the Confederacy and its leadership: Southerners are in league with the undead (and very nearly overwhelm the North through this devilish alliance). Men like Jefferson Davis, a hero of the Mexican-American War and two-time senator, knowingly participate in a perverse rebellion that can only result in vampiric overlords assuming power in the New World, while soldiers loyal to the South fight on in ignorance of the identity of their true masters. The novel and the film engage in overt spatial distancing of the South from the rest of the country through the promotion of "derogatory images of the Other," which in turn "reinforces and supports a positive image of the self, which becomes the stereotype of all that is good, honest, desirable, and superior."[32] While Grahame-Smith's book is able to skirt the connivance of the Rebs who fight alongside blood-sucking fiends, the motion picture leaves no middle ground. With fangs and claws extended, gray-clad vampires charge the lines of blue-uniformed Union soldiers, running shoulder-to-shoulder with fresh-faced recruits from Tennessee and Florida who seem happy to have the hell-spawn as their brothers-in-arms. In the dramatically staged battle scenes at Gettysburg, viewers of *ALVH* see a radical retelling of the so-called last invasion[33] of the US homeland: monsters and men working in cooperation to destroy America. While it is tempting to write off *ALVH* as harmless summer entertainment, we should remember that the "cinematic landscape is not . . . a neutral place of entertainment or an objective documentation or mirror of the 'real,' but an ideologically charged cultural creation whereby meaning of place and society are made, legitimized, contested, and obscured."[34] Furthermore, the very genre of horror is rooted in xenophobia, with its monsters standing in for any "predatory Other"[35] that might threaten the social fabric of our ordered world.

Adding to the monstrosity of the South, there is also an overlay of imperialism, just in case any viewers are still left wondering for whom they should root. As film scholars have pointed out, there is a close relationship between vampirism and imperialism in film (one that is only deepened through the trope of slavery): "No other monster has been more closely linked to the expansion of empires and the fear of imperial decline than the vampire."[36] While the notion of "empire" is nearly absent in the book, it is a recurrent theme in the film. In one scene, Henry shows Abraham a map of North America with the Southern states shaded in magenta, ominously noting that "they [vampires] have built an empire in the South," while in another, the diabolic Jack Barts informs Lincoln, "There's thousands of us here. We won't stop 'til this whole country is ours."[37] This is an interesting inversion of the actual political economy of the antebellum and Reconstruction periods, which more closely resembled an imperial structure

Evidence of vampires in the Confederate ranks. *Courtesy of Grand Central Publishing/Abraham Lincoln: Vampire Hunter by Seth Grahame-Smith. Copyright © 2010 by Seth Grahame-Smith. All rights reserved.*

wherein the industrializing North benefited from the raw materials and cheap labor of the agrarian South.

Grahame-Smith and Bekmambetov's "hostile imagination" presents a slave-holding South that is, for all intents and purposes, dehumanized and monstrous. In some ways, this is not particularly surprising, as the South has long been the subject of intense fascination for filmmakers, who frequently engage in "internal orientalism" when touching on issues of race, culture, and history, thus producing an "exalted national identity" on the part of the larger country.[38] As David R. Jansson argues, the "South" is often treated as fundamentally different from the rest of the nation, producing an "imagined space" that is not genuinely "America." By othering the South in filmic depictions, the United States is thus able to reaffirm a "national identity that emphasizes tolerance, enlightenment, and respect for law and human rights."[39] In the words of one reviewer of the film: "Outside of Nazis and zombies . . . nothing says easily disposable villains like slave-trading vampires. And there is, no question, something satisfying—as the pleasure of the story's pop conceit hits your deep historical outrage—about watching Lincoln decapitate a slave-trading ghoul."[40] In its utter simplicity, *ALVH* thus absolves America of its guilt for the historical crimes of slavery by pawning off the peculiar institution on supernatural villains, while simultaneously unambiguously elevating the sixteenth president to superhero status.

Films such as *Mississippi Burning* (1988), *Fried Green Tomatoes* (1991), and *A Time to Kill* (1996) similarly depict an othered South that supports a hegemonic status quo through the productive capacity of film to render the South as "a landscape of violence and death, intolerance and hatred, corruption and complicity."[41] By indexing Dixie as a land of supernatural threats, *ALVH* operates in the same vein as "Southern Gothic" horror films like *Angel Heart* (1987) and *Interview with the Vampire* (1994) and television programs such as *True Blood* (2008–) and *The Walking Dead* (2010–), sculpting a South that is a place of otherworldly monstrosity.[42] However, unlike these works, *ALVH* goes beyond the use of a Southern setting as a backdrop to horror, it effectively re-writes history through monstrosity, therein altering the "moral cartography"[43] of American national identity. This form of "monstrous othering,"[44] when viewed through a postcolonial lens, allows for a fuller understanding of the construction of "civilization" through remapping borders in the collective mind. In *ALVH*, we see—through the fictive retelling of the most analyzed event in American history—the making of the known (the Confederacy) into the "unknown" (a "vampirial" conspiracy). In a pivotal scene, a young US soldier kisses a tintype portrait of his beloved just as Gettysburg gets under way. Across the field, the Confederate battle flag flutters in slow motion as vampire "Seceshes" ominously advance on the Yankees, then disappear. A moment later, the lovesick private and his comrades are scattered corpses in a scene reminiscent of actual carnage of

Federal dead after the first day of the Battle of Gettysburg. *Courtesy of the Library of Congress.*

the first day of Gettysburg, leaving only their bewildered officer on the field of war as the "ghost soldiers" continue their wanton killing, winning the day for the South (a grisly outcome foreshadowed earlier in the film when Adam spills his goblet of blood on the map of Pennsylvania he is studying with Jefferson Davis).

This is the true essence of othering, wherein something that is near and well understood becomes a "repressed unfamiliar familiar, or the uncanny." In the words of Jansson, such cinematic propaganda allows the South to "serve as a receptacle for the country's shadow."[45] By presenting the Southern military forces as a monstrous hybrid of living and undead soldiers, Grahame-Smith and Bekmambetov's imaginary follows a well-trod path in popular culture that presents a demonic threat emanating from civilization's southern reaches. One need only think of medieval portrayals of "wicked Saracens"[46] or more recently Tolkien's "cruel Haradrim."[47]

A Vampiric South and Its Discontents

According to its author, the genesis for *ALVH* stemmed from the curious conflation of the bicentennial of Lincoln's birth (1809–2009) and the peaking popularity of the *Twilight* saga, a tale of young vampires and werewolves and the chaste teenager who loves them.[48] While on his book tour for *Pride and Prejudice and Zombies*, Grahame-Smith[49] noticed that in every bookstore he spoke, there was table of books celebrating the life and times of the sixteenth president positioned next to a table hawking *Twilight*, and thus was born the idea for *Abraham Lincoln, Vampire Hunter*. For an author riding high on the success of his first literary mashup, the idea for—in the author's own words—a "crazy," "ridiculous" genre conceit whereby the most heavily researched figure in American history had a secret "superhero origin story"[50] that involved battling the undead might have seemed a natural evolution; however, the accompanying notion that the Confederacy was a willing ally of vampire imperialists did not go without its critics.

From a metaphorical standpoint, there is certainly a fundamental truth to the "vampiric" nature of the institution of slavery. The rise of chattel slavery was concomitant with European imperialism: as the maritime powers of Portugal, Spain, and England ventured down the coasts of Africa and across the Atlantic to the Americas, there developed a parallel political economy of bondage whereby slaver traders—both African and European—profited from the capture and sale of humans for delivery to the plantations of the New World. This parasitic process ultimately depleted Africa not only of human but also physical resources, creating conditions that still hamper the socioeconomic development of the continent to this day.[51] Conversely, it is generally accepted that Early Modern Europe's "economic miracle" would have been impossible without the free labor of enslaved Africans in the Caribbean, the United States, and Latin America,[52] and that the foundations of the Industrial Revolution were laid by the fiscal benefits of the Triangular Trade,[53] a fact that was tacitly affirmed by British prime minister Tony Blair's quasi-apology to the descendents of slaves in 2006.

In the film, this dark coupling is made real during the kairotic "mural scene," conceived by director Bekmambetov, when Adam schools Abe on the omnipresence of slavery in world history. As the figures in a large mural adorning a plantation manor come alive, Adam recounts, "I have seen Jews build Egypt's glory, seen Christians thrown to the lions with my own eyes, and I've seen Africans sell their own kind to Europeans. We are all slaves to something."[54] While the book attributes vampires' lusty enthusiasm for the American republic to both push *and* pull factors (namely, the post-Báthory backlash and the geographic expanse of the United States), the film attempts to simplify the (faux) historical narrative by positioning Adam and his kind as *übermenschen* on the verge of "ending their millennium of darkness"[55] and assuming their "rightful" role as masters of humanity. As one reviewer points out, this is where the film stumbles into tricky territory: "The institution of slavery revealed something about the true face of young America, something unspeakable, but literalizing it in the form of a vampire turns out to not get us any closer to understanding what it is."[56] Ostensibly, the film completely exonerates the North from the crime of slavery, while multiplying the shame of the South by adding a monstrous overlay to their martial defense of the peculiar institution.

Johnny Reb's "deal with the devil," not surprisingly, provoked a backlash from certain quarters in the American South. Perhaps the most eloquent critic was Michael Cushman of the Southern Nationalist Network, a pro-secessionist website:

> The vampire obsession in the United State [sic] has officially gone crazy . . . [a]nd unsurprisingly in the modern USA it is Southerners, who in reality defended their right of self-determination in the 1860s against outside aggressors, who are the vampires. Our ancestors are portrayed as blood-sucking demons to be eradicated from the face of the planet. Of course, no other ethnic or culture group in modern Amerika [sic] could be portrayed as such. [Imagine] a movie where Blacks, Jews, Hispanics or Asians are all depicted as vampires who have to be exterminated by the US president and his army. Yes, it's impossible to imagine. But no insult is too gross when it comes to Southerners, the perpetual whipping-boy of the United States. . . . It might be just a movie but it certainly points towards the contempt in which Southerners are held by US society today.[57]

Cushman's comments—which were accompanied by a satirical, faux movie poster for *Jefferson Davis: Yankee Hunter*—reflect a perception among Southerners, and many conservative whites in other parts of the United States, that they have become the only acceptable "other" in a politically correct, "post-racial" society. While this may be an instance of rather common "self-othering" of the Southerner,[58] perhaps there is more to it, given that "the demonizing of the monster serves the ideological function of demonizing those who fall outside of socially dominant identity categories."[59]

Applying the lens of popular geopolitics to *ALVH* and the political milieu in which it was produced, it is readily apparent that Hollywood's "manipulation of the popular imagination"[60] has political implications here. Mediated popular culture (particularly blockbuster films) is absolutely vital to the "narration" of national life.[61] Such mediated representations also have a powerful didactic component that "situates and positions knowledge"[62] and produces key national values, promotes certain national codes, and reinforces national myths.[63] Adding horror to the mix only heightens the tension, given that "monstrous narratives not only shape our identities, they provide a place to hold conversations about our public anxieties."[64] Given that "representation is always an act of power,"[65] that Lincoln is frequently used as "a metaphor for ideas and values" of which particular moviemakers approve,[66] and the accompanying notion that Jefferson Davis—a paragon of states' rights and foe of federalism—was the agent of a vampiric-imperial

WHEN THE BLOOD-THIRSTY LINCOLNITES INVADED, THERE
AROSE A LEADER WHO STOOD AGAINST THE YANKEE HORDE...

Jefferson Davis
YANKEE HUNTER

Jefferson Davis, Yankee Hunter. *Courtesy of Southern Nationalist Network/Michael Cushman.*

conspiracy to enslave all of the peoples of America, it is nearly impossible to avoid contextualizing *ALVH* in contemporary US politics, and specifically, the conflict between the Tea Party and the presidency of Barack Obama. This is not insignificant, given that a "movie can lead to personal identification with a political actor" encouraging viewers to "step into their shoes."[67] Prior to the release of the film,

Lincoln (Walker) begins healing a riven nation. *Courtesy of Photofest/Twentieth Century Fox.*

the linking of Abraham Lincoln and Barack Obama in popular culture was well established.[68] From their Illinois roots, slim builds, and "teams of rivals"[69] to the more seminal nature of the connection between the author of the Emancipation Proclamation and the first African American president, Obama and Lincoln are viewed in parallel. Consequently, Obama's rivals—Tea Party Republicans and other critics of "big government"—are tacitly linked with the vampiric Rebs, at least in the darkness of the movie theater where that Lacanian "forgetting of ourselves" so often occurs.[70] Therefore, when we see Abe making the Gettysburg address on a battlefield where the secessionist foe has been dispatched and his vampire allies destroyed, we—the audience—can rest assured that our own "war between the states" will eventually come to an end, and the nation—free of slavery and vampires alike—will be whole again.

Notes

1. Faust, *This Republic of Suffering*, xi.
2. *ALVH* is the second in Seth Grahame-Smith's mashup novels, the first being the wildly popular *Pride and Prejudice and Zombies* (2009), a parodic adaptation of Jane Austen's classic novel of manners. In *Unholy Night* (2012b), Grahame-Smith went on to reimagine the birth of Christ as a sword-and-sorcery epic centered on the exploits of a triad of ne'er-do-wells posing as the Three Kings of biblical fame.

3. Sharp, "Hegemony, Popular Culture and Geopolitics"; Dodds, "Screening Geopolitics"; Grayson, Davies, and Philpott, "Pop Goes IR?"; Dittmer, *Popular Culture, Geopolitics, and Identity.*

4. Here I borrow Shelby Foote's enmity-laden construct for Confederate soldiers from his seminal three-volume work, *The Civil War: A Narrative* (1958–1974).

5. Keen, *Faces of the Enemy.*

6. Jansson, "A Geography of Racism."

7. Halberstam, *Skin Shows.*

8. Poole, *Monsters in America,* xvi.

9. Grahame-Smith, *Abraham Lincoln, Vampire Hunter,* 1.

10. Grahame-Smith, audio commentary on *Abraham Lincoln: Vampire Hunter.*

11. Rather importantly, the film version does not end with an undead Lincoln.

12. Grossman, "Ax Man."

13. Foner, *Our Lincoln.*

14. Grahame-Smith, *Abraham Lincoln, Vampire Hunter,* 203.

15. Ibid., 53.

16. Grahame-Smith, audio commentary on *Abraham Lincoln: Vampire Hunter.*

17. Grahame-Smith, *Abraham Lincoln, Vampire Hunter,* 252.

18. Ibid., 270.

19. Ibid., 273.

20. Ibid., 274.

21. Ibid., 292–93.

22. Ibid., 307.

23. Ibid., 337.

24. While reviews of the novel tended to be quite good (particularly given the "demigod" status of Lincoln in the American national psyche), the critical reception of the film was poor, with the notable exception of Roger Ebert, who described the performances as "earnest and sincere" and was impressed that the subject matter was treated with "an admirable seriousness." Conversely, Peter Travers of *Rolling Stone* quipped the movie "deserves a stake through the heart," while Manohla Dargis of the *New York Times* lamented that with such "a smashing title," it was "too bad someone had to spoil things by making a movie to go with it." Perhaps most famously, Colin Covert of the Minneapolis *Star Tribune* described the motion picture as "the worst thing to happen to Abe Lincoln in a theater since he attended 'Our American Cousin.'"

25. Grahame-Smith (audio commentary on *Abraham Lincoln: Vampire Hunter*) commented that the film needed a "central villain" (Adam) and "big third-act set piece" (a climactic train scene involving a grand battle between Lincoln, Henry, and Adam), two things that his novel lacked.

26. Poole, *Monsters in America,* xvi.

27. Levina and Bui, "Toward a Comprehensive Monster Theory," 2.

28. Wetmore, *Post-9/11 Horror.*

29. Poole, *Monsters in America,* 12.

30. According to the author and scriptwriter Grahame-Smith (audio commentary on *Abraham Lincoln: Vampire Hunter*), it was "important" to address race and oppression in the film adaption, thus resulting in the introduction of a character, Will Johnson

(Anthony Mackie), who "fights back" rather than simply being a victim in the vampiric structure of American slavery.

31. Lincoln, "Speech at Columbus, Ohio," 402.

32. Douglas, "Political Structures," 155.

33. Guelzo, *Gettysburg*.

34. Hopkins, "A Mapping of Cinematic Place," 47.

35. Carroll, *Philosophy of Horror*, 196.

36. Byron and Stephanou, "Neoimperialism and the Apocalyptic Vampire," 190. The paragon of vampires, Bram Stoker's Dracula (1897), was in fact a slave master, attended to by a retinue of Gypsy slaves, while the "real" Dracula, the Wallachian ruler Vlad the Impaler, is reported to have brought more than 10,000 Romany slaves to his capital to be "tortured and executed for his entertainment." Kenrick, 222.

37. *Abraham Lincoln: Vampire Hunter*, directed by Timur Bekmambetov.

38. Jansson, "A Geography of Racism."

39. Ibid., 266.

40. Dargis, "Slaying with Silver."

41. Jansson, "A Geography of Racism," 272.

42. Saunders, *Darker Angels of Our Nature*.

43. Shapiro, "Ethics of Encounter."

44. Rai, "Identity and Its Monsters."

45. Jansson, "A Geography of Racism," 268.

46. Higgs Strickland, *Saracens, Demons, and Jews*.

47. Sinex, "Monsterized Saracens."

48. The books, written by American author Stephenie Meyer, were published between 2005 and 2008; however, they were adapted into a series of motion pictures beginning in late 2008, thus resulting in a spike in sales. To date the series has sold over 100 million copies.

49. Grahame-Smith, audio commentary on *Abraham Lincoln: Vampire Hunter*.

50. Ibid.

51. Manning, *Slavery and African Life*.

52. Wallerstein, *The Modern World-System I*.

53. Wright, *Slavery and American Economic Development*.

54. *Abraham Lincoln: Vampire Hunter*.

55. Ibid.

56. Grossman, "Ax Man."

57. Cushman, "*Abe Lincoln: Vampire Hunter*."

58. Burton, "The South as 'Other,' the Southerner as 'Stranger.'"

59. Sibielski, "Gendering the Monster Within," 127.

60. Higson, "The Concept of National Cinema."

61. Dittmer, *Popular Culture, Geopolitics, and Identity*.

62. Gregory, *Geographical Imaginations*.

63. Dijkink, *National Identity and Geopolitical Visions*.

64. Poole, *Monsters in America*, 23.

65. Bleiker, "Aesthetic Turn," 515.

66. Stokes, "Abraham Lincoln and the Movies," 224.

67. Engert and Spencer, "International Relations at the Movies," 85.

68. See Dallek, "Barack Obama and Abraham Lincoln"; Hirschkorn, "The Obama-Lincoln Parallel"; Malcolm, "Barack Obama and the Abraham Lincoln Comparison."

69. Throughout Obama's first term, Lincoln biographer Doris Kearns Goodwin (2006) made a case for their similar "genius" in governing through a "team of rivals," the title of her book upon which the Oscar-winning biopic *Lincoln* (2012) was based.

70. Dittmer, *Popular Culture, Geopolitics, and Identity*, 36.

Bibliography

Abraham Lincoln: Vampire Hunter. Directed by Timur Bekmambetov. 2012. Los Angeles: 20th Century Fox Home Entertainment, 2012. DVD.

Austen, Jane, and Seth Grahame-Smith. *Pride and Prejudice and Zombies*. Philadelphia: Quirk Books, 2009.

Bleiker, Roland. "The Aesthetic Turn in International Political Theory." *Millennium: Journal of International Studies* 30, no. 3 (2001): 509–33.

Burton, Orville Vernon. "The South as 'Other,' the Southerner as 'Stranger.'" *Journal of Southern History* 79, no. 1 (2013): 7–50.

Byron, Glennis, and Apasia Stephanou. "Neoimperialism and the Apocalyptic Vampire: Justin Cronin's *The Passage*." In *Transnational and Postcolonial Vampires: Dark Blood*, edited by Tabish Khair and Johan Höglund, 189–200. New York: Palgrave Macmillan, 2013.

Carroll, Noël. *The Philosophy of Horror, or Paradoxes of the Heart*. New York: Routledge, 1990.

Covert, Colin. "'Vampire Hunter': Put a Stake in It." *Minneapolis Star Tribune*, June 22, 2012. http://www.startribune.com/entertainment/movies/159895575.html.

Cushman, Michael. "*Abe Lincoln: Vampire Hunter*." Southern Nationalist Network, March 19, 2012. http://southernnationalist.com/blog/2012/03/19/abe-lincoln -vampire-hunter/.

Dallek, Matthew. "The Comparisons between Barack Obama and Abraham Lincoln." *US News & World Report*, November 20, 2008. http://www.usnews.com/opinion/ articles /2008/11/20/the-comparisons-between-barack-obama-and-abraham-lincoln.

Dargis, Manohla. "Slaying with Silver in 19th Century South." *New York Times*, June 22, 2012. http://www.nytimes.com/2012/06/22/movies/abraham-lincoln-vampire-hunter.html?_r=0.

Dijkink, Gertjan. *National Identity and Geopolitical Visions: Maps of Pride and Pain*. New York and London: Routledge, 1996.

Dittmer, Jason. *Popular Culture, Geopolitics, and Identity*. Lanham, MD: Rowman & Littlefield, 2010.

Dodds, Klaus. "Screening Geopolitics: James Bond and the Early Cold War Films (1962–1967)." *Geopolitics* 10 (2005): 266–89.

Douglas, Neville. "Political Structures, Social Interaction, and Identity Change in Northern Ireland." In *In Search of Ireland: A Cultural Geography*, edited by Brian Graham, 151–73. London and New York: Routledge, 1997.

Ebert, Roger. "[Review of] *Abraham Lincoln: Vampire Hunter.*" RogerEbert.com. 2012. http://www.rogerebert.com/reviews/abraham-lincoln-vampire-hunter-2012.

Engert, Stefan, and Alexander Spencer. "International Relations at the Movies: Teaching and Learning about International Politics through Film." *Perspectives* 17, no. 1 (2009): 83–104.

Faust, Drew Gilpin. *This Republic of Suffering: Death and the American Civil War.* New York: Random House, 2009.

Foner, Eric. *Our Lincoln: New Perspectives on Lincoln and His World.* New York: Norton, 2008.

Foote, Shelby. *The Civil War: A Narrative.* 3 volumes. New York: Random House, 1958–1974.

Grahame-Smith, Seth. *Abraham Lincoln, Vampire Hunter.* New York: Grand Central Publishing, 2010.

———. Audio Commentary on *Abraham Lincoln: Vampire Hunter.* DVD.

———. *Unholy Night.* New York: Grand Central Publishing, 2012.

Grayson, Kyle, Matt Davies, and Simon Philpott. "Pop Goes IR? Researching the Popular Culture-World Politics Continuum." *Politics* 29, no. 3 (2009): 155–63.

Gregory, Derek. *Geographical Imaginations.* Cambridge, MA: Blackwell, 1994.

Grossman, Lev. "Ax Man." *Time* 175, no. 9 (2010): 56.

Guelzo, Allen C. *Gettysburg: The Last Invasion.* New York: Random House, 2013.

Halberstam, Judith. *Skin Shows: Gothic Horror and the Technology of Monsters.* Durham, NC: Duke University Press, 1995.

Higgs Strickland, Debra. *Saracens, Demons, and Jews: Making Monsters in Medieval Art.* Princeton, NJ: Princeton University Press, 2003.

Higson, Andrew. "The Concept of National Cinema." In *Film and Nationalism*, edited by Alan Williams, 52–67. New Brunswick, NJ: Rutgers University Press, 2002.

Hirschkorn, Phil. "The Obama-Lincoln Parallel: A Closer Look." *CBS News.* 2009. http://www.cbsnews.com/news/the-obama-lincoln-parallel-a-closer-look/.

Hopkins, Jeff. "A Mapping of Cinematic Place: Icons, Ideology, and the Power of (Mis)representation." In *Place, Power, Situation, and Spectacle: A Geography of Film*, edited by Stuart Aitken and Leo E. Zonn, 47–66. Lanham, MD: Rowman & Littlefield, 1994.

Jansson, David R. "'A Geography of Racism': Internal Orientalism and the Construction of American National Identity in the Film *Mississippi Burning.*" *National Identities* 7, no. 3 (2005): 265–85.

Kearns Goodwin, Doris. *Team of Rivals: The Political Genius of Abraham Lincoln.* New York: Simon & Schuster, 2006.

Keen, Sam. *Faces of the Enemy: Reflections of the Hostile Imagination.* New York: Harper & Row, 1991.

Kenrick, Donald. *Historical Dictionary of the Gypsies (Romanies)* (2nd ed.). Lanham, MD: Scarecrow Press, 2013.

Levina, Marina, and Diem-My T. Bui. "Toward a Comprehensive Monster Theory in the 21st Century." In *Monster Culture in the 21st Century: A Reader*, edited by Marina Levina and Diem-My T. Bui, 1–31. New York: Bloomsbury, 2013.

Lincoln. Directed by Steven Spielberg. 2012. Burbank, CA: Walt Disney Studios Home Entertainment, 2013. DVD.

Lincoln, Abraham. "Speech at Columbus, Ohio." September 16, 1859. In *Collected Works of Abraham Lincoln,* volume 3, edited by Roy P. Basler, Marion Dolores Pratt, and Lloyd A. Dunlap, 400–425. New Brunswick, NJ: Rutgers University Press, 1953. http://quod.lib.umich.edu/l/lincoln /lincoln3/1:137?rgn=div1;view=fulltext.

Malcolm, Andrew. "Barack Obama and the Abraham Lincoln Comparison." *Los Angeles Times,* February 13, 2009. http://latimesblogs.latimes.com/washington/2009/02/obama-lincoln.html.

Manning, Patrick. *Slavery and African Life: Occidental, Oriental, and African Slave Trades.* Cambridge: Cambridge University Press, 1990.

Poole, W. Scott. *Monsters in America: Our Historical Obsession with the Hideous and the Haunting.* Waco, TX: Baylor University Press, 2011.

Rai, Shailza. "Identity and Its Monsters: Borders Within and Without." In *Cartographies of Affect: Across Borders in South Asia and the Americas,* edited by Debra A. Castillo and Kavita Panjabi, 325–45. Delhi: Worldview Publications, 2011.

Saunders, Steven. *The Darker Angels of Our Nature: The South in American Horror Film.* Jackson, MS: UMI Dissertations Publishing, 2013.

Shapiro, Michael J. "The Ethics of Encounter: Unreading, Unmapping the Imperium." In *Moral Spaces: Rethinking Ethics and World Politics,* edited by David Campbell and Michael J. Shapiro, 57–91. Minneapolis: University of Minnesota Press, 1999.

Sharp, Joanne P. "Hegemony, Popular Culture and Geopolitics: *The Reader's Digest* and the Construction of Danger." *Political Geography* 15, nos. 6–7 (1996): 557–70.

Sibielski, Rosalind. "Gendering the Monster Within." In *Monster Culture in the 21st Century: A Reader,* edited by Marina Levina and Diem-My T. Bui, 115–30. New York: Bloomsbury, 2013.

Sinex, Margaret. "'Monsterized Saracens,' Tolkien's Haradrim, and Other Medieval 'Fantasy Products.'" *Tolkien Studies* 7, no. 1 (2010): 175–96.

Stoker, Bram. *Dracula: A Mystery Story.* New York: W. R. Caldwell, 1897.

Stokes, Melvyn. "Abraham Lincoln and the Movies." *American Nineteenth Century History* 12, no. 2 (2011): 203–31.

Travers, Peter. "[Review of] *Abraham Lincoln: Vampire Hunter.*" *Rolling Stone,* June 21, 2012. http://www.rollingstone.com/movies/reviews/abraham-lincoln-vampire-hunter-20120621.

Wallerstein, Immanuel. *The Modern World-System I: Capitalist Agriculture and the Origins of the European World-Economy in the Sixteenth Century.* Berkeley: University of California Press, 2011.

Wetmore, Kevin J. *Post-9/11 Horror in American Cinema.* New York: Continuum, 2012.

Wright, Gavin. *Slavery and American Economic Development.* Baton Rouge: Louisiana State University Press, 2013.

CHAPTER 2

Cry "Havoc!" and Let Slip the Vampires of War

Cynthia J. Miller

An old Russian folktale tells the story of the village of Uryupin—a town infested by a plague of rats. There had always been rats in the summer months, but in winter, the bitter Russian cold would kill off most of the vermin and maintain balance in the town. Recently, however, the winter months had little effect on the rats, and their numbers increased dramatically. By the third summer the rats were everywhere, and the townspeople resolved to abandon Uryupin, and not return until the rats had starved or moved elsewhere.

But before the people had a chance to leave, a traveling merchant, driving a crude wagon pulled by a single mule, arrived in the town. He told the townsfolk that he had heard about their problem and could help, but would not tell them how until they had entered into a bargain with him. Once the town had agreed to his price, the merchant revealed the contents of his wagon: a dozen small monkeys. Warning the villagers to keep their animals inside, he let the monkeys loose in the town.

No one saw the monkeys at work, but each time one of them found another rat, it let out a screech that cut through the silence of the town. On the fourteenth day, when there was nothing left in the town for them to eat, the monkeys returned to the wagon; the merchant locked their cage, took his payment, and left. The townspeople were glad to be rid of the rats, and even more glad to be rid of the murderous screaming of the monkeys. They basked in the newfound quiet, until its unnatural depth struck them—it was not just the absence of the screeching, but the absence of all sounds—absolute, total silence. Finally, a young child observed that there was silence because there was no birdsong. Not a single bird remained alive in Uryupin after the monkeys had carried out their task. None ever returned.[1]

This tale, with its warning of unanticipated consequences—the loss of beauty and grace in the eradication of a reviled foe—opens Jasper Kent's saga of human war and supernatural intervention, *Twelve*. The novel begins as Russia prepares to make a final stand against invading French forces, led by Napoleon Bonaparte. A band of twelve mercenaries are covertly summoned in a desperate effort to turn the tide of the battle; as the folktale foreshadows, however, their aid comes at an unexpected cost.

There are hidden forces at play in nearly all wars—unseen agents that sow the seeds of peace or chaos—shifting power and affecting outcomes in ways that history seldom records. Speculative casting of supernatural beings in that role not only challenges received knowledge of these historical processes, but religious faith, existential beliefs, and the framework of national identity, as well. In *Twelve*, Kent uses the undead to interrogate all of these, as he weaves together the monstrous of history, myth, and legend to create an undead menace that draws on Russian horrors and heroes that have persisted for centuries. The result is a terror that both stabilizes and threatens to destroy the soul of Holy Rus'.

The Twelve

Kent's novel takes the form of a sprawling epic that chronicles a desperate covert Russian response to the invasion of Napoleon's Grande Armée during the Patriotic War of 1812. Aleksei Ivanovich and his comrades-in-arms—Dmitry, Vadim, and Maks—are a small band of soldiers charged by their general to carry out "irregular operations": given free rein to carry out missions of espionage and sabotage, and sow the seeds of chaos behind enemy lines between tactical engagements. Their task is to defeat Napoleon's advancing troops before Moscow itself is overtaken—to save Russia at any cost.

Dmitry summons a group of twelve mercenaries with whom he has fought in the past. Hailing from the farthest reaches of Christian Europe, they are mysterious figures that work only under the cover of darkness, leaving a trail of mutilated corpses in their wake. Dmitry's explanations of their nature fall short: They are like the Cossacks of myth and legend, but not; even more similar to the Oprichniki, Ivan the Terrible's dark enforcers, but again, not. These comparisons make the Twelve comprehensible, though, and leave Aleksei and his comrades wondering if perhaps the strangers can, in fact, make good on their promise to turn the tide of the war.

As the narrative unfolds, the war becomes intimate, tracing the silent footsteps of street-level encounters rather than the bold marching of regiments. As the war focuses on the interplay of individual combatants, predators and prey, the insecurity of the four Russians—their fears, weaknesses, limitations—is increasingly contrasted against the seeming lack of vulnerability and concern on the part of the Twelve, who possess speed, stealth, and great power. The play of light, darkness, and shadow in the text similarly foregrounds the limitations of the soldiers' senses, calling into question their dependence on frail human abilities. In contrast to the four Russians' alienation from the natural world, the Twelve seem to melt into their surroundings, their stillness and silence rendering them invisible until ready to strike. An increasing tension exists between the impermanence of the human condition and the seeming invincibility of the mercenaries; the latter's physical brutality highlights the soldiers' flawed idealism as they cling to fragile beliefs about nature and nation. As Matfei, one of the Twelve, chides Aleksei, "you don't have the stomach to do what we do, and you don't have the guts to stop us."[2]

As Kent's alternate history unfolds, Aleksei and his comrades become increasingly suspicious of the motives and methods of the mercenaries, sensing that their respective motivations for fighting Napoleon's forces may align, but are not the same. Victims are found with their throats torn out, their flesh ripped apart as if they had been set upon by wild dogs, but it is not until Aleksei witnesses the carnage for himself that he realizes what his friend Dmitry had been keeping from him all along—the true nature of the Twelve—that they are *voordalaki*. Vampires. They do not kill for God or for country, but for hunger and bloodlust. After following Matfei in an attempt to discover the mercenaries' secrets, Aleksei observes him in the midst of a kill, crouching over the still-struggling body of a French soldier, wolflike teeth buried in his victim's neck, and drinking his blood:

> As Matfei raised his head, so the neck and the head of the soldier began to move with it. Matfei pushed against the body beneath him and I saw that his teeth were still sunk deeply into the man's throat. As he strained upwards, the skin suddenly ruptured and gave way and Matfei's head rose rapidly, a lump of flesh trailing from his bloody mouth.[3]

The sight immediately evokes deep childhood memories of tales told by his grandmother, as her words come flooding back, filling his mind with the realization that: "Now I had seen it with my own eyes . . . the creatures truly existed."[4] His understanding of the Twelve is immediately infused with legends handed down for generations—stories that he, as an educated man, had long ago dismissed as remnants of the "Old World" to which his grandmother belonged. In many ways, the Twelve conform to her ancient tales: they nest in cellars and other out-of-the-way places, sleeping in crates and coffins, and can only be killed by "traditional" means: a wooden stake through the heart, consumption by flames, or exposure to sunlight. In other respects, however, they redefine the horror of the *voordalaki* for Aleksei: particularly in that they are subject to the same anger, mistrust, and resentment as men, and lend their predatory skills to those desperate enough to pay. They have joined forces with the Russians only because, as Iuda, another of the Twelve, later confirms, "If Napoleon had defeated Russia, it would have meant French hegemony over the whole of Europe. And that would have meant peace—a peace you and I would have despised for different reasons."[5]

These mercenaries, or others like them, may, Aleksei realizes, have been covertly turning the tides of wars for generations. Their interest is not in the outcome, but in war's perpetuation, ensuring their ability to continue on as predators. Aleksei's awareness of the *voordalaki* adds a new dimension to his understanding of the battle that is occurring around him. It is no longer simply a geopolitical conflict, but an eternal one between humanity and consummate evil. Dmitry initially does not share his revulsion. When Aleksei confronts him about the true identities of the mercenary band he has summoned, he replies:

> So? We fight alongside Prussians, Austrians, Englishmen. We don't care who they are as long as they are on our side. . . . They are the most accomplished killers I have ever met. I knew that my country was threatened with invasion. . . . I knew that we needed them. . . . This is our country we're fighting for; it's not a time to be picky about how we fight.[6]

As the Russians' sentiments gradually turn against the Twelve, both sides suffer casualties, and Aleksei watches his fellow soldiers die at the hands of the *voordalaki*. The final conflict is set against a backdrop of chaos as the weight of retreating French forces collapses one of their hastily made bridges over the Berezina River. Hundreds plunge to their death in the icy waters, while thousands more surge toward the one remaining bridge, just ahead of the rapidly advancing Russian troops.

Aleksei and Iuda, the only two remaining actors in the drama of clandestine warfare, battle in the river amid the throngs of panicked and drowning Frenchmen. As they fight to the death, it is revealed that the aptly named Iuda (Judas, in English) is, in fact, an imposter, a traitor to his species—not a vampire at all, but a human who was never turned—passing as one of the supernatural beings to satisfy his pathological desires. Their struggle in icy waters ends as Iuda is torn from Aleksei's grasp by the fierce current, and his status—living or dead—is once again rendered a mystery.

Creatures of Myth and Legend

"*Voordalak!*" The word that sent a shudder through some long-forgotten corner of Aleksei Ivanovich's soul carries the weight of centuries of cultural meaning.

Thought by many to be the ancestor of all European vampires, the *voordalak* is an inhabitant of the pantheon of the Old Religion of the Slavs. Its terrifying name, coined by Russian author Alexandr Pushkin in the early nineteenth century, was borrowed from Slavic folklore. The term *vukodlak* first appeared in a thirteenth-century Serbian manuscript, describing a vampire/werewolf creature that devoured the sun and moon, while chasing clouds.[7] As the centuries passed, the Old Russian *upyr* (*vampir*) and Serbian *vukodlak* became colloquially synonymous, and stood interchangeably for the supernatural creatures invoked by the folklore of the region.[8] These creatures emerged from a wide range of origin stories, and were associated with a variety of signs, works, and moral messages, but their essence—of pure, otherworldly evil—remained constant.

> At the dead of midnight, leaving their graves where they lie as undecayed corpses, the vampires take on various forms. They . . . raise cain [*sic*] and frighten travelers, or they enter the peasants' cottages and suck blood from those sleeping, who always die from it afterwards.[9]

Long-interred bodies, found dripping with blood . . . gates branded with crosses, denying entry to the unholy . . . aspen stakes driven through corpses, preventing their reanimation. Tropes such as these filled traditional Slavic literature, spreading Slavic lore about vampires throughout the Balkans, Russia, Ukraine, and elsewhere, as far north as the Baltic Sea, and west to the Elbe River, and giving rise to the Slavic cult of the vampire. Far from the cloaked, fanged figure that would later be popularized by Bram Stoker's *Dracula*, Slavic vampires most often took the form of ordinary individuals—family members, the elderly, strangers on the road—who later revealed their evil nature.

Perhaps the best known of these early Slavic vampire stories is Aleksey Tolstoy's *Family of the Vourdalak* (*La famille du vourdalak*). Set in the year 1759, Tolstoy's novella tells a gothic tale of love, death, and the supernatural, in rural Serbia. A traveling soldier arrives in a small village and seeks out hospitality from a local family. While making him welcome, the family is anxious and sad. The eldest son explains that, ten days earlier, his elderly father, Old Gorsha, had taken his gun down from the wall and joined the search for a Turkish bandit that had been terrorizing the village. Old Gorsha carefully instructed his sons:

> Wait ten days for me, and if I do not return on the tenth, have a funeral mass said for me, for in that case, I shall have been killed. But . . . if (in this case, God protect you) I should return after the ten days have passed, for your own sakes, under no circumstances must you allow me to enter the house. I command you in that case to forget that I was your father and to pierce me with an aspen stake . . . for in that case I will be only an accursed vurdalak who has come home to drink your blood.[10]

Ten days later, the convent bell chimes eight o'clock, just as it did when Old Gorsha departed. As the bell ceases its tolling, his figure reappears at the edge of the woods. The family is overjoyed, but then troubled, wondering whether Gorsha's return had slipped just beyond the sound of the last peal, leaving his status as human or *voordalak* in question. In a short time, the answer becomes clear to all, and the family's demise begins, the result of their failure to accept the true nature of the undead and the actions that must be taken.

As Tolstoy's tale illustrates, the Old World Slavs viewed the boundary between the living and the dead as fluid and permeable. These beliefs find their roots, at least in part, in notions of the nature of the soul. In ancient Slavic belief, the soul is independent of the body, and free to come and go, during sleep, fainting, or other losses of consciousness. Thirsty, hungry, or lonely souls may wander off to fulfill their needs, opening up possibilities for countless tales of not only the acts of wayward souls, but also "undeath." Souls of the dead remain active, as well. For forty days the soul dwells on earth, seeking out familiar people and places, and wreaking havoc on those who had been enemies in life.[11] At the end of forty days, tradition tells of the soul approaching the body, trying to enter it and live again.[12] The dead, then, even for a finite period of time, maintain an active relationship with the living—sometimes benign, other times malevolent—blurring the boundary between the two states. The attempt to reinhabit deceased bodies further complicates the status of the dead. The introduction of the *voordalaki*—the undead—in the form of familiar figures of those once living, is simply a small step in an already established existential direction.

Defenders of the Sacred Nation

Kent draws on the ambiguities of these folkloric traditions, along with the (perhaps even greater) ambiguities of Russian history, to craft an alternate, hidden history significantly influenced by the violent, unseen power of the *voordalaki*. The mysterious band of mercenaries has been called upon to aid in the salvation of Russia from forces seeking to overtake the land and its people, in direct parallel with conventional historical narratives of the Patriotic War of 1812. Under cover of darkness, the Twelve silently infiltrate enemy camps, slaughtering soldiers and leaving terror in their wake as they move across the country.

Far from simplistic, two-dimensional constructs of evil, however, the *voordalaki* are complex figures that embody opposition—salvation and destruction, stability and chaos, the sacred and the profane. In this, their existence is as much a product of fact as fantasy, following a long Russian tradition of brutal warriors who carried out their missions unfettered by moralistic rules of combat. Kent creates an explicit link between the *voordalaki* and one such group—the

Oprichniki, a dark, ruthless brotherhood drawn together by Ivan IV, "Ivan the Terrible" (1533–1584)—crafting them as a fantastic embodiment of real historical terror.

Ivan's crowning in 1557 began the reign of Russia's first Orthodox tsar, and the birth of the historical mission of all the tsars that would follow: the realization of God's realm on earth in the land of the one true faith.[13] Moscow Metropolitan Macarius, who conducted the coronation ceremony, charged the new tsar:

> O Grand Prince Ivan Vasilievich, God-crowned Tsar of the whole of Russia, accept from God as a gift this scepter to rule the standards of the Great Empire of Russia, watch over and protect it [the Empire] with all your strength.[14]

Ivan the Terrible thus framed his reign in the rhetoric of the Chosen, embarking on nothing less than a holy mission to secure and maintain the land of true believers. The glorification of the Orthodoxy, and the punishment of all "wrong-believers," gave rise to a tyranny toward those within the Russian homeland and a hostility toward those outside its borders unlike anything experienced in the

Ivan the Terrible's murderous Oprichniki, as portrayed in Pavel Lungin's *Tsar* (2009).

past. From within this context, the Oprichniki, the most trusted of the tsar's bodyguard units, were created to sanctify the country and enforce Ivan's holy mandates. Dressed in black and riding dark horses, these agents of death spread terror as they sought to purge Russia of the enemies of the tsar—and by extension, of Holy Rus'. Each hung a severed wolf's head slung on a rope around his horse's neck, and carried a whip, emblazoned with a bundle of wool or a broom, signifying that the Oprichniki "fell upon the Tsar's enemies like wolves, and then swept into oblivion everything unnecessary."[15] The Oprichniki served as warrior monks, collapsing the realms of spirituality and savagery in the name of the tsar and the homeland. Clergy, nobility, and commoner—none were safe from their holy purge of treason, as they carried out their missions to protect and stabilize the tsar's sacred political doctrine.

Another, more familiar, thread also stitches the figures of Kent's *voordalaki* into the fabric of Russian history as well, through the culture, myth, and legend of the Ukraine Cossacks, defenders of holy Mother Russia, whose fearsome exploits merged soul and savagery. With a heritage that the *Istoriis Rusov*, the major historical and political work of the late eighteenth and early nineteenth centuries, traces back to a son of Noah, Cossacks are often framed as romantic freedom fighters tied to the origins of the Russian people—principal upholders of the Russian Orthodox faith, and preservers of the purity of Rus'[16]—heroes who evoke the soul of Russian civilization and serve as a reminder of the continuity of all that is truly Russia. Pokrova icons from Orthodox towns such as Pereiaslav and Deshky feature Cossack commanders—*hetmans*—in company with tsars and surrounded by saints, sheltered beneath the grace of the Virgin Mary.[17] Cossacks thus form a vital part of Russians' self-image; as Tolstoy suggested, "the Russian people all desire to be Cossacks."[18] As warriors, they were bold, fearless, and disciplined. They were largely responsible for routing Napoleon's army in the War of 1812, and pursued the retreating French all the way to Paris. It is this iconic image that moves Aleksei to make the connection, "They sound like *Kazaki*" when Dmitry first describes their new allies.[19]

As border people, the *vol'nyi kazaki*—ontologically "free Cossacks"—incorporate elements of both wilderness and civilization. They stand as liminal figures, both at the heart and on the margins of the Russian empire, providing service, but defying control, and by combining these opposites, the Cossack becomes an ideal and a vital whole.[20] As Kornblatt observes, this "seamless combination of opposing traits is a hallmark of the Cossack myth; it raises the hero above the fragmented human level."[21] Larger, stronger, less vulnerable than normal men, they transcend the boundaries imposed on mortals, be they spatial, temporal, moral, or metaphysical.[22]

Defenders of, and rebels against, order, Cossacks are immortalized in classic literature as noble warriors who embody Enlightenment ideals of individualism

Pokrova icon from the village of Deshky, featuring Cossack Hetman Bohdan Khmalnytskyi (far right). *Courtesy of the National Museum of Fine Art, Kyiv.*

and are tied to a sense of romantic nationalism and pan-Slavism—an image that has served throughout history as a counter to oppression and an abiding sense of futility.[23] At their most essential level, Cossacks are "of the land" rather than of its people. Their spirit is tied to the geography and nature that surrounds them; they are one with the soul of the country.[24] Classic authors from Glinka to Gogol have all written into being Cossack warriors modeled after the *bogatyri*—medieval heroes of Russian folklore. Poet Alexandr Pushkin argued that Sten'ka Razin, the most popular Cossack in Russian folk poetry, was "the only poetic figure in Russian history."[25] Razin and other celebrated Cossack warriors provided Russians with a vital, potent, and colorful figure to represent themselves and their past.

In the "Poetical Tale about the Azov Siege, 1642," Cossacks are cast as "holy-Russian heroes, defenders of the land when her purity is attacked by 'heathen'

Turks, 'infidel' Tatars, and 'heretical' Poles supported by the 'unholy' Jews."[26] Similarly, Gogol's Cossacks are larger than life. When preparing for battle, "the Cossack commander grew a whole yard," to become a "limitless leader."[27] The souls of dead Cossacks ride up to heaven in the arms of angels, and a corpse in "A Terrible Vengeance" grows to mammoth proportions, struggling to burst from his confinement underground.[28]

Much like these historical figures, the *voordalaki* of *Twelve* are not summoned on a mission of destruction, but rather, one of preservation. They are called upon to aid in the protection of the Russian homeland from invaders, to halt Napoleon's progress across the land by means prohibited by the morality of honor-bound soldiers. The result, however, is not the much-hoped-for stability, but complete destabilization and chaos.

Violence and the Sacred Aesthetic

Just like the villagers of Uryupin, who sought the help of the traveling merchant and his monkeys, Aleksei and his band of brothers remain unaware of the consequences of engaging the Twelve until their horrible devastation is done. Dmitry initially explains that they are similar to the Oprichniki, that they "understand that violence is of itself a weapon" and carry out their missions "unhindered by scruple or fear." Little does he realize that the horrors brought about by the *voordalaki* will exceed even the tales handed down through generations about the deeds of the Oprichniki. They are, as Dmitry relates, "expert in working behind enemy lines. Always attacking when they are least expected. Always causing maximum disruption at minimum risk."[29]

In historical fact, the tsar's monks came to be seen as embodiments of death and destruction. As Dmitry continues to explain to his comrades, "their faith gave them the fanaticism that Ivan needed."[30] Stories persist into the present day of the Oprichniki's sacrilegious masses, followed by extended orgies of sex, rape, and torture. In the fulfillment of their holy mission, the Oprichniki were said to have killed priests and high-ranking clergy, murdering many in front of their altars. When rumors that the city of Novgorod, a center of the Orthodoxy, intended to break away from the tsardom in 1570, it was the Oprichniki that delivered Ivan's ruthless punishment for treason against the tsar and the Church, massacring all of its residents.

> Novgorod's archbishop was first sewn up in a bearskin and then
> hunted to death by a pack of hounds. Men, women and children
> were tied to sleighs, which were then run into the freezing waters of
> the Volkhov River. The mass of corpses made it flood its banks.[31]

These vicious acts of suppression, born out of the corruption of cherished ideals, merged extreme violence and the sacred, creating an aesthetic that may be seen across holy wars, crusades, and inquisitions—and that also infuses the terror of the *voordalaki* of Kent's *Twelve*. The leader of the Twelve, Zmyeevich, a menacing figure whose name literally translates as "son of the serpent," introduces his twelve followers to Aleksei and his comrades through pseudonyms: Pyetr (Peter), Andrei (Andrew), Ioann (John), Filipp (Phillip), Matfei (Matthew), and so on, evoking, for even the least religious among the band of Russians, an identification with the twelve apostles. He explains that he and Dmitry first fought together years ago, against "the old enemy from the east," and prefaces their new mission with rhetoric befitting a holy conflict:

> While the unchristian Turk . . . cannot be blamed for his heresy, having learned it from this father and his father before him, Bonaparte has led his country to an abandonment of the Christ, Whom that nation had long known and loved. . . . So now we must face the common enemy.[32]

Dark, brooding, and disinterested, the Twelve appear to be all physicality and instinct, their pseudonyms a mockery of, rather than homage to, their apostolic forbearers. Zmyeevich, however, assures the Russians that "They have the desire—the lust to succeed."[33] Like the Oprichniki with whom they are identified, the twelve undead mercenaries not only wreak havoc and destruction among the living, they also take a perverse, sadistic delight in their horrors, whether carried out on soldiers or unfortunate passersby, such as a peasant woman whose mutilated corpse was discovered by Aleksei on the side of a deserted road:

> There were bites everywhere. Not just bitemarks, but actual missing pieces of flesh, torn away by the vampires' hungry teeth. Both her cheeks were missing, along with parts of her throat, her breasts, her belly, her buttocks, her thighs, and her calves. They had not been thorough in their devouring of her. There was plenty of flesh still remaining. From the look of torment on her face, I could imagine only one reason why they had decided to stop eating. It was that she had died.[34]

The *voordalaki*'s carnage inscribes the war—of Russians against Napoleon's troops, and the undead against the living—across the landscape in blood and mutilated corpses as the Twelve pursue their prey, and then ultimately become prey themselves as Aleksei and his compatriots gradually realize the horrors that they have invited into their homeland. As the Twelve rise each night from the grave, they reenact the resurrection at the center of the sacred beliefs of Holy

Rus'. Like the warrior monks of the old tsar, the undead apostles bring the sacred and the profane into communion through the blood of Russians and French, soldiers and civilians.

In yet another parallel from classic folklore and literature, Cossack violence forms a similar kind of sacred aesthetic, and suggestions of carnage, resurrection, and the defiance of death abound: In Slowacki's *Mazeppa: A Tragedy*, the hero remains walled up in a shrine referred to as a "tomb," only to emerge in the next scene as "a very Lazarus," risen from the dead to continue his profane, but valiant ways; in Ryleev's *Voinarovskij*, the hero's horse collapses by a mass grave, but even as he feels his life slipping away in the midst of death, the rider is resurrected, affirming that "I arose renewed from my deathbed" to ride again; in Bulgarin's *Mazepa*, the hero, Palei, remains imprisoned in a coffin in a basement in a monastery—a triple-walled tomb; Neon, in Narezhnyi's *The Seminarist*, sleeps unnaturally deeply due to a serious wound, but awakens at the sounds of spring and renewed life; and in "St. John's Eve," Gogol's Cossack, Petro, falls into a "deathlike sleep," only to awaken on the third day. Perhaps most dramatically, the eponymous Cossack hero of Gogol's *Taras Bul'ba and Other Tales* rides to Warsaw enclosed in a tomblike pile of bricks. His Cossack spirit dies and his heart stops beating, yet he recovers, stronger than ever, and avenges the death of his son. At the novel's end, his figure is portrayed elevated, with his hand nailed to a tree trunk, in a crucifixion that implies his later resurrection.

Just as the heroic Cossack Razin, featured in countless songs and stories, lays claim to immortality: "You needn't waste your gunpowder and burst your shells—/The little bullet won't touch me, the shot won't take me,"[35] the *voordalak*, whom Dmitry describes to his friends as being worth ten Cossacks each in battle,[36] evoke and adapt this folkloric association with resurrection: They die, yet live again, to bring death to others. At the same moment, they are, like the Oprichniki, the wolves who hunt their prey in the night, committing foul acts as amoral warriors, purging not only the vermin that threaten the safety of Holy Rus', but the innocents who, like Uryupin's birds, sing her praises, as well.

Conclusion

The alternate history recounted in *Twelve*, then, offers far more than merely a supernatural backstory for the defeat of Napoleon's Grande Armée in 1812, or a melodramatic commentary on the horrors of war. Rather, its carefully crafted adaptation of the struggle to save Russia from the French illustrates the timelessness and complexities of Russia's true horrors. The Oprichniki, the Cossacks, and Kent's *voordalaki* mercenaries all merge the sacred and the profane through acts of grisly violence carried out in the name of the Orthodoxy and the Russian homeland. While the vampires of Russian folklore are simplistic creatures who merely rise from the grave to prey on the living, the Twelve are all the more terrifying—and compelling—as a result of their shared politico-religious associations. They are warriors motivated by power, pride, bloodlust, and a cause—the "desperate measures" necessitated by desperate times. The summoning of the *voordalaki* speaks to a deep, abiding nationalism rooted in the Orthodoxy, one that justifies the use of extreme violence to punish and purge its enemies, and demands that the Holy Rus' be maintained as a sacred homeland of the only true believers. The unanticipated cost of the Russians' pact with supernatural evil, on the surface, is chaos and death, among Russians as well as the French invaders. The deeper, more intimate, cost is, for Aleksei, the irrefutable knowledge that the undead evil of his ancestors' lore not only exists, but persists in his lifetime, and beyond, altering the destinies of men and nations. The havoc raised by the *voordalak* may have turned the tide of the battle around him, saving Russia and the Orthodoxy from geopolitical conquest, but in so doing, it has also shaken his faith in God and nation, sowing the seeds of doubt and granting evil a foothold in the land of true believers.

Notes

1. Adapted from Kent, *Twelve*, 9–12.
2. Ibid., 181.
3. Ibid., 172.
4. Ibid., 174.
5. Ibid., 418.
6. Ibid., 196–97.
7. Perkowski, *The Darkling.*
8. For a thorough discussion of this merging of terms, see Perkowski, *The Darkling*, 37–38.
9. Afanas'ev, "Poetic Views of the Slavs."
10. Tolstoy, "The Family of the Vurdulak." See also: Garza, *The Vampire in Slavic Cultures*, 383–400.
11. Perkowski, *Vampires of the Slavs*, 23.
12. Ibid., 24.
13. Filjushkin, *Ivan the Terrible.*
14. Ibid., 11.
15. Shpakovsky and Nicolle, *Armies of Ivan the Terrible*, 44.
16. Plokhy, *Tsars and Cossacks*, 17.
17. Ibid., 45–48.
18. Kornblatt, *Cossack Hero in Russian Literature*, 13.
19. Kent, *Twelve*, 16.
20. Kornblatt, *Cossack Hero in Russian Literature*, 5.

21. Ibid., 46.
22. Ibid., 41.
23. Ibid., 4, 16, 18.
24. Ibid., 48.
25. Ibid., 22.
26. Ibid., 39.
27. Ibid., 44.
28. Ibid.
29. Kent, *Twelve*, 16.
30. Ibid., 18.
31. Meissner, "Absolute Terror." See also: Payne and Romanoff, *Ivan the Terrible*, 345, and Dmytryshyn, *Medieval Russia*.
32. Kent, *Twelve*, 45.
33. Ibid., 47.
34. Ibid., 336.
35. Kornblatt, *The Cossack Hero*, 22.
36. Kent, *Twelve*, 18.

Bibliography

Afanas'ev, Aleksandr N. "Poetic Views of the Slavs Regarding Nature." In *Vampires of the Slavs*, edited by Jan L. Perowski, 160–61. Cambridge, MA: Slavica Publishers, 1976.

Dmytryshyn, Basil, ed. *Medieval Russia: A Source Book, 900–1700*. 2nd edition. Orlando, FL: Holt, Rinehart and Winston, 1973.

Filjushkin, Alexander. *Ivan the Terrible: A Military History*. Yorkshire, UK: Frontline Books, 2008.

Garza, Thomas J. ed. *The Vampire in Slavic Cultures*. San Diego, CA: Cognella, 2010.

Kent, Jasper *Twelve*. Amherst, NY: Pyr, 2010.

Kornblatt, Judith Deutsch. *The Cossack Hero in Russian Literature*. Madison: University of Wisconsin Press, 1992.

Meissner, Daniel J. "Absolute Terror: Ivan the Terrible." http://academic.mu.edu/meissnerd /ivan-terrible.htm.

Payne, Robert, and Nikita Romanoff. *Ivan the Terrible*. Lanham, MD: Rowman & Littlefield, 2002.

Perkowski, Jan L. *Vampires of the Slavs*. Cambridge, MA: Slavica Publishers, 1976.

———. *The Darkling: A Treatise on Slavic Vampirism*. Columbus, OH: Slavica Publishers, 1989.

Plokhy, Serhii. *Tsars and Cossacks: A Study in Iconography*. Cambridge, MA: Harvard University Press for Harvard Papers in Ukrainian Studies, 2002.

Shpakovsky, V., and D. Nicolle. *Armies of Ivan the Terrible*. Oxford, UK: Osprey Publishing, 2006.

Tolstoy, Aleksander. "The Family of the Vurdulak." In *Vampires of the Slavs*, edited by Jan L. Perkowski, 248–71. Cambridge, MA: Slavica Publishers, 1976.

CHAPTER 3

Vampire Pilots and Industrialized War in *The Bloody Red Baron*

A. Bowdoin Van Riper

We remember the war, but forget the horror. Memories of the Crimean War—the first in which the tools of the nascent industrial age were used for state-sponsored killing—revolve around the saintly image of Florence Nightingale, and the valiant, doomed Light Brigade of Tennyson's famous poem. Reenactments of the American Civil War capture the intricate rhythms of volley firing, but erase the impact of metal on flesh and bone. The ghastly landscapes of Sevastopol and Antietam, which so shocked nineteenth-century audiences, have long since faded into a sepia-toned blur. The battlefield horrors of World War II have likewise been wrapped in a gauzy shroud of patriotic memory, or declared necessary to the task of preventing still-greater horrors. The carnage wrought by American forces in post–Cold War conflicts, visited almost exclusively on brown-skinned residents of distant lands, has gone un- or underreported, and likewise failed to lodge in popular memory.[1]

World War I is the perpetual, striking exception to this pattern. No other war of the modern era has been so completely and consistently defined by its horrors, and none is so regularly presented as a brutal, traumatic experience that scarred individual participants and combatant nations alike. The popular visual image of World War I is woven from the stuff of nightmares—mud, blood, rot, rats, darkness, and chaos—and studded with icons of bleakness and destruction: trenches and seas of shell-churned mud, shattered villages and tangles of barbed wire.[2] Stirring tales of courage, daring, and narrow escape are rare in literary and cinematic depictions of the war. Iconic works such as Wilfred Owen's "Dulce et Decorum Est," Erich Maria Remarque's *All Quiet on the Western Front*, and Stanley Kubrick's *Paths of Glory* revolve, instead, around shared trauma and futile, pointless death. Tales of World War I fighter pilots are a lone, conspicuous exception to this pattern. Their pilot-heroes, though also shadowed by trauma and death, meet one another in thrilling duels high above the trenches. Styled "knights of the air," they re-create an older, more chivalrous, more personal style of combat amid the industrialized slaughter of the wider war.

Fantastic retellings of World War I proceed from the idea that, horrific as the battlefields of 1914–1918 were, they could have been worse. Kim Newman's *The Bloody Red Baron* (1995)—second in a quartet of novels mixing alternate history and literary pastiche—falls squarely into this category, positing that Count Dracula, driven out of Britain in 1897, moved to Germany and allied himself with Kaiser Wilhelm in order to foment a Europe-wide war. Aided by an all-star team of fictional mad scientists, he turns the famous "flying circus" led by Manfred "The Red Baron" von Richthofen into a cadre of ruthless, near-invincible vampire fighter pilots. He deploys them, in 1918, in a desperate effort to turn the tide of the war and ensure vampire dominance in Europe. Only a team of heroic Allied fighter pilots, Cundall's Condors, and Edwin Winthrop, a secret agent turned aviator, stand in their way. *The Bloody Red Baron* takes aim at the "knights of the air" mythology, erasing the purported distinction between fighter pilots and others and turning the war in the air into a struggle every bit as desperate, destructive, and traumatic as that played out in the trenches below. Cundall's men, vampires themselves, are as coldly ruthless as von Richthofen's in battle. Far from being throwbacks who practice an older, more chivalrous form of warfare, they are enmeshed in a brutal total-war struggle with all the hallmarks of World War II.

The Cult of the Ace

"The heavens are their battlefield," prime minister David Lloyd George said of aviators in the fall of 1917. "High above the squalor and the mud, so high in the firmament that they are not visible from earth, they fight out the eternal issues of right and wrong." Addressing the House of Commons in a speech that praised, in turn, every group that contributed to Britain's war effort, he imagined airmen as the "cavalry of the clouds," as "armed sparrows," and as "the winged hosts of light" from *Paradise Lost* before settling on a more familiar comparison. They were, he concluded, "the knighthood of this war, without fear and without reproach," who called to mind the knights of legend "not merely by the daring of their exploits, but by the nobility of their spirit."[3]

Lloyd George was working well-tilled rhetorical ground. Comparisons of pilots—specifically those who flew single-seat fighters—to knights was commonplace by the fall of 1917. Officials of virtually all the warring states did it, journalists and wartime biographers did it, and—at least when writing for public consumption—some of the pilots themselves did it. "Chivalry!" declared Canadian ace Billy Bishop in his best-selling memoir *Winged Warfare*, "Of course it existed! The bitterness and hatred between the armies and navies engaged in the war, as well as in the intense feeling of the civilians, was not present in the air forces of the countries involved. In its place was a healthy respect for and interest in the opposing flying men."[4] Albert Ball recounted how he and a German adversary, having fought until their ammunition was exhausted, burst into laughter and waved to one another before retiring.[5] American "ace of aces" Eddie Rickenbacker assured audiences that he went into battle thinking "may the best man win!"[6]

The image of pilots as knights was born during the war, as part of the same process that enshrined the "ace" as a cultural hero.[7] Charles Lindbergh, an aviation-obsessed boy during the war, recalled scouring the news for reports of Bishop, von Richthofen, René Fonck, and other aces. "Attacking enemy fighters, bombers, and balloons in mortal combat," he recalled, they "represented chivalry and daring in my own day as did King Arthur's knights in childhood stories."[8] In the two decades that followed, the knightly image not only persisted but grew. Postwar pilot memoirs like Rickenbacker's *Fighting the Flying Circus* (1919) and sensationalized popular biographies like *The Red Knight of Germany* (1927), Floyd Gibbons's romanticized account of Manfred von Richthofen, used it as a central theme. The filmmakers behind *Wings* (1927), *Lilac Time* (1928), and *The Dawn Patrol* (1930, 1938)—who used war-veteran pilots and war-surplus aircraft to re-create the skies over the Western Front in the skies over California—wove it into the films' spectacular aerial sequences and the ground-based melodrama that separated them.[9] Even pulp magazines like *G-8 and His Battle Aces* and *Air War Stories*, devoted to straightforward adventure plots and pugnacious adventurer-heroes, borrowed the central convention of the "knights of the air" mythology: a vision of aerial warfare as a series of individual duels and small-group battles with identifiable foes.[10]

The knightly image of fighter pilots became the war's most enduring myth, in part because it differed so sharply from the realities of the ground war. The fighter pilots' war, according to the myth, was a throwback to an earlier time: a clean, honorable, rule-bound, and limited conflict utterly unlike the relentless, anonymous industrialized slaughter that took place in the trenches. Fighter pilots died too, the myth acknowledged, but their deaths were imagined to be quick, dignified, and both physically and morally "clean." The death of French ace Georges Guynemer, whose plane went down in a chaotic section of the front and whose body could not immediately be found, inspired a flurry of poems and images in which angels lifted the dead hero from his cockpit and carried him away to heaven without ever touching the earth.[11]

The reality of the air war was far less immaculate, and far more complicated. There *were* acts of aerial chivalry—German ace Ernst Udet is said to have broken off a dogfight with Guynemer when he realized the Frenchman's guns had jammed—and fliers on both sides of the war observed full military courtesies in burying, or acknowledging the deaths of, their fallen opponents. Death, however, was far from the gentle ascent to heaven imagined for Guynemer. Machine gun bullets mutilated combatants' bodies as thoroughly in the air as they did on the ground, and the lack of parachutes left a pilot whose plane caught fire with an unenviable choice: burn alive in the cockpit, or take his own life by jumping or pistol shot. The fighter pilots were, like the machine gunners and artillerymen in the trenches, professional soldiers whose job was killing. They strafed troop concentrations on the ground, dropped fragmentation bombs into the trenches, and regularly attacked slow-moving bombers and observation planes that had no hope of outmaneuvering them or fighting back on even terms. The leading aces were less likely to seek out combat with their equals than to look for easy victories that would increase their personal "score." Many of the most successful approached aerial combat like big game hunting, coolly and clinically stacking the odds in their favor by approaching in the enemy's blind spot, holding fire until a hit was assured, and firing at the most vulnerable targets: the engine, fuel tank, or crew.[12]

Manfred von Richthofen, whose eighty confirmed victories made him the war's top-scoring ace, is by far the best-remembered World War I fighter pilot. Bishop and Mannock, Ball and Rickenbacker, Guynemer and Udet have all faded from popular culture, but the "Red Baron" (as the British dubbed him) remains. He is immortalized in books, films, songs, and air shows; pressed into service as the unlikely emblem of a line of frozen pizzas; and familiar to generations of *Peanuts* fans as the once-and-future adversary of the "famous World War I flying ace" that Snoopy dreams of being. Richthofen was, as historians and biographers have shown, an especially ruthless practitioner of the pilot-as-hunter style of aerial warfare. His wartime autobiography, Robert Wohl notes, "is enough to shake anyone's faith in the idea that the air war between 1914 and 1918 was a chivalric contest free of those aspects of technological mass murder that alienated and numbed a generation of men." Yet the Baron has—simply because he is so widely remembered—become interwoven, in popular memory, with the "knights of the air" myth.

Monsters Made for War

The Bloody Red Baron uses its reimagined, undead version of the Baron to deliberately, systematically demolish that myth. Far from exemplifying humankind's best qualities—boldness and daring, tempered with compassion and restraint—Richthofen and the members of his squadron are barely even human. Vampires all, they behave like haughty supermen on the ground and transform into giant batlike creatures when they take to the air. Far from being exemplars of chivalrous single combat in an era of mechanized slaughter, they are themselves products of Germany's nascent military-industrial complex: monsters made for war.

Vampires are, in Kim Newman's fictional universe, occasionally born but far more often made: created when one who is already a vampire bites and "turns" one who is not.[13] Individual vampires thus possess two sets of "blood ties": the metaphorical ones that bind them to their birth family, and the literal ones that bind them to the vampire who turned them. Newman posits that, while all vampires have some qualities in common—vulnerability to sunlight and silver, for example, and a thirst for the blood of the "warm"—certain vampiric traits are confined to particular bloodlines. Dracula and those in his direct line, for example, possess the ability to shape-shift. The vampire-pilots of Richthofen's squadron are members of Dracula's line who have been deliberately "bred"—by mad scientists acting under the direction of the Count himself—to maximize their shape-shifting abilities. They are, therefore, "made" in a second, more literal sense: the "get" not just of Dracula, but of Germany's nascent military-industrial complex.

Richthofen's men—a mixture of real-world aces and fictional characters[14]—are capable of transforming themselves, at will, into monstrous hybrid creatures, retaining their human cunning while acquiring superhuman strength and aerial agility. They go to war not by climbing aboard aircraft, but by becoming weapons themselves:

> Something grew inside Richthofen. His shoulders broadened, his spine extended. He became wider and taller. Muscles swelled like wet sponges. Veins rose like firehoses under pressure. Fur swarmed over his skin, coating now-leathery hide with a thick pelt. Bones distended, lengthened and reshaped. The face darkened. Horny skull spurs prodded out around the eyes and the jaw. Bat-ears unfurled. The Baron's eyes opened, large as fists. The calm blue was unmistakable, a continuity between man and superman. Joints grew spindly as leather curtains fell, coalescing into wings.[15]

The creatures that Richthofen and his men become are as fast and maneuverable in the air as the most advanced fighter planes, equally capable of tearing an enemy aircraft apart with their teeth and claws or blasting it out of the sky with the twin Spandau machine guns strapped to their chests by leather harnesses.

The vampire pilots combine human cunning with an animal-like instinct to hunt, kill, and consume their prey. They regard their opponents not as worthy adversaries, but as prey no more worthy of consideration than a stag or wild boar. They pluck enemy pilots from their cockpits in midair, drain them of blood and life, and toss aside the empty husks of their bodies the way a human hunter would toss aside a bone he had picked clean. The Baron himself—the most ruthless of all—draws the parallel explicitly in a conversation with his biographer, comparing his hunting of Allied pilots over the battlefield to his hunting of wild game on his family's Silesian estate.[16] Richthofen's goal, the writer notes to himself, is not simply to defeat his opponents but to destroy them. He hunts not for the sport, but for the pleasure of the kill.[17] "When I have killed an Englishman," the Baron declares on another occasion, "my hunting passion is satisfied for a quarter of an hour. Then, the urge returns."[18]

Driven by their insatiable vampiric appetites, the men of *Jagdgeschwader 1* trample the unwritten rules that, according to legend, kept aerial combat civilized. To merely defeat an enemy—to drive him away from the battle, force him to land with a dead engine, or allow him to retreat because his guns have jammed—is to lose the opportunity to feed. As eager for blood as for victory, they specifically attack enemy pilots rather than enemy machines, inflicting wounds every bit as grotesque as those suffered by the infantrymen in the trenches. The body of Captain James Albright, killed in battle with Richthofen's men early in the story, falls to earth "ripped open from neck to crotch," with "lids shrunk from staring eyes" and his throat laid open by "a sucked-dry wound the size of an orange, exposing vertebrae, pale sinew, and the underside of the jawbone."[19]

Richthofen's own hunting instinct is interwoven with a sadistic streak that renders him doubly monstrous. A familiar "knights of the air" legend involves fighter pilots who bury a fallen adversary with full military honors and drop a memorial wreath over his home base as a gesture of respect. The Baron, having killed Albright, enacts a dark burlesque of the legend, dropping not a wreath but the man's mutilated corpse onto the grass runway of Condor Squadron's aerodrome at Maranique. Later, attacking a slow-moving British reconnaissance aircraft in which Edwin Winthrop (the viewpoint character, and nominal hero, of the story) is flying as an observer, Richthofen deliberately plucks the pilot from behind the controls, leaving the (seemingly) helpless Winthrop to plummet to his death in the rear cockpit of the intact but unguided plane. The ultimate expression of the Baron's cruelty, however, comes not in the skies over the Western Front, but at his own base. There, in the midst of a conversation with an appalled brother officer, he draws his service revolver and casually shoots "a sad-eyed white beagle" that comes begging for scraps.[20] His killing of the harmless dog is a grotesque reminder that, even in human form, he remains monstrous in nature, but it is also—because his victim is clearly meant to be Snoopy—a symbolic killing of the romanticized vision of aerial warfare that is embodied in Snoopy's World War I fantasies.

Mad Science and Super Soldiers

Traditional vampires are manifestations of an ancient evil. The Red Baron and his men, however, are products of a uniquely modern evil: science, backed by the resources of a nation at war and unhindered by ethical constraints. Their ability to shape-shift—the thing that sets them apart from "ordinary" vampires and makes them into terrifying, unstoppable weapons—is the product of an elaborate selective-breeding program overseen by a consummate mad scientist: Professor Ten Brincken. Invented for the novel, Ten Brincken could easily be Dr. Frankenstein, working under an assumed name. A rival describes him as "a charlatan . . . practically an alchemist," whose mind has been warped by mysticism and gothic fantasies. He is "a daring thinker. But none of his results are verifiable. He surrounds himself with Teuton blood ritual. No control group, no hygienic conditions, no proper records."[21] Assisting him are a corps of equally mad scientists led by three notorious figures "borrowed" by Newman from other period fictions: Caligari, Mabuse, and Rotwang.

All three members of this unholy trinity are products of a single milieu: Weimar Germany. Caligari, the title character in Robert Wiene's film *The Cabinet of Dr. Caligari* (1920), is the director of an insane asylum who, insane himself, uses a sleepwalking henchman under his control to commit murders on his behalf. Mabuse—a criminal mastermind featured in Norbert Jacques' novel *Dr. Mabuse, the Gambler* (1921) and Fritz Lang's film of the same name (1922)—carries out his schemes through a network of minions he controls through telepathic hypnosis. Rotwang, the crazed inventor in Lang's *Metropolis* (1927), builds a robot in the form of a woman to "resurrect" his dead wife, then complies with a dictator's order to transform it into an *agent provocateur* that he can use to disrupt a nascent workers' rebellion. Their penchant for mingling science and mysticism, as well as their obsession with controlling others, makes them natural allies of Ten Brincken, and links them to another product of the Weimar era: Adolf Hitler.[22]

The specter of Nazism permeates the German war effort in Newman's alternate World War I. Kaiser Wilhelm, always offstage, remains the weak, befuddled figure that postwar history has traditionally painted him as: a nineteenth-century prince, tragically out of his depth and unwittingly leading his nation to ruin. Count Dracula, in contrast, is an explicitly Hitlerian figure: a charismatic visionary—a "fiend for modernity" in the words of his former lover Mata Hari[23]—determined to remake Germany in his own image. In an era when aristocratic heads of state routinely wore gaudy military uniforms bedecked with medals, "Graf von Dracula" wears a simple officer's tunic and breeches topped by a gray cloak, a peaked cap, and a holstered pistol. "While his generals advised the tactics of Waterloo and Borodino, the Graf deployed machine guns against cavalry charges and ordered the digging of trenches across the whole of Europe. He was the great adapter, the supreme pragmatist."[24]

The Count's military pragmatism extends to the use of weapons and tactics chosen for their efficiency, and without regard to whether they are outlawed by treaty or tradition. As they did in the real war, zeppelins cruise over British cities by night, raining death on the (supposedly sacrosanct) civilian population in the expectation that indiscriminate bombing will break their will to resist. The attacks in the novel, however, go well beyond those of history. On some nights, the German airships carpet the cities below them with incendiary bombs, anticipating the massive fire raids that Allied bombers unleashed on Axis cities during World War II. On other nights, a survivor remembers, they release an unquenchable flaming liquid that, as one observer recalls, "adhered to living flesh" and "burnt to the bone."[25] The liquid—though never called by this name in the text—is clearly meant to be Napalm, which became a symbol of the horrors of modern warfare in World War II, Korea, and especially Vietnam.[26]

Richthofen and his squadron—a different kind of terror weapon, used to break the morale of Allied pilots—are Dracula's proudest creation. Ten Brincken may have orchestrated their creation—bringing the fliers together with elder members of ancient, distinguished vampire bloodlines and telling them whom to feed on, and for how long—but Dracula is their ultimate master. His blood flows in their veins, enhancing their powers, and binding them to him. "He is the ringmaster of the Flying Circus," Mata Hari explains, "and the Red Baron is his star act."[27] Overruling military advisors who consider them more useful as a psychological weapon, lurking in the shadows and building a fearsome reputation that corrodes Allied morale, Dracula places the Flying Circus in the vanguard of a massive, million-man attack on Paris. Gliding over the French countryside, they—along with Dracula's giant airship, the *Attila*—are not merely a weapon but a symbol of a modern Germany and its expanding dominion over Europe.

The vampire pilots—like the mad scientists who created them, and the portrayal of Dracula himself—paint Newman's phantasmagoric version of World War I Germany as Nazi-like without actually wrapping it in the trappings of the Third Reich. The pilots are part of a long tradition of fictional Nazi supersoldiers, and their origins in a state-sponsored selective-breeding program echoes interwar Germany's fascination with eugenics—a fascination that, as Newman subtly suggests, the Germans shared with the British and Americans.[28] Professor Ten Brincken's obsession with "Teutonic blood rituals," and Dracula's with the purity of vampire bloodlines, suggest Hitler's own obsession with preserving the purity of Germany's "Aryan" gene pool. There are no campaigns to drive the "warm" from Dracula's Germany, no camps to which they are exiled, and no dark design for eradicating them from the face of the earth, but—if they were to appear—they would strike few historically aware readers as out of place.

A Squadron of Survivors

Defending the West from such epic evil compels the Allies to abandon their pre-war notions of civilized war, and embrace ruthless efficiency instead. Too much is at stake for them to do otherwise. Midway through the book, for example, Winthrop visits a secret underground laboratory where Doctor Moreau and his American assistant, Herbert West, conduct vivisection experiments on captured vampires in order to discover their secrets and develop better ways to kill them.[29] The laboratory is, like Condor Squadron and Winthrop himself, controlled by the Diogenes Club—the secret "shadow cabinet" that directs the Allies' covert war against Dracula. When Dracula launches his great offensive, the leaders of the club order the Condors to intercept the *Attila* and shoot it down in flames: an assassination-by-aircraft that will "cut off the head" of wartime Germany and allow the body to wither. Croft, the spokesman for the Diogenes Club, is blunt about the nature of the plan, which foreshadows the American assassination of Admiral Isoroku Yamamoto in 1943.[30] When one of the pilots makes a light-hearted remark about looking forward to "a spot of Zep-busting," Croft sternly corrects him. "This is not sport . . . this is war. In this instance, this is murder. Make no mistake."[31]

The pilots of Condor Squadron are, nominally, the "good guys" in *The Bloody Red Baron*. Their ranks, as if to underscore the point, include both real World War I aces like Albert Ball and A. P. F. Rhys-Davids and fictional heroes such as Captain Midnight and The Shadow.[32] The mixture of characters reflects the diversity of sources—comic books, pulp magazines, and boys' adventure novels, along with romanticized histories and memoirs of the air war—that shaped the "knights of the air" mythology, but there is nothing knightly about the characters themselves. They are cold, cynical, and fatalistic: "a squadron of survivors, almost a squadron of sole survivors" who have "outlive[d] their fellows many times over,"[33] laying aside their youthful romanticism and idealism along the way. Aerial combat is, for them, just a job, to be completed with the greatest possible efficiency and the fewest possible risks.

Winthrop senses this coldness in his first encounter with the Condors, whom he finds unnerving "even for vampires."[34] Although he knows "the crucial differences between war as waged in the jingo press and war as waged in France," he is startled when his request for a pilot to fly a dangerous night reconnaissance mission does not lead to "a dignified competition of volunteers."[35] Forced to choose, he is surprised again when the pilot he picks merely responds "fair enough." The men of Condor Squadron have no shortage of skill, bravery, or daring, but those qualities manifest themselves as icy professionalism rather than swashbuckling romanticism. Their references to the legends that the press has created around them are laced with irony, and a young lieutenant named

Bigglesworth is visibly upset when a comrade implies that he takes his press-conferred status as a "knight of the air" seriously. When bad weather grounds the enemy, one pilot declares it "unsporting of the Hun, not coming out to play,"[36] but his tone is one of mockery. Well aware of the dangers they face, the pilots seek every possible advantage in combat. They use darkness, clouds, or the enemy's blind spots for cover; hold their fire until the last possible moment to ensure a hit; and concentrate their fire on vulnerable points such as engines, fuel tanks, and the enemy pilots themselves. Returning from missions, they empty their machine guns into enemy trenches—killing the enemy while lightening their own planes for landing.[37] One of the Condors, after attacking enemy fliers who have just landed and are unable to fight back, is unperturbed that his tactics were unsporting and his victory over the enemy will not be recorded. "One of the monsters [is] gone," and nothing else matters.[38] The goal is not victory rendered honorable by adherence to a particular set of conventions, but victory, period.

These tactics leave no room for respect or honor between individual pilots on opposite sides of the conflict. Cundall's men rarely refer to the members of the Flying Circus by name; they see them not as individual adversaries, but as interchangeable targets, all more or less equally needing to be killed. When they *do* invoke an individual, it is to curse his name (the sobriquet "Bloody Red Baron" taking on a triple meaning[39]) or—as Ball does with the Red Baron's brother Lothar, who shot him down—spit contemptuously on the floor and wish them dead. Winthrop, once a principled man appalled by their ruthlessness, is transformed when Richthofen leaves him to die in the plunging, pilotless reconnaissance plane. Crawling toward the front cockpit through a hundred-mile-per-hour slipstream, he reaches the controls determined—if he survives his ordeal—to "return to filthy Hunland, slaughter the evil bat-thing that had taken Courtney, and drink the Kaiser's stinking blood from a bowl made of the fucking brainpan of the Graf von Dracula."[40]

Fighting a war this way takes its toll, and—among the Allied pilots—Newman uses vampirism as a proxy for that toll. Winthrop's mental transformation from chivalrous gentleman to ruthless killer unfolds alongside his decision to embrace, rather than continue to resist, the entreaties of his lover Kate (a vampire) to let her turn him. Initially repulsed by the prospect of becoming a vampire himself, he gradually comes to see it as a matter of wartime expediency: a source of strength, physical resilience, and other qualities that will serve his ultimate goal of killing the Red Baron and, ultimately, his master, Count Dracula. Newman frames Winthrop's twin transformations as intertwined and inseparable: physical and mental/moral degradation unfolding simultaneously, forced upon Winthrop by the mortal threat posed by Germany and the all-consuming demands of total war. The pilots of Condor Squadron have all,

Newman implies, undergone similar transformations, and Albert Ball symbolizes the price they have paid. Deadly in the air—the squadron's finest pilot, and the Allied "ace of aces"—Ball is a virtual cripple on the ground, a grotesque figure with twisted limbs and a shambling, apelike gait.[41] He himself is too far gone for any imaginable postwar future—and he dies midway through the story, literally tearing himself apart in order to help Winthrop escape from a group of psychotic deserters who have captured them both—but it is no stretch to see, in the members of Condor Squadron who *do* survive, the Lost Generation in the making.

Conclusion: A Different Kind of War

The death of innocents, and of innocence itself, is the central theme in the *ur-narrative* of World War I. The theme emerged, even before the guns fell silent, in the work of soldier-poets like Wilfred Owen and Siegfried Sassoon, and was canonized in postwar novels and memoirs like Ernest Hemingway's *A Farewell to Arms*, Robert Graves's *Good-Bye to All That*, and Erich Maria Remarque's *All Quiet on the Western Front* (all 1929). It suffuses Rudyard Kipling's poem-cycle "Epitaphs of the War": the bitter, anguished work of a grieving father who lost his only son to a war that he himself had enthusiastically supported. The young men who came of age during and just after the war lived out their lives in a world transformed, emerging into adulthood to find, as F. Scott Fitzgerald put it: "all Gods dead, all wars fought, all faiths in man shaken."[42]

The "knights of the air" legend exists within, and draws its power from, that larger cultural narrative. It presents fighter pilots as embodiments of the world that World War I swept away, and their chivalrous behavior toward one another as a valiant (if ultimately futile) attempt to hold back the tides of history. The war in the trenches is modernity embodied: streamlined, mechanized, efficient, and dehumanizing. The war in the air is the last refuge of Edwardian gentility and Progressive-Era idealism. The "knights of the air" may fight their war at a hundred miles per hour, in sophisticated flying machines armed with twin machine guns, but they fight it with gentlemanly restraint, according to an agreed-upon set of rules. Their determination to treat enemy pilots as adversaries rather than targets, and the air war as a series of duels rather than a win-at-all-costs street fight, is thus an implicitly political statement: an assertion that the world the war destroyed was better than the world it made.

The Bloody Red Baron imagines an alternate World War I in which Dracula and his minions have made such idealism an unaffordable luxury. The kaiser, embracing the count and his vampire legions, takes on monstrous allies whom the West can defeat only by throwing away the old rules of war and, like Winthrop and the vampire pilots of Condor Squadron, becoming monsters themselves. Newman's tale of ruthless aerial combat—of machine guns loaded with silver bullets and pilots' bodies ripped open and sucked dry in mid-flight—turns the fighter pilots of World War I into harbingers of a second, more terrible war yet to come.

Notes

1. On this process at work in American culture see, for example: Slotkin, "Continuity of Forms" on the Crimean War; Blight, *Race and Reunion* and Horwitz, *Confederates in the Attic* on the Civil War; Roeder, *The Censored War* and Nobile, *Judgment at the Smithsonian* on World War II; and Poole, *Unspeak*, 101–25, on America's post–Cold War conflicts.

2. Fussell's *The Great War and Modern Memory*, the classic survey of literary responses to World War I, should be read in light of the revisions proposed in Quinn and Trout, *Literature of the Great War Reconsidered*, and the broader view offered in Winter, *Remembering War*.

3. Lloyd George, "A Nation's Thanks," 212.

4. Quoted in Pisano et al., *Legend*, 27. Bishop, with an official total of seventy-two victories, was the highest-scoring ace in the Royal Flying Corps, and the third-highest-scoring pilot of the war, after René Fonck (seventy-five victories) and Manfred von Richthofen (eighty victories).

5. Briscoe and Stannard, *Captain Ball*, 213.

6. Rickenbacker, *Fighting the Flying Circus*, 136.

7. Pisano et al., *Legend*, 31–41; Fritzsche, *A Nation of Fliers*, 59–101; Robertson, *Dream of Civilized Warfare*, 87–114.

8. Lindbergh, *Autobiography of Values*, 63.

9. Paris, *Wright Brothers to Top Gun*, 24–54.

10. On *G-8 and His Battle Aces*, arguably the most famous of the aviation pulps, see Carr, *Flying Spy*.

11. Pisano et al., *Legend*, 39; Wohl, *A Passion for Wings*, 229–38. The image of the dying aviator lifted directly into heaven became an established part of aviation folklore and popular culture. On its persistence after World War I, see Van Riper, *Imagining Flight*, 123–26, and Van Riper, ". . . And Touched the Face of God," 99, 104–5.

12. See, for example, Fritzsche, *Nation of Fliers*, 82–101. Wohl, Robertson, and Pisano offer similar deconstructions of the myth.

13. Spies recruited to work for their (former) enemies are said to be "turned"; members of organized-crime families rewarded for their fealty are said to be "made men." Given Newman's penchant for thickly layered allusions, his use of those terms—and their connotations of moral corruption—may well be deliberate.

14. Aside from the Red Baron himself, the *staffel* includes Herman Goering and Von Richthofen's younger brother Lothar, who were both members of it in the real world;

Ernst Udet, Germany's second-ranked ace, who flew with another squadron; and Bruno Stachel, the ambitious young antihero created by Jack D. Hunter in his novel *The Blue Max* (1964) and played by George Peppard in the film adaptation (1966).

15. Newman, *Bloody Red Baron*, 243.

16. Ibid., 217–18.

17. Ibid., 218.

18. Ibid., 253. The quote is genuine—taken from Richthofen's wartime memoir.

19. Ibid., 26.

20. Ibid., 254.

21. Ibid., 117.

22. Goodrick-Clarke, *Occult Roots of Nazism*, 19–22.

23. Newman, *Bloody Red Baron*, 100.

24. Ibid., 83.

25. Ibid., 90.

26. A form of jellied gasoline that burns at high temperatures while clinging tenaciously to whatever it touches, napalm was first used against Japanese fortifications in 1944 and Japanese cities in 1945. Widely employed by American forces in Vietnam as an antipersonnel weapon, it became a potent symbol of the destruction wrought by that war, particularly after the publication of a news photo showing a naked, burned Vietnamese child fleeing in terror after a napalm attack.

27. Newman, *Bloody Red Baron*, 108.

28. See Kevles, *In the Name of Eugenics*.

29. Moreau, in H. G. Wells's science-fiction/horror novel *The Island of Doctor Moreau*, surgically transforms animals into humans; West, in H. P. Lovecraft's novella "Herbert West—Reanimator," uses a chemical serum to revive the dead.

30. Having learned, by reading decoded communications, that Yamamoto planned to fly to the Philippines at a specific day and time, senior US commanders dispatched a squadron of long-range fighters to intercept his transport and shoot it down.

31. Newman, *Bloody Red Baron*, 302.

32. Both characters appear in the novel under their "real" names—James Albright and Harry Allard, respectively—but Newman includes abundant clues to their secret identities.

33. Newman, *Bloody Red Baron*, 4.

34. Ibid., 4.

35. Ibid., 6.

36. Ibid., 7.

37. Ibid., 310.

38. Ibid., 292.

39. Bloody as in murdering; bloody as in vampire; and bloody as in "fucking."

40. Newman, *Bloody Red Baron*, 158–59.

41. The effect is heightened by comparison with the most widely reproduced image of the real-world Ball: a posed photograph, taken at the height of his fame, depicting him as a handsome, clean-cut twenty-year-old in an immaculate uniform—the epitome of Edwardian youth.

42. Fitzgerald, *This Side of Paradise*, 218.

Bibliography

Blight, David W. *Race and Reunion: The Civil War in American Memory*. Cambridge, MA: Harvard University Press, 2009.

Briscoe, Walter Alwynn, and H. Russell Stannard. *Captain Ball, V.C.* London: Jenkins, 1918.

Carr, Nick. *Flying Spy: The History of G-8*. Rockville, MD: Borgo Press, 2007.

Fitzgerald, F. Scott. *This Side of Paradise*. 1948. Rockville, MD: Serenity Publishers, 2008.

Fritzsche, Peter. *A Nation of Fliers: German Aviation and the Popular Imagination*. Cambridge, MA: Harvard University Press, 1992.

Fussell, Paul. *The Great War and Modern Memory*. New York: Oxford University Press, 1975.

Goodrick-Clarke, Nicholas. *The Occult Roots of Nazism: Secret Aryan Cults and their Influence on Nazi Ideology*. New York: NYU Press, 1992.

Horwitz, Tony. *Confederates in the Attic: Dispatches from the Unfinished Civil War*. New York: Vintage, 1998.

Kevles, Daniel J. *In the Name of Eugenics*. Baltimore: Johns Hopkins University Press, 1986.

Lindbergh, Charles A. *Autobiography of Values*. New York: Harcourt, 1978.

Lloyd George, David. "A Nation's Thanks." In *The Great Crusade: Extracts from Speeches Delivered during the War*, edited by F. L. Stevenson, 199–215. New York: Doran, 1918.

Newman, Kim. *The Bloody Red Baron*. New York: Carroll & Graf, 1995.

Nobile, Philip, ed. *Judgment at the Smithsonian: The Uncensored Script of the Smithsonian's 50th Anniversary Exhibit of the* Enola Gay. New York: Marlowe and Company, 1995.

Paris, Michael. *From the Wright Brothers to* Top Gun*: Aviation, Nationalism, and Popular Cinema*. Manchester, UK: Manchester University Press, 1995.

Pisano, Dominick A., Thomas J. Dietz, Joanne M. Gernstein, and Karl S. Schneide. *Legend, Memory, and the Great War in the Air*. Seattle: University of Washington Press, 1992.

Poole, Steven. *Unspeak: How Words Become Weapons, How Weapons Become a Message, and How That Message Becomes Reality*. Boston: Little, Brown, 2006.

Quinn, Patrick J., and Steven Trout, eds. *The Literature of the Great War Reconsidered: Beyond Modern Memory*. London: Palgrave, 2001.

Rickenbacker, Eddie. *Fighting the Flying Circus*. New York: Stokes, 1919.

Robertson, Linda Raine. *The Dream of Civilized Warfare: World War I Flying Aces and the American Imagination*. Minneapolis: University of Minnesota Press, 2003.

Roeder, George H. *The Censored War: American Visual Experience during World War Two*. New Haven, CT: Yale University Press, 1995.

Slotkin, Richard. "The Continuity of Forms: Myth and Genre in Warner Brothers' *The Charge of the Light Brigade*." *Representations*, no. 29 (Winter 1990): 1–23.

Van Riper, A. Bowdoin. "'. . . And Touched the Face of God': Memorializing Disaster in the U.S. Space Program." In *We Are What We Remember: The American Past through*

Commemoration, edited by Jeffrey Lee Meriwether and Laura Mattoon D'Amore, 94–113. Cambridge: Cambridge Scholars Publishing, 2013.

———. *Imagining Flight: Aviation and Popular Culture*. College Station: Texas A&M University Press, 2003.

Winter, Jay Murray. *Remembering War: The Great War between Memory and History in the Twentieth Century*. New Haven, CT: Yale University Press, 2006.

Wohl, Robert. *A Passion for Wings: Aviation and the Western Imagination, 1908–1918*. New Haven, CT: Yale University Press, 1994.

CHAPTER 4

Nazis on the Moon! Nazis under the Polar Ice Cap!

AND OTHER RECENT EPISODES IN THE STRANGE CINEMATIC AFTERLIFE OF THE THIRD REICH

James J. Ward

> The enemy can make dust and ashes of our houses; but this makes the hearts of our population burn with hatred, but not to burn to ashes. One day the hour of retribution will come.
>
> —Joseph Goebbels, June 1943[1]

By every objective standard, it was clear by the middle of 1944 that Germany had lost the war. The military conspiracy to assassinate Hitler on July 20, reenacted in the 2008 Tom Cruise film *Valkyrie*, was but one symptom of the growing recognition throughout Germany that the war could no longer be won, the claims of Joseph Goebbels's Propaganda Ministry notwithstanding. While it was still capable of effective rear-guard actions and of occasional tactical successes, the Wehrmacht had been worn down in the huge battles of the preceding years against an ever-stronger Soviet adversary.[2] Weakened by its efforts to resupply the doomed Sixth Army at Stalingrad in the winter of 1942–1943, the Luftwaffe had been forced to concede control of the air space over Germany to British and American bomber squadrons.[3] With the country's war industry nearly defenseless against heavy bombardment, the strategic bombing campaign against German cities assumed more and more massive dimensions, forcing the Nazi leadership to divert human and material resources to antiaircraft defenses, the repair of rail lines and marshalling yards, and the restoration of some measure of "normality" to a war-weary civilian population.[4] Even more daunting than the military situation were Germany's economic prospects. While armaments production reached its highest levels in the second half of 1944, the effort could not be sustained. Crucial materials like steel, aluminum, copper, and magnesium were in short supply, and when new deliveries did reach front line troops, the weapons frequently proved unreliable and no spare parts accompanied them.[5] As the collapse of the German war economy became increasingly likely, the administrative chaos that had always been implicit in the structure of Nazi rule asserted itself. Where government officials faltered, fanatical party members stepped in. The result was what has been called the "cumulative radicalization" of the Third Reich as it entered its death throes.[6]

Amid this spectrum of defeat and disintegration, the Nazi leaders' determination to continue the war regardless of material destruction and human suffering has defied attempts at rational explanation. If the effect of Goebbels's propaganda machine was wearing thin, fear of the Gestapo and—with the collapse of the eastern front in 1944—fear of reprisals by the Red Army combined to prevent the emergence of any serious opposition to the regime. The war could not end with anything short of the total destruction of the Nazi state, and the German people were both complicit and compliant in continuing a futile struggle. To the extent that any hope existed for a less catastrophic outcome, it was based in the promise that new and terrible weapons—"wonder weapons"—were about to go into large-scale production. The reality of these secret weapons programs fell far short of the promises trumpeted by Goebbels's propaganda. Even those technological triumphs that were genuine, like the Me-262 jet fighter and the V-2 rocket, had little effect on the military and strategic balance in the last stages of the war, as they were neutralized by competing resource and labor priorities, pointless infighting among party satraps, and lack of development time.[7]

The secret nature of the Nazis' advanced weapons programs, together with their fierce determination to fight to the end against overwhelming odds, explains the quasi-mythic quality these projects acquired after 1945 and still possess today. This is nowhere better seen than in the spate of recent films that combine some measure of historical plausibility about the Third Reich with essays in the arcane and the occult, scientific and medical experiments outside any credible limits, and staples of exploitation cinema such as zombies, robots, and hybrid beings. These creatures and the films they inhabit may not belong in the usual catalog of horrors associated with World War II, but they reinforce the suspicion that we may not be finished with the Nazis, or that they may not be finished with us.

Nazi Zombies and Werewolves in . . . Ohio?

Given that he was fighting Nazis in *Inglourious Basterds* in 2009 and fighting zombies in *World War Z* in 2013, it might have seemed inevitable that the next stop in Brad Pitt's career would be to fight Nazi zombies. Unfortunately, it appears that this project is yet to be pitched. At an equivalent level of star power, Jenna Jameson—although her two crossovers so far, *The Evil Breed* in 2003 and

Zombie Strippers in 2008, dropped with a thud—should perhaps be thinking about a leading role in *Nazi Zombie Strippers*. After all, Sybil Danning came out of retirement to tease us in Rob Zombie's faux trailer for *Werewolf Women of the SS*, included in the theatrical release of Quentin Tarantino's and Robert Rodriguez's *Grindhouse* (2007), raising expectations that a new round of *Ilsa, She-Wolf of the SS* (1974) look-alikes might be in the offing. For years, viewers waited eagerly for Dutch filmmaker Richard Raaphorst's two award-winning trailers for his Nazi zombie opus, *Worst Case Scenario*, to materialize in a full-length film, only to be disappointed when the necessary funding failed to come through. But in 2013 some of Raaphorst's most ingeniously contrived Wehrmacht zombots finally made it to the screen in *Frankenstein's Army*, released on DVD and broadcast on several North American video-on-demand networks. So there might still be hope for *Nazi Zombie Strippers*, with or without Jenna Jameson and Brad Pitt.

In the last few years two scholarly anthologies have appeared on the continuing popularity of Nazi-related themes in entertainment, the mass media, and other cultural outlets, along with several scholarly articles addressing the same subject.[8] Obviously, interest in the Third Reich reaches well beyond the self-referential communities of Wehrmacht enthusiasts, SS fetishists, and World War II computer gamers.[9] Of the several subcategories of films about the Nazis, the one involving zombies shows no signs of loosening its grip on its fans and their appetite for un-killable Wehrmacht soldiers and SS men.[10] Following up on the success of the first

Working for the Nazis, Victor Frankenstein's grandson fine-tunes one of his Wehrmacht zombots, a hammer-headed killing machine. *Frankenstein's Army* (2013).

Dead Snow film (2009), in which some unwitting Norwegian medical students have a fatal run-in with a thawed-out corps of Waffen SS troops, *Dead Snow 2*, released in 2014, has the subtitle *Red vs. Dead*, which might be open to multiple interpretations. The original subtitle, *War of the Dead*, had to be scrapped when a Finnish-made film of the same title went into DVD distribution in 2011. Reportedly the most expensive film ever shot in Lithuania (€1 million), this *War of the Dead* was finished in 2008 but was delayed by cast and funding problems. The narrative is confused at best, involving a four-way struggle among Finns, Germans, Americans, and Russians and never explaining what Americans are doing fighting in Finland in 1941. A backstory, set in 1939, informs viewers that the Nazis had carried out "anti-death" experiments on Russian POWs in a secret facility on the Finnish-Russian border—again the history is indecipherable given that Germany and Russia were allies from August 1939 to June 1941—that enabled them to create indestructible super-soldiers. The main story focuses on the efforts of a British-American commando squad to locate the Nazi installation, abandoned on Hitler's orders when German weapons research was redirected to other projects, and destroy any of the super-soldiers who might still be concealed there. The plot remains muddled since it is never entirely clear whether the zombie soldiers who fight the titular war are Russians or Germans. Eventually the always useful SS insignia resolves the question.

Given their historical experience with the Nazis, it may be understandable why the Finns, Norwegians, and Lithuanians remain haunted by the threat of their return, even if in zombie form.[11] It requires a greater stretch of the imagination to locate German troops in Ohio, especially when the filmmakers' attempt to simulate northern France is so half-hearted. Yet this is what transpires in the American-made *Horrors of War*, released for theatrical distribution in 2006 and available on DVD a year later. Despite the catchy title and a plot that seems to have been lifted from Steven Spielberg's Oscar-winning *Saving Private Ryan* (1998), *Horrors of War* has largely escaped critical attention other than to be roundly denounced by the Internet Movie Database's user reviewers and message boards. According to the production history included with the DVD edition, *Horrors of War* was originally planned as a three-film anthology about Nazi research into the supernatural during World War II. Because of creative differences among its writers and producers, the project eventually collapsed into a single film, unified by the character of Lieutenant John Schmidt, an OSS operative assigned to carry out a secret mission behind German lines in occupied France. Predictably, Schmidt and a squad of misfit GIs from the First Infantry Division—nicknamed the "Big Red One"—encounter some terrifying creatures after they are air-dropped into enemy territory.

Schmidt has a backstory, having filed reports on something he saw in the fighting after the D-Day landings that no one else in his unit would confirm. In a grainy flashback, some American soldiers come upon the horrifically mutilated corpses of a German machine gun unit along with a single traumatized GI. The Germans have a creature that walks on all fours, the American tells his rescuers, some kind of wolf or giant cat. The beast turned on the machine gunners, killing everyone but him. There was also a mysterious German in civilian clothes, who seemed to be in command and whose appearance suggested that he was a Gestapo agent. The Americans move on, engage in a firefight with a German artillery unit, and reach a farmhouse inhabited by two women. In keeping with the "Dirty Dozen" impersonation, the officer in charge, Captain Mitchell, rapes one of the women and then kills her, even as the growls of an animal are heard outside the farmhouse. The other woman gives one of the more sympathetic soldiers four silver bullets, telling him he will need them. The following night, having set up camp, the Americans come face-to-face with the werewolf that has been stalking them. Captain Mitchell gets what is coming to him, and Sergeant Gary is bitten. But the silver bullets work and the dead werewolf reverts to his human form as the brother of the two French women. The film then jumps to an American base camp where Lieutenant Schmidt is being given his assignment. Feeling the pressure of the Allied advance, Hitler has ordered his scientists to step up their efforts to develop new weapons that can reverse the flow of battle before it is too late. At a laboratory east of Metz, Dr. Heinrich Schaltur has been put in charge of Operation Osiris, the details of which are a closely guarded secret. Dr. Schaltur has to be captured and his research brought to a halt.

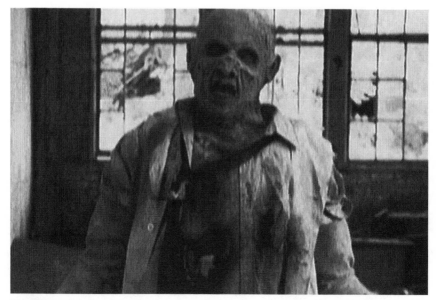

Nazi scientist Dr. Schaltur demonstrates the effects of his research in the science of zombification. *Horrors of War* (2006).

Now teamed up with Captain Joe Russo, played by Joe Lorenzo, who had his own encounter with some kind of Nazi super-soldier on Omaha Beach, Lieutenant Schmidt and his team succeed in locating Schaltur's laboratory. After another firefight and a run-in with a monstrous German soldier who proves difficult to kill, the Americans find Dr. Schaltur amid the evidence of his handiwork. "I gave them soldiers that were impervious to bullets, to pain," the scientist discloses. "I gave them two prototypes. They have abnormal strength and stamina. They wanted stronger soldiers, so I made another test of the formula. It must have been too strong." Suddenly it is clear that Schaltur's final test has been upon himself. As the Americans try to subdue the zombie scientist, Sergeant Gary reappears, in werewolf form. While the two monsters wrestle, Captain Russo injects himself with the formula. Transformed at once, Russo manages to kill Schaltur before, at Russo's own pleading, Schmidt kills his fellow officer. Back at the base camp, Schmidt is commended for the success of his mission, then told that he will have to "go back in . . . if there's more of those things."

Made on a budget of $300,000 and filmed entirely in Ohio, *Horrors of War* leaves a lot to be desired as a World War II horror or science fiction epic.[12] The locations are unconvincing—the site of Schaltur's laboratory looks exactly like what it is: a rusting factory in Youngstown—and the firefights between the Americans and the Germans are almost comical. At best there are three or four zombie super-soldiers, and the two werewolves look as if they are outfitted with department store Halloween masks. In a generally muddled plot, various cinematic borrowings are obvious. The werewolf story echoes Neil Marshall's *Dogs of War* (2002), where it was handled more convincingly, and with a larger budget. The gratuitous rape and murder recalls Brian DePalma's *Casualties of War* (1989), and there are a number of egregious rip-offs from *Saving Private Ryan*, including a captured German soldier who professes his admiration of Babe Ruth in hopes of staying alive. The film's greatest failing, however, is that its zombie super-soldiers are both unconvincing and unscary; and since there are only three or four of them—and they can be killed—it is unlikely that they will have much effect on the course of the fighting in western Europe.

The Phantom Reich: Mystics, Necromancers, and Nazi Satanists

Another subcategory of Nazi cinema that appears to be flourishing is that involving the occult. Unlike Nazi zombies, Nazi occultism has drawn serious scholarly attention in recent years, in part because powerful figures like Alfred Rosenberg and Heinrich Himmler took a personal interest in the subject, but also because of its susceptibility to distortion and exploitation by journalists, filmmakers, and television producers.[13] Joel Schumacher's 2009 film *Blood Creek* transports a Nazi archaeologist with an obsessive interest in the occult to 1930s West Virginia, where he bribes a rural family of German descent to shelter him while he pursues his research into necromancy, reincarnation, and runic magic. The result, seventy years later, is to unleash a horde of Nazi vampire-zombies on the unsuspecting locals. Most critics felt that the director of *Lost Boys* (1987) and *Flatliners* (1990) had lost his way with this essay into Nazi supernaturalism, even if the idea of Nazis lurking in the West Virginia backwoods offered a welcome change from the usual fare of overprivileged college kids running into families of inbred psychopaths and cannibalistic moonshiners.

The Nazis' interest in the occult has long provided a rich fund of material for filmmakers, especially since the success of the first *Indiana Jones* movie (1981) and more recently that of the *Hellboy* series (2004 et seq.). Along the way there have been a couple of standouts, most notably *The Keep* (1983), written and directed by Michael Mann, and the much underrated *The Ogre* (1996), with direction by Volker Schlöndorff and starring John Malkovich in the title role. While *The Ogre* only flirts with occultism, primarily through the presence of Hermann Göring, its setting in the East Prussian districts so bitterly fought over by the Germans and the Russians—part of what Timothy Snyder has labeled "The Bloodlands"—provides a pivot for several more recent films in which the Nazis' efforts to master the dark arts leaves a legacy that persists to the present day.[14] In this regard the 2001 British-made *The Bunker*, scripted by Clive Dawson and directed by Rob Green, is an outlier—it is set in the Ardennes as retreating German forces try to find defensible positions in the face of the Allied advance—and more of a study in fear, claustrophobia, and paranoia than an essay in the occult. Still, its allusions to supernatural forces and to vengeance exacted over an unspecified, but presumably wide, arc of historical time place it among Nazi occult films even if its principals are lowly Wehrmacht soldiers who, by unknowingly entering the crypt to which the title obliquely refers, find themselves in way over their heads. And, as Steffen Hantke points out, there is specific reference to atrocities committed by German forces in eastern Europe, which now return to haunt some of those responsible.[15]

Considerably more successful have been the first two films in the *Outpost* series, both directed by Steve Barker for Glasgow-based Black Camel Pictures. In *Outpost* (2008), Irish-born Ray Stevenson (a kind of everyman George Clooney) leads a mixed-nationality band of mercenaries into an unspecified eastern European country to locate a World War II German bunker in which the scheming business executive who has hired them has taken an interest. While the film is rooted in the category of Nazi science run amok, incorporating a lengthy disquisition on the military applications of unified field theory, the Wehrmacht soldiers with whom the mercenaries are soon doing battle are more phantomlike than they are standard-issue zombies in World War II uniforms. Admittedly, the miniature cyclotron the Nazis installed in the bunker lends some credibility to the film's theoretical premise, and the super-soldiers it yielded represent more than a mere nuisance in their capability to materialize and dematerialize at will. A never-explained civil war, corporate greed, and vague references to a UN rescue mission also impart plausibility, at least for anyone who remembers the 1990s in southeastern Europe. *Outpost: Black Sun* (2012) is similarly set somewhere in the Balkans and returns us briefly to the closing stages of World War II before fast-forwarding to the present where a NATO mission is under way to bring a halt to an inexplicable wave of violence. Again, there's a good measure of science involved, including the use of an electromagnetic pulse as a last-ditch defense against otherworldly threats, while the indestructible Nazi super-soldiers have somehow acquired a greater measure of materiality. The film straddles the line between science turned to monstrous ends and the forces of the occult.

The Nazis' excursions into the occult were examined with greater attention in the New Zealand–made *The Devil's Rock* in 2011. In advance of the D-Day invasion, two New Zealand commandos land on Forau Island, off the coast of the Nazi-occupied island of Guernsey, to spike the guns that otherwise would be firing on Allied troop carriers as they crossed the English Channel. At first impression a low-budget replay of *The Guns of Navarone* (1961), *The Devil's Rock* soon veers in a different direction as the intrepid commandos discover the bodies of slaughtered German soldiers inside an abandoned bunker. In no time one of the New Zealanders is dead and the other is being tortured by an SS scientist whose research into the island's supernatural properties has gotten out of hand. The remainder of the film involves Satanic rituals, shape-shifting, and

An SS occultist meets his match in the "hell-whore" his incantations have summoned from the dead, on the eve of D-Day. *The Devil's Rock* (2011).

a seductive female demon. Directed by Paul Campion, who earned his earlier film credits for special effects, *The Devil's Rock* does a respectable job in revisiting ground already covered by *The Keep*, *The Bunker*, and the *Outpost* films, with the added frisson of a flesh-craving female lead getting the better of the SS man who has invoked her presence on the führer's behalf. Played by New Zealand actress Gina Varela, who supplies a passable impersonation of the better-known Famke Janssen (of the *X-Men* series), the Nazi succubus leaves the screen strewn with blood splatter, body parts, and thwarted desire.

A Fourth Reich? Above the Earth? Inside the Earth?

The two most ambitious attempts to extrapolate a future for the Third—or Fourth—Reich fall squarely in the much-trafficked domain of Nazi science. Like the Nazis' interest in the occult, their research in the hard sciences has been a subject for serious academic study as well as for cinematic exploitation.[16] Particularly in light of competing American and Russian efforts to capture as many German scientists as possible in the first months after the war, scholars have sought to determine just how much the nuclear arms and space races depended on research done under the Nazis.[17] Most of the films made in the 1950s and 1960s were both cheap and cheesy, filled with hackneyed characters, implausible plotlines, and grotesque experiments that borrowed from medical practices the Nazis had employed in some of their death camps. Occasionally a more credible film would emerge, only to sink into obscurity until it was retrieved decades later thanks to the revival of both popular and scholarly interest in exploitation cinema.[18] Yet the factual evidence of what the Nazis were able to accomplish during the war—despite scarce resources and constant turf wars among government, party, and military agencies—continues to provide points of departure for films that stretch viewers' credulity to the breaking point, or beyond.[19]

Several years in the making and funded in part with contributions by supportive fans (the model Richard Raaphorst tried to use for *Worst Case Scenario*), the Australian-Finnish-German coproduction *Iron Sky* finally made it to theatrical release in 2012, followed by global DVD distribution.[20] Building on the fact that no small number of Nazi officials had escaped the collapse of the Third Reich in 1945, usually to one or another South American country, *Iron Sky* constructs an entire scientific and military complex on the far side of the Moon where, for seventy years, weapons are forged for the eventual reconquest of the Earth. The film's production history is itself of considerable interest, as the original concept of putting Nazis on the moon—an update on the "Nazis in space" theme, which has a history of its own—was expanded to incorporate political and social developments its principals saw as fair game for satirical comment.[21] The result is a film that resists easy categorization and is probably best placed in the questionable confines of Nazi science fiction–comedy, putting it in proximity to some of the most laughable Nazi-themed movies from the first couple of decades after the war. *Iron Sky* is in fact a better film than such an association might suggest and, had it appeared earlier, could justifiably have been included among the films discussed at the 2008 symposium on "Imagining Outer Space, 1900–2000" held in Germany at the University of Bielefeld's Center for Interdisciplinary Research.[22]

In the seven-year interim between developing the initial concept in 2005 and premiering the final version at the Berlin Film Festival in 2012, *Iron Sky* evolved from a twenty-first century CGI-assisted version of a "Nazis in space" movie to a highly topical (if quickly dated) political satire that left few if any of its several targets standing. The Nazis, predictably, come off poorly: arrogant, ideologically blinded, and overconfident of their military superiority, but also given to fratricidal rivalries and incapable of recognizing when they have lost. Both Hitler stand-ins, "Moon Führer" Wolfgang Kortzfleisch (Udo Kier) and SS intelligence officer Klaus Adler (Götz Otto) expect an easy reconquest of the earth once a few technical difficulties are resolved. Their military strategies differ, with Kortzfleisch planning to launch a "meteor-Blitzkrieg" against the defenseless planet using a fleet of space Zeppelins and Adler intending to employ the ultimate Death Star weapon, the *Götterdämmerung*, as soon as an adequate power source can be found. In the visually impressive space battle that follows, neither strategy is successful since the rival Moon Führers have failed to factor seventy years' progress in terrestrial weapons technology into their planning.[23] Even so, the *Götterdämmerung*, a space battleship fifteen miles in diameter, looks as if it might do the trick once its propulsion problem is solved by the insertion of a single iPad. But after blasting off from the lunar surface, the only thing the *Götterdämmerung* manages to accomplish before it crashes back to its point of origin is to blow out a large enough section of the Moon's curvature so that the earth becomes an easy target for what, if there is an *Iron Sky II*, will presumably be the next attack from its satellite's far side.[24]

Neither the Udo Kier and Götz Otto characters nor the Sarah-Palin lookalike US president (Stephanie Paul)—who sends a black astronaut to the moon as a stunt in her reelection campaign only to discover that a space war against the Nazis works even better—are the real leads in *Iron Sky*. Instead, the Nazi schoolteacher Renate Richter, played by French-German actress Julia Dietze, is the focus as she transforms from an ideologically convinced true believer into what is probably cinema's first post-racial Nazi, signaled by her romantic embrace before the surviving members of the Nazi moon colony with the black-turned-white-turned-black-again US astronaut (Christopher Kirby) after she has dispatched new Moon Führer Adler with a spiked heel in the forehead. Richter's ideologi-

After seventy years of waiting, the Nazi space battleship *Götterdämmerung* rises from the surface of the moon to begin its assault on the Earth. *Iron Sky* (2012).

cal conversion is facilitated not only by her romance, but also by her exposure, during a brief expedition to Earth, to a non-bowdlerized version of Charlie Chaplin's *The Great Dictator* where she sees her former führer for the first time through (as it were) American eyes. Chaplin's film is only one of several Nazi cinematic inside jokes we see in *Iron Sky*; there are references to *Dr. Strangelove* and *Downfall* as well, along with an oddly sympathetic replay, by Udo Kier, of Rutger Hauer's replicant death scene in *Blade Runner*.[25]

As a commentary on fascism, whether in the form of the Nazi moon colony or in the more contemporary version of the Sarah Palin–like US presidency, *Iron Sky* can be seen as a descendant of the first *Star Wars* film (1977) and, at closer distance, of Paul Verhoeven's *Starship Troopers* (1997). Unlike the earlier films, *Iron Sky* dispenses with surrogates and symbols and instead gives us the real thing: not simply the Nazis attacking from space but—as director Timo Vuorensola puts it—"the stupidity of the human race, from the Nazis all the way to our wonderful international leaders today."[26] Rather than tossing off the film as a high-tech oddity—much of the €7.5 million budget went into visual effects—scholars might be advised to read it as a prolegomenon to the potential implications of the imperialistic conquest of outer space whether in pursuit of scarce resources, strategic advantage, or additional "living space." And it gives us Julia Dietze as a sexy blonde Nazi not out of the Dyanne Thorne/Sybil Danning dominatrix school, but as a Nazi with a heart who does the right thing.[27]

Frequently mentioned in the same breath as *Iron Sky* is *Nazis at the Center of the Earth*, released in 2012 by The Asylum, best known for producing films that are shown first on the SyFy Channel and then put into DVD distribution. Again, a film with a seemingly ludicrous plot rests upon fragments of pseudo-historical information, in this case reputed Nazi expeditions to Antarctica that have been debunked by serious scholars and yet persist in popular imagination.[28] Outlasting the end of a Cold War culture that encouraged fantasies about Nazi ice-breaking submarines, nuclear-propelled UFOs, and an underground complex of frozen caverns inhabited by refugee scientists from the Third Reich, such stories persist on the Internet and in faux documentaries given new life by concerns about global warming.[29] The fact that the Russians had begun an aggressive exploration of the Arctic as early as the 1930s and that these expeditions had fueled the Soviet propaganda machine has lent additional, although specious, credibility to claims that the Nazis were not about to be left behind in exploiting the military potential of the polar regions.[30]

Out of this jumble of history, pseudo-history, and geopolitical speculation writer Paul Bales and director Joseph Lawson construct a film that pushes almost every button in the inventory of Nazisploitation cinema. *Nazis at the Center of the Earth* begins with the quintessential evil scientist, Josef Mengele, notorious for the medical experiments he conducted at Auschwitz, making his escape from the defeated Third Reich as American troops overrun an airfield somewhere in western Germany.[31] With him he takes a sinister metal canister, the contents of which can easily be surmised by anyone familiar with Nazi science fiction movies, comic books, and men's "action" magazines from the 1950s. Then, with a fast-forward to the present, a group of Antarctic researchers discover a secret Nazi fortress in an unknown world beneath the ice, Dr. Mengele performs brain surgery without anesthesia, one of the female scientists is raped by a gang of Nazi zombies, and the Nazis launch a flying saucer to bomb the Falkland Islands with flesh-eating bacteria.

Without a strong central character to cover its many plot holes, *Nazis at the Center of the Earth* ends up as a series of genre splices—war movie, "lost world" adventure movie, horror movie, science fiction film.[32] Christopher Johnson plays Mengele in a satisfyingly menacing fashion, but the inevitable aging process eventually takes its toll. Jake Busey as Mengele's henchman who procures new victims for his experiments by organizing phony expeditions to Antarctica contributes little more than his trademark grin. The other characters are forgettable and disposable. Making the Falkland Islands the first target for a bacteriological attack is a nice touch, as is using a V-1 "flying bomb" as an escape vehicle when the Nazi space vessel is shot down by Royal New Zealand Air Force fighters. The film's centerpiece is a giant robot that looks like a cheap *Transformers* knockoff but carries the head—remember the metal canister—of Adolf Hitler. Reactivated by an injection of fetal brain tissue and given to histrionic speeches vow-ing world domination, the Hitler robot is no more effective than its fanaticized followers, although the last glimpse we get of the führer appears to promise a sequel with the Nazis lurking on the sea floor.[33]

Dismissed by critics who specialize in science fiction and horror films and as well by a majority of the online community of fans who might be attracted by its title, *Nazis at the Center of the Earth* leaves a void in the ongoing post-history of the Third Reich that waits to be filled by the next novel concept. If more than a half-century of moviemaking is a predictor, it is unlikely that Nazis are going to disappear from film, television, and computer screens anytime soon. The current generation of Nazi zombie films may tap out, although the mass zombie assault on Jerusalem in *World War Z* opens up narratological and cinematographic possibilities—that is, a Nazi dream come true.[34] Implicating the Nazis in the regional conflicts and small-scale wars of the early twenty-first century, or in the "global war on terror," would give them new opportunities for realizing their long-deferred program of racial-imperialist expansion. More ambitiously, what could not be achieved in the hinterlands of Eastern Europe might yet be accomplished in the stellar reaches of the universe. If conditions on our overcrowded and overheated planet spur a new era of deep space exploration in pursuit of alternative living environments, does it stretch the imagination that much to expect to see a film with Nazi jihadists commanding intergalactic vehicles, a scenario for which, as historian Jeffrey Herf reminds us, the groundwork was laid decades ago?[35]

It would not represent that big a technological step for a future cadre of Nazi Islamist terrorists to move from hijacking jumbo jets to seizing control of military intelligence satellites or orbiting space stations. The suicidal nature of an attack from space would be wholly in keeping with the ideological underpinnings of 9/11, which were arguably colored by the influence of Nazi propaganda.[36] Nor would it be the first time that the Nazis tried to exploit the ideological potential of the Islamic faith to advance their military and geopolitical objectives.[37] If they could promote their terrestrial agenda in the Middle East and on the frontiers of Asia in the mid-twentieth century, why couldn't they try it again in the cosmic tracts that space technology promises to make accessible in the twenty-first century? It might just be that the coming crop of Nazi movies may exhibit more historical substance than those that put Hitler's die-hard followers on the moon or under the polar ice cap. Nazi *zombie* jihadists in space, though, might be a stretch.

Notes

1. "Goebbels's Call for Retribution, June 5, 1943."
2. Citino, *The Wehrmacht Retreats.*
3. Hayward, *Stopped at Stalingrad.*

4. Evans, *Third Reich at War*, part 5, "The Beginning of the End." On the effectiveness of the bombing war, see also Friedrich, *The Fire*, and Overy, *The Bombing War*.

5. Tooze, *Wages of Destruction*.

6. Mommsen, "Cumulative Radicalisation." For a further development of this concept, see Mommsen, "The Dissolution of the Third Reich."

7. Kershaw, *The End*.

8. Buttsworth and Abbenhuis, *Monsters in the Mirror*; Magilow, Bridges, and Vander Lugt, *Nazisploitation!* Sabine Hake's study, *Screen Nazis*, might also be cited, although its subject is the representation of history through film rather than exploitation cinema alone. Representative essays include Kingsepp, "Thrills of the Third Reich"; Petley, "Nazi Horrors"; and Hartman-Warren, "Fashionable Fascism."

9. See especially Kingsepp, "Fighting Hyperreality with Hyperreality"; and Hayton, "Digital Nazis."

10. Cf. Miller, "Rise and Fall."

11. The Germans refused the Finnish government's plea for military assistance during the Russo-Finnish War in the winter of 1939–1940. Following the German attack on the Soviet Union in June 1941, Finland effectively became a German satellite. Norway was invaded in April 1940 and was governed by a collaborationist regime headed by Vidkun Quisling from 1942 until the German surrender in May 1945. Resistance by Norwegian villagers against the Germans serves as a plot device in the first *Dead Snow* film. Lithuania was annexed by the Soviet Union in 1940 and occupied by the Germans between 1941 and 1944. The country was the site of some of the worst brutalities inflicted on the native Jewish population.

12. In a "documentary" extra on the DVD edition, producer Phil Garrett describes *Horrors of War* as a "war/science fiction/horror/action drama."

13. Cf. Kurlander, "Hitler's Monsters," and Kingsepp, "The Power of the Black Sun."

14. Snyder, *Bloodlands*. See also Bergfelder, "Shadowlands."

15. Hantke, "The Military Horror Film."

16. See, for example: Walker, *Nazi Science*, and Cornwell, *Hitler's Scientists*.

17. Cf. Gordin, *Red Cloud at Dawn*, and Maddock, *Nuclear Apartheid*.

18. Ward, "Utterly without Redeeming Social Value?"

19. See, for example: Neufeld, "The Guided Missile and the Third Reich," and Giffard, "Engines of Desperation."

20. The operative term is "crowdfunding." See *Iron Sky* director Timo Vuorensola, cited in Graham, "Storm Fronts and Filmmaking." See also Bartlett, "From Grassroots to Moon Nazis."

21. In their commentary included with the DVD edition, *Iron Sky* producer Samuli Torssonen and director Timo Vuorensola describe it as "a war comedy, not a science fiction film." See also MacFarlane, "Stooges from Space."

22. See the conference report "Space in Europe, Europe in Space." At the conference Werner Suppanz presented a paper on "Nazis in Space: Distant Worlds as Projection Screens of Cultural Memories," which unfortunately is not included in the published proceedings. See Geppert, *Imagining Outer Space*.

23. Apart from the *Götterdämmerung*, the Nazis' technology is surprisingly anachronistic and replicates that available in the 1930s and 1940s, including an early Volkswagen

for Moon Führer Kortzfleisch and some side-valve BMW military motorcycles for the local storm troopers.

24. The film's final frames, showing the crippled Moon as seen from an Earth being wracked by nuclear exchanges between the United States and its erstwhile UN partners, suggest however that a sequel, if made, may put the Nazis on Mars instead. An analysis by graduate-program physicists at the University of Leicester argues that the debris created by the lunar explosion and the consequent degradation of the moon's orbit would render any notion of reconquering the earth moot, for the planet would already be irretrievably doomed, nuclear war or not. See Bryan, Forster, and Stone, "The Falling Iron Sky."

25. All of these are acknowledged in the commentary on the DVD edition, along with an admission that until Sarah Palin erupted onto the American political landscape in 2008 the lead character in the White House was going to be Jenna Bush, the "alcoholic daughter of George W. Bush."

26. Timo Vuorensola in the commentary on the DVD edition of *Iron Sky*. On the use of fascist and Nazi tropes in *Starship Troopers*, see Crim, "A World That Works."

27. The Julia Dietze character might be anticipated by that of Dr. Elsa Schneider (Alison Doody) in Steven Spielberg's *Indiana Jones and the Last Crusade* (1989), although with a more ambiguous conclusion. See Kozma, "Ilsa and Elsa."

28. The Nazis did finance one expedition to Antarctica, in 1938–1939, primarily for purposes of geographic charting in anticipation of securing a German share in the global whale-oil industry. See Lüdecke and Summerhayes, *Third Reich in Antarctica*.

29. These stories are discussed in detail in Summerhayes and Beeching, "Hitler's Antarctic Base." See also Krapp, "Cold Culture."

30. McCannon, *Red Arctic*.

31. Despite decades of cinematic overexposure, Mengele remains the embodiment of Nazi biomedical research and—as a result—another link between the Third Reich and the scientific establishment today, however much the latter has tried to dissociate itself from the former. See, for example: Weiss, *The Nazi Symbiosis*.

32. In the commentary on the DVD edition of *Nazis at the Center of the Earth*, director Joseph Lawson claims to have made "four films in one, maybe five."

33. A familiar enough theme, going back to *Shock Waves* (1977) and a couple of Franco-Spanish underwater Nazi zombie films in the 1980s.

34. Cf. Mallmann and Cüppers, *Nazi Palestine*.

35. Herf, *Nazi Propaganda for the Arab World*.

36. Küntzel, *Jihad and Jew-Hatred*.

37. Cf. Motadel, "Islam and Germany's War."

Bibliography

Bartlett, Myke. "From Grassroots to Moon Nazis: How Fan Support Kickstarted a Ten Million Dollar Movie." *Metro Magazine: Media & Education Magazine*, no. 173 (2012): 38–40.

Bergfelder, Tim. "Shadowlands: The Memory of the *Ostgebiete* in German Film and Television." In *Screening War: Perspectives on German Suffering*, edited by Paul Cooke and Marc Silbermann,123–42. Rochester, NY: Camden House, 2010.

Blood Creek (also released as *Town Creek*). Directed by Joel Schumacher. 2009. Santa Monica, CA: Lionsgate Home Entertainment, 2010. DVD.

Bryan, M., J. Forster, and A. Stone. "The Falling Iron Sky." *Journal of Physics Special Topics* 11, no. 1 (2012). Accessed October 23, 2013. https://physics.le.ac.uk/journals/index.php/pst/article/view/591/410.1.

The Bunker. Directed by Clive Dawson. 2001. Miami, FL: MTI Home Video, 2004. DVD.

Buttsworth, Sara, and Maartje Abbenhuis, eds. *Monsters in the Mirror: Representations of Nazism in Popular Culture*. Westport, CT: Praeger, 2010.

Citino, Robert M. *The Wehrmacht Retreats: Fighting a Lost War, 1943*. Lawrence: University Press of Kansas, 2012.

Cornwell, John. *Hitler's Scientists: Science, War, and the Devil's Pact*. New York: Viking, 2003.

Crim, Brian E. "'A World That Works': Fascism and Media Globalization in *Starship Troopers*." *Film & History* 39, no. 2 (2009): 17–25.

Dead Snow. Directed by Tommy Wirkola. 2009. New York: IFC Films, 2009. DVD.

Dead Snow 2: Red vs. Dead. Directed by Tommy Wirkola. 2014. Plano, TX: Well Go USA Entertainment, 2014. DVD.

The Devil's Rock. Directed by Paul Campion. 2011. Toronto, ON: Entertainment One, 2011. DVD.

Evans, Richard J. *The Third Reich at War*. New York: Penguin, 2009.

Friedrich, Jörg. *The Fire: The Bombing of Germany, 1940–1945*, translated by Allison Brown. New York: Columbia University Press, 2006.

Geppert, Alexander C. T., ed. *Imagining Outer Space: European Astroculture in the Twentieth Century*. New York: Palgrave Macmillan, 2012.

Giffard, Hermione. "Engines of Desperation: Jet Engines, Production, and New Weapons in the Third Reich." *Journal of Contemporary History* 48, no. 4 (2013): 821–44.

"Goebbels's Call for Retribution, June 5, 1943." *German History in Documents and Images*. Accessed December 12, 2013. http://germanhistorydocs.ghi-dc.org/sub_document.cfm?document_id=1584.

Gordin, Michael A. *Red Cloud at Dawn: Truman, Stalin, and the End of the Atomic Monopoly*. New York: Farrar, Straus and Giroux, 2009.

Graham, Gregory. "Storm Fronts and Filmmaking: Cloud Computing Regulation and the Impact on Independent Filmmakers." *Pittsburgh Journal of Technology Law and Policy* 13 (2012): 1–15. Accessed August 26, 2013. http://d-scholarship.pitt.edu/17861.

Hake, Sabine. *Screen Nazis: Cinema, History, and Democracy*. Madison: University of Wisconsin Press, 2012.

Hantke, Steffen. "The Military Horror Film: Speculations on a Hybrid Genre." *Journal of Popular Culture* 43, no. 4 (2010): 701–19.

Hartman-Warren, Kylee M. "Fashionable Fascism: Cinematic Images of the Nazi before and after 9/11." In *Fashion and War in Popular Culture*, edited by Denise N. Rall, 35–55. Chicago: Intellect, 2014.

Hayton, Jeff. "Digital Nazis: History and the Displacement of Evil." In *Nazisploitation! The Nazi Image in Low-Brow Cinema and Culture*, edited by Daniel H. Magilow, Elizabeth Bridges, and Kristin T. Vander Lugt, 199–218. New York: Continuum, 2011.

Hayward, Joel S. A. *Stopped at Stalingrad: The Luftwaffe and Hitler's Defeat in the East, 1942–1943*. Lawrence: University Press of Kansas, 1998.

Herf, Jeffrey. *Nazi Propaganda for the Arab World*. New Haven, CT: Yale University Press, 2009.

Horrors of War. Directed by Peter John Ross and John Whitney. 2006. Deerfield Beach, FL: Maverick Entertainment, 2007. DVD.

Iron Sky. Directed by Timo Vuorensola. 2012. Toronto, ON: Entertainment One, 2012. DVD.

Kershaw, Ian. *The End: The Defiance and Destruction of Hitler's Germany, 1944–1945*. New York: Penguin, 2011.

Kingsepp, Eva. "Fighting Hyperreality with Hyperreality: History and Death in World War II Digital Games." *Games and Culture* 2, no. 4 (2007): 366–75.

———. "The Power of the Black Sun: (Oc)cultural Perspectives on Nazi/SS Esotericism." Paper presented at the First International Conference on Contemporary Esotericism, Stockholm, August 27–29, 2012. Accessed August 20, 2013. http://contern. org/cyberproceedings/papers-from-the-1st-international-conference-on-contemporary -esotericism/eva-kingsepp-the-power-of-the-black-sun-occultural-perspectives-on -naziss-esotericism.

———. "Thrills of the Third Reich: Contemporary Popular Culture Approaches to Nazi Germany and the Second World War" (2007). Accessed August 6, 2013. http://ci-tation.allacademic.com//meta/p_mla_apa_research_citation/1/7/1/4/5/pages171450/ p171450-1.php.

Kozma, Alicia. "Ilsa and Elsa: Nazisploitation, Mainstream Film, and Cinematic Transference." In *Nazisploitation! The Nazi Image in Low-Brow Cinema and Culture*, edited by Daniel H. Magilow, Elizabeth Bridges, and Kristin T. Vander Lugt, 55–71. New York: Continuum, 2011.

Krapp, Peter. "Cold Culture: Polar Media and the Nazi Occult." *Proceedings of the Digital Arts and Culture Conference "After Media: Embodiment and Context,"* University of California at Irvine, December 2009. Accessed August 30, 2013. http://escholarship .org/uc/item/7nz0j5p5.

Küntzel, Matthias. *Jihad and Jew-Hatred: Islam, Nazism, and 9/11*, translated by Colin Meade. New York: Telos Press, 2007.

Kurlander, Eric. "Hitler's Monsters: The Occult Roots of Nazism and the Emergence of the Nazi 'Supernatural Imaginary.'" *German History* 30, no. 4 (2012): 528–49.

Lüdecke, Cornelia, and Colin Summerhayes. *The Third Reich in Antarctica: The German Antarctic Expedition, 1938–39*. Norwich, UK: Erskine Press, 2012.

MacFarlane, Kit. "Stooges from Space: '*Iron Sky*' and the Pursuit of Lowbrow Propaganda." *Metro Magazine: Media & Education Magazine*, no. 173 (2012): 34–37.

Maddock, Shane J. *Nuclear Apartheid: The Quest for American Atomic Supremacy from World War II to the Present*. Chapel Hill: University of North Carolina Press, 2010.

Magilow, Daniel H., Elizabeth Bridges, and Kristin T. Vander Lugt. *Nazisploitation! The Nazi Image in Low-Brow Cinema and Culture*. New York: Continuum, 2011.

Mallmann, Klaus-Michael, and Michael Cüppers. *Nazi Palestine: The Plans for the Extermination of the Jews in Palestine*, translated by Krista Smith. New York: Enigma Books, 2010.

McCannon, John. *Red Arctic: Polar Exploration and the Myth of the North in the Soviet Union, 1932–1939*. New York: Oxford University Press, 1998.

Miller, Cynthia J. "The Rise and Fall—and Rise—of the Nazi Zombie in Film." In *Race, Oppression, and the Zombie: Essays on Cross-Cultural Appropriations of the Caribbean Tradition*, edited by Christopher M. Moreman and Cory James Rushton, 139–48. Jefferson, NC: McFarland, 2011.

Mommsen, Hans. "Cumulative Radicalisation and Progressive Self-Destruction as Structural Determinants of the Nazi Dictatorship." In *Stalinism and Nazism: Dictatorships in Comparison*, edited by Ian Kershaw and Moshe Lewin, 75–87. New York: Cambridge University Press, 1997.

———. "The Dissolution of the Third Reich: Crisis Management and Collapse, 1943–1945." *Bulletin of the German Historical Institute Washington, DC* 27 (2000): 9–23.

Motadel, David. "Islam and Germany's War in the Soviet Borderlands, 1941–45." *Journal of Contemporary History* 48, no. 3 (2013): 784–820.

Nazis at the Center of the Earth. Directed by Joseph Lawson. Los Angeles: The Asylum, 2012. DVD.

Neufeld, Michael J. "The Guided Missile and the Third Reich: Peenemünde and the Forging of a Technological Revolution." In *Science, Technology, and National Socialism*, edited by Monika Renneberg and Mark Walker, 51–71. New York: Cambridge University Press, 2002.

Outpost. Directed by Steve Barker. 2008, Culver City, CA: Sony Pictures Home Entertainment, 2009, DVD.

Outpost: Black Sun. Directed by Steve Barker. Los Angeles: XLrator Media, 2012. DVD.

Overy, Richard. *The Bombing War: Europe, 1939–1945*. New York: Penguin, 2014.

Petley, Julian. "Nazi Horrors: History, Myth, Exploitation." In *Horror Zone: The Cultural Experience of Contemporary Horror Cinema*, edited by Ian Conrich, 205–26. New York: I. B. Tauris, 2010.

Snyder, Timothy. *Bloodlands: Europe between Hitler and Stalin*. New York: Basic Books, 2010.

Summerhayes, Colin, and Peter Beeching. "Hitler's Antarctic Base: The Myth and the Reality." *Polar Record* 43, no. 224 (2007): 1–21. Accessed August 30, 2013. http://art-desiderata.co.uk/lazarus/Lazarus/downloads/Antarctic%20base.pdf.

Suppanz, Werner. "Nazis in Space: Distant Worlds as Projection Screens of Cultural Memories." Paper presented at the Symposium on 20th-Century Astroculture, "Space in Europe, Europe in Space," Center for Interdisciplinary Research, University of Bielefeld, February 6–9, 2008. NASA History Division newsletter *News & Notes* 25, no. 2 (2008): 1–12. Accessed August 28, 2013. http://history.nasa.gov/nltr25-2.pdf.

Tooze, Adam. *The Wages of Destruction: The Making and Breaking of the Nazi Economy*. New York: Penguin, 2006.

Walker, Mark. *Nazi Science: Myth, Truth, and the German Atomic Bomb*. New York: Basic Books, 2001.

War of the Dead. Directed by Marko Mäkilaasko. 2011. Toronto, ON: Entertainment One, 2013. DVD.

Ward, James J. "Utterly without Redeeming Social Value? 'Nazi Science' beyond Exploitation Cinema." In *Nazisploitation! The Nazi Image in Low-Brow Cinema and Culture*, edited by Daniel H. Magilow, Elizabeth Bridges, and Kristin T. Vander Lugt, 92–112. New York: Continuum, 2011.

Weiss, Shelia Faith. *The Nazi Symbiosis: Human Genetics and the Third Reich.* Chicago: University of Chicago Press, 2010.

Part II

THE DEAD DON'T REST

CHAPTER 5

The Wages of War
SPECTRAL CHILDREN IN
THE DEVIL'S BACKBONE

Michael C. Reiff

A man tells his psychiatrist that the ghosts of children are haunting him and are driving him mad. Another man is unable to sleep because of the constant crying of children he hears night after night. Yet another, terrified of spectral reprisals for the sins of his past, cries out on his deathbed that at this most vulnerable moment his victims have come to take their revenge: *"They're coming to get me!"*

These sound like scenarios from ghoulish horror films, narratives replete with specters and ghosts that do more than merely appear and frighten, but reach out, accost, and even attack their victims. They are not fictions, however, but legacies of the Spanish Civil War (1936–1939), in which military forces led by Francisco Franco overthrew the left-leaning government of Spain, plunging the country into years of bloody turmoil, replete with civilian massacres. The perpetrators of the war's mass killings and extra-judicial executions are, as historian Paul Preston notes, haunted to this day by their victims, especially the children they left in roadside ditches and unmarked graves.[1] Even more troubling than these individual hauntings, however, is the extent to which Spain as a whole has not yet grappled with this specific part of its past. During the decades-long dictatorship that followed the Civil War, histories not approved by the Franco regime were suppressed, and false memories were propped up in their place: memories on "which the regime was reliant for its survival."[2]

As Spain has modernized and democratized in recent decades, emerging artistic voices have begun to uncover and re-create those lost memories, and craft narratives of the true cost of the Spanish Civil War. Cinema has been at the forefront of this movement, with the transnational film *The Devil's Backbone*, directed by Mexican director Guillermo del Toro, a particularly notable example. The film, set during the last throes of the Spanish Civil War, examines the long-suppressed histories of the war, but with an eye toward the specters indicated above, and especially the toll that the war took upon Spain's children.

This essay considers how del Toro's *The Devil's Backbone* examines the history of this still contentious war through spectral characters and objects, violent eruptions within a microcosmic setting, and the ways in which the living both search for and deny violent and difficult truths during wartime. It uses hauntological readings[3] to explicate the complexity and meaning of the characters' interactions with the specters within their midst, and considers how, by mixing the war and horror genres, the film achieves its peak impact, shedding light on the ontological and historical issues that a seventy-five-year-old war continues to raise today.

Historical Background, Textual Purpose

The Spanish Civil War remains a ripe ground for reinterpretation. The conflict ostensibly pitted the "Republicans"—loyal to the democratically elected socialist government—against the "Nationalists" led by fascist general (soon to be president-cum-dictator) Francisco Franco. The political reality, however, was far more complex. Fighting between Franco's forces and the numerous communist, anarchist, and socialist factions that backed the loyalist cause took the lives of uncounted innocents and noncombatants. It also led to the deaths of countless who were merely suspected of being (or giving aid to) loyalists or fascists. These non-battlefield killings were, as Preston notes, carried out in ways that made them nearly impossible to track:

> There were the executions of those registered as killed "without trial" in reference to those who were discovered harboring a fugitive, and so were shot just on military orders. There was also a systematic effort to conceal what had happened. Prisoners were taken far from their hometowns, executed and buried in unmarked mass graves.[4]

Those actions—and the postwar narratives created to downplay, disguise, or erase them—have clouded and complicated the historical memory of the war from 1939 to the present.

The postwar rewriting and suppression of Spanish Civil War history remains at issue today. There are, Preston argues, "two sets of historical memory: the homogeneous Francoist one imposed on the country during four decades of dictatorship and the diverse Republican ones, repressed until recent years."[5] The tension between a powerful, yet false fascist narrative, and emerging minority narratives continues to pervade Spanish culture. The "memory war" is not the straightforward replacement of one narrative with another, but an ongoing and contentious battle in which historical narrative hegemony is at stake.[6] One side effect of this war is what Jonathan Blitzer describes as "social amnesia," common among younger generations of Spaniards who "would just as soon relegate it all to a vague memorial blur."[7] The "memorial blur" is exactly what *The Devil's Backbone*, with its blending of horror and war genres, attempts to counteract. It shakes audiences by first scrambling their expectations, then luring them in through familiar tropes, and finally delivering a visual and aural experience that breaks through their "social amnesia" and asserts a specific point of view about the horrors of war.

Guillermo del Toro's affinity for the horror genre is well known, and his ability to mine the genre for allegorical and existential questions is evident in films such as *Cronos* and *Pan's Labyrinth*.[8] His decision to make *The Devil's Backbone*, however, was driven by the less-discussed war elements of the story, and by his specific interest in the Spanish Civil War.[9] In fact, he requested a rewrite of the original script of *The Devil's Backbone*, in order to move the narrative's location from his own native Mexico to Spain and so capture the immediacy of the conflict.[10] The film's melding of the two genres may therefore be seen as a natural outgrowth of the director's predilections, but current critical conceptions of communal and postwar memory suggest other reasons for rooting and melding the two genres within each other in *Backbone*, a film set during a historically fraught conflict in European history.

In the past decade, Spanish cinema has begun to revisit the Spanish Civil War for the first time since the post-Franco era of the late 1970s. These recent productions, however, often neutralize or gloss over the still-lingering traumas of the conflict. They have, as José Colmeiro notes, the "look and feel of conventional heritage drama productions," and are "too palatable and too comfortable, thus neutralizing their potential as instruments for social intervention."[11] They "suture the discontinuities of the fragmented past, made out of silence and voids . . . paradoxically [seeming] to replicate the straight and smooth official historical narratives that avoid challenging the status quo."[12] The ghost in *The Devil's Backbone* stands in opposition to this: a character who jarringly stares back at the hiding viewer, the raw punch and puncturing nature of his gaze troubling the smoothed-over, cleaned-up narratives of modern Spanish war cinema.

The main characters in *The Devil's Backbone*—a group of orphaned boys, disempowered and adrift in a crumbling, forgotten (and bombed) orphanage—emphasize the distinctly "collective" nature of the film. It is, however, the film's horror elements—the ghost, the shocking imagery, and the sense of gothic and impending dread—that make it an effective antidote to "collective forgetting." Without the horror, del Toro's vision would be closer to being yet another "normative historical account"[13] of the type that Colmeiro critiques. *Backbone*'s generic horror elements are, therefore, the root of its historically disruptive and reorienting effect.

Narrative Overview and Critical Reception of *The Devil's Backbone*

The Devil's Backbone takes place during the closing phase of the Spanish Civil War, as the Republicans are losing to the Francoists. The plot itself unfolds mostly at an orphanage in a barren Spanish countryside, where the children of dead, dying, or endangered loyalists are sent. Running the orphanage is the avuncular Casares, a part-time teacher, and part-time concoctor of vaguely mystical potions and tinctures. Also present is a governess-like teacher, Carmen: instructor to orphans at night and erstwhile lover of Jacinto, the longest-residing of them, who serves as groundskeeper. Concurrently, Carmen carries on an unfulfilled romance with Casares, who is considered sexually impotent, while also hiding gold bars earmarked for the leftist ideology she once fervently supported, and for which her late husband died.

Jacinto is the instigator of the narrative. On the same night that a Francoist bomb is dropped in the courtyard—where it does not explode, but remains as a ghostly relic—a young orphan named Santi finds Jacinto attempting to rob the orphanage of Carmen's hidden cache of gold. Jacinto chases Santi into the basement of the kitchen, strikes the boy's head against a rock pylon, and (when Santi begins to convulse violently) slips his body into a large pool in the basement to drown, an event witnessed covertly by another, younger orphan named Jamie. Soon after this event, a new child, Carlos, arrives at the orphanage. Immediately, the ghost of Santi visits Carlos, and Carlos undertakes a quest to learn his story. Throughout his investigation of the dead, Carlos is directly and indirectly harmed by the living residents of the orphanage, young and old alike. In various scenes, he is taunted and harassed by the orphanage bully Jamie, attacked by the groundskeeper/oldest orphan Jacinto, and largely ignored by the adults running the orphanage. By the end of this quest, Jacinto has destroyed the orphanage with a makeshift bomb, mortally wounding Casares and killing Carmen along with many children, all in search of the rebels' gold. Carlos has, by now, learned the killer's initial crime, and a band of boys led by Carlos and Jamie assault Jacinto in the same basement where Santi died. As Jacinto slips into the pool, weighed down by the gold he so fervently sought, the ghost of Santi grasps him tightly, dragging him down into the depths of their shared tomb.

The Devil's Backbone has been read and criticized closely since its release in 2001. Critical attention has often focused on the film's allegorical nature, which is framed by del Toro's own admissions that he envisioned the orphanage's protectors as loyalists, Jacinto as a Fascist/Francoist, and the children as Spain.[14] Juan Gu's wider allegorical reading ranges more widely, contending that the "orphanage is the microcosm of Spanish society torn by Civil War," and that its

The ghost of Santi stands over his watery tomb in the orphanage catacombs.

placement in the Spanish landscape "mirrors this void of order and civilization which is a war situation outside the orphanage," especially by the end of the film.[15] This emphasis on the location of the film and its allegorical architecture and contents is important in linking the work not only to a specific moment in the Spanish Civil War, but also to the war's effects and outcomes. The film's violent climax, which many find as troubling as it is cathartic, has become especially contentious in the reading of the film. It raises the question of whether the film, with its combination of war and horror genre elements, can be deemed antiwar and confrontational toward wartime horrors when Jacinto meets a vicious and violent end at the hands of initially innocent children.

The violent climax to the film, and the moral questions that it raises, encourages a closer hauntological reading of *The Devil's Backbone*: one that attempts to examine the placement of the film in relation to both of the genres it utilizes, as well as the historical context it is reflecting. Gu notes that the climax, with its mixture of live and undead participants (the boys, Santi, and the ghost of Casares) "undermines the anti-war theme, since the film does not query clearly the legitimacy of the children's [and victimized ghost's] use of violence."[16] If antiwar readings of *The Devil's Backbone* are compromised by the climax, however, so too—to an even greater degree—is Anne Hardcastle's view of the film's final violent act as a "cathartic confrontation."[17] Such an emphasis on catharsis, Lazaro-Reboll has noted, echoes official historical discourses, "which have endorsed reconciliation, compromise, and consensus in an exercise of collective amnesia"[18]—a problematic outcome, and the antithesis of the film's overall purpose. *The Devil's*

Backbone is best examined more deeply, and through a more nuanced lens, with particular attention to the way in which it uses ghosts and specters in a wartime setting to develop purpose and understanding.

A Wealth of Specters

The ghost of Santi is the lynchpin of the narrative in *The Devil's Backbone*, and will be central to the hauntological reading in the next section, both for what it signifies in the active historicism of the film, and for what it provokes within the other characters. Additionally, the figure of Casares is a double phantom. In life, the avuncular caretaker and spurned lover floats about the orphanage, a figurative ghost relegated to the margins of the struggle he once took part in as a loyalist (indeed, witnessing the extrajudicial killing of international Republican fighters late in the film, Casares does nothing but look on, a detached spectator of the war). In death, murdered by Jacinto and transformed into a literal ghost, he paradoxically becomes more active, gaining agency (he releases the imprisoned boys from a Jacinto-fashioned cell) and corporeal tethers (a boy receives a monogrammed handkerchief indicating his presence) and becomes an enduring watchful presence in the setting (the final shot shows him standing in the orphanage doorway). He serves as the narrator of the film, and what is not yet clear at the beginning of the film is brought full circle at the end: The narrative has actually been related by a ghost, one who self-reflexively analyzes the role of ghosts within the story, within a specific space, and within war itself.

Two other important nonhuman specters need to be noted: the bomb and the orphanage itself. The unexploded bomb—a constant presence in the courtyard of the orphanage, and a constant reminder of the vulnerability of the setting—is itself a ghost, and also a powerful symbol of the transition between the war and horror/ghost genres. The bomb, buried and "deactivated" in the heart of the orphanage, is a reminder to the adults of the war that rages around the orphanage, but to the boys it is a ticking, communicating being, a ghostly figure with a tangible physical presence but an unknowable personality. The bomb is first seen falling from the belly of a plane—a classic image from war films—but once it lands in the orphanage, the location of the ghost story, it becomes a ghost itself: one genre's tropes transmuted into another's.

Finally, the orphanage itself becomes a ghost, a transition that takes place in tandem with the transition of the bomb. As the bomb becomes a ghostly apparition once it enters the space of a ghost story, the orphanage becomes a ghost once it is visited by the bomb, a symbol of the war story. The orphanage, shattered by Jacinto in his attempt to break open a vault and steal the gold, becomes a ghost of its past self—an echoing and empty shell. It is this concurrent creation

A constant reminder of impending war: an unexploded bomb in the orphanage courtyard—a ghostly ordnance.

of ghosts, then, through both horror and war genre elements, that shows the importance of the specter in binding the narrative in a literary sense, and points to the importance of reading the ghosts deeply to fully explicate this text.

This preponderance of specters makes the study of hauntology, and its varied interpretations, useful in understanding the role of horror genre elements in this war film, and the film's response to, and involvement in, the fragmentation of lost minority histories. Hauntology, in contrast, allows for a more direct and inquisitive approach to the horror element found in *The Devil's Backbone* and the traumatic historical destruction found after the Spanish Civil War.

Hauntological Readings

The theoretical framework of hauntology—applied both to a close reading of the film, and to the characters' own approaches to specters—aid in reconsidering and readdressing the traumas of the Spanish Civil War. Before beginning, however, a distinction should be made. For Jacques Derrida, hauntological readings of ghost narratives are a way of further examining issues outside of a film's frame, or, at most, the issues a narrative evokes; hauntological readings are not necessarily a way of dealing with the ghosts themselves. For Nicholas Abraham and Maria Torok, however, the ghost itself points toward deeper avenues of understanding the work at hand. Both will be important here, as *The Devil's Backbone* points both outward toward Spain's fraught history, and inward to an allegorical narrative that illuminates humanity's differing approaches to experiencing guilt, specters, and the inscrutability of the past.

Derrida's outwardly inquisitive approach to hauntology gestures toward the initial impetus of the film, to shock the audience and encourage them to view specters as manifestations of Spanish history itself. As Colin Davis writes in a study of hauntology, "Derrida's specter is a deconstructive figure hovering between life and death, presence and absence, and making established certainties vacillate."[19] The initial part of that description of a ghost seems obvious, but the secondary aspect is particularly important. Ghosts make "established certainties vacillate," forcing both character and viewer to grapple with a world in which ghosts exist as one that itself is temporally, historically, and culturally unmoored—not quite as rigid and structured as initially presented.

Indeed, for Derrida, and, as we will see, in *The Devil's Backbone*, the importance of the specter is its ability to compel one to engage in the practice of inquiry itself, even if no clear answer will necessarily be revealed. As Derrida notes, a specter is a figure "*On ne sait pas si c'est vivant ou si c'est mort*,"[20]—an entity that the characters (and perhaps even viewers) cannot readily understand as either being alive or dead. Therefore this entity, and its initially baffling nature, provokes an investigator to look outside of normal boundaries and narratives for answers. Davis notes that Derrida "calls on us to endeavour to speak and listen to the specter, despite the reluctance inherited from our intellectual traditions."[21] Ghosts, for Derrida, are useful in creating a "productive opening of meaning" and a conversation with them should not be "undertaken in the expectation that they will reveal some secret. . . . Rather, it may open us up to the experience of secrecy as such: an essential unknowing."[22] This "essential unknowing" is a crucial factor to confront and to become aware of, and is an important element to both the ending of *The Devil's Backbone* and the film's place within the larger discourse on the Spanish Civil War's fragmented historical narrative that is evolving today.

The work of Abraham and Torok, however, presents a more narrative-based approach to the ghost and hauntology. Specters, they argue, are confrontational entities that leave historical and memory gaps within a narrative's characters that must be explored, investigated, and answered for.[23] This view of the specter is indeed present in *The Devil's Backbone*, but Abraham and Torok's emphasis on interacting with ghosts is also important. In Davis's reading of Abraham and Torok, this investigation of spectral gaps leads to "noxious effects on the living [being] exorcized,"[24] a sense of narrative, if not corporeal, putrefaction in dealing with the presence of ghosts. The process of intra-narrative inquiry undertaken by characters in ghost stories is as key to Abraham and Torok's reading as the fact that the process dispels "noxious effects"—not only for the narrative, but also, I will argue, for the characters and the viewer.

Denying and Investigating the Ghosts of War

To properly identify how the film uses the specter to evoke a specific position or truth, it will be useful to closely read three characters in *The Devil's Backbone*, from three different generations, each of whom interacts with a different type of denial and, through engagement with specters, comes to understand truths about wars, both national and private.

The first character to consider is obviously Jacinto. The film's accidental murderer, and instigator of internal and external violence, Jacinto has the most to lose by engaging directly with specters. Yet, by the end of the film, this is exactly what takes place. For Jacinto, admitting to the killing of Santi would mean not only expulsion from his close-knit surrogate home and family, but also the end of his opportunity to acquire the rebels' gold. Denying the existence of Santi's ghost is, for him, a logical extension of these realities. It is therefore fitting that Jacinto's resultant fate is both the least introspective and the most gruesome. He is skewered like a hunted animal by the living boys, dragged into the depths of the orphanage's murky pool, grasped by the spectral hands of Santi, and held down by his pilfered gold. He is also shocked, in the last moments of his life, by the full awareness of his guilt and the specter he has created.

Jacinto seems to be a crude, yet effective, warning to those who would blindly deny truths—a warning that to not wrestle with the costs and implications of war early in life is to risk facing horrific, unexpected revelations later. As Jacinto is not engaged in an investigation of the specter of Santi, his character is a clear example of the forces Derrida is interested in puncturing and provoking through hauntological readings and inquiries, individuals who hold on to a "reluctance inherited from [their] intellectual traditions," as much as personal motivations for rejecting the potential truth of a specter. Additionally, once others investigate the spectral presence and history, Jacinto himself is exorcized (reminiscent of Abraham and Torok's hauntological investigative outcome) from the boys' life and the countryside in general. Jacinto himself is the noxious effect that is purged from the film's war narrative by contact with a specter from the horror narrative.

The path that the orphanage bully Jamie takes in dealing with spectral and violent events is more directly related to the interweaving of horror and war genre tropes. Jamie is a boy with two sides. One is romantic, evidenced by Jamie's unrequited devotion to Jacinto's girlfriend Conchita, another orphanage caretaker. Whenever he interacts with this older woman his outwardly brusque persona is tempered, though his every attempt to woo Conchita is frustrated by her, and Jamie's own, fear of Jacinto. Perhaps because of this romantic frustration, or more likely his guilt and fear over witnessing Santi's death, Jamie's other side is militaristic, covetous of loyalty and dominance within his age group.

These desires come into play when Carlos arrives and begins to investigate the spectral presence of Santi. Jamie's initial urge is not to aid Carlos by informing him of Santi's past, but to socially torment and isolate him. Jamie's need for loyalty from his group is closely tied to his need for social and historical dominance. He is determined to not only suppress the history of Santi, but to contain his importance within the present social framework: that Jamie was Santi's true friend in life and not the individual who stood by and let Santi be slipped into the pool.

By the end of the film, of course, Jamie uses these three impulses—social dominance, demands for loyalty, and historical containment—to destroy Jacinto. Along with Carlos, he leads the charge to kill their oppressor. Jamie's direct linkage to the specter of Santi also, however, reveals another important element of his bullying nature, and another role of the ghost in the story. It is true that having grappled openly and fully with the truth of Santi's demise, Jamie is, amid the other boy's dawning awareness of Jacinto's crime, able to expunge the "noxious" elements of his past, as Abraham and Torok stipulate. In his initial attempt to submerge the truth and thwart Carlos's inquiry, however, he once more works against the searching for answers provoked by specters—what Derrida considers to be the purpose of hauntological experiences.

It is therefore understandable why, throughout the film, Carlos is seen as expressing far more agency than Jamie—though often, paradoxically, to his own detriment and Jamie's benefit. In a key scene, when Jacinto interrupts the boys' investigation of Santi's pool, Jamie is paralyzed, unable to speak of his true purpose at the pool (as he, himself, has been attempting to submerge spectral truths). Carlos, however, is fully aware of what his encounter with the specter has driven him to do. He is thus able not only to sacrifice both his self (he receives a cut on his face for his inquisitiveness) but also to achieve power over Jamie—the power not of historical or social domination, but of moral astuteness. It is Carlos who is willing to uncover the ghastly truths of war and horror, and therefore Carlos who is able to fully uncover the truth, though he is an outsider not present at the initial moment of crisis.

The role played by Casares should, likewise, be considered carefully. In the film, he is the wartime caretaker of a group of children, as well as the film's only witness to wartime violence outside the orphanage. His proximity to those who should be protected, and his knowledge of the dangers of unrestricted violence, render his non-role in the investigation of a violently created specter important. In a key scene, Carlos asks Casares whether or not he believes in ghosts. Casares answers him obliquely, discussing how ghosts, like the potions he concocts in his laboratory for nearby villagers, are a matter of superstition, and not to be taken seriously. Carlos leaves, but the camera lingers on Casares, who drinks some of the potion he had moments before derided. Shortly afterward, Casares views a moment of violence in a nearby town, as Republican rebels are lined up against a wall and summarily executed. He locks eyes with one of the rebels in the moment before his death, gaining awareness of the man's torment (for he, in the moment, has become a living ghost), but saying nothing. This moment of impotence haunts Casares, and compels him to lead the children from the orphanage, which sets into motion the climactic moments of the film. Aware that Casares is evacuating the orphanage, Jacinto decides to finally blow open the vault, which he believes contains the rebels' gold. Jacinto only succeeds in destroying the orphanage (the vault remains sealed), killing Carmen and children, and wounding Casares and other orphans. In the ultimate ironic twist in Casares's impotence, his one moment of decisive action brings even more brutality and death to his own small community.

It is this impotence in the face of haunting events and spectral figures that is perhaps the most important characteristic of Casares, however. As he tells Carlos, the potion he creates is supposedly good for curing both "impotence" as well as "blindness." These terms have a double meaning, however, for Casares himself is both sexually impotent (it is implied) and, more importantly, existentially impotent. He is unable to intervene on behalf of the soldiers in the town, and, it is implied, has left the Republican resistance behind as well (Casares does not even hide the rebels' gold—Carmen does that). His "blindness" is even more problematic, however. Casares seems to be willfully blind to the relationship between Jacinto and his mistress, Carmen, but he is even more blind to the murder that has taken place in his own orphanage, and the spectral presence that has erupted out of it, even as children investigate its specific outcomes.

Casares's inaction (in contrast to Jacinto's active suppression) makes him an anti-hauntological actor: He does not investigate the underlying truths evoked by a specter, nor is he able to expunge the "noxious" elements in his midst. His actions could be seen as those of a man attempting to safeguard what is left of his crumbling refuge. His impotent silence in the face of hegemonic and personal war enables the repression of narrative and truth—forces that reassert themselves explosively toward the end of the film, killing him, his lover, and many of the children. His actions evoke the passively repressive processes undertaken both during the Franco era by those determined to maintain power and afterward by modern Spaniards (suffering from "social amnesia") determined to preserve what is left of a stable Spain.

Ironically, neither of the two major characters in the film, Carlos and Santi, have crucial roles as Derridaian investigators or as active expungers of the "noxious elements" that Torok and Abraham focus on. Carlos is the driving investigative force among the living characters in the film, wholly invested in the process of investigating the truths the spectral presence is provoking. Santi himself acts as a hauntological instigator, not merely by confronting the intellectual and logical faculties of Carlos and those around him, but also by directly engaging

Santi speaks to Carlos, yearning for reckoning and resolution.

with Carlos. In one key scene, Carlos locks himself in a linen closet, terrified of the approaching ghost of Santi. In a dramatic close-up, replete with screeching violins on the sound track, del Toro presents a bulging, bloodshot eye, gazing directly at Carlos (and the camera). This look, shocking as it is, is also the moment in which Carlos begins to fully engage in his investigation. The spectral truth is not merely something to be found, but something that looks back. It is as intellectually illogical as it is narratively motivating for Carlos to uncover the deeper understandings of the specificity of the crime Santi is the victim of, as well as a deeper understanding of what men are capable of during wartime.

The last spectral issue that requires attention is the enduring nature of the spectral elements within the film, particularly the fate of Santi, Casares, and the bomb. In the film's final montage, Santi has not dissipated, but merely stands guard over his (and now Jacinto's) watery grave. Viewers are left to assume that, were any new visitors to arrive, Santi would remain an active spectral force. Additionally, Casares is an unresolved spectral force by the film's close. He, as well, remains at the threshold of the broken orphanage, though his "role" as narrator (revealed at last) has come to an end. Finally, the hollow ghost of the bomb remains, lodged in the courtyard of the orphanage. Therefore, as the boys hobble out of their home (now a ghost of its former self) a critical question remains: Why, in a film concerned with wrestling, and hopefully coming to peace with, spectral forms and truths, are entities themselves still haunting, still wandering, still unresolved even after the perpetrators of violence have been eliminated?

The answer may be that the true sources of this violence have not been eliminated at all, and that the spectral warnings themselves therefore should not, and indeed cannot, be eliminated. Colin Davis points out that in the conventions of the horror genre ghosts often point toward a "temporary interruption

Santi beckons to Carlos, standing at the threshold of the catacombs, and violently repressed knowledge.

in the fabric of reality, a glitch in the matrix" that, once resolved, allows for the restoration of the "proper moral and epistemological order of things."[25] Indeed, as Enrique Ibarra notes, a ghost reveals "unfinished symbolic business; it seeks closure for itself and the living subject by coming back in the form of a haunting."[26] What, then, does it say that the numerous spectral figures in *The Devil's Backbone* are still unresolved by the end of the film, that many have achieved "revenge" but have not been re-submerged into the "fabric of reality," and that they remain consistent "glitches in the matrix" of the orphanage's reality?

Unlike a ghost story in which the specters are eliminated once answers or revenge has been achieved, del Toro's film emphasizes the ghosts' enduring legacy, pointing toward the unresolvability of the acts of violence committed during war. Even after they have killed Jacinto, Santi and his spectral accomplice Casares still cannot rest. They remain figures of agency and spectral form, even after the living children have left. They are husks of their former selves, much like the unexploded bomb that also remains at the orphanage. All three are able to provoke action, and at points exhibit limited agency, but without the participation of the boys, nothing would have been achieved. Their lingering nature, however, points also to the unresolved, and perhaps unresolvable, nature of the costs of and destructive forces associated with war. Like the bomb, the ghosts of Santi and Casares function, at the end of the film, not as active figures but as monuments to the effects of war, with the former standing resolute over his burial place as a spectral marker, and the latter literally narrating the story, which must be continuously repeated and wrestled with. These omnipresent ghosts act as both continual provocateurs (in Derrida's hauntological readings) and as a continual testament to what can be achieved through Abraham and Torok's outcome-oriented hauntological processes. If these remaining specters have a purpose, therefore, it is not to solve a specific unresolved glitch in the matrix of life, but to stand as testament to the enduring costs of war, as horrific and ghastly spectral forms that cannot, and will not, be submerged again.

Conclusion

Malcolm Gladwell, in his book *David and Goliath*, describes the work of psychologist J. T. MacCurdy on the psychological effects of German bombing on the British during World War II. After the initial German bombing campaign, MacCurdy discovered, the surviving civilians were not only not frightened by subsequent campaigns, but exhibited a degree of drive and certainty in their lives inconsistent with a city under still-constant attack.[27] MacCurdy explained this phenomenon of seemingly illogical calmness by an effect he called "remote misses": Those who had experienced a bombing, but had not felt its immediate traumatic results (death) had a better understanding of both its force and the *effects of fear* of that force, as well as a new understanding of the limitations and true nature of the perpetrators of that force.[28] Continual experience of near misses allowed for the British to overcome their anxieties and carry on in profound ways throughout the war, even in the face of continuing losses and catastrophic property damage. It allowed them to understand the Luftwaffe's limitations, and their own strengths.

The boys in *The Devil's Backbone* experience something similar. Those remaining at the end of the film—especially those most clearly in this "remote misses" category like Carlos and Jamie—are the ones who turn on their oppressor with the most gusto, even though he is just as dangerous in the basement as he ever was before. They are also the ones who lead the remaining children out of the orphanage, into an uncertain future and onto unfriendly terrain teeming with new bombs, new horrors, and new Jacintos.

The horror elements of *The Devil's Backbone* provoke this sense of "remote miss" strength and resolve within the viewer as well. Confronted not only with the violence of war (rebels gunned down without trial, a bomb dropped on an orphanage, children killed for Republican gold) but also with its spectral results, the viewer is simultaneously confronted by horrors and distanced from the events. By integrating and combining these genre elements, del Toro creates "remote miss" situations for viewers as well, pulling them through psychologically terrifying sequences so that they emerge with a sense of relief and an emboldened nature, having faced not only the horrors of war but the horrifying specters that war creates.

Notes

1. Preston, *Spanish Holocaust*, 523–24.
2. Ibid., 519.
3. "Hauntology" is a term coined by philosopher Jacques Derrida in his discussion of the purpose of specters in literature and cultural readings. Discussed at length in his 1994 essay "What Is Ideology?" hauntology has been further discussed in myriad works of film criticism, notably those of Nicholas Abraham and Maria Torok. Hauntology, Derrida, Abraham, and Torok are all discussed later in this essay.
4. Preston, *Spanish Holocaust*, xvii.
5. Ibid., 519.
6. As Paul Preston elaborates eloquently, these new narratives "challenge the integrity of the reassuringly unified but ultimately false memories upon which the regime was reliant for its survival." Preston, *Spanish Holocaust*, 521.
7. Blitzer, "*The Devil's Backbone*," 45.
8. Chun, "What Is a Ghost?," 29.
9. Ibid.
10. Ibid.
11. Colmeiro, "A Nation of Ghosts?," 29.
12. Ibid.
13. Ibid., 30.
14. Chun, "What Is a Ghost?," 30.
15. Gu, "Children in Anti-War Films," 787.
16. Ibid., 798.
17. Hardcastle, "Ghosts of the Past and Present," 119.
18. Lazaro-Reboll, "Transnational Reception," 47.
19. Davis, "Hauntology," 376.
20. Derrida, "What Is Ideology?," 26.
21. Davis, "Hauntology," 376.
22. Ibid., 377.
23. Abraham and Torok, *L'encore et le noyau*, 427.
24. Davis, "Hauntology," 378.
25. Davis, *Haunted Subjects*, 3.
26. Ibarra, "Permanent Hauntings," 61.
27. Gladwell, *David and Goliath*, 131.
28. Ibid., 132.

Bibliography

Abraham, Nicholas, and Maria Torok. *L'encore et le noyau*. Paris: Flammarion, 2009.
Blitzer, Jonathan. "*The Devil's Backbone*: Charting the Legacies of Franco's Brutal Rise to Power." *Bookforum* 19, no. 2 (2012): 45.

Chun, Kimberly. "What Is a Ghost?: An Interview with Guillermo del Toro." *Cineaste* 27, no. 2 (2002): 28–31.

Colmeiro, José. "A Nation of Ghosts? Haunting, Historical Memory and Forgetting in Post-Franco Spain." *452°F. Electronic Journal of Theory of Literature and Comparative Literature* 4 (2011): 17–34.

Davis, Colin. *Haunted Subjects: Deconstruction, Psychoanalysis and the Return of the Dead.* Basingstoke, UK: Palgrave Macmillan, 2007.

———. "Hauntology, Specters and Phantoms." *French Studies* 59, no. 3 (2005) 373–79.

Derrida, Jacques. "What Is Ideology?" In *Specters of Marx, the State of the Debt, the Work of Mourning, and the New International.* Trans. Peggy Kamuf. London: Routledge, 1994.

The Devil's Backbone. Directed by Guillermo del Toro. 2001. Culver City, CA: Sony Pictures Classics, 2004. DVD.

Gladwell, Malcolm. *David and Goliath.* Boston: Little, Brown, 2013.

Gu, Juan. "Children in Anti-War Films; Guillermo del Toro's *The Devil's Backbone* and *Pan's Labyrinth.*" *Literature and Visual Society Bulletin* 9, no. 3 (2008): 779–801.

Hardcastle, Anne E. "Ghosts of the Past and Present: Hauntology and the Spanish Civil War in Guillermo del Toro's *The Devil's Backbone.*" *Journal of the Fantastic in the Arts* 15, no. 2 (2005): 119–31.

Ibarra, Enrique Ajuria. "Permanent Hauntings: Spectral Fantasies and National Trauma in Guillermo del Toro's *El espinazo del diablo* [The Devil's Backbone]." *Journal of Romance Studies* 12, no. 1 (2012): 57–71.

Lazaro-Reboll Antonio. "The Transnational Reception of *El espinazo del diablo.*" *Hispanic Research Journal* 8, no. 1 (2007): 39–51.

Preston, Paul. *The Spanish Holocaust.* New York: Norton, 2012.

Ruffles, Tom. *Ghost Images: Cinema of the Afterlife.* Jefferson, NC: McFarland, 2004.

CHAPTER 6

Traversing the Afterlife Fantasy

THE HAUNTED SOLDIER IN *JACOB'S LADDER*

Thomas Robert Argiro

> He wasn't even sure that he was alive, because he was living like a dead man.
>
> —Albert Camus, *The Stranger*

> The most frightening thing about Jacob Singer's nightmare is that he isn't dreaming
>
> —*Jacob's Ladder* film poster

The threat of chemical weapons remains one of the most horrific elements of modern warfare. In 2003, the United States went to war with Iraq on the pretext that the Bush administration was seeking to prevent Saddam Hussein from developing the capacity to use chemical weapons. More recently, the US government confronted Syria over a similar issue, this time involving the actual use of chemical weapons in the country's ongoing civil war. The United States, however, has its own history of chemical weapons use—both agents, which burn and asphyxiate, and reagents, which inflict their damage psychologically, causing hallucinations and psychotic breaks. The history of these weaponized reagents, deployed as part of psychological warfare, haunts America's cultural memory.

Jacob's Ladder (1990), a psychological war/horror drama, opens an imaginative window on such drug-related issues. The film's plot involves a secret US Army drug experiment, apparently directed by the CIA, conducted on a combat unit on patrol in Vietnam. Jacob Singer (Tim Robbins), the film's protagonist, is among the soldiers unknowingly victimized when their field rations are laced with a powerful hallucinogen. Under its influence, the men believe that their unit is under enemy attack, and turn against each other in a psychotic killing frenzy. During this mass hallucination, Jacob is fatally bayoneted by one of his deranged comrades. His long, drawn-out struggle with death is complicated by an ominous, otherworldly trip, during which he envisions himself back in a stateside life, working as a postal employee and in a relationship with a mysterious Latina lover, "Jezzie" (Elizabeth Peña). However, this hallucinated otherworld is inexplicably haunted by hideous, demonic figures that menace Jacob, signifying his harrowing inner struggles, as he wanders through a series of surreal events and disturbing confrontations. Some of the individuals he meets are sinister strangers, and some are from his former life: members of his Vietnam unit, Veteran's Administration (VA) personnel, and his ex-wife and children. Jacob's plunge into this disconcerting unreality is an experience he must eventually transcend, in order to find a path to spiritual release through willing surrender to death. His bizarre, drug-induced delirium is both an obstacle to this path, and an ironic allegory of his complex psychic predicament.

Vietnam on Drugs

Jacob's Ladder features characters with multiple drug-related problems, while parading the drugs' various effects in scenes—both realistic and surrealistic—that combine in a startling matrix of hallucinations, paranormal events, near-death visions, and demonic hauntings. The film refers to the powerful psychoactive agent surreptitiously used on Jacob and the members of his unit as "the Ladder."[1] That this drug is a thinly veiled stand-in for the hallucinogen "BZ" is made evident by the film's postscript: "It was reported that the drug BZ was used in experiments on soldiers during the Vietnam War. The Pentagon denies this."[2]

BZ is a powerful psychotropic drug that the military sought to weaponize as an incapacitating agent. Mark Unno explains that "incapacitating agents are usually defined as chemical agents that produce reversible disturbances in the central nervous system that disrupt cognitive ability."[3] BZ typically sets off profoundly disorienting and psychically perplexing responses:

> A serious effect of poisoning with BZ, as also with other atropine-like substances, is an increased body temperature. Deterioration in the level of consciousness, hallucinations and coma occur subsequently. Incapacitating after-effects may remain 1–3 weeks after the poisoning.[4]

Detailed information about the military's experiments with BZ has emerged in recent years, validating claims that the testing of the drug transpired under questionable circumstances. James S. Ketchum, MD, an expert in the field of secret military drug experiments involving hallucinogens, notes a critical distinction—germane to the film's portrayal of psychic disturbances in its unwitting victims—between BZ hallucinations and the effects of LSD. The latter, Ketchum argues:

are really not hallucinations—they're more illusions. People generally know that they're not real, but produced by the drug. Whereas with BZ, the individual becomes delirious, and in that state *is unable to distinguish fantasy from reality.*[5]

Jacob's Ladder replicates both the shadowy history and the clinical effects of BZ. During a key moment in the film, the character Michael Newman (Matt Craven) reveals to Jacob that he was previously arrested for running an illegal LSD lab, and that while under arrest, he was offered a way out if he would work as a chemist for the CIA in Vietnam. Spirited away to Saigon, he developed a drug called "the Ladder," designed to cause exposed subjects to tap into their deepest primal fears and aggression. According to Newman, the Army believed that US troops were less combat-motivated than the enemy and expected that this drug would tip the balance in favor of US forces. Preliminary tests, according to Newman, proved horrifically effective, as test subjects indiscriminately attacked anyone in their presence with animalistic savagery.

Newman's descriptions indicate precisely the kind of rampant viciousness that strikes Jacob's unit, causing them to wantonly kill each other in a crazed friendly-fire melee. This terrifying scene delivers viewers into utter chaos as men succumb to the drug, some falling ill, others plunging wildly into combat. Prior to this sudden outbreak of mass insanity, members of Jacob's squad have been casually smoking marijuana. This is historically accurate: drug use among GIs in Vietnam was widespread, and soldiers serving there used marijuana and other, harder drugs, including amphetamines, opiates, and psychedelics.[6]

Marijuana use, in particular, is a recurring theme in Vietnam War films such as *Apocalypse Now* and *Platoon*, where it is treated as an expression of the cultural milieu and *l'esprit du temps*, but also as a symbol of larger issues related to the domestic political conflicts brought on by the Vietnam War, and the social changes that followed from them in America. Drug use in Vietnam War films also acts as a countercultural motif, informing the films' often-critical view of the war itself. *Jacob's Ladder* engages with this history, but it treats drug issues not merely as an expression of anarchistic rebelliousness, but rather from the perspective of soldiers becoming hapless victims of a secret US Army drug experiment.

The BZ experiments carried out at the Army's Edgewood Arsenal provide an unsettling backdrop to the bizarre events of *Jacob's Ladder*:

> The drug's effect lasted for days. At its peak, volunteers were totally cut off in their own minds, jolting from one fragmented existence to the next. They saw visions: Lilliputian baseball players competing on a tabletop diamond; animals or people or objects that materialized and vanished. "I had a great urge to smoke and, when I thought

about it, a lit cigarette appeared in my hand," a volunteer given a drug similar to BZ recalled shortly after the experiment. "I could actually smoke the cigarette."[7]

Moreover, "soldiers on BZ could remember only fragments of the experience afterward. As the drug wore off, and the subjects had trouble discerning what was real, many experienced anxiety, aggression, even terror."[8]

As the film progresses, the survivors of this tragic, drug-fueled Vietnam debacle return in Jacob's hallucinated, otherworldly reality. One squad member, Paul, contacts Jacob about what has happened to them during their awful moment. Immediately after the meeting, Paul dies under suspicious circumstances, in what other members of the unit believe was an intentional car bombing. Gathering after Paul's funeral, the rain-drenched graveyard scene enhancing the film's themes of death and dying, this group also meets with Jacob. Its members appear alienated, distrustful, stunned, and without necessary recourse to moral or medical support. Their talk reveals something extra-normal shadowing their lives, Jacob realizing from their dialogue that "the paranoid visions of demonic persecution to which he has been subjected have been shared by all the survivors of the decimated platoon."[9] These ominous paranormal phenomena function as an extended metaphor for the unqualified otherness of residual psychic damage.

The film dramatizes the marginalization of real-world veterans who, according to a recent ruling by a California district court: "are not entitled to additional government-funded medical care for any long-term health effects they might experience as a result of [Army drug] experiments. They must wait their turn for standard care from the Department of Veterans Affairs."[10] Typically, "applying for this care, however, is a difficult and lengthy process, says Ben Patterson, a lawyer representing the veterans, and many people never receive the care they need."[11]

The members of Jacob's unit who appear in his fantasized life back home face similar barriers. They cannot obtain the necessary information that might qualify what has happened to them, nor comprehend why they are troubled by disturbing, inexplicable experiences. Their attempts to learn the cause of their problems are consistently stonewalled and subverted. When Jacob joins with his former comrades in an attempt to pressure the government for an explanation through a lawyer named Geary (Jason Alexander), Geary tells him, during their acrimonious encounter in a courthouse, that the government indicated to him that Jacob and his squad "were never in Vietnam," and were instead involved in some weird experiment "in Thailand."[12] In the face of this clearly conspiratorial body of lies, Jacob's intimidated Vietnam comrades quickly withdraw their support, leaving Jacob the only one left trying to fight against whatever has turned his life into a vision of hell.

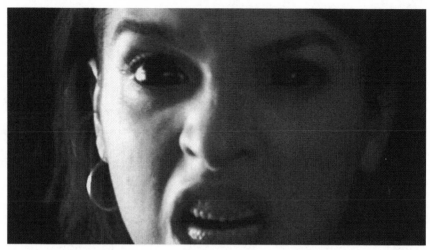

Demon lover!

Life then becomes truly dangerous for Jacob, who is seized outside the courthouse by unknown agents and muscled roughly into the backseat of a sedan. One of these thugs mocks Jacob: "Singer, what a name for a guy who can't keep his mouth shut."[13] These mysterious men batter Jacob, who bravely fights back, causing the car to careen, and thereby manages to make a painful, desperate escape from their malevolent clutches.

Ken Jurkiewicz, responding to the film as a "political conspiracy thriller"[14] that condemns nefarious covert government practices, posits a series of relevant rhetorical questions:

> Are Jacob's angels and demons functioning as supernatural muckrakers, transcendent investigative reporters who are cluing Jacob and us in on another Vietnam-and-Watergate-era outrage? And what is supposed to be our reaction to this further duplicity and government conspiracy? Is being told about this meant somehow to be a call for action on our part or merely another good reason to wish we could join Jacob and Gabe on their one-way trip to oblivion?[15]

Jurkiewicz's criticism of the "ultimately soporific"[16] New Age resolution to the disquieting ethical and political issues raised by the film has merit. His skeptical response refers to the appearance of Jacob's dead child, "Gabe" (Macaulay Culkin) during the denouement of Jacob's hallucinated postwar life, which he experiences just as he is dying in the real world. Gabe takes Jacob's hand and leads him lovingly up a stairway filled with golden light, indicating his ascent into heaven. While Jurkiewicz's dismissive view of this redemptive, supernatural moment is in line

The shock of alterity.

with his focus on the film's more concrete political aspects, there is a more conceptually appropriate and politically engaged way to relate to the film's message, beyond merely indicting its sentimental recuperation, or putting off its rhetoric to mere paranoia. In fact, the film delivers a candid testimony to the unsolved problems of veterans being ill-used, marginalized, and abandoned.

A Dance with Camus

The film's framework of an existential crisis is made obvious in the scene following Jacob's wounding in combat, in which he suddenly appears riding in a New York subway car, reading Albert Camus's *The Stranger*. The presence of this existential work suggests that its themes operate in articulation with those of the film. The overriding message of *The Stranger* is that we inhabit an unpredictable and indifferent universe, one in which we can neither expect justice nor obtain understanding of why things happen as they do. *The Stranger*'s main character, the emotionally detached Meursault, kills a man while suffering from the effects of imminent heatstroke, and feels no remorse about the matter. Later tried for the crime, he is unexpectedly sentenced to death, and yet defiantly rejects a final effort by a priest to bring him solace through faith. Meursault's disconsolate vision insists that one must come to terms with a life that offers no real meaning or purpose, or final answer for why things are that way.

Camus's deeper theme thus bears a salient relationship to the weird and uncertain world that Jacob inhabits during his hallucinatory near-death state, in which incredible events plague him during his descent into a frightening psychic

Tartarus.[17] Both *Jacob's Ladder* and *The Stranger* speak to the problem of never obtaining any final understanding about hidden forces at play, what they may portend, and the reason behind mysterious outcomes, apparently orchestrated by unknowable entities. While Meursault is cynical about his fate, Jacob resists death to the bitter end in his Vietnam field-hospital bed, and yet Meursault's life, like Jacob's weirdly fantasized stateside role as a postal worker, exemplifies a struggle with the banality of a meaningless existence.

Queried by a priest about what he would hope to find in an "other life," Meursault shouts, "One where I could remember this life!"[18] For a time, Jacob seeks precisely the same thing. As he wanders through a series of supernatural and demonic episodes, Jacob seems disconnected from himself, confused, unable to make sense of anything, lacking recourse to certainty. At times he becomes ill, spikes a high fever, and seems near death. Laid up in traction in a demonically run hospital, Jacob is rescued by Louis (Danny Aiello), a chiropractor who adjusts the deep displacements of Jacob's spine and offers him helpful advice in the form of paraphrases from Meister Eckhart. He urges Jacob to release himself from battling whatever strangeness he is undergoing, and choose a proper course of action in line with higher powers. Louis thus plays a role similar to the priest attending Meursault, although he is certainly more effective.

While the intractable Meursault has been received as a figure of "indifference," who embodies an "unexplained mixture of inability to feel and protest against inauthentic emotion,"[19] Jacob most certainly feels; indeed, he is something of a romantic. Yet he is caught in an illusion that he does not initially realize is inauthentic at every level. In this way he is like Meursault, who "shuns introspection and is devoted to sensuous experience."[20] *The Stranger* signifies precisely what Jacob must resist: a fall into accepting an in-between existence, like Meursault's, that affirms neither life nor death, but signifies an un-deadness. The artificial world of Jacob's hallucinations are such a middle realm, wherein his life will never be normal—since it is not really a life at all, but a desperate fantasy calculated to avoid confronting death and whatever lies beyond, cast as a projection of quotidian quasi-normalcy. Moments of epiphany eventually allow Jacob to move beyond the dire existentialism expressed by Meursault, who remains the immovable architect of his own negativity. Jacob undergoes a final spiritual redemption, represented in the film by an uplifting encounter with the spirit of his dead son, just as he is dying on the field-hospital operating table in Vietnam.

Traversing the Afterlife Fantasy

Jacob's passage through deep horror is multivalent, bespeaking not merely an individual's mental aberrations during a stoned delirium, but the fact that we all inhabit a political reality in which the true nature of what may be happening to actual victims, those like Jacob Singer, is camouflaged by hidden forces without ethical imperative. The *X-Files*-type paranoia conveyed by the film can now be situated in relation to recent revelations by insiders who worked in the realm of secrets that the film invokes. A lawsuit leveled against Edgewood Arsenal contends that "whether out of military urgency or scientific dabbling, the Army recklessly endangered the lives of its soldiers—naïve men, mostly, who were deceived or pressured into submitting to the risky experiments."[21] More significantly, "the soldiers were never told what they were given, or what the specific effects might be, and the Army made no effort to track how they did afterward. Edgewood's most extreme critics raise the spectre of mass injury—a hidden American tragedy."[22] These covert and controversial experiments often damaged the lives of their dubiously informed participants: "for some of the surviving test subjects, and for the doctors who tested them, what happened at Edgewood remains deeply unresolved. Were the human experiments there a Dachau-like horror, or were they sound and necessary science?"[23] *Jacob's Ladder* poses a similar set of ethical questions.

The ethical and political dimensions of these issues militate against the film's final spiritualized recuperation, foreshadowed by its title's multifold reference to the Old Testament, the Kabbalah, and Judeo-Christian theology. In view of Jacob's unutterable suffering through a phantasmagoric hell, his ultimate recovery through personal mystical salvation lures viewers into a seductive metaphysical reverie. Even so, for those preferring the film's proffered resolution, serious research into after-death experiences abounds.[24]

The New Age ending is easily received as righteous deliverance, since Jacob is not at all responsible for any of the hideous events that have precipitated him into his gothic otherworld, and he is sympathetically portrayed as a hapless victim of evil forces beyond his control. Various evil and monstrous figures (secret agents, demonic doctors) attempt to capture him. His "solidly carnal"[25] lover, "Jezzie," holds him in erotic thrall and misleads and abuses him. His lawyer betrays him, and other strange figures try to deceive him and influence his behavior. By telling him that he's dead, the demonic doctors who menace Jacob in their operating-room-cum-torture-chamber force him into a baffling confrontation with his denial over his dying state. Previously, a palm reader at a wild party tells Jacob that his life line shows he is "already dead."[26] These demons drive Jacob to confront, and ultimately reject, his self-comforting fantasy that he is "still alive."[27]

The film thus reproduces a "talking cure" scenario, first through Jacob's tenacious clinging to his fantasy of life back home, and then through his realization that things are not right, since his world is ontologically strange. Finally, he gains the insight that he is dying, and is thereby able to recognize "the true ephemeral nature of his problems"[28] and embrace an end to his struggle. Jacob's moves toward agentive self-awareness recall the psychoanalytic process: the traversing of a fantasy that does not serve one's purpose and keeps one in a repetitive cycle of suffering, mobilized by the death drive.

The film, early on, cues viewers to this psychic predicament by relaying the Lacanian trope of the Letter: Jacob first appears in his hallucinated otherworld wearing a postal worker's uniform. This transition from his combat fatigues to a postal worker's garb, along with its geographical shift, signals a displacement, but merely from one official (paternal law) responsibility and role to another. One of Lacan's most famous essays is "The Agency of the Letter in the Unconscious, or Reason since Freud."[29] It focuses on the material support that the signifier provides to the subject's field of identity and selfhood. Confirming a Lacanian allegory, the US Postal Service is, quite literally, the Agency of the Letter, *par excellence*, most especially in terms of its *official authority* to deliver "the Letter." A scene at the post office shows Jezzie holding a number of letters.

Jacob's split soldier/postal worker identity works a wry twist on Lacan's paradigm, since his unconscious fantasy identity, conjured within a tormented, drug-induced delirium, inevitably operates as another "Instance of the Letter," a chain of signifiers perpetually disrupting his understanding.[30] Jacob allegorizes the unconscious, fantastically morphed under the demand of the drive. As in Lacan's "Seminar on 'The Purloined Letter,'" the sought-for signifier remains invisible at the place of its most obvious presentation, hidden only by Jacob's inability to see it.[31] Jacob demands answers to his troubling questions along the path of the signifier, but this search is futile, since he will only encounter additional signifiers metonymically passing along his chain of desire. His demand (drive) for a reason regarding his uncertain condition cannot be satisfied within the topography of his fantasy, since there is no final signifier that would call a halt to the parade of inconclusive and discomforting signs he confronts.

The film likewise signals another Lacanian allusion: as Jacob searches for a missed subway exit, he winds up crossing the tracks to get to it. He crosses the tracks in his *desire* to find his way home. His attempt to move across the subway line, the bar of repression between signifier and signified, is deferred when he is confronted by an oncoming train, the true danger of the Real, an impending death. He then falls down on the adjacent tracks, becoming, quite literally, and as Lacan puts it, "caught in the rails—eternally stretching forth towards the *desire for something else*—of metonymy."[32] Jacob is adamant in his quest and never stops seeking for a final answer from every *authority*, even though he finds himself following a track of failures, stymied at every turn in his search for full self-knowledge, an absolute manifestation of the death drive.

Jacob orbits his own black hole of lack, all the while constructing an elaborate dream-work fantasy narrative of denial that serves to shield him from the inadmissible truth that he's actually dying.[33] His fantasy bears all the traces of a psychotic hallucination. Lacan explains that in psychosis "the lack of one signifier necessarily brings the subject to the point of calling the set of signifiers into question."[34] Jacob interrogates the range of signs he encounters exactly at this level of dissatisfaction. Lacan notes that "in psychosis [. . .] what is there to protect the subject appears in reality. The subject places outside what may stir up inside him the instinctual drive that he has to confront."[35] Small wonder that many of the terrifying "creatures" that Jacob encounters during his surreal delirium, including eyeless monsters with vibrating heads and figures with serpentine appendages, are freakishly undead, either maimed or disfigured in some grotesque way.[36] They are the stuff of nightmares, signifying Jacob's condition of being in between life and death.

Neither is Jacob's hallucinated otherworld a random collection of fragmented gothic terrors. Its construct is entirely specific to Jacob's total life-world. It represents not merely an escapist fantasy, but rather Jacob's projection of what life would have been like for him had he survived and returned home. The problem is that it bears no real relation to who he actually is, except in terms of a phantasmagoric attempt to regain a sense of equilibrium in the face of an unacceptable trauma. Yet his hallucination is ironically saturated with the interrogative imperative that would have no doubt driven his response to his victimizing, had he lived to pursue it. The dream-work thereby discloses a double discourse, with a dual wish-fulfillment function: It protects Jacob from the realization that he is dying, and also responds determinedly to the injustice responsible for his death. He is caught in the double-bind of this fantasy narrative, but he must learn that it is not the sine qua non of his being.

The psychic force driving Jacob's repetitive, hallucinated memory montage is the death drive, in its most self-deceptive aspect—a determination to recover that which can never be regained. Jacob's perpetuating of his otherworldly fantasy signifies the death drive hooked into a demand to know the reason for the Real lack in the Other: the Army's failure to validate his query. It is Jacob's own lack that forces this demand, disclosing how his fantasy masks precisely what he refuses to see: that the object of the drive is a phantasm, a non-Thing, but also a force that hollows out Jacob's entire economy of desire. One cannot inhabit a life beyond time, filled only by fantasized memories—a substitute immortality. That "ladder" runs in the wrong direction, back to an impossible fantasy of plenitude. Paradoxically, Jacob's undead plunge into the Real, as he seeks to comprehend the function of the Other in relation to the Real, is a fruitless search, signifying his ultimate lack, an answer explaining the annihilation of his being.[37] Utter terror haunts the limits of this conception, heralded by Jacob's distorted demons.

Jacob is not totally without support in his otherworldly fantasy life. His need for traversing his undead, hallucinated state is facilitated in a benevolent way by Louis, a guardian angel figure who explains to Jacob that only by letting go of his futile attempt to cling to a false life will he attain a desirable state. Louis is cast in the role of the analyst. His perspective leads Jacob to the realization that he is in charge of his fate, that he has a choice. He can stay in hell and fight for a life that is not viable, or he can let go of his hallucinated torment and reach for an alternative path. At each juncture of Jacob's bizarre Harrowing of Hell, he is faced with conditions that alienate him, frighten him, and threaten him. This is the non-world that he has projected during his dying trip, a delirious plunge into a de-realized consciousness that is anything but a reassuring Elysium.

Junctures of Trauma

Jacob's exit with Gabe up the stairway to heaven conveys his profound need to be done with his cumulative and corrosive traumas. This ending closes off Jacob's trauma of a painful death; the trauma of his unit's catastrophe and their failure to gain any subsequent answers, resolution, or support; and the trauma of mourning for his dead son. These closures allow him to move beyond the morbid, undead realm of his own psychic conjuring. All of this confirms that the film explores numerous traumas. Trauma informs and underlies much of its action, as the film's rhetoric extends a serious message about various traumas and their lingering legacies among veterans in post-Vietnam America.[38]

All of Jacob's symptoms are intertwined in a trifecta of traumatic effects: his fatal wounding, his struggle to beat death, and his hallucinated fantasy of a vexing otherworldly existence. Jacob's fevered mind inflicts very real pain as his otherworldly nightmare continues. After suffering brutal assaults by mysterious agents and a depraved Salvation Army "Santa Claus," the physical trauma of his terror reaches its apex as demonic doctors pierce him between the eyes with a needle—in a scene that evokes both alien experimentation and the symbolism of an attack on his "third eye." His arguments with Jezzie are equally traumatic: She dehumanizes Jacob, harassing and insulting him while mocking his insecurities and search for truth. When confronted scornfully by her as he peruses books on demonology and passages from Dante's *Inferno*, Jacob screams, "Who are you?" As if in answer, her face morphs into a hideously demonic visage.[39] The real question, however, remains: Who is Jacob?

Each of these traumatic incidents bears traces of the others, creating a theme of horror and suffering that runs throughout *Jacob's Ladder*. Even Jacob's more humanely envisioned moments are fraught with emotional uncertainty. He wakes up in bed with his ex-wife, who chides him for cheating on her in his dreams. During his hospital visit with his family, he hears a haunting voice telling him to "dream on."[40] His treatments by Louis are a metaphorical reference to his traumatic combat wound, and his dialogues with his former Vietnam

PTSD blues.

buddies are perturbed, since the survivors of his unit cannot agree on the source of their anguish. Jacob's hallucinations are a self-induced coping mechanism, disclosing the psychic swerve his mind produces in response to his mortal trauma and its attending confusion. Cathy Caruth explains the mind's defensive dream-work response to a death threat:

> The shock of the mind's relation to the threat of death is thus not the direct experience of the threat, but precisely the *missing* of this experience, the fact that, not being experienced *in time*, it has not yet been fully known. And it is this lack of direct experience that, paradoxically, becomes the basis of the repetition of the nightmare.[41]

This is exactly what Jacob's nightmare fantasy reveals: an attempt to conjure away the threat by creating an alternative reality in which the terror of death is perpetually reexperienced in surreal encounters with substitute danger and pain. The multiplicity of demons; strange figures; mysterious people, places, and events are the stuff of an inner theater of denial, a fantasy simulacrum:

> The return of the traumatic experience in the dream is not the signal of the direct experience but, rather, of the attempt to overcome the fact that it was not direct, an attempt to master what was never fully grasped in the first place. Not having known the threat of death in the past, the survivor is forced to confront it over and over again. For consciousness then, the act of survival, as the experience of trauma, is the repeated confrontation with the necessity and impossibility of grasping the threat to one's own life.[42]

Jacob's violent and threatening otherworldly experiences corroborate that "traumatic disorder is indeed the apparent struggle to die."[43] Of course, Jacob never survives long enough to experience actual PTSD, a disorder affecting combat survivors and surviving victims of other traumas.[44] It is made obvious during Jacob's barroom meeting with his former comrade, Paul, and later with former unit members following Paul's funeral, that their troubled discourse in these scenes is that of veterans attempting to negotiate PTSD. Dr. Carlson, a VA psychiatrist who has been counseling Jacob and others in his former unit, remains a significantly present absence. The group is shocked to learn that his sudden death occurred in the same manner as Paul's strange and suspicious end. The film thus highlights the problem of veterans failing to receive necessary counseling or therapy, which is not a hallucinated reality but a significant issue very much of our own time.[45]

This element of reality points to one of the film's more evident contradictions: If Jacob is hallucinating events and circumstances that he has never, in fact, experienced, then how is he able to apprehend real-world issues that are historically accurate in relation to the film's treatment of Vietnam, secret drug testing, PTSD, and conspiracies? This question is underscored by his discovery of his discharge papers in a box of memorabilia stored at his ex-wife's apartment—impossible if he was killed in action. One possible explanation is that Jacob's nightmare is entirely plausible, since his life might well have turned out this way if he had lived.

Jacob's Ladder may be viewed as a signpost pointing to the need for further investigations into the troubling legal and political questions raised by America's shadowy experiments in chemical warfare. The hallucinated, otherworldly psychodrama of the film relays an important message, affirming that our society must achieve an informed understanding of the scope and importance—ethical as well as medical—of these issues.

Viewers may read its testimony to the real horrors of war in the actualities interwoven throughout Jacob's haunting psychic odyssey. In reality, BZ has the ability to induce seamless hallucinated realities that seem utterly real, and so, Jacob's combat ordeal could also be interpreted as a result of the drug's hallucinatory properties, which may also—depending on the subjects and circumstances—cause insanely violent behavior. Similarly, the psychic afflictions that affect Jacob and the other members of his unit reflect the frequency of PTSD, which is also frequently accompanied by psychotic hallucinations, among veterans of Vietnam and other conflicts. Finally, and most significant to the film's political message, the film's plot reflects the historical reality that US military and clandestine intelligence agencies engaged in dangerous secret drug experiments, during the Vietnam era and after, that left their subjects wracked by psychic and physical maladies—horrors of war for which there is no redress.

Notes

1. *Jacob's Ladder*, directed by Adrian Lyne.
2. Ibid.
3. Unno, "The Story of the Drug BZ."
4. Ibid, 2.
5. "Hallucinogenic Weapons." Italics mine.
6. Calhoun, "Silencing of Soldiers," 250.
7. Khatchadourian, "Operation Delirium," 47. See also "Bad Trip to Edgewood," a series on the Edgewood experiments, https://www.youtube.com/watch?v=IgS6QUltnI0.
8. Ibid.
9. Fry, Craig, and Jurkiewicz, "Three Viewers Viewing," 231.
10. Reardon, "Government vs. Guinea Pig," 6.
11. Ibid.
12. *Jacob's Ladder*.
13. Ibid.
14. Fry, Craig, and Jurkiewicz, 230.
15. Ibid., 232.
16. Ibid.
17. Tartarus refers to the lowest infernal region of classical Greek mythology. I use the term here because this realm was inhabited by numerous monsters cast down by the gods. Jacob encounters various ghastly monsters during his delirium, hence the appropriateness of the reference.
18. Camus, *The Stranger*, 120.
19. McCarthy, "Historical Contexts," 10.
20. Ibid., 9.
21. Khatchadourian, "Operation Delirium," 40.
22. Ibid.
23. Ibid.
24. Fry, Craig, and Jurkiewicz, 222. Fry's section of this "Symposium" on the film is devoted to what he calls "New Age Salvation," 222. See also Greyson, "Near-Death Experiences and Spirituality," 393–414.
25. Fry, Craig, and Jurkiewicz, 225.
26. *Jacob's Ladder*.
27. Ibid.
28. Fry, Craig, and Jurkiewicz, 231.
29. See Lacan, "The Agency of the Letter," 146. The original translation of the essay's title uses the word "Agency," implying an operative authority. This notion is relevant to my understanding of the Lacanian allusion in the film. More recent translations use the term "Instance," hence my referencing of both titles.
30. Lacan, "The Instance of the Letter," 412. My reading and use of "Instance" here implies the effects of the signifying chain at any moment.
31. Lacan, "Seminar on 'The Purloined Letter,'" 11–47.
32. Lacan, "Agency of the Letter," 167.

33. See Dutta, "Repression of Death Consciousness," 341: "But when one is faced with the imminence of death, this anxiety cracks open in all its floridness, the paradoxical stance of the death wound undoing the birth wound conditions itself once again."

34. Lacan, *The Psychoses*, 203.

35. Ibid.

36. *Jacob's Ladder*.

37. My discussion here is indebted to Chiesa, *Subjectivity and Otherness*, 141–44. He notes (144) that "as long as desire and drive remain associated in relation to the real lack, they perpetuate the subject of the fantasy that veils this lack." Jacob's condition, precisely.

38. See Bernet, "The Traumatized Subject," 160–79. Bernet, elucidating Lacan's theory of trauma, explains that "the trauma is traumatic for the subject, specifically because it is at once proper and improper, because it touches the subject in its most singular intimacy all the while remaining a foreign body. The traumatized subject is thus submitted to an excessive tension, because it remains torn between two contradictory imperatives: appropriating the foreign to itself and rejecting it in order to preserve that which is its own" (169–70). This is virtually the allegory of Jacob's torment throughout the film.

39. *Jacob's Ladder*.

40. Ibid.

41. Caruth, *Unclaimed Experience*, 62.

42. Ibid.

43. Ibid., 63.

44. See Kaštelan, "Psychotic Symptoms," 274: "In 18 of 91 subjects (20%), hallucinations and delusions were established. Auditory hallucinations were most frequent, followed by tactile and olfactory hallucinations. Referential and paranoid delusions were the most common delusions."

45. Calhoun, "Silencing of Soldiers," relates (251) that "soldiers find it necessary to numb their critical faculties and to anesthetize themselves emotionally in order to accept what they are being asked to do and to live with what they have seen and done. When they do not succeed in rendering their experience surreal enough to be tolerable, they sometimes take their own lives. In 2005 alone, more than 6,000 U.S. troops are known to have committed suicide."

Bibliography

"Bad Trip to Edgewood 1/4." *Exposing Mind-Control*. YouTube. October 14, 2012. https://www.youtube.com/watch?v=IgS6QUltnI0.

Bernet, Rudolf. "The Traumatized Subject." *Research in Phenomenology* 30 (2000): 160–79.

Calhoun, Laurie. "The Silencing of Soldiers." *Independent Review* 16, no. 2 (2011): 247–70.

Camus, Albert. *The Stranger*. Translated by Matthew Ward. New York: Vintage, 1989.

Caruth, Cathy. *Unclaimed Experience: Trauma, Narrative, and History*. Baltimore: Johns Hopkins University Press, 1996.

Chiesa, Lorenzo. *Subjectivity and Otherness: A Philosophical Reading of Lacan.* Cambridge, MA: MIT Press, 2007.

Dutta, Varsha. "Repression of Death Consciousness and the Psychedelic Trip." *Journal of Cancer Research and Theraputics* 8, no. 3 (2012): 336–42.

Flannelly, Kevin J., Christopher G. Ellison, Kathleen Galek, and Nava R. Silton. "Belief in Life-After-Death, Beliefs about the World, and Psychiatric Symptoms." *Journal of Religious Health* 51 (2012): 651–62.

Fry, Carrol, Robert Craig, and Ken Jurkiewicz. "Three Viewers Viewing: A Viewer-Response Symposium on *"Jacob's Ladder."* *Literature Film Quarterly* 26, no. 3 (1998): 220–35.

Greyson, Bruce. "Near-Death Experiences and Spirituality." *Zygon* 41, no. 2 (2006): 393–414.

"Hallucinogenic Weapons." *10 Zen Monkeys.* January 10, 2007. http://www .10zenmonkeys.com /2007/01/10/hallucinogenic-weapons-the-other-chemical-warfare/.

Jacob's Ladder. Directed by Adrian Lyne. 1990. Santa Monica, CA: Lionsgate Home Entertainment, 2010. DVD.

Kaštelan, Ana. "Psychotic Symptoms in Combat-Related Post-Traumatic Stress Disorder." *Military Medicine* 172, no. 3 (2007): 273–77.

Ketchum, James S. *Chemical Warfare Secrets Almost Forgotten: A Personal Story of Medical Testing of Army Volunteers.* Santa Rosa, CA: ChemBook, 2006.

Khatchadourian, Raffi. "Operation Delirium." *New Yorker* 88, no. 40 (2012): 46–65.

Lacan, Jacques. "The Agency of the Letter in the Unconscious, or Reason since Freud." In *Écrits: A Selection*, translated by Alan Sheridan, 146–79. London: Routledge, 1977.

——. "The Instance of the Letter in the Unconscious, or Reason since Freud." In *Écrits: The First Complete Translation in English*, translated by Bruce Fink. New York: Norton, 2006.

——. *The Psychoses: The Seminar of Jacques Lacan.* Book III, 1955–1956, translated by Russell Grigg. London: Routledge, 1993.

——. "Seminar on the '"The Purloined Letter.'" In *Écrits: The First Complete Translation in English*, translated by Bruce Fink, 11–48. New York: Norton, 2006.

McCarthy, Patrick. "Historical Contexts." In Albert Camus, *The Stranger*, 5–11. New York: Cambridge University Press, 2004.

Reardon, Sara. "Government vs. Guinea Pig." *New Scientist* 219, no. 2928 (2013): 6–7.

Unno, Mark. "The Story of the Drug BZ." March 1998. http://pages.uoregon.edu/munno /OregonCourses/REL353W05/BZStory.htm.

CHAPTER 7

The Haunted Tank

Paul O'Connor

Not every ghost is malevolent, and not every haunting is the work of a ghost. For almost three decades, DC Comics' Haunted Tank fought its way across the battlefields of World War II, guided by the spirit of a Confederate general, and driven by the fears and anxieties of its very mortal crew. Despite its title, The Haunted Tank, a regular feature of the *G. I. Combat* series, was less a ghost story than it was a prime example of how wars are romanticized, and serves to show how the tacit acceptance of war as a generational rite of passage contributes to the perpetuation of war itself.

The post–World War II era saw a boom in popular entertainment about the war—novels, movies, and television shows catered to GIs returning from overseas with tales that were usually (but not always) about the agreed-upon fiction of that conflict, rather than its grim realities. War tales were no less a presence in the comics of the 1950s, catering not so much to soldiers as to the children of those veterans, who were eager for tales of the conflict that defined their fathers' generation. With the cancellation of EC's *Two-Fisted Tales* and *Frontline Combat* comics in the mid-1950s, owing to complications following implementation of the Comics Code, a void appeared that DC Comics filled with what came to be known as their "Big Five" war books: *Our Army at War, Our Fighting Forces, Star Spangled War Stories, G. I. Combat*, and *All-American Men of War*. These titles reached their peak under Robert Kanigher, who began editing and writing the line in 1952.[1]

Following the tradition of those earlier EC titles, the DC war books concentrated on the human face of war, with comic book combat action leavened by sometimes quite sophisticated stories of men under fire. They were, as Bob Schelly notes, "an early example of comic books for older readers."[2] A host of dog-faced soldiers marched through these books—along with iconic DC war heroes like Sgt. Rock, Gunner and Sarge, and Johnny Cloud—before the Haunted Tank made its first appearance, in *G. I. Combat* #87 (May 1961). That the Haunted Tank was introduced into a mature war book market is significant, in that reader tastes were changing and experimentation with the form had become a characteristic of the day. Possibly owing to the success of the science fiction–infused "War That Time Forgot" series that Kanigher debuted in *Star Spangled War Stories* the year before, "The Haunted Tank" was a further attempt to expand the war comics genre with fantastic elements, though the typical Haunted Tank adventure was considerably more traditional than the soldiers-versus-dinosaurs action of that other series.

The premise of The Haunted Tank was as simple as it was far-fetched: a World War II tank is haunted by the spirit of a legendary Confederate cavalry commander, who acts as a protector and mentor to its crew. Despite the title, however, the first appearance of "The Haunted Tank" had a limited supernatural element. The initial story showed the crew overcoming impossible odds on a mission to clear an enemy town of superior armored forces, and taking out an enemy tank even though they had all been knocked unconscious. The tank commander, stunned by this improbable survival and success, was left to surmise that some divine force was protecting him.

It didn't take the commander long to connect the dots. He remembered back to his boyhood, when he played at being a Confederate soldier, and thought he heard ghostly laughter—laughter that was repeated when he joined the army, and when he first saw his tank. The pieces came together when it was revealed that the spirit in question must be his own ancestor, Confederate brigadier general (and celebrated cavalry commander) J. E. B. "Jeb" Stuart—a fitting guardian, since the tank itself was an M3 Stuart (like its commander, named for the famous cavalryman). In the issues that followed, further coincidences would bind all the tank's crew together through their boyhood friendship and the shared experience of their fathers' service in World War I, but there was also a touch of destiny involved, as Stuart was assigned to haunt this particular tank by the ghost of Alexander the Great, himself part of a kind of supernatural chain-of-command providing otherworldly support for all the nations contesting the war.

In time, the series' cosmology would become complicated, with the spirit of Attila the Hun supporting the Nazi cause in combat with the Haunted Tank, but the comic was rarely better than when it told simple war stories with minimal supernatural influence. Most tales were complete in one issue, and followed a familiar formula, with the ghostly J. E. B. Stuart offering oracular advice to his tank-commanding namesake, and with poor Lieutenant Stuart (and the reader) left to puzzle out how that advice would again save the day. For example, in "Time-Bomb Tank!" (*G. I. Combat* #105), General Stuart tells his charges that they should "Beware of history repeating itself," but then stays mute when Lieutenant Stuart likens his defeat of a German tank to the historical tale of the Roman soldier Horatio defending a bridge. Only at the end of the tale (and after several

The ghost of J. E. B. Stuart, and memories of their own fathers' WWI service, connected the men of the Haunted Tank to the military heroes of the past. *Courtesy of DC Comics and © DC Comics.*

more scrapes with death and disaster) does the lieutenant understand that the general's advice related to the Trojan Horse, with the capture of an Allied tank explained by the discovery that Nazi soldiers were masquerading as wounded GIs.

This contorted supernatural element of the series was additionally contained by the convention that only Lieutenant Stuart could usually see and hear his ghostly guardian—a ghost trope at least as old as Shakespeare, and familiar to twentieth-century audiences thanks to movies like *It's a Wonderful Life* (1946), *The Ghost and Mrs. Muir* (1947), and *Harvey* (1950), all of which featured main characters who alone were able to see their spiritual guardians or companions, and were forever having to explain away their one-sided, out-loud conversations with empty air.

This convention afforded a kind of deniability to the supernatural element of The Haunted Tank, grounding the series as a war book, rather than a ghost story. The war record of the Haunted Tank—with its endless series of victories over superior opposition—did not especially strain credulity in the context of a 1960s war comic, and no hard evidence was left behind when some ghostly intervention saved the day. The Haunted Tank's crew was favored with spiritual guidance and protection, but J. E. B. Stuart's ghostly powers were limited. It was still men, and not ghosts, that had to fight the war—and since no one but Lieutenant Stuart saw the ghost, the lieutenant's behaviors might be explained away as eccentricities, excused by a crew who cared only that their leader kept them alive. Soldiers have carried lucky charms into battle in every age, and viewed from a distance, the rituals and behaviors of the Haunted Tank's crew might even pass for elaborate superstitions—but "The Superstitious Tank" lacks the drama of the actual series title.

The idea of a spirit from the past helping warriors of a later day was not unique—comics historian Don Markstein notes a similar role for a spirit of the Revolutionary War in the 1940s-era Startling Comics series *Fighting Yank*[3]— but in The Haunted Tank, the concept found its most successful form. The Haunted Tank was DC's longest-running recurring war feature (aside from Sgt. Rock, which eventually became a series in itself), lasting all the way to the cancellation of *G. I. Combat* in 1987. The book's iconic years were primarily drawn by artist and cocreator Russ Heath—a run the artist concedes was probably the longest of his career, though he didn't much care for the assignment, growing tired of the series' repetition and limited cast, saying he "couldn't believe kids kept wanting to look at it."[4]

The stories may have been repetitive, but Heath's art had extraordinary appeal, far outstripping the requirements of the genre. An old-school comic book professional, and largely self-taught, Heath began his comics career while still in high school.[5] He drew tanks and aircraft so accurately, according to Joe Kubert—cocreator of *Sgt. Rock* and himself the artist of many "Haunted Tank" adventures—that they "looked more like the real thing than if they were photographed. I used to check my photo references for tanks and equipment against Russ' drawings. Any question of authenticity and I'd always opt for the drawing that Russ did."[6] Heath's art even achieved indirect critical acclaim when it was sourced by artist Roy Lichtenstein, who based his iconic "Blam!" and "Brattata!" upon work Heath created for *All-American Men of War* #89.[7]

The primary author of the Haunted Tank stories was editor and cocreator Robert Kanigher, a core DC Comics writer also credited with creating the Metal Men and the Black Canary, and known for long runs on the Sgt. Rock feature and *Wonder Woman*. Kanigher worked rapidly, as befitted a genre author writing several comics a week, sometimes composing a story over his lunch hour.[8] Given the many thousands of war stories Kanigher wrote, a reliance on formula was inevitable, but Kanigher's work had a distinct power and a rhythm. When reading several Haunted Tank stories in a row, the repetition of story elements—like a surprise Stuka attack, or a gun hidden in a haystack—took on the aspect of a chorus, with a kind of musicality reinforced by Kanigher's strong storytelling voice, where heroes narrated their stories directly to the audience, and seemingly every line ended with an exclamation point. When underscored by the visual "Clankety Clank" sound effects of the Haunted Tank's treads endlessly crawling the battlefield, the whole of Kanigher's Haunted Tank adventures takes on the aspect of a campfire song, where repetition doesn't betoken lack of originality, but rather a familiar, expected, and beloved recurring touch point of an interconnected work.[9]

Keen readers (and comics historians viewing the series in retrospect) could spot a larger, historical narrative in The Haunted Tank. The crew fights in both North Africa and Europe; crew members are killed and replaced; even the tank itself is refitted and upgraded, at one point becoming a "Jigsaw Tank" assembled from parts scavenged from a vehicle graveyard. But specific campaigns and events were not central to Kanigher's tales, which cast his heroes into a kind of "eternal now" rather than a war history. Kanigher's World War II was a crucible where the spirit and courage of men were tested on the field of battle, and strange destinies were fulfilled through the agency of suddenly appearing mythic characters.

One such character is the nameless "old soldier" who provides key sniper support in "Battle Window" (*G. I. Combat* #102). A veteran of the Franco-Prussian war, the soldier spends his days in a rocking chair, rifle close to hand, in front of a window looking out onto a bell tower in a nameless French village. When German troops lay an ambush for the Haunted Tank by occupying the town, the old soldier halts his ceaseless rocking to first fire a warning shot, alerting the Haunted Tank to danger, and then to gun down a German sniper who has Lieutenant Stuart in his sites. His mission accomplished—without the crew of the Haunted Tank ever fully aware of his presence—the old soldier then returns to his rocker, and closes his eyes (perhaps in death), while the ghost of J. E. B. Stuart observes that his waiting was over at last.

Stuart didn't always rely on intermediaries like the "old soldier" to work his will. Like a ghostly father, Stuart let the crew make their own mistakes, but also intervened directly when there was no alternative, as in "Battle of the Tank Graveyard" (*G. I. Combat* #109) when he guided his namesake's hand to the trigger when courage failed him. In this, and in the mysterious appearances like the sniper from "Battle Window," The Haunted Tank followed a rich folkloric tradition that saw invisible saints protecting their mortal charges in battle.[10]

Against this endless panoply of war, Kanigher concentrated on the small but meaningful stakes of men in battle. Readers could count on the Haunted Tank completing its mission, but whether the crew would conduct themselves with courage was another thing entirely, and much was made of the virtues and demands of a soldier's duty. The tank's crew received minimal characterization, but their fears were vividly depicted, soldiering on in a light, under-gunned tank that was inferior to those of their Axis foes, and from the very first issue, sometimes derided by Allied soldiers and crews as being boys sent to do a man's job. For the crew of the Haunted Tank, the greatest fear was not that they would fail in their duty, but that they would not measure up to the expectations of their fellow soldiers, or be judged unmanly for failing to shoulder their share of the burden of war.

In this, The Haunted Tank stories came down on the side of tradition in the culture war fought in America during the 1950s and 1960s. The definition of masculinity was a battlefield in postwar America, with social critics like Philip Wylie coining the term "momism" to describe what he considered an epidemic of overprotective mothers that threatened the moral fiber of America. So great was this threat that, in the hyperbolic words of one Army Air Force information education officer, overprotective mothers had, in World War II, produced soldiers so unfit for combat that "Mom and her pies (had) killed as many men as a thousand German machine guns."[11] Not so with the crew of the Haunted Tank, who certainly loved their mothers in a red-blooded, American way, but never let it interfere with their mission, serving as prime examples of the "best of men"—the "hero image that the postwar generation of American men grew up revering."[12] The crew members of the Haunted Tank were the prototypical GIs of post–World War II fiction—not heroes in and of themselves, but heroic in that they did their duty without question, expressing masculine virtues of courage and self-sacrifice in the terrible crucible of war.

The Haunted Tank had an unfair advantage, of course, in the form of its guardian spirit. Like many ghosts, J. E. B. Stuart was capricious, and not just because he spoke in riddles. He was bound by some unseen code of conduct from offering too much direct information, and would go silent or keep a respectful distance from the action as the story required. At other times, ghostly Stuart

Icons and eras merge in the series' stories of duty, honor, and courage. *Courtesy of DC Comics and © DC Comics.*

would characterize his aid as instructional, or deflect credit for his guidance back onto the soldiers in his care. Sometimes he seemed as powerless as his human charges to control his fate. Stuart was always presented as a mythic character, setting a critical example of how the soldiers were expected to conduct themselves, but over time, the old general became friendly and familiar, bestowing fatherly affection on his charges, and excusing his patronage of a "Yankee" tank by noting it was crewed by Southern boys.

The American Civil War cast a shadow over "The Haunted Tank," both in the minor culture clash of a Confederate spirit looking out for a Yankee tank, and more overtly in tales such as "Two-Sided War," (*G. I. Combat* #106), where the Civil War and World War II were granted equivalency in stories told literally side by side on the page. In this, however, the creators were just leveraging a cultural touchstone from America's past—scant attempt was made to explore the nuances of these conflicts, and the root causes of the Civil War were treated as little more than the basis for good-natured ribbing and trivial disagreement between Stuart and his charges. Neither the Civil War nor World War II was examined, in the series, in terms of their justification or place in history. Instead, all soldiers (at least, all American soldiers) were treated as equivalent in their courage and sacrifice, regardless of the cause they served, following the pattern used in popular mid-century histories of the Civil War and in films like *The Great Locomotive Chase* (1956) and *Shenandoah* (1965). The issue of race in the Civil War—or the attitudes of a ghostly general who might reasonably reflect the views of that time—were rarely examined, but race and racism were touched upon in select stories, such as the sensitive-for-its-era "Let Me Live . . . Let Me Die!" (*G. I. Combat* #141) where a nameless black soldier was lauded for showing the same, or greater, courage as his white counterparts, or later in the series, when a member of the Haunted Tank's crew was killed, and replaced by a black soldier. Meaningful female characters, the impact of war on civilians, corruption in the ranks or at headquarters, and the long-term, traumatic effects of battle are likewise addressed rarely, if at all.

In this, "The Haunted Tank" differed little from other juvenile war stories of the 1950s and early 1960s. The anti–Vietnam War movement had yet to mobilize, and renewed scholarly attention to the role of race in the Civil War was still years in the future. At heart, these were adventure stories for boys, with plenty of action and slim reflection on what larger forces drove young men, generation after generation, to lay down their lives on the field of battle. And aside from their supernatural elements—the whispered warnings of a ghost, the semi-hallucinatory moments when the crew seems to travel through time to briefly intervene in some past conflict, or the appearance of some ancient soldier from the mists of time to save the tank and crew—these might be like any other comic book war stories of the era: exaggerated and often bloodless for our heroes,

DC's revival of The Haunted Tank, set during the Iraq War and
featuring an African American hero, failed to find an audience.
Courtesy of DC Comics and © DC Comics.

with nonstop action papering over cracks in the narrative. More sophisticated stories were left for a later age: DC Comics would return to the Haunted Tank from time to time—a 2009 revival saw the Haunted Tank as an M1 Abrams in modern-day Iraq, helmed by African American tank commander Jamal Stuart, and an ancient Lieutenant Jeb Stuart himself briefly returned as part of DC's "New 52" relaunch of *G. I. Combat* in 2012—but the series never reclaimed the popularity it had enjoyed in the 1960s.

The Haunted Tank was a product of its era, and its supernatural elements were slim, but it would be a mistake to claim that the series has nothing to offer modern readers. Russ Heath's art offers spectacular battle vignettes, and Robert Kanigher tells stories in powerful-but-economical style. Where The Haunted Tank stories offer the most insight (for readers of any era), however, is through their indirect examination of why men fight. Written at a time when military service was a near-universal generational experience (and before America's societal rebellion against the military-industrial complex during the Vietnam War), it reinforces the notion of combat as duty, and as a manly virtue—a virtual requirement for men coming of age, whether in World War II or in some earlier time. It is not just the ghost of J. E. B. Stuart that sits in judgment of the Haunted Tank's crew, but it is their fellow soldiers and, more notably, the spirits of soldiers from past wars, who expect that our heroes will live up to their example. These honored dead are an invisible jury that pass verdict on the Haunted Tank crew, and, by extension, validate these stories as a model of behavior for a generation of young readers finding their own place in the world. In The Haunted Tank, war is a terrible inevitability, but a man's role is to fight for his side with honor, courage, and an unexamined faith in the cause he serves, whether he is the ghost of a Civil War general, the flesh-and-blood commander of the World War II tank, or a young reader who might someday be called to service in a future war.

In the end, the Haunted Tank is not haunted by a ghost so much as it is by its crew's own sense of having to live up to past examples of martial glory. Just as the crew of the Haunted Tank romanticized the Civil War through the guiding spirit of J. E. B. Stuart—dreaming, as children, of the glory of battlefields past—so, too, did The Haunted Tank stories offer a romanticized view of World War II to its young readers. Robert Kanigher's scripts were far from flag-waving propaganda, and his stories could be frank and unflinching when they touched on the cost of war, but they tacitly accepted war itself as an inevitable condition of life, consecrated by the acts of men and ghosts alike. It was a worldview that perfectly aligned with the adventures of the Haunted Tank as it ceaselessly clanked its way across a battlefield haunted less by ghosts than by the expectations of a generation of fathers who viewed war as a noble civic duty, as well as the truest test of manhood.

Notes

1. Schelly et al., *Art of Joe Kubert.*
2. Schelly, "Foreword," 6.
3. Markstein, "Fighting Yank."
4. Cooke, "T. Russ Heath of Easy Co."
5. Dueben, "Living Legend."
6. Kanigher et al., "Foreword," 6.
7. Dueben, "Living Legend."
8. Stroud, "Russ Heath Interview."
9. Schelly, "Foreword," 6.
10. Brunvand, *American Folklore,* 766.
11. Coontz, "When We Hated Mom."
12. Davis, *Understanding Manhood in America.*

Bibliography

Brunvand, Jan Harold. *American Folklore: An Encyclopedia.* New York: Garland, 1996.

Cooke, Jon B. "T. Russ Heath of Easy Co." *TwoMorrows.* http://www.twomorrows.com/comicbookartist/articles/spheath.html.

Coontz, Stephanie. "When We Hated Mom." *New York Times.* May 7, 2011.

Davis, Robert G. *Understanding Manhood in America: Freemansonry's Enduring Path to the Mature Masculine.* Lancaster, VA: Anchor Communications, 2005.

Dueben, Alex. "Living Legend: Why You Should Know the Work of Russ Heath." *Comic Book Resources.* http://www.comicbookresources.com/?page=article&id=53313.

Kanigher, Robert. *Showcase Presents: The Haunted Tank, Vol. 2.* New York: DC Comics, 2008.

Kanigher, Robert, and Russ Heath. *Showcase Presents: The Haunted Tank, Vol. 1.* New York: DC Comics, 2006.

Kanigher, Robert, Bob Haney, and Joe Kubert. "Foreword." In *The Sgt. Rock Archives. Vol. 1.* New York: DC Comics, 2002.

Markstein, Don. "Fighting Yank." *Don Markstein's Toonopedia.* www.toonopedia.com/f_yank.htm.

Schelly, Bill. "Foreword." In Robert Kanigher, Bob Haney, and Joe Kubert, *The Sgt. Rock Archives, Vol. 2.* New York: DC Comics, 2003.

Schelly, William, Joe Kubert, Gary Groth, and Kim Thompson. *The Art of Joe Kubert.* Seattle, WA: Fantagraphics, 2011.

Stroud, Bryan, ed. "Russ Heath Interview (Pt. 1)." *Russ Heath Interview* (Pt. 1). Accessed July 23, 2014. http://www.wtv-zone.com/silverager/interviews/heath_1.shtml.

CHAPTER 8

(Re)Remembering the Great War in *Deathwatch*

Marzena Sokołowska-Paryż

Michael J. Bassett's *Deathwatch* (2002) was intended to be both an unconventional horror film and a meaningful war film. Remembering the images of "dead guys, people blown apart, soldiers eating their breakfasts next to their dead comrades and not caring" he had seen as a child in his grandfather's copy of *Covenants with Death*,[1] Bassett decided that not only would the infamous trenches of the Western front work perfectly as a "contained environment" to substitute for the haunted house setting, but also that the horror convention would powerfully convey "the human horror of World War One."[2] The plot is relatively straightforward. A squad of British soldiers, apparently the only survivors of a company decimated in a disastrous attack on German forces, is lost in enemy territory and cut off from support. Wandering in a fog-enveloped forest, the men come across a complex network of enemy trenches—undefended, because all but three of the Germans occupying them are dead. How they were killed, however, is shrouded in mystery. The British soldiers soon discover that malevolent forces—capable of killing and making men kill— haunt these all-too-easily captured trenches. What remains unclear is whether or not the men who enter the trenches are, in fact, already dead: forced, in death, to reenact the horrors of killing and being killed.

   Deathwatch is a product of cultural memory, drawing together all the paradigmatic themes of Great War literature, the canonical iconography of the cinematic representations of the Great War, and some of the most enduring legends of this conflict. According to one reviewer, "Bassett can't decide whether he's making a horror film, a psychological thriller or a wartime drama, and consequently tries to pitch *Deathwatch* somewhere between all three, which will please no one."[3] However, it is precisely this generic hybridity that constitutes the film's greatest asset, successfully proving that the path to understanding *how* and *why* the Great War is "remembered" as "horror" in literature, drama, and film leads through the horror genre. As Karen Randell writes, "[the film's] tropes of horror stand in for the unknowable horrors of war."[4] In their own way, cultural representations of the Great War aim for the same effect as horror, to "prompt the emotions of fear, sympathy, revulsion, dread, anxiety or disgust. And in doing so, they also stimulate thoughts about evil in many varieties and degrees: internal or external, limited or profound, physical or mental, natural or supernatural, conquerable or triumphant."[5]

The Western Front as Horror-Scape: Cultural Contexts

The opening scene in *Deathwatch* evokes memories of Delbert Mann's *All Quiet on the Western Front* (1979). It begins with close-ups of soldiers assembled in a trench, awaiting the dreaded whistle that will be their signal to leave its shelter and begin their attack. The camera moves gradually to show the faces of the lead characters: Charlie Shakespeare (Jamie Bell), Colin Crevasse (Rúaidhrí Conroy), Captain Bramwell Jennings (Laurence Fox), Willie McNess (Dean Lennox Kelly), Barry Stravinsky (Kris Marshall), Jack Hawkstone (Hans Matheson), Anthony Bradford (Hugh O'Connor), Corporal Doc Fairweather (Matthew Rhys), Thomas Quinn (Andy Serkis), and Sergeant David Tate (Hugo Speer). This is not, however, a case of mere appropriation from another film. In Mann's film, the attack and counterattack take place in glaring daylight. In contrast, Bassett's soldiers are engulfed in sombre darkness, their faces half-visible, only briefly illuminated by the fleeting light of a flare. It is only later that the viewer grasps the meaning of this oppressive darkness as "the locus of torment, punishment, mystery, corruption and insanity,"[6] a foreshadowing of what awaits the men as they scramble out into no-man's-land, doomed never to return.

According to Randell, the various ways in which the soldiers face the menacing inevitability of the oncoming attack—"shakily light[ing] a cigarette," "down[ing] alcohol from a flask," "star[ing] catatonically into the distance"—are manifest "signs of neurosis."[7] She contends that "the film's engagement with depictions of war trauma—neurotic symptoms—ensures that the horror awaiting the soldiers is understood within the context of war, rather than the 'slasher movie' that the film becomes."[8] *Deathwatch*'s Great War trauma-scape has its literary and cinematic precedents, however, such as Wilfred Owen's "Mental Cases":

> Surely we have perished
> Sleeping, and walk hell; but who these hellish?
> These are men whose minds the Dead have ravished[9]

or G. W. Pabst's *Westfront 1918* (1930), with its climax—"one of the most powerful and disturbing [scenes]" in the history of the war film—showing "the rapid descent into madness" because "war is undoubtedly hell—on the battlefield and off. On the battlefield, death is the only result whether it is from artillery, combat, mechanized warfare or grenade."[10] Randell's analysis of *Deathwatch* clearly indicates that Bassett's soldiers are entrapped within the confines of their own personal mental hells. However, hell is also a conspicuously physical space in Bassett's film.

When the signal for attack has been given, Charlie Shakespeare is unable to move. After he is threatened with execution for cowardice, he manages to climb over the top, but freezes when he realizes what is going on. A fellow soldier turns to him and says: "Welcome to hell, Private Shakespeare."[11] The attack takes place in the darkness of the night, occasionally illuminated by the light from explosions. Fires erupt around shell-holes filled with water, creating the impression of burning lakes. This is the hell-scape of war; an eerie space of physical torment, with bodies torn apart or disappearing into nothingness; a meticulous visualization of one of the most recurrent metaphors in Great War literature. Owen does not even come close to a realistic description of no-man's-land, offering instead a visionary projection of hellish attributes onto the battlefield: "slimy paths [. . .] trailed and scraped / Round myriad warts that might be little hills. / From gloom's last dregs these long-strung creatures crept, / And vanished out of dawn down hidden holes."[12] A. D. Gristwood writes of "a lunar landscape, lifeless, arid and accursed," "a hideous welter of dust and smoke," and "region of desolation."[13] Within the confines of the "grey pandemonium," the men undergo an ordeal that leaves them "helpless, agonized, hopeless, frozen with terror, tortured with wounds."[14] Bassett transfigures this metaphor of war as hell into the Real.

The attack ends with a huge explosion, followed by an abrupt change of scene. It is not clear how the men all got to be where they are, but it is altogether a different space. The soldiers are shown walking through woods, all wearing gas masks. When one soldier loses his mask, all the men realize that what they took for gas was just a fog. What happens later looks like an adaptation of the opening scene from Gristwood's *The Somme*:

> The trenches had been abandoned by the Germans only yesterday, and everywhere lay scattered arms and clothing. [. . .] Sprawling over the parapets were things in rags of grey and khaki that had once been men. [. . .] Everywhere they found carrion and ordure [. . .]. Sometimes the Germans had buried their dead in the floor of the trench [. . .]. A foot treading unwarily here sunk suddenly downwards, disturbing hundreds of white and wriggling maggots. In one place a hand with blue and swollen fingers projected helplessly from the ground. [. . .]

> Thus there lay in the billows of tumbled earth a company of dead men half-buried.[15]

Approaching the apparently abandoned enemy trenches, McNess steps on a corpse, his boot sinking deep into the rotten flesh. What Bassett's soldiers are first unable—and then unwilling—to see, is "the ease with which [their] bod[ies] could become a corpse."[16] The trenches are a labyrinth, a typical "space of punishment, symbolic of unresolved fears."[17] Considering what the men experience in the trenches, their passage through the fog must be considered a crucial moment in the film, indicating a blurring of boundaries, which, in the trenches, takes on the form of the "weird blends of life and death"[18] typical of the Great War.

When Bradford manages to get a German radio working again and hears a British voice announcing that Company Y no longer exists, the thick enveloping fog gains—retrospectively—a new meaning. Fog such as this has long been a staple trope of horror films, obscuring the distinction between absence and presence, visibility and invisibility, the knowable and the unknowable. Yet, Bassett's use of fog is also reminiscent of the legend of the Vanished Battalion, which tells of the seemingly inexplicable disappearance of the Fifth Battalion of the Norfolk Regiment during the Gallipoli campaign. According to the legend, "when [the men] arrived at [a] cloud they marched straight into it, with no hesitation, but no one ever came back."[19]

The final scene of Julian Jarrold's *All the King's Men* (1999), based on the story, shows what appears to be a wall of fog spreading between the British and Turkish positions, having the same gaslike appearance as in *Deathwatch*. Whether this similarity was intended or not, it adds an interpretative dimension to what Bassett's soldiers become after passing through the fog and what

Soldiers attempt to find their way through the fog.

they encounter in the trenches. The men do not see—since the enshrouding fog obstructs visibility—that they may have crossed the borderline between life and death. As David Clarke writes, it was a common belief among soldiers that "the spirits of the dead continued to fight alongside them [. . .]. This appears to have been a psychological by-product of living in trenches so close to the dead, many of whom were buried in shallow graves or remained visible in the walls of the trenches or in No Man's Land."[20] In Bassett's horror version of such legends, these are, however, neither phantoms nor "angel helpers in times of peril,"[21] but visual embodiments of death—the undead, whose presence bespeaks the truth of what it means to be soldier.

The trajectory of the characters' movement in *Deathwatch* is of utmost significance: After having moved upward from their own trench into the hell of battle, they now climb down into an apparently hellish enemy trench, where they are subjected to physical, spiritual, and psychological torment. Bassett's horror-scape proves to be another level of the same hell of war, beneath which there is yet another, as the earth sucks in the pile of corpses. Charlie, as he attempts to run away, suddenly finds himself sliding down a tunnel that takes him below to another abode of the dead, where he sees all his killed comrades, seemingly alive, sitting and talking. In this respect, *Deathwatch* is an obvious appropriation of Owen's "Strange Meeting":

> It seemed that out of the battle I escaped
> Down some profound dull tunnel, [. . .]
> Yet also there encumbered sleepers groaned,
> Too fast in thought or death to be bestirred.
> [. . .]
> And by his smile, I knew that sullen hall;
> By his dead smile I knew we stood in Hell.[22]

The fact that only Charlie manages to leave the sinister trenches may have much to do with the fact that he is the only one in the group of British soldiers who shows empathy for the enemy, recognizing the bond forged out of common suffering. Significantly, it is the German (undead) soldier Friedrich who lets Charlie go back over the top: "Only you tried to save me. That is why you are free."[23] It is a matter of speculation whether Charlie's surname is a deliberate reference to the famous evocation of comradeship in William Shakespeare's *Henry V*, yet his character undoubtedly represents an attitude common enough on the Western Front: "in a war in which all combatants were victims of material, in which an industrial technology was the 'true' aggressor, identification with the enemy and his dominant motif—survival—was logical, even necessary."[24]

Trench Warfare through the Lens of the Horror Genre

Literary evocations of the Great War describe newly buried corpses "suffering untimely resurrection"[25] when unearthed by exploding shells. In Bassett's horror, this resurrection is a literal one, and the continuous rain signifies that something fundamental to the place itself is horribly wrong.[26] The corpses "come back to life," most vividly in the scene in which the undead, ensnared in barbed wire, attack Starinski, the animated wire moving to entangle and destroy yet another body. In an earlier scene, the soldier fights with a mud-coated figure he initially assumes to be just another harmless corpse. The infamous mud on the Western Front tortured the soldiers from both sides of the conflict, and Henri Barbusse readily used it as a means of promoting a transnational sense of comradeship binding antiheroic "workers in battle" clothed in the "foul armour of mud."[27]

In *Deathwatch*, however, the impossibility of distinguishing the soldiers in the fight scene—their uniforms cannot be seen under the mud—serves a different purpose altogether, more in tune with Frederic Manning's pessimistic supposition that "war is waged by men, not by beasts or by gods. It is a peculiarly human activity. To call it a crime against mankind is to miss at least half its significance; it is also the punishment of a crime."[28] In *Deathwatch*, Bradford says that "God is nowhere near this place,"[29] and this is true, but not because the trench is a haunted space that emerged from nowhere. Men dug the trenches and the tunnels beneath them, and invented poisonous gas. In other words, mankind created conditions where primal instincts overcome reason and empathy.

Quinn represents a different side of human nature, which is elicited by the circumstances of war—an inherent propensity for cruelty, a pleasure in inflicting pain, a lust for killing. It is Quinn who tells Charlie that: "This war is murder. I love it."[30] He readily indulges in an orgy of violence, culminating in the torture of Friedrich tied to a branchless tree, a quasi-crucifixion scene reminiscent of the myth of the Crucified Canadian propagated among the Allies to "underline the ruthless actions of a Godless foe who would stop at nothing, not even the most painful form of killing devised in 2,000 years."[31]

Stravinsky's indulgence in sexual self-satisfaction after killing the enemy—he masturbates while looking at erotic photographs—and Quinn's orgasmic pleasure in murder and torture represent the Eros/Thanatos's duality of wartime experience, for as Lt. Col. Dave Grossman has written, "The linkage between sex and killing becomes unpleasantly apparent when we enter the realm of warfare. . . . The sexual aspects of killing continue beyond the region in which both are thought to be rites of manhood and into the area in which killing becomes like sex and sex like killing."[32] A similar message is conveyed in James Hanley's *The German Prisoner*

(1931), where two British soldiers are cut off from their unit during an attack due to a descending thick fog. Lost in no-man's-land, they find themselves trapped in a shell hole. Suddenly, a young German soldier emerges, weaponless, with his hands up in a gesture of surrender. The three soldiers sit together surrounded by an impenetrable fog, ubiquitous mud, and multitudes of corpses, and the setting begins to takes its toll: "Make the funkin' fog rise. [. . .] Make all this mud and shite vanish. [. . .] We are [. . .] going mad. We are going to kill ourselves," Elston complains to the German. And O'Garra exclaims, "FOG. FOG. Oh hell, we are all going crazy. FOG. FOG."[33] What happens next is "as dehumanizing a scene as can be found in literature,"[34] the torture of the German youth: "The two men now fell upon the prisoner, and [. . .] began to mangle the body. They worried it like mad dogs. [. . .] In complete silence O'Garra pulled out his bayonet and stuck it up the youth's ass. [. . .] They stuck the horse-hair up his penis."[35]

It is highly significant that Stravinsky and Quinn—whose degradation to the lowest form of being is the most conspicuous in the film—are punished by the cruelest of deaths in the Great War: They are both killed by barbed wire, which is very much "alive," and capable of reaching out and wrapping or piercing the human body. Even so, its existence and use is man's idea: "All that is needed to understand World War I in its philosophical and historical meaning is to examine barbed wire—a single strand will do—and to meditate who made it, what it is for, why it is like it is."[36] The barbed wire in Bassett's film—a man-made object that becomes monsterlike—signifies the monster within man himself. The ultimate punishment inflicted by whatever haunts the hellish trenches is liberating the "monster" within the soldiers (hatred or fear) that will lead them to kill each other.

The soldiers' fate—killed as punishment because they, themselves, have killed—makes it most appropriate that they are judged by the (un)dead. The

Barbed wire seems to come alive as a murderous entity.

return of dead soldiers as the judges of human conduct harks back to both Abel Gance's *J'accuse* (1918–1919) and Hans Clumber's *Wonder um Verdun* (*Miracle at Verdun*) (1930), though there is a meaningful difference. In the case of *J'accuse*, "[the] sequence of the dead rising from their graves is one of the great scenes of early cinema. Its force is made even more poignant when we realize that most of the men we see on the screen were actual French soldiers lent to Gance by the French army to play in his film. . . . Many of the soldiers . . . had returned to the front in the last months of the war and had been killed. . . . Representation and reality became one."[37] The protagonist summons the dead as a punishment upon their families, neighbors, and friends, who are not worthy of the blood sacrifice made in their name. *Wunder um Verdun* is preceded by a fragment from the book of Ezekiel wherein the resurrection of the dead leads to the restoration of the human body: "and the bones came together, bone to his bone [. . .] the sinews and the flesh came up upon them, and the skin covered them above; [. . .] and the breath came into them, and they lived, and stood up upon their feet, an exceeding great army."[38] The Messenger summons the dead German and French soldiers to rise from their graves to confront their families and politicians with the sacrifice they had made in order to prevent another war from happening. Significantly, neither the soldiers' families nor the politicians want the dead to return because they disrupt the new lives the families have started and pose a threat to the national politics dependent on "the war dead [as] a central symbol of a national identity."[39] Yet, if in *J'accuse* and *Wunder um Verdun* the dead soldiers return to judge the complacent civilians, in *Deathwatch* they return to judge and punish their former adversaries in combat.

Friedrich is revealed, in the final scenes, to be the eerie judge of the British soldiers' conduct: How they treat him determines their fate. Depending on how their passage through the fog is interpreted, the British soldiers may either be living, but doomed to die in the trenches, or trapped on the threshold between two realms (a life-in-death state), or, finally, already dead, but still (like Charlie) possessing a chance of escaping hell.

Regardless of whether the German trenches are interpreted as a death-trap for the living or hellish punishment for the dead, who must repay sins committed in life, they work effectively within the narrative template of the prototypical horror movie, which Noël Carroll has subdivided into "onset," "discovery," "confirmation," and "confrontation." The "onset" takes place when "the monster's presence is established for the audience" by means of "scenes and sequences involving the manifestations of the monster, . . . often in the form of murders or other disturbing events [that] pile up before anyone (living) has a glimmering of what is going on,"[40] whereas the "discovery" occurs "when one character or group of characters comes to the warranted conviction that a monster is at the bottom of the problem."[41] In *Deathwatch*, what threatens the group is a condition common to all soldiers, best illustrated in the biblical citation opening Innes and Castle's 1934 *Covenants with Death*, the photographic (hi)story of the Great War that inspired Bassett: "We have made a covenant with Death, and with hell are we at agreement."[42] This covenant is endowed with a dual meaning, for soldiers are both the victims and agents of death. Friedrich warns the British soldiers that the trench is a trap—declaring that: "You shouldn't come here"—and the British soldiers soon sense something is not right about the place: "What happened here?" "So much death!" Friedrich also warns them that they will turn against each other," for "there is something evil in the ground, something wrong."[43]

Bassett perfectly renders the psychological impact of trench warfare where "the dominance of long-range artillery, the machinegun, and barbed wire had immobilized combat, and immobility necessitated a passive stance of the soldiers before the forces of mechanized slaughter."[44] The soldiers think they hear the shouts of attacking troops and the sounds of an artillery barrage. Captain Jennings is depicted from the beginning of the film as an officer on the verge of a mental breakdown under the duress of combat, drinking and unable to exercise his authority over the men under his command, and the unseen attack is the last straw. He goes insane and shoots one of his own men. The "invisibility" of the other side is one of the most iconic tropes of Great War literature: "The air screams and howls like an insane woman. [. . .] we [. . .] grovel like savages before this demonic frenzy. [. . .] I recover and hear the roar of the bombardment. It screams and rages and boils like an angry sea. [. . .] A shell lands with a monstrous shriek in the next bay." "The air overhead whistles, drones and shrieks."[45]

The stage of "confirmation" in the horror movie "involves the discoverers of or the believers in the existence of the monster convincing some other group of the existence of the creature and of the proportions of the mortal danger at hand."[46] It is Bradford who tells Charlie that "Death is in the earth, in the rats, in the flies, in you and me. We're dead, Charlie, I know that now. I can't hear my heartbeat anymore. I died, I just didn't realize it."[47] Death is not, however, just a state of nonbeing, it is also a state of mind. In *All Quiet on the Western Front*, Paul Bäumer speaks of himself and his comrades as "dead men with no feelings, who are able by some trick, some dangerous magic, to keep running and keep on killing."[48] Similarly, Alfredo Bonadeo focuses on transnational representations of "beastliness" as an inescapable psychological condition imposed by the realities of trench warfare: "Life in the trenches, exposure to death, and the prospect of mass slaughter . . . took away from man his human self. He then found the will and the strength to fight and to face extermination, and he became instead a soldier."[49]

Deathwatch is about the moral degradation of men under the duress of trench warfare ("This place is making us kill each other"[50]), yet Bassett takes the "descent to the beast" theme to its most extreme meaning, with a literary precedent to be found in Liam O'Flaherty's *Return of the Brute* (1929). Private

Quinn, who kills both his sergeant and lieutenant, is very much like O'Flaherty's William Gunn, whose deteriorating state of mind leads him straight to murder: "with his chest pressed against the Corporal's writhing body, he slowly sought the throat, found it and enlaced it with his fingers and pressed fiercely [. . . .] Then, uttering queer sounds, he began to mangle the body with his bare hands. Now he was really an animal, brutish, with dilated eyes, with his face bloody."[51]

The final stage of the horror movie is "confrontation," where "humanity marches out to meet its monster." It "may assume the shape of an escalation in intensity or complexity or both. Furthermore, the confrontation movement may also adopt a problem/solution format."[52] The only character who confronts the "death" inside him is Charlie. He is the only soldier who has retained his moral integrity amid the ensuing chaos. His character evolves from a cowardly boy, unable to help disentangle his sergeant from barbed wire, to a resolute young man who tries to stop Quinn from killing Tate, and Bradford from blowing up the trenches. In the strange underworld, he sees himself among the dead soldiers. Charles Derry writes that:

> The horror itself is both distanced from man and, what is more important, highly symbolic. The horror may be a metaphorical mani-festation of man's animal instincts . . . , his evil desires . . . , or his fear of being dead yet not at rest. . . . But the horror is certainly not man itself. This separation usually enables man in the horror films to confront directly his evil enemy as surely as one could confront one's reflection in a distorted mirror. Almost always the horror is vanquished.[53]

It remains an unanswerable question whether Charlie manages to conquer his own "death," for although he gets out of the tunnel and the trenches, it is not clear what his disappearance in the fog enveloping no-man's-land actually means, the soldier becoming "[a war body] made invisible again."[54]

The *Unheimliche* Western Front and the Traumatic "Realness" of the (Un)Dead Body

In *Deathwatch*, the horror convention accentuates the *Unheimliche* nature of "the troglodyte world"[55] of the Western Front by evoking the fears specific to that world: being exposed to a gas attack, sucked in by the mud, stuck on barbed wire, or lost in no-man's-land. All this underscores the exceptionality of the Great War, which no later war even faintly resembled. And yet, within the frames of his eerie "other world," Bassett perfectly captures the essence of the most enduring Great War legacy that has come also to define all future conflicts: sacredness overcome by the profane—by the reduction of the human being to sheer corporeality. The most repulsive scene in the movie is where Charlie removes the blanket covering Chevasse's legs and sees rats eating away at the flesh. The ever-present rats in the trenches are an iconic trope in Great War literature and film: "In warding off the rats, the soldiers struggle against the impending disintegration of their own humanity. The assault by the corpse rats—animals that fed on human bodies—aptly represents the depth and ugliness of the decay that devours soldiers."[56]

The Great War altered perceptions of the human body: "The severity of [the] mutilations was unprecedented: nothing in . . . history . . . was adequate preparation for the physical devastation of the First World War. All parts of the body were at risk: head, shoulder, arm, chest, intestines, buttock, penis, leg, foot."[57] Unparalleled losses at the Western Front made swift and proper burial a challenge, with the decomposing dead creating "corpsescapes"—"worlds constructed, literally, of corpses."[58] This meant a further degradation of the human body: "The dead were underfoot; they were used to reinforce the parapets of the trenches. . . . Some turned up in bizarre places, such as the latrine, holding up a fragile doorway, or up a tree."[59] Corpses, Julia Kristeva writes, are emotionally and psychologically alienating: "The corpse, the most sickening of wastes, is a border that has encroached upon everything. . . . In that thing that no longer matches and therefore no longer signifies anything, I behold the breaking down of a world that has erased its borders. . . . The corpse, seen without God and outside of science, is the utmost of abjection. It is death infecting life."[60]

One could say that the plot of *Deathwatch* revolves around the horror of confronting "corpse[s] as abject [and] mark[ing] the threshold between the subject and object and threaten[ing] to contaminate or dissolve the subject."[61] When Quinn pokes his club into the mud-covered bodies, he creates an ontological distance be-

A pile of bodies, part of the horrific "corpsescape" of *Deathwatch*.

tween himself and the corpse. Likewise, when the soldiers pile up the dead in one place, they try to restore "the distinction between being and non-being," since "the corpse [also] marks the border that confirms the living person as alive."[62]

The corpse heap is shown in a manner that brings to mind the harrowing images of piles of bodies discovered in concentration camps. The collapse of this pile into the depths of the earth is a scene remarkably similar to one envisaged by Sebastian Faulks's protagonist in *Birdsong*: "The difference between living and dying was not one of quality, only of time. . . . He saw a picture in his mind of a terrible piling up of the dead . . . the row on row, the deep rotting earth hollowed out to hold them."[63] And it was the author's explicit intention to show the Great War as the first stage in the process of "degradation [of man]; further degradation was awaiting in concentration camps."[64] It is highly significant that the Thiepval Memorial to the Missing of the Somme plays a prominent role in Faulks's novel, for it commemorates more than seventy thousand men whose bodies were never found. Bassett's soldiers have disappeared from the moment they find themselves in the fog-enveloped forest, and the trenches they find are only a fulfilment of their inevitable destiny to become cadavers that will disappear within the depths of the monster-earth, greedily waiting to suck them in. The film ends by reenacting the scene of a soldier stepping into a decaying corpse, and this "circular structure away from and neurotic return to the trampling of the German corpse suggests two things about representing war. First, the dead and decomposing war body is a locus of trauma . . . whose visceral abjectness presents an impossibility of assimilation. Second, war will only be recovered from traumatic memory by its continued reinterpreting and reinvention of the war body."[65]

The concept of embodied memory gains an entirely new meaning in relation to the horror, for the assumption of "the importance of the body and its habitual and emotional experiences as both a reservoir of memories and a mechanism of generating them"[66] applies to the dead body. The truth of the war experience is "embodied" in the corpse, and trauma is located in the vulnerability of the human body, with the undead signifying the impossible restoration of the human body in its pre-death completeness. If we interpret the soldiers' passage through the fog as one from life to death, then, with the exception of Chevasse, they become undead with intact bodies, which once again must go through physical degradation to become cadavers. Whatever happens to the soldiers' bodies in the trenches, they are ultimately seen by Charlie in the Owen-like underworld as men intact, their bodies bearing no sign of the mutilations they endured.

This is an interplay similar to the "dehumanization/reanimation"[67] that can be found at the core of the memorialization of the Great War dead through an unidentified soldier's body. The completeness of the corpse assures its eternal "beingness." As Wittman argues, "one of the main images of how the Unknown Soldier tremendously increases the disquieting nature of corpses is that bare bones grow new flesh just as mutilated bodies acquire prostheses; somehow the Unknown Soldier's body is reanimated, undead, even as he is dead, and able to contaminate the living not just with mortality but with the abject mortality of the trenches."[68] The idea behind the construction of tombs for single unidentified soldiers across various countries was to restore "dignity [to] the body itself, which is no longer seen as passive but active; the body is the agent that transcends social constructions and names,"[69] yet, as Wittman writes, this memorialization practice was also "associated with an experience of radical loss and horror beyond words," which explains "why the materiality of the Unknown Soldier's body was both so fascinating yet so repressed."[70] In *Deathwatch* we encounter a similar tension between the need to restore the traumatic "monstrosity of soldiers' bodies"[71] and the desire to "contain" abjection through conjuring a "mystical body"[72] which is "purified," bearing no sign of mutilation or decay.

It is significant that "monstrosity" in Bassett's horror is located in the corpse, the barbed wire, and the mud, yet the undead are not depicted in a zombielike manner. When Friedrich, waiting for another group of British soldiers to enter the trenches, stares straight at the camera with a sinister expression in his eyes, he is frightening but not monstrous.

Conclusion

One of the major concerns of many Great War veterans was whether civilians in the time of the conflict, as well as future generations, would understand—and believe in—the "horror" and "hell" of trench warfare. The major challenge facing writers and filmmakers across time and space has always been how to capture the "other-worldliness"[73] of the Western Front. The horror genre is all about the impossible, the implausible, and the irrational, and these are precisely the categories that lie at the heart of the literary and cinematic representations of the Great War. Horror films are "narratives built on suspense, surprise, and shock,"[74] elements equally crucial for war narratives intent on evoking "empathic unsettlement," which "disturbs disciplinary protocols of representation and raises problems bound up with one's implication in, or transreferential to, charged, value-related events."[75] Concomitantly, "horror is insecurity, horror is uncertainty; and horror is also the dawning conviction that our worst fears cannot hold a candle to the enormity of the reality they half reveal, half conceal from us."[76] The Great War put the human body at the center of attention, with commemorative practices and cultural representations trapped between the ethical obligations to convey the truth of violent death and, concomitantly, to "restore" dismembered and disappeared bodies.

Daniel Quinn's epigraphs for each part of his alternate history dystopia, which correlates the disappearance of memory with the disappearance of bodies, perfectly summarize Bassett's use of the horror convention for rendering a truth about war, remembrance, and modern-age insecurities relating to corporeality: *Forgotten*: "Bodies do not always stay buried"; *Found*: "It is much easier to dig one large grave than to dig many small ones"; *Risen*: "The dead, as we have seen, can quite literally emerge from their graves if the conditions are right"; and *Epilogue*: "People can simply never get used to what a corpse can do."[77] These epigraphs—taken from Paul Barber's *Vampires, Burial, and Death: Folklore and Reality*—bespeak an attitude toward death and the dead that has come to dominate twentieth- and twentieth-first-century historical consciousness: "[loss of] confidence in the stability of death and a corpse's embodiment of death."[78] The subversion of traditional ontological boundaries is the key point of convergence between the cultural representations of the war and horror genres: "corpses sprout, fluctuate in and out of consciousness, appear to sleep or to speak. They camouflage themselves as pieces of the material world but then emerge from that camouflage and pronounce themselves emphatically separate from the landscape."[79]

Notes

1. Bassett, Interview by Dareen Rea.
2. Bassett, Interview by Phil Davies Brown.
3. "*Deathwatch* Review."
4. Randell, "Welcome to Hell," 126.
5. Freeland, *The Naked and the Undead*, 3.
6. Cavallaro, *The Gothic Vision*, 27.
7. Randell, "Welcome to Hell," 123.
8. Ibid., 122.
9. Owen, "Mental Cases," 73.
10. Kelly, *Cinema and the Great War*, 93.
11. *Deathwatch*, directed by Michael J. Bassett.
12. Owen, "The Show," 70.
13. Gristwood, *The Somme*, 20, 22.
14. Ibid., 26, 59.
15. Ibid., 17–18.
16. Booth, *Postcards from the Trenches*, 54.
17. Cavallaro, *The Gothic Vision*, 30.
18. Booth, *Postcards from the Trenches*, 54.
19. Hayward, *Myths and Legends of the First World War*, 67. For a "rational" historical explanation of the allegedly "supernatural" disappearance of the British soldiers, see Travers and Celik, "Not One of Them Ever Came Back."
20. Clarke, *The Angel of Mons*, 192–93.
21. Ibid., 192.
22. Owen, "Strange Meeting," 74–75.

23. *Deathwatch.*
24. Leed, *No Man's Land,* 107.
25. Gristwood, *The Somme,* 23.
26. What Randell terms a "signifier of a dysfunctional environment." Randell, "Welcome to Hell," 126.
27. Barbusse, *Under Fire,* 315, 318.
28. Manning, "Author's Prefatory Note," in *The Middle Parts of Fortune,* n.p.
29. *Deathwatch.*
30. *Deathwatch.*
31. Hayward, *Myths and Legends,* 103.
32. Grossman, *On Killing,* 135–36.
33. Hanley, *The German Prisoner,* 33–34.
34. Meyer, "Introduction," x.
35. Hanley, *The German Prisoner,* 35.
36. James Dickey, quoted on the second page of all the books published in the Joseph M. Bruccoli Great War Series.
37. Winter, *Sites of Memory, Sites of Mourning,* 15.
38. Chlumberg, *Miracle at Verdun.*
39. Piehler, "The War Dead and the Gold Star," 168.
40. Carroll, *Philosophy of Horror,* 101.
41. Ibid.
42. Innes and Castle, *Covenants with Death.*
43. *Deathwatch.*
44. Leed, *No Man's Land,* 164.
45. Harrison, *Generals Die in Bed,* 13, 102.
46. Carroll, *Philosophy of Horror,* 101.
47. *Deathwatch.*
48. Remarque, *All Quiet on the Western* Front, 83.
49. Bonadeo, *Mark of the Beast,* vii.
50. *Deathwatch.*
51. O'Flaherty, *Return of the Brute,* 138.
52. Carroll, *Philosophy of Horror,* 103.
53. Derry, *Dark Dreams 2.0,* 22–23.
54. Randell, "Welcome to Hell," 130.
55. See Fussell, *The Great War and Modern Memory,* 36–74.
56. Bonadeo, *Mark of the Beast,* 45.
57. Bourke, *Dismembering the Male,* 33.
58. Booth, *Postcards from the Trenches,* 50.
59. Tate, *Modernism, History and the First World War,* 66.
60. Kristeva, *Powers of Horror,* 3–4.
61. Tate, *Modernism, History and the First World War,* 69.
62. Ibid.
63. Faulks, *Birdsong,* 72.
64. Faulks, "Interview by Harriet Gilbert."
65. Randell, "Welcome to Hell," 131.

66. Misztal, *Theories of Social Remembering*, 79.
67. Wittman, *The Tomb of the Unknown Soldier*, 153.
68. Ibid., 137.
69. Ibid., 11.
70. Ibid., 150–51.
71. Ibid., 153.
72. Ibid., 11.
73. Gristwood, *The Somme*, 20.
74. Corrigan and White, *The Film Experience*, 308.
75. LaCapra, *History in Transit*, 136.
76. Taylor, "Foreword," 16.
77. Quinn, *After Dachau*, 1, 93, 177, 219.
78. Booth, *Postcards from the Trenches*, 63.
79. Ibid.

Bibliography

Barbusse, Henri. *Under Fire*. Translated by Robin Buss. London: Penguin Books, 2003.

Bassett, Michael J. Interview by Phil Davies Brown. *The Horror Asylum*. August 14, 2006. http://www.horror-asylum.com/interview/michaeljbassett/interview.asp.

———. Interview by Dareen Rea. *Sci-fi Online*. March 5, 2008. http://www.sci-fi-online .com/Interview/03-05-08_MichaelJbassett.htm.

Beidler, Philip D. "Introduction." In *Company K*, edited by William March, vii–xxvi. Tuscaloosa: University of Alabama Press, 2006.

Bonadeo, Alfredo. *Mark of the Beast: Death and Degradation in the Literature of the Great War*. Lexington: University Press of Kentucky, 1989.

Booth, Allyson. *Postcards from the Trenches: Negotiating the Space Between Modernism and the First World War*. New York: Oxford University Press, 1996.

Bourke, Joanna. *Dismembering the Male: Men's Bodies, Britain and the Great War*. London: Reaktion Books, 1999.

Carroll, Noël. *The Philosophy of Horror or Paradoxes of the Heart*. New York: Routledge, 1990.

Cavallaro, Dani. *The Gothic Vision: Three Centuries of Horror, Terror and Fear*. London: Continuum, 2002.

Chlumberg, Hans. *Miracle at Verdun*. Translated by Edward Crankshaw. In *Famous Plays of 1932–33*. London: Victor Gollancz, 1934.

Clarke, David. *The Angel of Mons: Phantom Soldiers and Ghostly Guardians*. Chichester, UK: Wiley, 2004.

Corrigan, Timothy, and Patricia White. *The Film Experience: An Introduction*. Boston: Bedford/St. Martin's, 2004.

Deathwatch. Directed by Michael J. Bassett. Neubiberg, Germany: ApolloMedia Distribution, 2002. DVD.

"*Deathwatch* Review." *TalkTalk.* http://www.talktalk.co.uk/entertainment/film/review/films /deathwatch/148.

Derry, Charles. *Dark Dreams 2.0: A Psychological History of the Modern Horror Film from the 1950s to the 21st Century.* Jefferson, NC: McFarland & Company, 2009.

Faulks, Sebastian. *Birdsong.* London: Vintage, 1994.

———. "Interview by Harriet Gilbert." *BBC World Book Club.* April 2008. http://www .bbc.co.uk/worldservice/specials/133_wbc_archive_new/page3.shtml.

Freeland, Cynthia A. *The Naked and the Undead: Evil and the Appeal of Horror.* Boulder, CO: Westview Press, 2000.

Fussell, Paul. *The Great War and Modern Memory.* Oxford: Oxford University Press, 1977.

Gristwood, A. D. *The Somme, Including Also The Coward.* Columbia: University of South Carolina Press, 2006.

Grossman, Dave. *On Killing: The Psychological Costs of Learning to Kill in War and Society.* New York: Back Bay Books/Little Brown and Company, 1996.

Hanley, James. *The German Prisoner.* Holstein, Ontario: Exile Editions, 2006.

Harrison, Charles Yale. *Generals Die in Bed: A Novel from the Trenches.* London: Definitions, 2004.

Hayward, James. *Myths and Legends of the First World War.* Stroud, UK: History Press, 2010.

Innes, T. A., and Ivor Castle. *Covenants with Death.* London: Daily Express Publications, 1934.

Kelly, Andrew. *Cinema and the Great War.* London: Routledge, 2007.

Kristeva, Julia. *Powers of Horror: An Essay on Abjection.* Translated by Leon S. Roudiez. New York: Columbia University Press, 1982.

LaCapra, Dominick. *History in Transit: Experience, Identities, Critical Theory.* Ithaca, NY: Cornell University Press, 2004.

Leed, Eric. *No Man's Land: Combat and Identity in World War I.* London: Cambridge University Press, 1979.

Manning, Frederic. *The Middle Parts of Fortune.* London: Penguin Books, 1990.

March, William. *Company K.* Tuscaloosa: University of Alabama Press, 2006.

Meyer, Bruce. "Introduction." In James Hanley, *The German Prisoner*, vii–xviii. Holstein, Ontario: Exile Editions, 2006.

Misztal, Barbara A. *Theories of Social Remembering.* Maidenhead, UK: Open University Press, 2003.

O' Flaherty, Liam. *Return of the Brute.* Dublin: Wolfhound Press, 1998.

Owen, Wilfred. "Mental Cases." In *The Wordsworth Book of First World War Poetry*, edited by Marcus Clapham, 73. Ware, UK: Wordsworth Editions, 1995.

———. "The Show." In *The Wordsworth Book of First World War Poetry*, edited by Marcus Clapham, 70. Ware, UK: Wordsworth Editions, 1995.

———. "Strange Meeting." In *The Wordsworth Book of First World War Poetry*, edited by Marcus Clapham, 74–75. Ware, UK: Wordsworth Editions, 1995.

Piehler, Kurt. "The War Dead and the Gold Star: American Commemoration of the First World War." In *Commemorations: The Politics of National Identity*, edited by John R. Gillis, 168–85. Princeton, NJ: Princeton University Press, 1994.

Quinn, Daniel. *After Dachau*. Hanover, NH: Zooland Books, 2001.

Randell, Karen. "'Welcome to Hell, Private Shakespeare': Trench Horror, *Deathwatch* and the Resignification of World War I." In *The War Body on Screen*, edited by Karen Randell and Sean Redmond, 120–33. New York: Continuum, 2008.

Remarque, Eric Maria. *All Quiet on the Western* Front, translated by Brian Murdoch. London: Vintage, 2005.

Tate, Trudi. *Modernism, History and the First World War*. Manchester, UK: Manchester University Press, 1998.

Taylor, John Russell. "Foreword to the Original Edition." In Charles Derry, *Dark Dreams 2.0: A Psychological History of the Modern Horror Film from the 1950s to the 21st Century*, 15–17. Jefferson, NC: McFarland & Company, 2009.

Travers, Tom, and Birten Celik. "'Not One of Them Ever Came Back': What Happened to the 1/5 Norfolk Battalion on 12 August 1915 at Gallipoli?" *Journal of Military History* 66, no. 2 (2002): 389–406.

Winter, Jay. *Sites of Memory, Sites of Mourning: The Great War in European Cultural History*. Cambridge: Cambridge University Press, 2006.

Wittman, Laura. *The Tomb of the Unknown Soldier, Modern Mourning, and the Reinvention of the Mystical Body*. Toronto: University of Toronto Press, 2011.

CHAPTER 9

The U.N.dead

COLD WAR GHOSTS IN
CAROL FOR ANOTHER CHRISTMAS

Christina M. Knopf

On December 28, 1964, the United Nations aired *Carol for Another Christmas*—the first in a series of four promotional television movies commemorating its twenty-fifth anniversary—on the ABC network.[1] Written by Rod Serling, produced and directed by Joseph L. Mankiewicz, underwritten by Xerox, and featuring an all-star cast, it is described as the darkest, most unusual retelling of Charles Dickens's *A Christmas Carol*, and one of the bleakest holiday specials, ever produced. It is not only a product of, but also an ideological weapon in, the Cold War—a downbeat and didactic propagandist plea for world peace through dialogue, involvement, and the U.N.[2] An apocalyptic twist on Dickens's Christmas tale of supernatural visitation and transformation, *Carol for Another Christmas* (*CFAC*) is a Victorian ghost story for the Atomic Age. It places themes of Cold War science fiction and atomic-bomb cinema into a Gothic package appropriate to post–World War II fantasy films and wraps it in holiday trappings. This chapter will walk through the story line of *CFAC*, demonstrating how and where the film borrows from these various genre traditions, and then discuss how the different genres shape the telling and reading of its bomb-anxious, antiwar message.

The ninety-minute, made-for-television production opens with a series of Christmas card images backing the credits, calling to mind the Victorian ideal of cozy, social Christmas celebrations,[3] before cutting to the cold and isolated exterior of an opulent house. The house is imposing and gloomy—the ideal setting for a ghost story. The haunted house is almost a fixture in the horror genre; hauntings can only take place when the familiar is interrupted and becomes unfamiliar.[4] In American narratives, including both horror and atomic-bomb stories, the house is a significant symbol of domesticity and status. As such, it is often used as a marker of the American Dream or its corruption, synecdochically representing society at large.[5] Throughout Serling's work on his contemporary television series *The Twilight Zone* (1959–1964), big, well-appointed houses were often used as façades for misery and even the means of destruction—reflecting Serling's own outlook that material success too often detracted from humanity and family.[6]

A Haunted House

It is the then-present day: Christmas Eve, 1964. Inside the mansion, a black butler, Charles (the closest thing to a Bob Cratchit character in this story, played by Percy Rodrigues), goes about his solitary business on the expansive ground floor. Above stairs the story's main character, Daniel Grudge, sits alone in a dim bedroom listening to a record player project the sound of the Andrews Sisters singing "Don't Sit under the Apple Tree." On the wall are a number of military decorations and photographs, framed in memoriam. As Grudge looks, stone-faced, at the memorabilia, shadows crisscross the space around him, creating the appearance of a gloomy cage as a visual symbol of Grudge's emotional state and political ideology. It is here that Grudge, and the audience, first encounter the uncanny. Grudge brings the music to a dying halt, sliding the needle from the record, and begins to leave the room. As he turns off the lights, the music restarts and loops on the lyrics, "'Til I come marching home," though the record does not spin.

Grudge continues downstairs, where his nephew Fred (Ben Gazzara) is waiting for him. The two proceed to have a conversation, with Fred delivering what has been described as "a sanctimonious speech"[7] about a cultural exchange program at the college where he is a professor of history. Grudge has, apparently, pulled strings to prevent the exchange, which would have brought in a professor from communist Poland. Their argument is held beneath the watchful portrait of Grudge's son Marley, who died on Christmas Eve during World War II, and the audience learns that Grudge is a wealthy and powerful man whose strongly isolationist views were triggered by that death. Bitter and cynical, he actively disparages and opposes any and all progressive, humanitarian, "bleeding heart" causes, whether domestic or international, while referring to political adversaries and foreigners as "those people" or "their kind." Fred chides his uncle that his epitaph will be, "Here lies Daniel Grudge, on his side of the fence," and observes that "there are certain fences the world can no longer afford." As Grudge throws Fred out and is wished, "Merry Christmas, by the way," Grudge says, "Tonight, especially tonight, I'm in no mood for the brotherhood of man."

Grudge, played by Sterling Hayden, is a right-wing villain who thinks the needy and oppressed should be told to help themselves. He wants "effort, sweat, and faith" put into development of "the fastest bombers and the most powerful missiles on Earth": weapons that "we're not too chicken to use," and that other nations will be unable to match. This endorsement of peace through armed strength is, perhaps not unintentionally, reminiscent of General Jack D. Ripper, the deranged, paranoid anti-communist character Hayden had played, that same year, in *Dr. Strangelove, Or How I Learned to Stop Worrying and Love the Bomb*. Such heavy-handed politicizing of the humanitarian/anti-isolationist message, a 1960s variation on Dickens's call for mercy and benevolence, has been criticized[8]—but it is not unsurprising given the credentials of the film's production team. The right-wing extremist was the bogeyman of Hollywood, thanks to the House Un-American Activities Committee's investigation into communist infiltration of the American movie industry from the late 1940s to the mid-1950s. The subsequent Congressional hearings were an effort to contain not only communism but also dissent, and because of Hollywood's global reach, it was an easy target. Hundreds of performers, directors, and writers suspected of association with radical causes were banned from the entertainment industry.[9] Mankiewicz and Serling were not only both liberals, but had also both struggled with the limits of censorship during their careers.[10]

Marley Was Dead

As Fred leaves, Grudge sees Marley's reflection in the window glass of the door, suggestive of the iconic Marley doorknocker. He turns, and now sees his son sitting at the dinner table. He calls out, but gets no answer. At this point, it is plausible that Grudge is hallucinating in his grief. His nephew has just observed that: "I feel you mourn the death of Marley less than you mourn your personal loss of him. You keep his room like a shrine. You set a place for him at dinner each Christmas Eve because he died on Christmas Eve. Those things are for you, not for him." Ghost stories and occult films of the World War II and postwar eras, such as *A Guy Named Joe* (1943) and *Between Two Worlds* (1944), were meant, in part, to ease the grief of the living by visually demonstrating life after death.[11] They were also, however, an acknowledgment of the psychological traumas experienced in war, and of the presence of death in life; many of the ghosts in stories of this genre and time frame *are* hallucinations.[12] Even Grudge seems to believe this is his case, as he runs his hands over his face and eyes as if to clear his head and vision. As these two apparitions are the only appearances of Marley's ghost—a significant departure from the original *A Christmas Carol* in which Marley's ghost is a damned herald from beyond with a specific and personal message to impart—Grudge may well be hallucinating, though the apparitions are only a hint at the visions yet to come.

Again, Grudge hears the Andrews Sisters record start playing and skipping—though his butler hears nothing. He rushes to Marley's room to find the record still and the needle resting to the side, and the music stops. That the media technology of the record player is so prominent in these first eerie encounters is more than uncanny. It is symbolic of the human-versus-machine struggle that was characteristic of the postwar years. In fact, technology became central to nightmares of the horror tales developed after World War I, during which mankind realized that it had used science to create a living, and dying, hell for itself. Antitechnology sentiment was renewed in narratives following the Cuban Missile Crisis.[13] Horror stories that feature ghosts in machines or "living" technologies tend to emphasize the soulless nature of the technological specter, however animate and sentient the technology may appear.[14] This mediated ghost/media ghost is also present in the looming portrait of the dead Marley (Peter Fonda, whose scenes were cut from the final film[15]), hovering lifeless over Grudge and his nephew throughout their Christmas Eve argument. The picture, like a ghost, is only a reflection, an image of what was once living. Photographs and other media technology, like ghosts, often operate in the liminal spaces between life and death.[16] While looking at the portrait, Grudge puts words to this idea of man and machine, of vitality and vessel. "The one solid, brief thing on this Earth that I cared anything at all for, and to what end? So that his life could be snuffed out? His fine, young body turned into a bundle of bleeding garbage, in return for which I'm sent his dog-tags, some medals, and a twelve-word telegram."

Christmas Past: Ghosts of War

Soon, the chandelier crystals begin to vibrate, making tinkling sounds. As Grudge watches the light fixture, baffled, his house and furnishings fade away into blackness and swirling fog, and the chimelike sound from the chandelier gives way to a ship's bell—ringing in the appearance of the Ghost of Christmas Past (Steve Lawrence), a World War I casualty with a hepcat attitude who plays a haunting tune on his harmonica. It is 1918 and Christmas Past and Grudge are on a troop transport ship going nowhere. The fog-shrouded deck is stacked with the coffins, draped with the flags of various nations, of those killed in action from all of history's wars. The ship's rails are lined with the silent, staring, spirits of the wars' dead, forever at attention. Past explains, "I'm all of 'em: All of 'em who rallied around the flag, any flag, all flags. [. . .] I'm the dead, all the dead." Around them in the misty black of night, the bells and horns from thousands of other ghost ships without a destination can be heard. Seeing men from World War II, "his war," on a nearby ship, Grudge remarks that Americans should have stayed out of both world wars—a sympathetic perspective for many Americans, resentful of how World War II had disrupted their lives,[17] and wary of militarism, particularly after the 1962 Cuban Missile Crisis brought home the threat of nuclear holocaust.[18] In a rare moment of patriotic sentiment, Past agrees that it would be better if American blood were not spilled around the world—but that America's un-involvement was, and is, not possible. He explains that not fighting will not keep wars—or destruction and death—from happening. "War is also a contagious disease, Mr. G. [. . .] The one thing we do know, the only chance to keep this particular disease from spreading is to keep talking. So long as you talk, you don't fight. Simple?"

During this sequence it is revealed that Grudge was a naval officer in the Pacific during World War II. It is the only visit by a Christmas ghost that touches directly and specifically on Grudge's life. Past echoes Grudge's words about the United States not being "too chicken" to use the Bomb and then directs him through the ship's hatchway. With a blinding flash, they are transported to Hiroshima, September 1945. The dead have been cleared away, and only silence remains. Grudge witnesses himself and his soft-hearted driver (Eva Marie Saint) viewing the stark aftermath of the bomb, visiting a ward filled with schoolgirls who suffered flash burns in the blast. The children are, figuratively and literally, faceless behind bandages, wrapped like mummies and shrouded by translucent netting. One sings a song in a clear yet incorporeal voice, suspended over an un-

The Ghost of Christmas Past, surrounded by the ghosts of wars past, acts as a voice for all the dead.

seen body. They are the living dead—victims of the disease of war and disfigured embodiments of the nuclear threat. Briefly, Grudge is reminded of the horror he felt that day, even as he tried to justify the scene as the "simple arithmetic" of military planning, and his driver suggests that "war is obsolete now."

Christmas Present: Shadows

Christmas Past tells Grudge to walk through the doorway of the medical ward saying, "I'm Then. In there, is Now." Grudge now finds himself in the company of the Ghost of Christmas Present (Pat Hingle), seated at a long dining table—Grudge's own dining table, lit by Grudge's own chandelier—laden with food. He is again enclosed in darkness. The Christmas Present sequence has been called one of the more successful scenes in the *CFAC*,[19] demonstrating individual responsibility and morality in world problems. Present is a rather coarse entity, clothed in a smoking jacket, alternating between expressions of compassion and callousness. "You might say that I'm as close to being a walking, eating image of the human race as it's possible for a man or phantom to be. Part of me feels a gnawing hunger. Part of me is satiated. I'm warm, contented, healthy, but much of me shivers in the cold. [. . .] Mankind includes extremes." Grudge is immediately suspicious of a lecture about charity and the "Haves" and the "Have-Nots"—until he is surrounded with the shadowy images of the Have-Nots. By ringing a servant's bell, Present produces a vision of displaced-person camps, where refugees huddle, hungry, in the cold, singing hopeful songs of the season despite their condition. Now, Grudge becomes enraged that Present can sit there eating and drinking his holiday feast while those around him starve. Present explains, "I'm a ghost. I don't have a heart. I don't have a soul, no nerve endings, no brain center. I'm just a reflection. But then, I've already told you that. Shall I now tell you how many times you've stuffed yourself while two-thirds of the world starved in a cage?" What follows is a sobering presentation of statistics on worldwide oppression, poverty, deprivation, and disease, highlighting mankind's "selective morality." Here, Present fulfills the ghostly function of filling the gaps between the living and dead, the Haves and Have-Nots, the known and unknown—between politics and humanity—underscoring communal relations, with human want and need as great equalizers.[20]

In a key piece of dialogue, Grudge proclaims: "Nothing on this Earth could force me to eat while starving people watch!" Present responds, "*Watching* makes all the difference, what? You never *saw* them while tearing into your mashed potatoes! They weren't actually there when you buttered your bread." Later, Grudge cries, "I don't want to see them! I don't want to look at them," and is commanded, "Do, Mr. Grudge! Look at 'em, now!" The visual, the sense of sight invoked, is particularly important. Dickens's version of the Ghost of Christmas Present was similarly concerned with vision, commanding Scrooge to look upon various things he had previously not seen.[21] In fact, visibility is at the very heart of haunting. Ghosts contextualize the distinctions between what people see and what people know, putting human senses, particularly vision, and belief systems into crisis. Specters may "appear when the trouble they represent and symptomize is no longer being contained or repressed or blocked from view" helping to demonstrate the connections between individual lives and the course of world history.[22] That Grudge and Present are surrounded by darkness and shadows, just as Grudge and Past were on the ship, and just as Grudge was in his son's room, underscores the importance of sight. Shadows are both the absence and the result of light. Every moment of illumination—that is, every insight for Grudge—supposes a shadow, a frightening cover to the unknown. Importantly for the narrative, the shadow is not only an indication of the uncanny but also a representation of the atomic threat. The shadow is at once a metaphor for the nuclear dangers of the Cold War,[23] a physical mark of a nuclear explosion—a flash-burned silhouette of people and things that have otherwise been erased[24]— and a symbol of the nuclear aftermath.[25]

Christmas Future: Walking Death

When Grudge can take no more horrors of the present, he runs through the darkness, only to find himself entrapped in the barbed-wire cage of a displaced-persons camp. Collapsing in defeat, he is found by the hooded Ghost of Christmas/World's Future (Robert Shaw). As he rises, Grudge discovers that he is now in the rubble of what was once his town's meeting hall. Future informs that, "Time happened here, Mr. Grudge. [. . .] A few passing catastrophes. Time! [. . .] It seemed we reached a moment in time when talk became superfluous. So now your town hall is past tense. But then again, if you step outside, most of what you see is past-tense, or rather, most of what you don't see. [. . .] The year is not important. Calendars are past-tense now, also." Dates may be irrelevant to the future, but time is quite significant to the journey that Grudge and the audience are taking. The Christmas ghosts bridge past, present, and future, moving not only through time but beyond it. Hauntings are about the experience of time and the spaces between times,[26] forcing people to revisit the past (i.e., the deceased) and face the future (i.e., mortality). The future necessarily includes revenants of the past; as Future explains, "When the first bomb dropped on Hiroshima, the fate of man could have been predicted by a cut-rate Gypsy."

In this unspecified future, which is a typical time frame for apocalyptic cinema,[27] doomsday has occurred because the talking stopped when "Somebody thought somebody had dropped some bombs, but by then, of course, everybody *had* The Bomb. [. . .] Nobody was really anybody if they didn't have The Bomb. What you see before you, Mr. Grudge, is a tiny part of a big, round, radioactive burying ground." Not even the United Nations kept talking, but, Future assures, "There were voices, Mr. Grudge. The world didn't lack for sound. Behind each separate fence, each separate wall, came screams of anger, suspicion, and prejudice. And they grew, and they grew. But there were no answers, remember, no discussion, no place for it. And so in the end, the world was filled with the noise of hate." Again, the ghostly presence calls human senses into question. This time, it is sound rather than sight—just as sound haunted Grudge through his record player, through the silence of Hiroshima broken by the faceless voice of the Japanese schoolgirl, and through the Christmas carols being sung in the refugee camps. Even the original ghostly works of Dickens "suggests that noises, real and unreal, reveal themselves through conscious, intent acts of listening. The nervous body fills the vacuum of silence with phantom sounds generated by its own hyperacuity. If we believe that what we cannot see, we cannot know, then the possibility exists that inert and lifeless objects may have a secret life that only reveals itself when we look away or fall asleep"[28]—but hearing stays awake, even while we sleep. By the assault on Grudge's ocular and aural senses, he is being encouraged to open himself up to the experiences of the world around him, to see and hear that to which he has previously turned a blind eye or a deaf ear.

Future introduces Grudge to a band of H-bomb survivors—a dirty, ragtag group of men, women and children marauders, calling itself the Individual Mes. The Mes are organized by the Non-Government of the Me People, and led by the flamboyant Imperial Me (Peter Sellers), who wears a sequined ten-gallon hat cut to resemble the points of a crown, symbolizing at once the lawlessness of the Old West and the authority of a monarchy. Partly because of the Imperial Me, the Christmas Future sequence has been called the *CFAC*'s "most bizarre."[29] Such peculiarity is not, however, atypical of many Cold War narratives which use the surreal to undermine political and social assumptions. In fact, by the 1960s many fictional nuclear narratives had shifted to the absurd, suggesting that audiences were no longer interested in straight or dramatic accounts.[30] Sellers, like Sterling Hayden, had appeared earlier that year in the absurd *Dr. Strangelove*. Sellers's over-the-top performance as the Imperial Me, a zealot with an extreme vision of a perfect post-bomb future, may deliberately recall his portrayal as the psychotic Dr. Strangelove, who also had ridiculous ideas of life after the nuclear holocaust.

It is quickly apparent that the group follows the Imperial Me with mindless fanaticism. They scream like teenagers at a rock concert at his appearance, ironically mimicking images of adoring female fans of the Beatles, who made their American debut in 1964. The Imperial Me announces that the People from

Down Yonder and the People from 'Cross River want to come and "talk about what they call our mutual problem, our common differences" and debate about solutions "until somehow they get their problems solved." He states that doing so would be a waste of time, that it would mean surrendering to "do-gooders" and "bleeding hearts" who would assume control with an "insidious doctrine of involvement." The Imperial Me goes on to claim that "We have now reached a pure state of civilization. The world of the ultimate Me is finally within our grasp. It's a world where only the strong will exist, where only the powerful will love, where finally, the word 'we' will be stamped out and will become 'I' forever. Because we are each the wise. We are each the strong. And we are each the Individual Mes." His followers yell like an angry mob in agreement. They obsessively chant, "Me! Me! Me! Me!" As the camera pans over the collected group of Individual Mes, the audience sees evidence of the former civilization—a sailor's cap, a policeman's hat, a lab coat, a hard hat, a tuxedo.

Into the fevered group walks Charles, Grudge's butler, holding the hand of a black woman the audience will learn is Grudge's cook, Ruby. Charles kisses the woman and then entreats the crowd to listen to him. "We have survived the holocaust," he says, "and if we are to go on surviving we must work together

The Imperial Me is a ghoulish symbol of lawlessness and authority leading doomsday survivors.

now. We must talk together." He says that ethics, honor, and decency were not destroyed by The Bomb. The crowd laughs hysterically at his impassioned argument and throws him about the room. The Imperial Me charges Charles with "the treason of involvement" and "the subversion of the Individual Me." Charles is given a chance to speak, with the instruction that he does not have to think about it, but just say it. He states: "I may be all the sanity that is left. I may be all the conscience that remains on Earth. I can't let you kill me." As the mob hypnotically calls for him to jump to his death, a mother (Brit Ekland) sits in the back and dispassionately knits, reminiscent of Dickens's Madame Defarge in *A Tale of Two Cities* knitting the names of those who would lose their heads, except that here reason is being lost instead and not to the guillotine. Her son, dressed as a cowboy—the ultimate symbol of rugged individualism—takes a gun from a box labeled "Just Like Daddy's" and kills Charles while his mother smiles approvingly before returning to her knitting. At this point, the Imperial Me calls for the disposal of the People from Down Yonder and 'Cross River before they "proceed with the most important business of all, which is the killing of each other until there remains only the one Individual Me. [. . .] Follow me, my friends, my loved ones, to the perfect society. The civilization of I!"

Grudge called the Individual Mes "insane" and "animals," echoing a common trope in atomic bomb cinema, where inhabitants of a nuclear or post-nuclear world, are often represented as mutants, monsters, aliens, or ghouls. The Individual Mes, in fact, resemble zombies. Though they are still human, they live among the ruins of a radioactive, worldwide, burying ground/cemetery. Like the living dead of Hiroshima, they are victims of the contagion of war and by condemning one another to die they have become the walking dead. Mindless, primitive, and bloodthirsty, their only motivation is their instinct to survive. Like the zombie, they are post-human, a monstrosity of self and humanity that has lost its volition and feeds on destruction of life—embodiments of society's fears of the nuclear holocaust, all the more terrifying because they still look like friends and neighbors. They represent a post-civilization of animalistic instinct and taboo, replacing the familiar civilization of enlightened humanity.[31] The breakdown, and ultimate destruction, of society is a recurring theme in atomic bomb cinema, which relies on the apocalyptic imagination to help people comprehend the nuclear threat. However, most often, the idea is explored by its more optimistic opposite—the necessity of group cooperation to guarantee survival of the community.[32] The Me philosophy in *CFAC* was, nonetheless, not unprecedented. In fact, the oxymoron of a perfect civilization or perfect society was a theme repeatedly explored in Serling's *The Twilight Zone*, several episodes of which put forth the idea that there could be no peace, no harmony, as long as there were people. So though cooperation would be necessary for survival, it was not likely, given the behavior of humankind.[33]

Doubtful Transformation

Grudge demands to know what happened to him and if the future must be like this, but he gets no answer. He awakes on the floor beneath his tinkling chandelier. The phone is beeping off the hook beside him, and church bells are ringing in Christmas morning. He pauses to look at Marley's portrait and opens the doors to a new day. Fred appears at the door on his way to church, having been called by his uncle at 3:00 in the morning—a call that Grudge does not remember making (adding further credence to the possibility that Grudge was in fact haunted by his own grief and misery rather than by any supernatural beings). Before they can talk, Grudge is distracted by the radio. The children of the United Nations delegates are singing native Christmas songs in a broadcast from New York; Grudge recognizes the tunes from his visit with the Ghost of Christmas Present. While the children sing in the background, Grudge and Fred remark that a "family of nations" may not be the final answer but it is a possible one and that as long as there are children there must be possibilities. Echoing the sentiment of W. H. Auden's poem *September 1, 1939*, which says, "We must love one another or die"—alluded to earlier in 1964 by the Lyndon Johnson "Daisy Girl" campaign ad that used bomb imagery, and a voice-over by Johnson that proclaims, "These are the stakes. To make a world in which all of God's children can live, or to go into the dark. We must either love each other, or we must die."—Grudge admits: "There must be involvement. [. . .] We find ourselves living in a world in which we either greet the morning or accept the night." After wishing Fred a Merry Christmas and a good morning, Grudge goes into the kitchen to have breakfast and listen to the U.N. children's choir in the company of his black servants—a nod to the race relations of the time, an important issue to Serling.[34] Many critics have questioned the plausibility of Scrooge's rapid and complete transformation in the original Charles Dickens tale.[35] Grudge's more hesitant acknowledgment of the need for engagement with others may be more believable—but it offers much less hope for humanity. While both Dickens and Serling ask their audiences to be the change represented by their main characters, Serling's narrative gives no evidence that such reformation will, or even can, avert a bleak and violent future—indicating that though the Ghosts of Past, Present, and Future represent a world in progress, everyone is predestined for mortality.

A Nuclear Winter Holiday

By 1964 the American public was tired of militarism, increasingly skeptical of the containment narratives of official Cold War discourse, and cautious of the escalating involvement in Vietnam. *Carol for Another Christmas* attempts to both respond to and circumvent these attitudes by joining more familiar Cold War formulas with a ghostly Christmas tale from another time and place. "The ghost story covertly invokes a form of spectatorship that meets the ghost on its own spectral terms. This silent invocation, however, is in the end little more than a reflection of nostalgic longing and frustrated desire for a metaphysical, theological model of vision that no longer seems plausible or believable."[36] *A Christmas Carol*, despite its graveyards and emissaries from hell, has never had the reputation of being a tale of terror; the cozy family and holiday warmth chase away any chills.[37] *CFAC* lacks such gloom-dispelling cheer, but the ghostly presences and seasonal setting do suggest nostalgia for simpler, more family- and community-centric times—a nostalgia that is seen throughout Serling's work.[38]

Adapting Dickens's story, and thus comingling multiple generic practices, offers the Cold War narrative several advantages by adding new layers to the story's themes. The Christmas setting and release date offer a stark juxtaposition between the bounty and goodwill of the season and the self-centered philosophies touted first by Grudge and then by the Imperial Me—just as the Dickens story juxtaposed Scrooge's greed with the charity of Christmas. Fantasy stories are often ideal frameworks for political messages—making them more palatable and less obvious to the audience—though with its litany of speeches, *CFAC* lacked subtlety in this regard. Indeed, Serling had long ago realized that the supernatural or fantastic made excellent story lines for masking controversial social commentary. Moreover, Mankiewicz, whose only television project was *CFAC*, had also realized the advantages of using classic English literature to make subtle political points.[39] Dickens himself was an activist and a subversive who—like Serling, a fan of Dickens—wrote to undermine accepted principles of his time,[40] and the themes of charity and forgiveness that Dickens wove into *A Christmas Carol* were easily translated to the political ideologies of advocacy and action.

A Christmas Carol is ultimately a story of a transformational supernatural journey—a format also common in atomic-bomb cinema, especially in the late 1950s to mid-1960s. Apocalyptic narratives often feature protagonists on otherworldly or mythological journeys of self-discovery in order to garner the wisdom needed for survival.[41] The apparently supernatural setting opens Grudge, and the viewing audience, to the experience of being haunted not only by the Christmas spirits and the ghosts of war, but also by the apparitions of the hungry and oppressed and the monsters of selfishness and hopelessness. This spectral take on atomic-bomb and apocalyptic cinema encourages thoughtful reflection on dominant Cold War narratives: the value of nuclear arsenals and the viability of civil defense, challenging the inevitability of future war. While other Cold War fictions do the same, the Christmas spirits and spirit of Christmas contextualize the debate with sentimentality and sympathy as opposed to the sex and science of *Dr. Stangelove* and sensationalistic Cold War shock films. By existing in the in-betweens, specters are representations of linkages between past and present, present and future, here and there, us and them. Ghost stories, therefore, offer a narrative form for defining community and continuity[42]—the central themes of *CFAC*'s message.

Carol for Another Christmas is not only another *Christmas Carol* but is also a wish that there might be another Christmas, and an imperative to ensure there is another Christmas. Despite criticisms of being didactic and its overt efforts at United Nations propaganda, *CFAC* is an often clever and subtle blending of classic English literature, American television holiday special, cultural hauntings, and apocalyptic fiction. With Dickensian allusions, science-fiction undertones, and horror themes in a Christmas Eve/Morning setting, *CFAC* is an entertaining, if pious, challenge to the militaristic containment culture of its day—with messages about the common dignity of mankind and the obsolescence of war that resonate into the current era. Like the tale upon which it is premised, *CFAC* is no more a classic ghost story than it is a traditional zombie movie, and perhaps this is what makes it so dark, so chilling. If hauntings occur when the familiar becomes unfamiliar, what could be more frightening than a deadly, monstrous world of man's own creation?

Notes

1. Hadley, "The UN Goes to the Movies"; *Carol for Another Christmas*.
2. Chitwood, "A Victorian Christmas in Hell"; Guida, *A Christmas Carol and Its Adaptations*; Hadley, "Carol for Another Christmas"; Vinciguerra, "Marley Is Dead."
3. It has been argued that the Victorians, and particularly the works of Charles Dickens, invented the cozy Christmas. See Briggs, *Night Visitors*, and Chitwood, "A Victorian Christmas in Hell."
4. Bailey, *American Nightmares*; Ruffles, *Ghost Images*; Wolfreys, *Victorian Hauntings*.
5. Seed, *Under the Shadow*.
6. Feldman, *Spaceships and Politics*; Serling, Interview with Mike Wallace.
7. Guida, *A Christmas Carol and Its Adaptations*.
8. Ibid.
9. Krutnik, Neale, Neve, and Stanfield, eds., *"Un-American" Hollywood*.
10. Lenihan, "English Classics for Cold War America"; Serling, Interview with Mike Wallace.
11. Norden, "America and Its Fantasy Films"; Snelson, "The Ghost in the Machine."
12. Porcelli, "City of Ghosts."
13. Briggs, *Night Visitors*; Mundey, *American Militarism and Anti-Militarism*.
14. Ruffles, *Ghost Images*; Sconce, "Excerpt from Introduction to *Haunted Media*."
15. Vinciguerra, "Marley Is Dead."
16. Pilar Blanco and Peeren, "The Ghost in the Machine."
17. DePastino, "Willie & Joe Come Home"; Leff, "The Politics of Sacrifice."
18. Suid, *Guts and Glory*; Mundey, *American Militarism*; Walt, "Two Chief Petty Officers."

19. Guida, *A Christmas Carol and Its Adaptations.*

20. Kwon, "The Ghosts of War and the Spirit of Cosmopolitanism"; Kwon, "The Ghosts of War and the Ethics of Memory"; Brogan, *Cultural Haunting.*

21. Chitwood, "A Victorian Christmas in Hell," 89.

22. Gordon, *Ghostly Matters,* loc. 195; Gunning, "To Scan a Ghost"; Mills, *The Sociological Imagination.*

23. As in Judith Merril's 1950 novel *Shadow on the Hearth* and the 2003 RAND policy report *Beyond the Nuclear Shadow.*

24. An image found in the city of Hiroshima, and in the pages of John Hersey's 1946 novel *Hiroshima* and Ray Bradbury's 1950 story "There Will Come Soft Rains." See Pilar Blanco, *Ghost-Watching American Modernity,* 149–50; Seed, *Under the Shadow.*

25. As represented by imagery in Pat Frank's 1959 novel *Alas, Babylon.*

26. Derrida, *Specters of Marx;* Gordon, *Ghostly Matters.*

27. Seed, *American Science Fiction.*

28. Toop, "Excerpt from *The Chair Creaks, But No One Sits There,*" loc. 6380–2.

29. Vinciguerra, "Marley Is Dead."

30. Seed, *American Science Fiction.*

31. Boon, "And the Dead Shall Rise"; Christie, "A Dead New World"; Bishop, "Raising the Dead"; Higashi, "*Night of the Living Dead.*"

32. Shapiro, *Atomic Bomb Cinema.*

33. Feldman, *Spaceships and Politics.*

34. Serling, Interview with Mike Wallace.

35. Gilbert, "The Ceremony of Innocence"; Ruffles, *Ghost Images.*

36. Smajic, "The Trouble with Ghost-Seeing," 1110.

37. Kendrick, *The Thrill of Fear.*

38. Feldman, *Spaceships and Politics.*

39. Kovacs, *The Haunted Screen;* Snelson, "Ghost in the Machine"; Serling, Interview with Mike Wallace; Feldman, *Spaceships and Politics;* Lenihan, "English Classics."

40. Engle, "Politics of Dickens' Novels"; Kirshner, "Subverting the Cold War," 40–44; Vinciguerra, "Marley Is Dead."

41. Shapiro, *Atomic Bomb Cinema.*

42. Ibarra, "Permanent Hauntings"; Kwon, "The Spirit of Cosmopolitanism"; Kwon, "The Ethics of Memory."

Bibliography

Bailey, Dale. *American Nightmares: The Haunted House Formula in American Popular Fiction.* Madison: University of Wisconsin Press, 1999. Kindle edition.

Bishop, Kyle. "Raising the Dead: Unearthing the Nonliterary Origins of Zombie Cinema." *Journal of Popular Film and Television* 34, no. 4 (2006): 196–205.

Boon, Kevin. "And the Dead Shall Rise." In *Better Off Dead: The Evolution of the Zombie as Post-Human,* edited by Deborah Christie and Sarah Juliet Lauro, 5–8. New York: Fordham University Press, 2011.

Briggs, Julia. *Night Visitors: The Rise and Fall of the English Ghost Story.* London: Faber, 1977.

Brogan, Kathleen. *Cultural Haunting: Ghosts and Ethnicity in Recent American Literature.* Charlottesville: University Press of Virginia, 1998.

Carol for Another Christmas. Directed by Joseph L. Mankiewicz. Written by Rod Serling. Television broadcast. TCM. Accessed December 20, 2013. http://www.tcm.com/tcmdb/title/963811/Carol-for-Another-Christmas-A/.

Chitwood, Brandon. "A Victorian Christmas in Hell: Yuletide Ghosts and Necessary Pleasures in the Age of Capital." *Dissertations (2009–),* Paper 181. Marquette University, 2012. http://epublications.marquette.edu/dissertations_mu/181.

Christie, Deborah. "A Dead New World: Richard Matheson and the Modern Zombie." In *Better Off Dead: The Evolution of the Zombie as Post-Human,* edited by Deborah Christie and Sarah Juliet Lauro, 67–80. New York: Fordham University Press, 2011.

DePastino, Todd. "Willie & Joe Come Home." In *Willie & Joe Back Home.* By Bill Mauldin, vii–xix. Seattle, WA: Fantagraphics Books, 2011.

Derrida, Jacques. *Specters of Marx: The State of the Debt, the Work of Mourning and the New International.* Translated by Peggy Kamuf. New York: Routledge, 1994. Kindle edition.

Engle, Monroe. "The Politics of Dickens' Novels." *PMLA* 71, no. 5 (1956): 945–74.

Feldman, Leslie Dale. *Spaceships and Politics: The Political Theory of Rod Serling.* Lanham, MD: Lexington Books, 2010. Kindle edition.

Gilbert, Elliot. L. "The Ceremony of Innocence: Charles Dickens' *A Christmas Carol.*" *PMLA* 90, no. 1 (1975): 22–31.

Gordon, Avery F. *Ghostly Matters: Haunting and the Sociological Imagination.* Minneapolis: University of Minnesota Press, 2008. Kindle edition.

Guida, Fred. *A Christmas Carol and Its Adaptations.* Jefferson, NC: McFarland & Company, 2000.

Gunning, Tom. "To Scan a Ghost: The Ontology of Mediated Vision." In *The Spectralities Reader: Ghosts and Haunting in Contemporary Cultural Theory,* edited by María del Pilar Blanco and Esther Peeren, chapter 13. London: Bloomsbury, 2013. Kindle edition.

Hadley, Mitchell. "Carol for Another Christmas." *TVparty!,* 2010. http://www.tvparty.com/xmas-carol-for-another-christmas.html.

———. "The UN Goes to the Movies." *TVparty!,* 2008. http://www.tvparty.com/fall-un.html.

Higashi, Sumiko. "*Night of the Living Dead*: A Horror Film about the Horrors of the Vietnam Era." In *From Hanoi to Hollywood: The Vietnam War in American Film,* edited by Linda Dittmar and Gene Michaud, chapter 11. New Brunswick, NJ: Rutgers University Press, 1990. Kindle edition.

Ibarra, Enrique Ajuria. "Permanent Hauntings: Spectral Fantasies and National Trauma in Guillermo del Toro's *El espinazo del diablo.*" *Journal of Romance Studies* 12, no. 1 (2012): 56–71.

Kendrick, Walter. *The Thrill of Fear: 250 Years of Scary Entertainment.* New York: Grove Press, 1991.

Kirshner, Jonathan. "Subverting the Cold War in the 1960s: *Dr. Strangelove, The Manchurian Candidate,* and *The Planet of the Apes.*" *Film & History* 31, no. 2 (2001): 40–44.

Kovacs, Lee. *The Haunted Screen: Ghosts in Literature and Film*. Jefferson, NC: McFarland, 1999.

Krutnik, Frank, Steve Neale, Brian Neve, and Peter Stanfield, eds. *"Un-American" Hollywood: Politics and Film in the Blacklist Era*. New Brunswick, NJ: Rutgers University Press, 2007.

Kwon, Heonik. "The Ghosts of War and the Ethics of Memory." In *Ordinary Ethics: Anthropology, Language, and Action*, edited by Michael Lambek, 400–413. New York: Fordham University Press, 2010.

———. "The Ghosts of War and the Spirit of Cosmopolitanism." *History of Religions* 48, no. 1 (2008): 22–42.

Leff, Mark H. "The Politics of Sacrifice on the American Home Front in World War II." *Journal of American History* 77, no. 4 (1991): 1296–1318.

Lenihan, John H. "English Classics for Cold War America." *Journal of Popular Film & Television* 20, no. 3 (1992): 42–51.

Mills, C. Wright. *The Sociological Imagination*. Fortieth Anniversary Edition. 1960. New York: Oxford University Press, 2000. Kindle edition.

Mundey, Lisa M. *American Militarism and Anti-Militarism in Popular Media, 1945–1970*. Jefferson, NC: McFarland, 2012. Kindle edition.

Norden, Martin F. "America and Its Fantasy Films: 1945–1951." *Film & History: An Interdisciplinary Journal of Film and Television Studies* 12, no. 1 (1982): 1–11.

Pilar Blanco, María del. *Ghost-Watching American Modernity: Haunting, Landscape, and the Hemispheric Imagination*. New York: Fordham University Press, 2012.

Pilar Blanco, María del, and Esther Peeren. "The Ghost in the Machine: Spectral Media/ Introduction." In *The Spectralities Reader: Ghosts and Haunting in Contemporary Cultural Theory*, edited by María del Pilar Blanco and Esther Peeren, chapter 12. London: Bloomsbury, 2013. Kindle edition.

Porcelli, Stefania. "City of Ghosts: Elizabeth Bowen's Wartime Stories." In *The Ghostly and the Ghosted in Literature and Film: Spectral Identities*, edited by Lisa Kröger and Melanie R. Anderson, 15–27. Newark: University of Delaware Press, 2013.

Ruffles, Tom. *Ghost Images: Cinema of the Afterlife*. Jefferson, NC: McFarland & Company, 2004.

Sconce, Jeffrey. "Excerpt from Introduction to *Haunted Media*." In *The Spectralities Reader: Ghosts and Haunting in Contemporary Cultural Theory*, edited by María del Pilar Blanco and Esther Peeren, chapter 14. London: Bloomsbury, 2013. Kindle edition.

Seed, David. *American Science Fiction and the Cold War: Literature and Film*. Edinburgh: Edinburgh University Press, 1999.

———. *Under the Shadow: The Atomic Bomb and Cold War Narratives*. Kent, OH: Kent State University Press, 2013. Kindle edition.

Serling, Rod. Interview with Mike Wallace. *The Mike Wallace Interview*, first broadcast September 22, 1959. *The Twilight Zone Definitive Collection*, season 2, disc 5. Chatsworth, CA: CBS Broadcasting, 2006. DVD.

Shapiro, Jerome F. *Atomic Bomb Cinema: The Apocalyptic Imagination on Film*. New York: Routledge, 2002. Kindle edition.

Smajic, Srdjan. "The Trouble with Ghost-Seeing: Vision, Ideology, and Genre in the Victorian Ghost Story." *ELH* 70, no. 4 (2003): 1107–35.

Snelson, Tim. "The Ghost in the Machine: World War II, Popular Occultism and Hollywood's 'Serious' Ghost Films." *Media History* 17, no. 1 (2011): 17–32.

Suid, Lawrence H. *Guts and Glory: The Making of the American Military Image in Film.* Revised and expanded edition. Lexington: University Press of Kentucky, 2002.

Toop, David. "Excerpt from *The Chair Creaks, But No One Sits There.*" In *The Spectralities Reader: Ghosts and Haunting in Contemporary Cultural Theory*, edited by María del Pilar Blanco and Esther Peeren, chapter 17. London: Bloomsbury, 2013. Kindle edition.

Vinciguerra, Thomas. "Marley Is Dead, Killed in a Nuclear War." *New York Times*, December 20, 2007. http://www.nytimes.com/2007/12/20/fashion/20CAROL.html.

Walt, Stephen M. "Two Chief Petty Officers Walk into a Bar . . ." *Foreign Policy*, April 7, 2014. Accessed April 9, 2014. http://www.foreignpolicy.com/articles/2014/04/07/why_cant_we_make_fun_of_the_military_anymore.

Wolfreys, Julian. *Victorian Hauntings: Spectrality, Gothic, the Uncanny and Literature.* New York: Palgrave, 2002.

Part III

MAKING MONSTERS

CHAPTER 10

Pall in the Family
DEATHDREAM, HOUSE, AND
THE VIETNAM WAR

Christopher D. Stone

> "Vietnam, I never thought I'd be coming back. I guess we never really can leave, can we?"
>
> —*Braddock: Missing in Action III* (1988)[1]

> "Wars can be fought and won only when the dead are buried and forgotten."
>
> —Irwin Shaw, *Bury the Dead* (1936)[2]

All wars leave their mark on human bodies, scarring them, obliterating them, and profaning them. This simple, yet unavoidable fact creates a challenge for societies at war: broken bodies and forfeited lives must be explained, and their loss inscribed with meaning. The "official" response to this challenge is, typically, to treat the dead as a collective and interpret their deaths as sacrifices that allow the nation to endure. Such remembrances, however, hinge on forgetting. They merge the individuals who died—people with specific connections, experiences, and memories—into an undifferentiated mass so as not to undermine the nationalistic aims of official commemorations. After all, if one conceives of war as extinguishing individual lives rather than sacrificing unnamed soldiers, grief and righteous anger might overwhelm patriotic pieties. This possibility explains official culture's insistent need to memorialize: Mourning cannot be allowed to overtake mythmaking, lest the ability of policy makers to wage future wars be compromised. In short, as Irwin Shaw notes, societies must bury the dead, both physically and metaphorically, or risk being haunted by them.

But what if the dead (or more precisely cultural imaginings of the fallen) fail to cooperate? This question becomes more pressing when dealing with the Vietnam War, which American culture obsessively revisited for nearly two decades

155

after it ended in 1973. This essay engages the issue by examining how filmmakers have used the undead to comment on the Vietnam War. The undead have figured into multiple Vietnam-themed productions, including *Zombie Brigade* (1986), *Flatliners* (1990), *Jacob's Ladder* (1990), and *Universal Soldier* (1992), but this chapter focuses on two lesser-known examples: *Deathdream* (1972) and *House* (1986).[3] Viewed together, these films speak to fundamental shifts in representations of the Vietnam War from the 1970s to the 1980s—shifts that exemplify the concurrent rightward turn in American politics and culture—while offering an extended commentary on masculinity and its relationship to the American family.

Deathdream: Father as Villain, Undead as Scourge

Deathdream had its origins in *Children Shouldn't Play with Dead Things* (1972), the first cinematic collaboration between director Bob Clark and screenwriter Alan Ormsby. Impressed by what the duo achieved with a miniscule budget, producers Peter James and John Trent of Quadrant Films offered to finance their next project.[4] Ormsby responded by pitching *Deathdream*. As Clark recalls, the producers did not see its antiwar message as a commercial stumbling block. If anything, they saw it as a selling point, assuming that its commentary would resonate with many filmgoers.[5] Indeed, according to Ormsby, the script generated buzz beyond Quadrant Films, with many hailing it as an interesting spin on David Rabe's Tony Award–winning *Sticks and Bones* (1971).[6]

Deathdream and *Sticks and Bones* do share similarities. Each text is the story of a scarred son returning home and threatening his family's bourgeois household both physically and ideologically.[7] Yet, it is unclear whether Rabe's play influenced the film. According to Ormsby, the basic premise for *Deathdream* goes back to an unproduced play he wrote in the late 1960s. He drew inspiration from three antiwar touchstones. The first was a political cartoon by Robert Minor that originally ran in *The Masses* in 1916. Minor lampooned the military by envisioning its "perfect soldier": a hulking body with no head—a creature that solely existed to do or die, utterly incapable of thinking, questioning, or challenging his orders.[8] The second was the 1918 Bertolt Brecht ballad "Legend of the Dead Soldier." In it, a procession of Germans, under orders from the kaiser, revive a dead soldier and redirect him to the front so he can fight anew for God and the fatherland.[9] The third source, and the one that most informs *Deathdream*, is Irwin Shaw's 1936 play *Bury the Dead*, which imagines what would happen if six dead soldiers stood up and refused to be buried. This play sought to dramatize the hypocrisy infusing remembrances of the fallen, to show that

In his audition, Richard Backus, star of *Deathdream*, was instructed to stare at a lamp and project all his hate upon it. Here, in the finished film, as the camera locks onto Andy's eyes transfixed in rage, it becomes clear why Backus landed the role.

memorials exist less to commemorate the dead than to silence them, ignoring what they can teach us about how men die in war and for whom and for what.

If *Bury the Dead* rages against generals, policy makers, and business interests, *Deathdream* targets a cultural mind-set. It opens with the shooting of Andy Brooks (Richard Backus) in Vietnam before shifting to his middle-class home, where a telegram informs the family that Andy—the son, the brother—is dead. Inconsolable, Andy's mother, Christine (Lynn Carlin), prays and chants all night, imploring her only son to return. He does, but he is detached, aloof, and uncommunicative. Only belatedly does the family grasp the truth: The Andy that came back is one-part zombie, one-part vampire who murders and siphons blood to partially delay decomposition. After killing five people and becoming increasingly ghoulish in appearance, Andy returns home one last time. Try as he might, his father, Charles (John Marley), cannot shoot him. After Charles turns the gun on himself, Christine asks Andy: "Where will you be safe?" He directs her to a graveyard where he begs her to cover him with dirt. Reluctantly, she complies, allowing Andy to die for good.[10]

Director and screenwriter alike emphasize that, in telling this story, they wanted to employ horror to address broader issues with a progressive voice.[11] For the most part, they succeed, but cultural texts are invariably unstable. They contain ambiguities and contradictions, which invite multiple readings, and *Deathdream* is no exception.

Much of the film, for example, centers on the notion of innocence betrayed and destroyed. The original theatrical trailer plays up this angle as it solemnly notes: "A boy went away to fight a war, a man came back, but something came back with him, something unspeakable."[12] A Vietnam War–themed narrative predicated on lost innocence, however, is inherently problematic. As historian Christian Appy observers, such narratives privilege a particular middle-class mind-set at the expense of the more jaded outlook of the working-class youths who actually fought the war.[13] In short, a fixation on innocence can displace class. *Deathdream* leaves itself open for criticism on this front by focusing on a comfortably middle-class family despite the fact that middle-class households produced only 20 percent of American personnel in Vietnam. Kids like Andy, especially those with parents who socialized with deferment-granting physicians, as Andy's did, were unlikely to go to Vietnam.[14] It appears the filmmakers made a commercial decision to better connect with average Americans who tend to define themselves, regardless of income, as "middle class."

Deathdream's use of innocence also raises a second troubling possibility, one often evident in Vietnam War films: a tendency to classify the war as a cultural pathogen infecting otherwise healthy "organisms," whether the American military, American society, or individual soldiers. At its most troubling, this tendency roots this malady within Vietnam itself, defining the country and its people in exceedingly Orientalist terms as corrupt, uncivilized, or barbaric, as seen in films such as *The Deer Hunter* (1978), *First Blood* (1982), and *Missing in Action* (1984). *Deathdream*, however, preceded these by several years.

Such Orientalism not only taints the film's cultural geography, but also infuses the only one of Orsmby's primary inspirations not forged by the crucible of World War I: the 1902 short story "The Monkey's Paw," by W. W. Jacobs. This titular object is a mummified paw imbued by a fakir with supernatural powers (it grants three wishes). The paw and the fakir hail from India, which the short story encodes as an exotic land of mystery, magic, and danger. A soldier-adventurer recently returned from India introduces the paw into a humble English household with tragic consequences. *Deathdream*'s debt to "The Monkey's Paw" resides with the fate of the family's son. Ignoring the soldier's advice, the father wishes for two hundred pounds. The paw delivers, but with a catch: the sum comes from the son's employer after a fatal industrial accident. A few days later, the mother uses the paw to resurrect the son slain by a shortsighted father, only to be foiled when her husband uses the final wish to send the son back to his grave.[15]

On the most obvious level, *Deathdream* and "The Monkey's Paw" share three characters: the deceased son, the complicit father, and the grieving mother who reanimates her fallen child. On a deeper level, these texts betray Orientalist trappings. Eastern mysticism brings despair and death to an English family in "The Monkey's Paw," while *Deathdream*, forgoing the fakir, suggests that Asian culture morally and physically compromised American soldiers by exposing them to potent and highly addictive drugs such as heroin. Such fears, in themselves, carry Orientalist baggage, as they harken back to the role of opium in the "yellow peril" discourse of the late nineteenth and early twentieth centuries.

Deathdream's references to heroin are exceedingly overt. To postpone decay, Andy needs blood, which he acquires through injections. The film hints at this fact when a coroner notices needle marks in the arm of Andy's first victim. Later, the audience witnesses Andy getting a fix. He fills a needle with blood, ties a tourniquet around his arm, shoots up, and experiences an exhilarating high. Here the film was responding to the news media, which after 1968 unleashed a torrent of grossly exaggerated reports about drug abuse among American servicemen in Vietnam.[16] The political right, especially President Richard Nixon, used this issue to castigate the counterculture and Great Society liberalism. Figures on the political left, including the makers of *Deathdream*, also joined this discourse, albeit on different grounds and with different objectives. In doing so, they unwittingly helped obscure and defuse, as historian Jeremy Kuzmarov notes, a potent wellspring of political radicalism, the GI resistance movement, by helping transform "the image of Vietnam veterans from agents of imperialism—as many came to see themselves—and dissenters to pathological victims of an unpopular war, upon whom public fears became transfixed."[17]

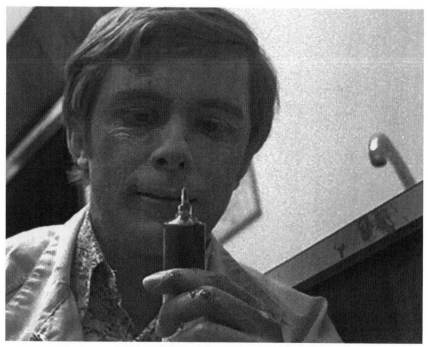

Having silenced another member of Nixon's complicit majority, Andy draws the victim's blood and prepares to inject it as if it were heroin.

In uncritically echoing sensational media reports about heroin, *Deathdream* evinces some of the Orientalist tendencies that profoundly informed American media coverage of Vietnam and the Vietnam War. It is important, however, not to overextend the Orientalist charge against the film. Traces exist, to be sure, but it is not the film's underlying message. According to *Deathdream*, Andy's victimization does not stem from a remorseless, savage enemy or from exposure to a debauched, primitive world. Indeed, the film says little about Vietnam itself; it never acknowledges, let alone depicts or discusses, the Vietnamese—a problematic fact in itself, but one typical of American representations of the Vietnam War.[18]

Who, then, is responsible for Andy's fate? The film answers "us." Like *Welcome Home, Soldier Boys* (1972), *The Visitors* (1972), and *Tracks* (1976), *Deathdream* brings the war home, metaphorically punishing Americans for actively supporting or passively allowing the bloodletting in Vietnam. It alerts the audience to this particular project in one of its first scenes. Howie (David Gawlikowski), a soon-to-be murdered trucker who picked up a hitchhiking Andy, stops at a diner. Noticing a uniformed passenger in his cab, an inebriated patron (Robert Cannon) asks: "What kind of soldier is he? Theirs or ours?" When Howie answers "ours," the relieved drunk remarks: "Good, I thought we were being invaded." This scene performs two functions. First, it references the ambivalent position of the Vietnam veteran in American discourse. Was he the idealized "us," selfless, idealistic, and triumphant? Or was he "them," alien, corrupt, and dangerous? Second, it draws upon popular anxiety about returning soldiers and the havoc they might wreak—worries stoked by extensive media coverage of violent outliers.[19] Andy is an invading force, but he is not a foreign agent. He is an American sacrificed needlessly; he is an undead avenger who turns the tables on his fellow countrymen by spilling their blood so he may endure. As he caustically informs one victim: "I died for you, doc. Why shouldn't you return the favor?"[20]

As grim as this retribution is, the filmmakers empathize with Andy. They deem his cause just; they cast him not as a monster or an aggressor, but as a victim and a scourge. But what exactly are Andy and, through him, the film excoriating? *Deathdream* directs its ire at two targets: the authoritarian, patriarchal family and the conservative mind-set that undergirds it. The film puts patriarchy on its agenda with the very first scene set in the United States: a dinner sequence featuring Charles, Christine, and their daughter Cathy (Anya Ormsby). As Charles carves the roast beef, Christine coos: "I think a man should always do the carving." She then advises Cathy not to wed a man who cannot fulfill that responsibility. Cathy resorts by noting that Joanne, Andy's girlfriend, makes a tasty vegetarian cutlet. Christine ignores this suggestion, fixating instead on her favorite subject: Andy.

This brief sequence performs several tasks. It taps into the gendered symbolism of meat, a food long associated, as Nick Fiddes notes, with such so-called manly virtues as "strength and aggression."[21] It links meat to the transmission of patriarchy. As Christine observes, Charles learned to properly cut meat from his father and, in turn, Charles passed that knowledge to Andy. Christine seeks a similar legacy when she implores Cathy to emulate her by embracing a patriarchal model where women prepare meals out of view, then cede the knife to men so they can openly assert their status as household head.[22] By stressing that patriarchy is not a given but has to be learned, this scene raises the possibility of change. Indeed, it suggests the younger generation, symbolized by Cathy and Joanne, were already exploring alternatives. Lastly, the unwillingness of either parent to acknowledge, let alone engage, Cathy's proposal suggests that the patriarchal home devalues daughters. The film amplifies this theme through a succession of scenes where Cathy's parents ignore, dismiss, or even manhandle her—a sequence that reaches its apex when Christine, utterly beset by worry for Andy, bellows: "I don't care about Catherine!"[23]

Christine occupies an ambiguous position in the film. She endures patriarchy's slings and arrows, but also embraces and reinforces some of its core tenets. The film is less ambivalent about Charles. He is an authoritarian who repeatedly defines the home as his castle and exhibits no qualms about bullying those who live within its walls. Andy may be a homicidal, blood-siphoning zombie, but Charles is the true enemy, the real threat. Even his name suggests as much. After all, most characters call him "Charlie," a reference that positions him as the enemy in the place of the absent Viet Cong guerillas ("Victor Charlie," or simply "Charlie," to American soldiers). According to screenwriter Alan Ormsby, Charlie embodies the psychology that produced the war, a conservative mind-set infused with machismo and belligerent patriotism.[24]

Maybe worst of all, Charlie killed his only son. The filmmakers levy the child-killer accusation through Christine. According to her, Andy was a sensitive soul whom Charlie labeled "effeminate." The father constantly needled and belittled the son, browbeating him until he emulated his father, who had served in World War II, by enlisting. Charlie, however, maintains that he did not coerce Andy; rather, he argues that Andy volunteered in order to free himself from a mother whose smothering affections threatened to unsex him, echoing Philip Wylie's popular argument that "momism" would extirpate the vitality of young males (and that of the United States), leaving them weak and susceptible to enemies foreign and domestic.[25] As an equally proud patriot and patriarch, Charlie celebrated Andy's decision and hoped the military would make a man out of his son by helping him recognize, loathe, and purge the feminine characteristics that shamed his father.

The film's climatic moments validate Christine's explanation. Charlie storms into the house, gun in hand, ready for a final showdown. He orders Andy to "stand up and face me," his voice echoing with confidence and righteous anger. Andy slowly complies, revealing his true condition. He is frail and decomposing. His face, with bones protruding from his flesh, is etched in fear—a pitiful, macabre sight achieved with the help of makeup artist Tom Savini, himself a Vietnam veteran.[26] An unnerved Charlie recoils. He expected to find an enemy to vanquish, a threat to eliminate, a monster to destroy; instead, he confronts the ruins of a son. He also grasps his culpability; he sacrificed his only son on an altar of antiquated ideals. With that realization, the father takes his own life. This suicide acts not just as a confession of guilt—and an indictment of an entire nation—but also as an expression of hope for the filmmakers, the hope that Charlie's mentality, what Ormsby dubs "John Wayneism," will expire just as Charlie did.[27]

Deathdream was hardly the only cultural text from this period making such wishes. Films such as Hail, Hero! (1969), Summertree (1971), and The Visitors (1979) looked to identify and assail perspectives they deemed culturally untenable. Moreover, like Deathdream, they mocked the father, who most definitely did not know best. In Summertree, the patriarch is an insurance-peddling Babbitt (Jack Warden) compelled by pride and patriotism to halt his son (Michael Douglas) from evading the draft. Betrayed by his father, the son dies in Vietnam. In Hail, Hero!, the family is headed by a racist, misogynistic, provincial blowhard (Arthur Kennedy) who expects his son to serve in Vietnam. Although opposed to the war, Carl Dixon (Michael Douglas, again) enlists. He wants to prove his ethical code can survive the ravages of combat. At film's end, it is unclear whether Carl will succeed. In The Visitors, the most interesting of the cluster, the patriarch is Harry Wayne (Patrick McVey), a successful novelist who lives with daughter Martha (Patricia Joyce) and her boyfriend Bill Schmidt (James Woods), a veteran who helped convict two soldiers for the rape and murder of a Vietnamese girl.[28] After a brief prison stay, the duo visits Bill, receiving a warm reception from Harry, a racist reactionary. They repay Harry's hospitality by pummeling Bill and raping Martha.

Like Charlie Brooks, Harry Wayne (another intentionally referential name) represents what Elia Kazan terms: "the dead end of an outdated philosophy."[29] These two films, as well as the two Michael Douglas vehicles, may have wanted to tramp the dirt down on the grave of this philosophy, but as Alan Ormsby concedes, they failed.[30] None achieved commercial success, with Deathdream never making it out of Southern grindhouses.[31] Yet despite its limited distribution, Deathdream did develop a cult following that grew after a high-quality reissue by Blue Underground in 2004. The rerelease elicited a flurry of online reviews, most of which hailed the film as an audacious, overlooked gem.[32]

House: Father as Hero, Undead as Threat

In the years after Deathdream, Bob Clark, not wanting to be pigeonholed, moved away from horror and achieved substantial success with Porky's (1982) and *A Christmas Story* (1983). Before those hits, however, he helmed one final horror film: *Black Christmas* (1974), which helped establish the groundwork for the slasher film, the dominant subgenre of horror in the early 1980s.[33] This subgenre gave Sean Cunningham, who directed, produced, and devised the story for *Friday the 13th* (1980), his greatest commercial success, even if he had qualms about the film's graphic violence.[34] Although he continued to produce lucrative sequels, he wanted to find a project that pushed back against the slasher film. He discovered such an idea from Fred Dekker, an aspiring filmmaker who saw low-budget horror as his ticket into the movie business.

Dekker developed an idea about a guilt-ridden Vietnam veteran battling his past and a haunted house. Preoccupied by another project, Dekker passed script-writing duties to his friend Ethan Wiley. Wiley gave *House* a more comic direction, diverging from Dekker's original vision of "a gritty, black-and-white, William Friedkin–style character-study-cum-balls-out-horror-film." The script's lighthearted touches proved a major selling point for both Cunningham and director Steve Miner.[35] With these established filmmakers attached, New World Pictures agreed to finance the project, which became a solid grosser when released in early 1986.[36]

House tells the story of Roger Cobb (William Katt), a best-selling horror author whose life began unraveling a year before the film begins, his career stalling once he gave up horror stories to struggle with a memoir about his experiences in Vietnam. Writer's block, however, soon became the least of his woes. As he wrestled with the book, his son Jimmy (Erik and Mark Silver) mysteriously disappeared from the Victorian mansion owned by Roger's Aunt Elizabeth (Susan French). Grief-stricken and frustrated with Roger, his wife Sandy (Kay Lenz), a successful television actress, then divorced him.

The final blow came with Aunt Elizabeth's suicide, the event that actually begins the narrative of *House*. After her funeral, Roger elects to return to the site of one trauma (his son's disappearance) to grapple with another trauma (the war). He soon discovers that the house is a living thing. It knows; it manipulates; it destroys. It exploits his guilt about "Big Ben" (Richard Moll), a soldier Roger failed in Vietnam. Memories of Ben haunt Roger whether he is writing or dreaming. To add horror to trauma, the house makes Roger's regrets corporeal. Indeed, of all the monsters that besiege Roger, none is more frightful than Ben's reanimated corpse, a zombie who billets deep in the interiors of the house in a fantastical jungle that symbolizes Vietnam. Roger eventually learns that zombie Ben kidnapped Jimmy in order to force Roger into a final confrontation. After a lengthy struggle, Roger overcomes his fears, exorcises his demons, and rescues his son.[37]

As this synopsis suggests, *House* has two fundamental subjects: memory and family. Although it quickly pairs these concerns, the film leads with memory, a theme it establishes at a book signing where Roger's fans exhibit little interest in his proposed memoir. His agent (Steve Susskind) cites their indifference as proof "nobody wants to read about the goddamn Vietnam War anymore." Roger holds firm. He knows he must master the past to move forward, but, as his agent remarks, this quest has disrupted his life, leading Sandy to leave him and threatening to derail his career.

Here *House* explicitly links Roger's troubled relationship to Vietnam to the deterioration of his household. It continually underscores this connection, most explicitly in its framing of Roger's returns to Vietnam. Whether they stem from nightmares, enactments of Roger's prose, or supernatural visitations, these returns are always preceded and/or followed by references to family. For example, a phone conversation with Sandy precedes the first return, which establishes the stakes for subsequent returns. In a scene that casts Vietnam as phantasmagoria, Roger envisions a boy playing beside a grave in a jungle clearing. A hand bursts through the ground and grabs the screaming child. Only later does the audience learn that the boy is Jimmy and the assailant is Ben.

As this scene suggests, *House* is not primarily interested in Vietnam as a historical or geographic reality. Nevertheless, the film does briefly address the war as an actual event, offering a problematic assessment of America's performance in Vietnam. The filmmakers announce this theme during Roger's first recollection of Vietnam. An officer awakens a slumbering Roger by declaring: "We got a war to lose, remember." His remark acknowledges defeat (and calls attention to that remembrance), but it also raises another question: Why did the United States lose the war? The film could be read as suggesting that American personnel in Vietnam were not up to snuff. Indeed, almost as soon as Roger's squad is introduced, they are ambushed by the Viet Cong. During the firefight, nearly the entire squad remains immobilized; only Ben and Roger return fire. While this scene might serve purely mechanical needs—setting the main characters apart from everyone else—it assumes greater meaning when conjoined with another moment. As the squad prepares for a night patrol, an officer asks two soldiers to take point. Both decline the assignment, one out of fear, and the other out of marijuana-induced insubordination, leaving Ben and Roger to shoulder the burden. These scenes not only cast American servicemen as impotent, cowardly, and irresponsible, but also deflect blame from the true architects of American defeat: elite policy makers who vainly endeavored to prop up an unstable, corrupt, unpopular, and repressive proxy regime.

House attempts to depict the actual war to a small degree, but mostly it strips the war and Vietnam itself of any historicity, reconfiguring both as an imaginary landscape where Americans can resolve their own traumas and conflicts.[38] To do so, Roger, representing the best of the United States, must return to the site of his (and "our") trauma. Only then can he recover what had been lost and achieve redemption. Roger literally wears the symbol of this quest. After battling his first monster, Roger dons his combat fatigues and continues to sport them as he defeats a series of ghouls, including zombie Ben.

Zombie Ben is Roger's guilt made corporeal, a decomposing memorial to Roger's failure, and perhaps the nation's. If not vanquished, it can destroy Roger and his family. These propositions drive *House*, but how exactly does the film define "failure"? This question becomes even more intriguing if one contrasts the film with Dekker's original premise. Dekker imagined a veteran haunted by what he did in Vietnam. During a firefight, he killed a mortally wounded comrade whose screams threatened to expose their position. Years later, after starting a romance with a VA psychologist, the veteran sees his buddy's reanimated corpse (the film was to be coy on whether these hauntings were real or imagined). The picture would end with the veteran's death, a product of either a guilt-induced suicide or a score-settling homicide by the undead soldier.[39] Screenwriter Ethan Wiley discarded this downbeat ending, which did not jibe with the "it's morning in America" optimism of the 1980s. He also altered Roger's "offense." Instead of killing to save his own skin, he refuses to finish off a badly wounded Ben, who pleads with him to stop the pain and ensure he is not taken alive by the enemy. Roger seeks assistance instead, but the Viet Cong seize Ben before he can return. While understandable, Roger's actions are not praised by the film. As zombie Ben notes, the enemy tortured him for weeks before killing him. One could read the film as tapping into a particularly corrosive narrative about the Vietnam War, a narrative that insists that the United States lost the war because it did not match the fervor and cruelty displayed by its foes.[40] Certainly, zombie Ben's taunts not only suggest such a reading, they gender it. Zombie Ben contends that Roger is a "wimp" who acted out of weakness. Ben further attempts to shame and unsex his former friend by snarling caustically: "Roger, you hit like a little girl."

After repeatedly fleeing, Roger makes his stand and prevails. In so doing, he completes three interrelated projects. First, he expunges the past, invalidating Ben's boast: "You can't get rid of me. You can't and you never will." Second, he reaffirms his impugned masculinity. Third, he rescues his son and, more than likely, restores the household. Granted, on this last point, the film does not explicitly state Sandy will rejoin the fold, but such a reunion would follow the narrative's emphasis on reversal. Roger's unconquered past cost him a wife and son. By regaining Jimmy and mastering the past, Roger has cleared the path for marital reconciliation—a possibility hinted at by the film's final moments as Sandy and Jimmy embrace under the watchful eye of a beaming Roger.

If this sounds like a fairly conservative endgame, it is. But one must be careful not to overextend this reading. *House* certainly wants to restore the masculine pride it believes the war damaged, but it does not advocate patriarchy. Before the divorce, Sandy was an independent career woman and she would remain so if she remarried Roger. Moreover, Roger is hardly *Deathdream*'s Charlie. Roger is sensitive, nurturing, and creative—a superior alternative to the film's other model of masculinity, Ben, who is reckless and brutish. Indeed, Ben partially functions as a parody of the super-warriors who often populated the right-wing Vietnam War films of the 1980s. The filmmakers underline this connection by having Ben lug an M60, the same massive, belt-fed machine gun toted by Chuck Norris in *Missing in Action* (1984) and Sylvester Stallone in *Rambo: First Blood Part II* (1985).

A shared affinity for oversized, highly phallic military hardware is hardly the most critical link between *House* and other conservative Vietnam-themed films from the 1980s.[41] In many ways, *House* fits snugly within what I term the "Reemerging Warrior" cycle. This cluster sought to rehabilitate a heroic, muscular brand of masculinity, while also positioning violence as the only way to overcome threatening foes.[42] Moreover, like many films in the cycle, *House* hinged on a return to the original site of trauma—returns frequently justified as missions to free the wrongly imprisoned. Here it should be recalled that Roger's final return was to retrieve his son, who in a deliberate nod to the iconography of POW/MIA films, was detained in a bamboo cage. In telling such stories, these films accomplished several ends. They ennobled American warriors by giving them a just cause.[43] They exploited and exorcised bitter memories of the Iranian Hostage Crisis, which many saw as an indictment of post-Vietnam America and its alleged weakness and vulnerability.[44] They cast the "other" as the aggressor,

Unlike *Deathdream*, the father is the hero of *House*. He rescues the son, reunites the family, and reasserts his masculine vigor. It is a story told by many right-wing films in the 1980s, especially the POW cycle, the iconography of which *House* invokes by encasing the imperiled son within a bamboo cage.

a move especially critical for films that exploited the POW/MIA issue to invert and rewrite the Vietnam War.

Conclusion: A Culture's Journey, 1972–1986

As symbols of the American war in Vietnam, Andy and Ben allow their respective films to define the war as unfinished business. This analogy suggests that the war's wounds will not heal until the past is mastered. However, if these films imagine the war as trauma, they differ not only in how they diagnose and treat that trauma, but how they define recovery.

For *Deathdream*, trauma resides in the sacrifice of thousands of Americans for an unworthy cause. Andy symbolizes these dead Americans—if not their Vietnamese, Laotian, and Cambodian counterparts. He is an avenging spirit consumed with anger.[45] Andy directs much of his fury toward Charlie, who, like the fathers of *Hail, Hero!*, *Summertree*, and *The Visitors*, represents retrograde values. While Andy does not kill Charlie, it is only because the filmmakers devised a symbolically richer endgame. Charlie kills himself upon realizing his culpability for Andy's fate, an action that underscores the bankruptcy and obsolescence of his worldview. Here we see the primary way *Deathdream* sought to overcome the trauma of war. By assisting in efforts to delegitimize the mentality that produced American intervention, it hoped to prevent future wars, spare countless Andys, and allow those killed in the Vietnam War to rest easier.

House emerged from a much different political and cultural moment than did *Deathdream*. Whereas *Deathdream* was produced at a time when the Vietnam War had minimal public support, *House* followed in the wake of a concerted effort to rewrite and rehabilitate the war as a "noble cause." While many films enlisted in this conservative counteroffensive, only a few such as *Hamburger Hill* (1987) and *The Hanoi Hilton* (1987) actually depict the Vietnam War. More commonly, films set their stories in the present and reduced Vietnam to a set of ideas and associations. Some such as *Nighthawks* (1981), *The Annihilators* (1985), *Eye of the Tiger* (1986), and *Lethal Weapon* (1987) pitted Vietnam veterans against criminals within the United States. Others, such as the *Missing in Action* trilogy, *Rambo: First Blood Part II*, and *Uncommon Valor* (1983), sent them back to Southeast Asia, usually in search of lost comrades. Both variations defined the war as a trauma to ameliorate. The trauma stemmed from defeat, which left the United States weak and beset by doubt. In response, the Reemerging Warrior cycle sought to reclaim what had been lost and did so through violence. In that sense, these films served as a ritualistic exercise in which foes could be humbled and the United States—symbolized by the masculine hero—could be reborn, no longer weak, afraid, or ineffectual.

House belongs to this cycle of films. Doubts and fears gnaw upon Roger Cobb and threaten his career and family. He tries to master the past through prose but fails. Confronted by zombie Ben, he repeatedly attempts to flee, but fails. He succeeds only when he fights. More specifically, he succeeds only when he conquers his fear—a moment underscored by the script when Roger boasts: "I'm not afraid of you anymore, Ben. I beat you and this goddamn house."

To complete his redemption, Roger must vanquish a fellow veteran, an undead avenger like Andy. Zombie Ben even echoes Andy. Just as Andy insisted it was only fair for a civilian to die for the soldier who perished for him, zombie Ben parries Roger's declaration that he would have died for Ben by cackling: "Well, here's your chance." Of course, zombie Ben has a different target than Andy. Rather than a cultural mind-set, zombie Ben hunts an erstwhile friend he deems weak and effeminate. By proving otherwise, Roger saves his imperiled home, reaffirms his masculine vitality, and puts the war behind him (and "us").

As understandable as that desire to move on is, it has also inspired many of the silences and evasions that haunt the American memory of the Vietnam War. Americans do not need to move on or forget; they need to engage and remember. They need to reconvene with the critical spirit of films like *Deathdream*. As a more recent Vietnam War–themed picture suggests: "Maybe ghosts need to upset people. It's that or disappear."[46] The ghosts of Vietnam do not need to be exorcised but, rather, held close, so that new generations might learn from them. Properly remembered, they will linger among us and, hopefully, help us become wiser and more humane.

Notes

1. *Braddock: Missing in Action III*, directed by Aaron Norris.
2. Shaw, *Bury the Dead*, 27.
3. *Deathdream* was theatrically released as *Dead of Night*. It has also been titled *The Night Andy Came Home* and *Night Walk*. *Deathdream* is the most common title.
4. "Audio Commentary #1 with Co-Producer/Director Bob Clark" and "Audio Commentary #2 with Screenwriter/Make-up Artist (Uncredited) Alan Ormsby," *Deathdream*, DVD.
5. Clark, "Commentary."
6. Ormsby, "Commentary." *Sticks and Bones* won Best Play in 1972. David Rabe served in Vietnam from February 1966 to January 1967. Kolin, *David Rabe*, 9–10, 35.
7. Both texts make it clear that their subject is middle-class America. In his script, Ormsby refers to the film's setting as "Pleasantville" (although eventually the filmmakers opted for the name of the Florida town where the movie was shot, Brooksville). Ormsby, "Commentary." Rabe describes the setting of *Sticks and Bones* as "an American home, very modern . . . there is a sense of space and, oddly, a sense also that this room, these

stairs, belong in the gloss of an advertisement." Of course, Rabe tips his hand even more overtly by naming his main characters after *The Adventures of Ozzie and Harriet*. Rabe, *Sticks and Stones*, 96.

8. Minor, "At Last a Perfect Soldier!"

9. Brecht, "Legend of the Dead Soldier."

10. *Deathdream*, directed by Bob Clark.

11. Clark, "Commentary"; Ormsby, "Commentary."

12. "Theatrical Trailer," *Deathdream*, DVD.

13. Appy, "Vietnam According to Oliver Stone," 188.

14. 4-F deferments indicated that a draft registration was found to be physically, mentally, or morally unqualified for service. Appy, *Working-Class War*, 17–38, 44–55.

15. Jacobs, "The Monkey's Paw."

16. Reporters and politicians made a litany of errors: They conflated all drugs, did not distinguish between casual and habitual use, ignored the fact that drugs were rarely used in combat situations, and overlooked alcohol abuse, which was more detrimental to the war effort. Kuzmarov, *Myth of the Addicted Army*, 15–36.

17. Ibid., 9.

18. Many commentators have lamented this tendency. Turner, *Echoes of Combat*, 67–68; Sturken, *Tangled Memories*, 104; Cawley, "The War about the War," 78; Boggs and Pollard, *The Hollywood War Machine*, 90–91. While I concur, it is important to distinguish between collective oversight and individual creative license. As infuriating as the cinematic erasure of Vietnam has been, a given movie has the right to tell the story it wants to tell. One just wishes the resulting choices were not so predictably myopic.

19. Turner, 50–51; Lembcke, *The Spitting Image*, 69–70.

20. The film never defines what Andy is, but the sequence with the doctor draws upon vampire mythology, particularly the tradition that claims vampires require an invitation before entering some spaces. Andy reminds doctor and audience alike that the physician invited him to his office. Likewise, the trucker invited Andy into his rig. The young people at the drive-in were killed after Andy accepted an invitation for a double date. Moreover, it should be noted that all of these killings took place at night.

21. Fiddes, *Meat*, 7.

22. In analyzing the symbolism of meat, Fiddes highlights the importance of meat carving in traditional families. Ibid., 16, 158.

23. Other examples include Charles bidding Cathy to serve a male guest despite the fact that each character was an equal distance from the refreshments. Charles, distraught that Andy killed his dog, pushes aside a concerned Cathy and barks, "Mind your own business!" Christine praises Cathy, but suddenly stops so she can refocus her thoughts on Andy.

24. Ormsby, "Commentary."

25. See Wylie's *Generation of Vipers* (1996; Original publication date,1942).

26. *Deathdream* was Savini's first film credit. While listed as the movie's makeup artist, he actually assisted Ormsby. Savini served as a combat photographer in Vietnam. Interested in special effects and makeup as a boy, his wartime experiences gave him a "lesson in anatomy," which shaped his work in films such as *Martin* (1976), *Dawn of the Dead* (1978), *Friday the 13th* (1980), *Creepshow* (1982), and *Day of the Dead* (1985). "Tom Savini: The Early Years," *Deathdream*, DVD; Skal, *The Monster Show*, 307–8.

27. Ormsby believes miscasting prevented the character of "Charlie" from achieving his full potential. While crediting sixty-five-year-old John Marley for a solid performance, Ormsby wanted a younger, more physically imposing actor in the role. Someone the audience could imagine playing football and forcing Andy to do the same. Ormsby, "Commentary."

28. The film originated from Daniel Lang's piece in the *New Yorker* about a conscience-stricken GI who testifies against his comrades. Lang's piece also inspired *Casualties of War* (1989).

29. Young, *Kazan*, 309.

30. Ormsby, "Commentary." Ormsby argues the United States has reverted back to the "with us or against us" mentality that brought the country to disaster in Vietnam.

31. "Deathdreaming: Interview with Richard Backus," *Deathdream*, DVD.

32. For a sample of the reviews inspired by the Blue Underground release, see Erickson, Corupe, Ebiri, and Bowman.

33. Nowell, *Blood Money*, 57–78; Rockoff, *Going to Pieces*, 42–44.

34. Sean Cunningham was not the only person from *Friday the 13th* involved in *House*. Steve Miner, director of *House*, helmed *Friday the 13th Part II* (1981) and *Friday the 13th Part III* (1982). Harry Manfredini, who did the music for *House*, scored *Friday the 13th*.

35. See "Interviews *House* Creator Fred Dekker" and "Essay," Roger Cobb's *House: The Website*, http://www.rogercobbshouse.com/htmlmain.htm (accessed, June 3, 2014). The interview is found under the tab "House Specials," while the essay is located under "Production Notes."

36. *House* was the second-highest-grossing film released by New World during the 1980s, bested only by another film directed by Miner in 1986, the infamous *Soul Man*. *House* made nearly $20 million, making it 1986's forty-seventh-most-popular theatrical release. New World, Boxoffice.mojo, http://www.boxofficemojo.com/studio/chart/?studio=newworld.htm (accessed, June 9, 2014); *House*, Boxofficemojo.com, http://www.boxofficemojo.com/movies /?page=weekly&id=house.htm (accessed, June 9, 2014).

37. *House*, directed by Steve Miner.

38. Turner, *Echoes*, 90–91, 98; Auster and Quart, *How the War Was Remembered*, xv, 70; Muse, *The Land of Nam*, 10–11; Franklin, *Vietnam and Other American Fantasies*, 32.

39. Roger Cobb's *House: The Website*, "Interviews *House* Creator Fred Dekker."

40. This narrative has surfaced often in the Vietnam War filmography. Cawley, 70–71; Dresser, "Charlie Don't Surf," 81–82.

41. As James William Gibson notes, one of the defining features of these films was the sheer size and destructive capacity of the weaponry employed. Gibson, *Warrior Dreams*, 81–82.

42. The films often conveyed these messages through a particular visual motif, which gives this cycle its name. In this sequence, the besieged hero, seemingly defeated, re-emerges, generally from water, which symbolizes his rebirth, before smiting his tormentors. Such sequences occur in *Nighthawks* (1981), *Missing in Action* (1984), *Rambo: First Blood Part II* (1985), *Let's Get Harry* (1986), *Lethal Weapon* (1987), *Braddock: Missing*

in Action III, and *Rambo III* (1988). *House* makes partial use of the motif. Roger's final journey to "Vietnam" begins when he is plunked into a river, from which he resurfaces, and ends when he reemerges from a pool in his backyard.

43. *Uncommon Valor* (1983) expresses this need most baldly. As he briefs his team, Colonel Cal Rhodes (Gene Hackman) reassures them: "So we're going back there, and this time, this time nobody can dispute the rightness of what we're doing."

44. Farber, *Taken Hostage*, 10–14.

45. Anger defines Andy. The ability to project that anger was so critical that actor Richard Backus received the following instructions from the casting director during his audition: "Stare at a lamp and convey as much hatred as I possibly could and then once I felt filled with hatred to turn it on her." Backus, "Deathdreaming."

46. *Guy X*, directed by Saul Metzstein.

Bibliography

Appy, Christian. "Vietnam According to Oliver Stone." *Commonweal*, 23 March 1990, 187–89.

———. *Working-Class War: American Combat Soldiers and Vietnam*. Chapel Hill: University of North Carolina Press, 1993.

Auster, Albert, and Leonard Quart. *How the War Was Remembered: Hollywood and Vietnam*. Westport, CT: Praeger, 1988.

Blue Underground. http://www.blue-underground.com/.

Boggs, Carl, and Tom Pollard. *The Hollywood War Machine: U.S. Militarism and Popular Culture*. Boulder, CO: Paradigm Publishers, 2006.

Cawley, Leo. "The War about the War: Vietnam Films and American Myth." In *From Hanoi to Hollywood: The Vietnam War in American Film*, edited by Linda Dittmar and Gene Michaud. New Brunswick, NJ: Rutgers University Press, 1990.

Cobb, Roger. *House*: The Website. Accessed June 3, 2014. http://www.rogercobbshouse.com/htmlmain.htm.

Deathdream. Directed by Bob Clark. 1972, West Hollywood, CA: Blue Underground, 2004. DVD.

Dresser, David. "'Charlie Don't Surf': Race and Culture in the Vietnam War Films." In *Inventing Vietnam: The War in Film and Television*, edited by Michael Anderegg, 81–102. Philadelphia: Temple University Press, 1991.

Farber, David. *Taken Hostage: The Iran Hostage Crisis and America's First Encounter with Radical Islam*. Princeton, NJ: Princeton University Press, 2005.

Fiddes, Nick. *Meat: A Natural Symbol*. London: Routledge, 1991.

Franklin, H. Bruce. *Vietnam and Other American Fantasies*. Amherst: University of Massachusetts Press, 2000.

Gibson, James William. *Warrior Dreams: Violence and Manhood in Post-Vietnam America*. New York: Hill & Wang, 1994.

House. Boxoffice.mojo. http://www.boxofficemojo.com/studio/chart/?studio=newworld.htm.

House. Directed by Steve Miner. 1986, Chatsworth, CA: Image Entertainment, 2011. DVD.

Jacobs, W. W. "The Monkey's Paw." *The Lady of the Barge and Other Stories.* Project Gutenberg, 2004. http://www.gutenberg.org/files/12122/12122-h/12122-h.htm.

Kolin, Philip C. *David Rabe: A Stage History and a Primary and Secondary Bibliography.* New York: Garland Publishing, 1988.

Kuzmarov, Jeremy. *The Myth of the Addicted Army: Vietnam and the Modern War on Drugs.* Amherst: University of Massachusetts Press, 2009.

Lembcke, Jerry. *The Spitting Image: Myth, Memory, and the Legacy of Vietnam.* New York: New York University Press, 1998.

Muse, Eben J. *The Land of Nam: The Vietnam War in American Film.* Lanham, MD: Scarecrow Press, 1995.

Nowell, Richard. *Blood Money: A History of the Teen Slasher Film Cycle.* New York: Continuum, 2011.

Rabe, David. *The Vietnam Plays: Volume One.* New York: Grove Press, 1993.

Rockoff, Adam. *Going to Pieces: The Rise and Fall of the Slasher Film, 1978–1986.* Jefferson, NC: McFarland, 2002.

Russell, Jamie. *Book of the Dead: The Complete History of Zombie Cinema.* Surrey, UK: Fab Press, 2007.

Shaw, Irwin. *Bury the Dead.* New York: Dramatists Play Service, Inc., 1970.

Skal, David J. *The Monster Show: A Cultural History of Horror.* New York: Norton, 1993.

Sturken, Marita. *Tangled Memories: The Vietnam War, the AIDS Epidemic and the Politics of Remembering.* Berkeley: University of California Press, 1997.

Turner, Fred. *Echoes of Combat: The Vietnam War in American Memory.* New York: Anchor Books, 1996.

Wylie, Philip. *Generation of Vipers.* 2nd edition. New York: Dalkey Archive Press, 1996.

Young, Jeff. *Kazan: The Master Director Discusses His Films.* New York: Newmarket Press, 1999.

CHAPTER 11

Strategic Military Reconfiguration in Horror Fiction

THE CASE OF F. PAUL WILSON'S *THE KEEP* AND GRAHAM MASTERTON'S *THE DEVILS OF D-DAY*

Fernando Gabriel Pagnoni Berns

In his text *Nietzsche, Freud, Marx* (1990), Michel Foucault describes these three thinkers as "masters of suspicion." What he is suggesting is that the three each approach cultural discourse with suspicion, viewing it as distorted by an underlying, concealed motive: the "will to power" (Nietzsche), sexual desire (Freud), and class interest (Marx). Foucault builds on this premise, contending, "language does not say exactly what it means. The meaning that one grasps . . . is perhaps in reality only a lesser meaning that shields . . . the meaning underneath it"[1]

Interpretation, therefore, becomes an endless task, always fragmented, and never able to access a true point of origin—as Foucault contends, "the further one goes in interpretation, the closer one approaches at the same time an absolutely dangerous region where interpretation is not only going to find its point of no return but where it is going to disappear itself as interpretation."[2] Thus, when a given text is interpreted, what the interpreter finds under it is just another interpretation. As a result, interpretation is inexhaustible, and never finished. Simply put, a (constructed) reality is merely superimposed upon another (constructed) reality. There is no original meaning; the interpretation, in fact, precedes the sign, and there is nothing to interpret *but* interpretations.

Military discourse works in a similar fashion, creating layers of meaning, superimposing one "reality" upon another. Military language, of course, has its own terminology—words, phrases, slang, and abbreviations—developed, as Maurice Matloff argues, in close connection with tactics.[3] These idiomatic constructions work in a specific context—a narrowly bound world composed of military installations and populated by soldiers—except in wartime, when they escape their peacetime boundaries and spread everywhere the war touches: not only the warring countries, but also the territories they occupy or merely pass through.

Then, reclassification of the wartime world begins. Everything that has some military value changes in both name and meaning. Forgotten roads become paths to victory, caves are reconfigured into places of ambush, and green pastures are changed into strategic sites for the final battle. Simultaneously, everything that does not have a use in the context of war is obliterated from the military vision of the world—pushed aside, covered up, or simply ignored. War thus constructs its own reality, which is superimposed upon the already existing realities of territories and lives. A geographical map redesigned in the service of war overwrites previous maps. The killing of civilians is converted, by the power of language, into "collateral damage," and devastatingly lethal weapons are given innocuous names like "Willie Pete" and "daisy cutter," or impenetrable acronyms that make sense only to those who participate in military culture and can speak its specialized language.[4]

There is only one thing that wartime shifts in language cannot reclassify: the supernatural. In horror/war fiction, undead and supernatural beings pass invisibly among the day-to-day horrors of war or, where visible, tenaciously resist classification. Monsters, by nature, are unclassifiable,[5] since they refuse to be relegated to existing cultural categories. Confronted with them, even the transformative power of wartime military language fails.

This chapter explores the confrontation of the military and the supernatural—the forces of order and the forces of chaos—through two horror novels: F. Paul Wilson's *The Keep* (1981) and Graham Masterton's *The Devils of D-Day* (1978). In Wilson's tale, the landscape is reclassified to serve wartime needs; the horrific "keep" of the title—a medieval stone tower—would have been left alone had it not stood in a strategically valuable site. The novel aptly illustrates Foucault's discussion of interpretation and dramatizes his contention that original "truth" remains beyond humans' grasp. Struggling to understand the supernatural forces that confront them in the keep, Wilson's soldiers find—as Foucault predicts—that finding the core truth they seek will lead to their destruction. Masterton's novel also involves a seemingly successful reclassification of supernatural beings to serve military needs: the American military's enlistment of demons as allies to help it win the Second World War. As in *The Keep*, however, the reclassification proves to be temporary. The supernatural beings defy classification, and their power easily overwhelms human attempts to control them.

Monsters in the Battlefield

The presence of supernatural beings in times of war can be framed in two different matrices: entities that use the surrounding chaos to pass unnoticed, and entities that are visible, but are militarily classified in such a way as to deny their supernatural character—even if this undertaking is, ultimately, unsuccessful. The former is illustrated in works such as Connie Willis's short story "Jack," about a vampire who, thanks to his remarkable supernatural senses, locates survivors trapped beneath the ruins of World War II bombings. His uncanny nature goes unnoticed because he lives in times when the horror of everyday life

In *The Keep*, by F. Paul Wilson (1981), German soldiers occupying a mysterious castle are slowly eliminated by an ancient sorcerer.

in wartime obscures all else. The latter is illustrated by works such as Wilson's *The Keep*, where the true nature of a figure of chaos and darkness is denied, even when doing so results in madness and death for those who seek to stop it.

The Keep takes place in 1941. A unit of the German army, led by Captain Klaus Woermann, has been ordered to occupy a keep—a structure historically used as a refuge of last resort—located at Dinu Pass in the mountains of Romania. After settling in, the soldiers begin to die during the night, their throats ripped out. Woermann, knowing that he is not facing a traditional enemy, requests that his company be moved elsewhere. The local German headquarters responds, instead, by sending out a contingent of elite SS troops, led by the despicable Nazi death camp commander Major Erich Kaempffer, whose assignment is to establish a new death camp in Romania. Kaempffer believes that Romanian partisans are responsible for killing off Woermann's men, but the enemy will turn out to be something darker and far more dangerous: A millennia-old creature named Rasalom, which the keep was built to imprison, has been liberated and is now wreaking horrible vengeance on the Nazi intruders.

The keep is deemed to have strategic value because it overlooks the pass and affords a clear view of anyone moving to or through the mountains. The tale opens with a German reconnaissance report that details the area's military significance, and makes reference to an "old fortification midway along the pass which should serve adequately as a sentry base."[6] This is the first reinterpretation that the military worldview imposes: A geographical location that has gone unnoticed, perhaps for centuries, is reconfigured into a strategic post with a new layer of significance. The keep, an old, forgotten fortification, is reclassified into a "sentry base," a new name for something that has suddenly acquired value, and is immediately integrated into the landscape of the war. "Woermann's practiced military eye immediately assessed the strategic values of the keep. An excellent watchpost."[7] The route to the keep is likewise redefined: deemed a suitable road for military vehicles, despite its limitations: "[T]his was not a road. He [Woermann] would have classed it as a trail or, more appropriately, a ledge. A road it was not."[8] Bit by bit, the local Romanian landscape is thus transfigured into a geography that serves the German occupiers' wartime needs.

The SS troops undertake a further transformation of the keep itself, turning a dead-end corridor at one end of the structure into a "compound for the prisoners from the village."[9] This seemingly modest military reconfiguration, directed by Kaempffer, is even more sinister than it appears: Although he was sent to aid Woermann and his troops, he covets the place as the future site of the death camp he has been ordered to establish. Its central location, readily accessible from many other parts of Romania, will, he believes, allow him to more efficiently carry out his mission of deportation and extermination—work that has, itself, been reconfigured by his superiors as the "final solution" to a national "problem."[10]

The old keep, however, harbors a supernatural being. It is an uncanny structure, castlelike in design, yet created as a prison, to keep the creature within trapped forever. Its bizarre nature compels the German occupiers to impose order on it, and yet frustrates every attempt to do so. The narrative's first description of the keep is steeped in contradictions that undermine a clear definition and embody ambiguity: It "had no name and that was peculiar. It was supposedly centuries old, yet it looked as if the last stone had been slipped into place only yesterday."[11] Even the nearby village has been recast, from local and familiar, to foreign and strange: "Woermann decided to reclassify that as well: This was no village in the German sense; this was a collection of stucco-walled, shake-roofed huts."

The Germans' seeming taxonomic mania is not innocent or capricious. Classification is an act of control, and an assertion of power. To name is to objectify, and even the smallest element must be tagged and labeled—in brief, classified—in order to exert some control over it.[12] That which has no name lives on the fringes of society, escapes surveillance, and can be potentially dangerous. In wartime—when chaos is ever-present and the need for control is overpowering—such elements are intolerable. They must be converted into something governed by rational, linear logic in order to be of use.

The keep, however, remains unclassifiable. In some passages, it is described as a "huge slumbering beast";[13] in others, it is a "tomb of stone."[14] Cuza, a local Jewish professor whom the German commandos drag to the keep as part of their effort to understand the nocturnal killings, will make explicit what no one wishes to acknowledge: that the structure cannot be classified, no matter how hard military officers try: "This structure isn't a keep. [. . .] This building [. . .] is unique. I don't know what you should call it."[15] The building refuses to be named and thus, refuses to be disempowered by the Nazi commandos.

Woermann, after observing the unique character of the building, approaches it in the same way he has been trained to approach any military problem, working back through its mysterious history to try to find something tangible; the very "source" of the keep.[16] He attempts to peel off layer upon layer of signs to get to the source where answers lie, but gets nowhere. When he questions who the owner of the building is, who pays for its maintenance, or at least, who gives orders to the building's caretakers, Cuza explains, "there is no link anywhere to the person or persons who opened the account; the money is to be held and the interest is to be paid in *perpetuum*."[17]

This is clearly a case of infinite semiosis in which the apparent deciphering of a sign only takes the interpreter to another sign, and another, and another. The source that the Germans are so desperately seeking is impossible to reach because it is not a social construct, but rather, an unreachable truth—not an interpretation and therefore not made for human eyes—opaque and impossible to decipher. The keep serves as a highly polyvalent, fluid sign: The building is "bigger than it looks"[18] and the rooms within "seemed to be everywhere."[19] The keep is of "unusual design"[20] and "odd."[21] Even the crosses that embellish its exterior walls are not "good, strong, symmetrical" things.[22]

Woermann approaches the reconfiguration of the place not only with the eye of a military officer, but with that of an artist: "a landscape lover's" eye.[23] He observes everything around him not just in terms of military use but also in hues and textures: "brown and gray, clay and granite, these were the colors, interspersed with snatches of green."[24] Freud identifies creativity with access to the unconscious.[25] An artist's subconscious slips out, not in the normative forms and conventionalities of works of art, but in the little details; odd hues or weirdly placed brushstrokes are slips from the artist's mind that say more about them than their entire oeuvre. These little slips are truly revealing of that zone that lies behind interpretation, that area that is impossible to grasp. So it is when Woermann decides to paint an image of the keep. There are tiny details in his work that hint at the uncanny depths lying just beneath the placid surface of the space. As Kaempffer notes, Woermann has inadvertently drawn an extra figure into his painting: the morbid image of a man hanging from a rope.[26] Woermann first denies that the figure is what Kaempffer claims, but the more he looks at the painting, more insecure he is about his denial.[27]

The horrors of the tale begin when the military (unsuccessfully) remaps Dinu Pass to serve their purposes, only to find out that something there resists their reclassification of it. The madness that resides in the "original truth" is the menace at the heart of the keep, threatening those who insist on seeking what lies beneath the surface. Doing so is their job as soldiers: They must find the culprit of the nighttime slaughter, since more and more of their comrades are dying gruesome deaths, and they must render the keep and its surroundings suitable for military use. With the arrival of the German soldiers, madness and death fill the fortress—the result of the commandos' insistence on "peeling off" the surface of the place to discover the truth that lies behind. In the process, a pair of soldiers—Grunstadt and Lutz—inadvertently liberate the supernatural being that had been trapped within the walls for years. Neither escapes unscathed: Grunstadt retreats into insanity, and Lutz is gruesomely killed. These events bring us back to Foucault's arguments about interpretation: If one succeeds in entering the depths that lie behind interpretation, the result will be "the disappearance of the interpreter himself"[28] through death or madness. The use of classification to evade the uncomfortable notion of sinister and powerful forces at work appears again when Kaempffer dismisses Grunstadt's condition as simple wartime "shock."[29]

The more the keep resists classification, the stronger the soldiers' need to find its true nature, and thus disempower it.[30] Woermann is afraid to descend into the cellar, with its "glistening walls and inky recesses."[31] Following Gaston Bachelard, cellars and subterranean spaces may be seen as the "subconscious" of buildings.[32] Woermann is afraid of descending that deep inside the keep's "mind" because he knows that no one escapes the depths that exceed human knowledge. He clings to the safety of his own interpretations, whether artistic or military. Magda, Professor Cuza's daughter, likewise felt that "some primal part of her brain was rebelling, trying to turn her around"[33] when she descends to the sub-cellar. The use of the word "primal" is interesting in this context, since something pre-social is always lurking within the keep and the surroundings, trying to escape.

Rasalom, the creature that has been liberated from the keep, is a monster so alien to human rationality that the creature presents itself to Professor Cuza as a vampire—a mythological creature whose nature is well known from folklore, by way of imagery and superstitions—in order to be comprehensible and gain the professor's help. It is truly a supernatural being, originating in a time before human interpretation. Cuza, however, fails to consider this possibility, thus committing the same mistake that the Nazi commandos make. Convinced that he can grasp an ultimate source—a "truth" not grounded in human interpretation—he instead concludes that the creature is one he has sought his whole life, the one true vampire "from which all Romanian vampire lore has originated."[34] Rasalom thus presents himself as just that—the original vampire that the professor so desperately wants to identify.[35] His intention is not merely to satisfy the professor, but to preserve him: If the monster were to present itself in its true form, it would drive Cuza to madness or death, and the creature needs him alive and sane. Even if vampires are supernatural creatures, at least they are firmly and unambiguously classified as such, and some ideas about their mythic nature circulate through society.

Cuza immediately classifies Rasalom as an evil being,[36] because that is the interpretation of the vampire myth[37] in folklore, but as the monster reveals itself as something much more complicated than the vampire of traditional European folklore, it begins to evade classification, and human rationality starts to crumble. The creature, and its longtime persecutor, Glaeken, both come from a time of pre-interpretation—a time before good and evil, an epoch free of social logos. When the novel reaches its climax, Cuza admits that he does not comprehend the creature anymore and the monster replies: "You are not expected to. You are not capable of it."[38] The monster is "a survivor of the First Age. He pretended to be a five-hundred-year-old vampire because that fit the history of the keep and the region. And because it generated fear so easily."[39]

Glaeken defines himself and Rasalom as two incomprehensible forces[40] beyond any human notions of good and evil. The vast divide between this and human conceptualizations is apparent when Magda insists that Glaeken, with whom she has fallen in love and frames as "good," must have some religion, even when he responds that he has none.[41] During the final battle between the creatures, Glaeken reveals himself to Magda as a force of Light, and Rasalom as one of Chaos. She immediately interprets their confrontation as one between Christianity and evil, drawing on the social symbolism that frames ideas as "light" or "chaos." These ideas, however, are merely social constructs that signify no more than what society has chosen them to represent.

As Glaeken says: "The keep was built to trap and hold him [Rasalom] . . . forever. Who could have foretold that it or anything else in the Dinu Pass might someday be considered of military value?"[42] This lament captures the essence of the novel: Until wartime, nothing in the landscape was of use, and so it remained ignored. The outbreak of war, however, cast the local geography in a new light and brought about a reconfiguration (or, rather, an attempted reconfiguration) of it. The presence of supernatural (and thus unclassifiable) forces lurking within the landscape meant, however, that reclassification for military use collided with a signifier that cannot be apprehended by reason or reconfigured by language. The horror of *The Keep* is born amid this tension between a taxonomic necessity and an unclassifiable monstrosity.

The Monster as a Military Weapon: The Case of *The Devils of D-Day*

Graham Masterton's novel *The Devils of D-Day* provides an interesting contrast with *The Keep* because in it the classification of the supernatural is successful, if only to a certain extent. Daniel McCook, the main character, is an American cartographer visiting Normandy to make a map that will illustrate a book about World War II.[43] His task is to draw a map that relates the topography of the area to the events of the war—replicating the actions of the armies that fought there, but ignoring the area as a whole—essentially rendering invisible those areas not of military interest. As Colin Flint argues, the relationship between geography and war is very important, not only during the war but also thereafter.[44] Topography illustrates the outcome of the war, and a map is nothing more than an interpretation or reading of the results of war that responds to the interests of those producing the map. Behind the fixed nature of a map, there are ambiguities and inconsistencies that do not come to the surface, but are obliterated. Maps, like all texts, are merely interpretations, and "mapmaking is an exercise in power."[45]

McCook's intense focus on wartime events eventually leads him beyond the area he has been assigned to map, however, and into the village of Pont D'Ouilly.[46] His attention is drawn there by an odd relic of the war: a lone Sherman tank abandoned in place by the US Army. Coming to the village to investigate, McCook meets the beautiful Madeleine Passerelle, who tells him that the

Was the rusting old tank only a relic of the war-torn past—or was it hiding an ungodly horror about to be released upon an unsuspecting world?

THE DEVILS OF D-DAY

GRAHAM MASTERTON

author of *The Manitou*

In Graham Masterton's *Devils of D-Day* (1978), a demon used by the Allies to turn the tide of war in World War II escapes from a US Army tank, and seeks to join its brethren in order to be their master.

tank has remained in the middle of nowhere since the Allied victory in 1945, unacknowledged and unclaimed by any military organization. The locals, she explains, have come to the conclusion that the tank is haunted and that its presence casts an evil influence over the village. Its mere mention turns milk sour, and those who approach it suffer from anxiety and hallucinations. Many villagers claim to have heard voices coming from inside it,[47] and that some—including Madeleine's mother—have even fallen victim to the evil that lurks within.[48]

The villagers' suspicions that evil forces are at work prove to be correct. The tank *is* haunted, containing a bag of bones that belonged to a hellish creature named Elmek: one of thirteen demons summoned by the US Army in order to help Allied forces break out of their beachheads in Normandy after D-Day. Thirteen black Sherman tanks (whose drivers were never seen) arrived at Pont D'Ouilly on September 13, 1944, and won a pivotal battle by annihilating a Nazi armored column. Twelve of the tanks withdrew after the battle, but the thirteenth broke a track and remained behind. The American army did nothing to remove it, and the tank remained, frozen in place for decades after the war. Villagers recall that the turret was welded shut by American soldiers. A priest then said some words over it, and the tank "was left to rot."[49] Each of the tanks was commanded by a different demon, and when the last tank was left behind, its demon, Elmek, was sealed inside in order to suppress knowledge of the lengths to which America went to win the war. The tanks were unstoppable in battle and even the abandoned one still pulsates with evil, long after being used as a supernatural weapon. Like the keep in Wilson's novel, the tank is infused with uncanny power derived from the evil residing within.

Daniel convinces the local priest to perform an exorcism, and after opening the tank, he retrieves the sack containing Elmek's bones. But the priest's ritual is not enough to vanquish the demon, and—when the tank is unsealed—Elmek breaks free and takes both Daniel and Madeleine as hostages. Seeking his twelve brothers, he forces the two to go in search of the Allied commanders who first summoned the creatures.

The couple eventually succeeds in the latter mission, discovering along the way that the demons were classified with the generic acronym for ANPs: "Assisting Nonmilitary Personnel."[50] This acronym both blurred the demons' identities, transforming them to "personnel" of the American military, and sidestepped any moral implications, reframing the demons and attempting to render them manageable. An old colonel who was involved with the tanks in Normandy makes explicit this negation of any moral implications when he says "we certainly never knew them as, well, devils. They were ANPs."[51] This childish insistence on redefining and disguising evil creatures with an acronym responds to the need of both classificatory urgency and moral neutrality. Under the bland name is hidden the fact that the "good" ones, the Americans, had made a pact with beings of pure evil. As an old priest reminds the couple, "people's standards are different in time of war."[52]

It could be argued that, ethical implications aside, the Allied high command succeeded in the reclassification of supernatural beings as weapons. Having won the war with their ANPs, the Allied commanders had no idea what to do with this "help" once the war was over and decided to simply "forget" the demons—the ultimate act of repression, covering the dark lengths to which America had gone to win the war. Significantly, the remaining twelve sacks of demon bones were stored in London, in the British War Office, and not in a church, indicating that the demons were still classified as weapons rather than supernatural creatures. Daniel and Madeleine find them there, decades later: evidence that the Army intended to leave these war crimes forgotten. Even the thirteenth tank, which lay exposed and threatened innocent people, remained unaddressed by villagers unwilling to confront the threat and become entangled with its dangers. As Madeleine says, the tank is "a terrible reminder of something that most of us now would prefer to forget."[53]

The novel ends with the revelation of another act of repression—a sign obscuring another sign. Madeleine is the reincarnation of Charlotte Latour, a girl who was given to demons "by General Patton in payment for Operation Stripes."[54] Armed with this knowledge, and with a new strength acquired from heaven, the young woman faces and destroys the thirteen demons, thus ending the legacy of a war crime that was still claiming victims decades after the war ended.

As with Woermann's paintings in *The Keep*, something in the landscape of *The Devils of D-Day* defies remapping. The tank has been harming the landscape for decades: as a reminder that classification and domination of supernatural beings is simply impossible. They have never really had control of the demons. The countryside and the people who inhabit it have suffered for years from the dark presence of those nonmilitary "personnel" who have caused deaths and pain since the end of the war. Impossible to integrate in the Allies' discourse of victory, the tank reminds readers of the ways in which wars are won. The military fails to repress the demons because, in fact, their reclassification has been just another temporal fiction.

Conclusion

In each of the two novels discussed here, the monstrous existed, dormant, long before the tale was told. It was "activated"—brought into play—by military attempts to classify and control it for their own purposes. The horror in Paul Wilson's *The Keep* begins when the German army takes an interest in a forgotten landscape, and tries to reach and defuse its primal signifier so that—by renaming the topography and all that lies within it—they can appropriate it for military use. The original sign, however—the root of the tale's evil—is impossible to grasp without interpretation because it is incomprehensible. The Germans succeed in shattering the keep's control over the entities imprisoned within, but fail to reimpose control over the keep or the monsters that they have released. In Graham Masterton's *The Devils of D-Day*, the horror begins when the US Army attempts to reclassify demons from hell as military weapons. The monsters are drawn, temporarily, under military control—their true nature obscured by an acronym—but that control, too, proves merely illusion, and horror ensues. In both tales, the supernatural creatures remain unclassifiable and uncontrollable because they embody that which lies beyond not only military, but human, comprehension, interpretation, and control.

Military discourse and practices attempt to exert power over enemies and allies alike, remapping reality in ways that are both ideological (removing ethical issues through the use of acronyms) and material (reformulating the topography of an area). This reformulation is an interpretation that is applied, sometimes by force, and overlaid on other, earlier interpretations. Its effectiveness is well established, but in war-horror fiction, it is the nature of the monster to resist and reject such an act. The monster illustrates, instead, how easily military discourse reformulates what can be useful—changing appearances or names, erasing or altering identities—and thus, accommodating all that they see to the aims and interests of war.

Civilians, who see war outside the military construction of acronyms and strategic names—Professor Cuza and Magda in *The Keep*, Daniel and Madeleine in *Devils*—can see that such classification is in fact impossible. They are not soldiers, so military language is as alien to them as the supernatural creatures. Despite their perceptions, however, their resistance to control by military forces is fraught with great peril; historically, it is always civilians who bear the greatest costs of battle. Only the supernatural can truly reveal the falseness of the military's acts of rewriting, by escaping from its interpretative framework, because only the supernatural has enough power to resist this repressive conversion.

Notes

1. Foucault, "Nietzsche, Freud, Marx," 59.
2. Ibid., 63.
3. Matloff, *American Military History*, 2:11.
4. Matheson, *Media Discourses*, 22.
5. Baumgartner and Davis, "Hosting the Monster," 2.
6. Wilson, *The Keep*, 10.
7. Ibid., 14.

8. Ibid., 12.
9. Ibid., 87.
10. Ibid., 81.
11. Ibid.
12. Bourdieu, *Language and Symbolic Power*, 243.
13. Ibid., 16.
14. Ibid., 7.
15. Ibid., 123.
16. Ibid., 100.
17. Ibid., 126. Emphasis in the original.
18. Ibid., 19.
19. Ibid., 21.
20. Ibid., 22.
21. Ibid., 23.
22. Ibid., 29.
23. Ibid., 14.
24. Ibid., 11.
25. Badley, "Darker Side of Genius," 226–27.
26. Ibid., 82.
27. Ibid., 84.
28. Foucault, "Nietzsche, Freud, Marx," 63.
29. Ibid., 47.
30. It is interesting to note that no high Nazi official within the keep wants to understand its secrets to gain power over these supernatural forces. They only want to know what the building exactly is to keep the soldiers safe and the place useful as a post of war.
31. Wilson, *The Keep*, 48.
32. Bachelard, *The Poetics of Space*, 17–19.
33. Wilson, *The Keep*, 241.
34. Ibid., 141.
35. Ibid., 194.
36. Ibid., 198.
37. Rasalom even fakes fear of Christianity to engage better within the human interpretations of vampirism. In truth, Rasalom is beyond religion.
38. Wilson, *The Keep*, 256.
39. Ibid., 359.
40. Ibid., 369.
41. Ibid.
42. Ibid., 360.
43. Masterton, *Devils of D-Day*, 4.
44. Flint, "Introduction," 4–5.
45. Lathrop, "O Taste and See," 44.
46. Masterton, *Devils of D-Day*, 7.
47. Ibid., 10, 24, 28–29.
48. Ibid., 29, 40.
49. Ibid., 28.

50. Ibid., 166.
51. Ibid.
52. Ibid., 162.
53. Ibid., 28.
54. Ibid., 231.

Bibliography

Bachelard, Gaston. *The Poetics of Space*. Boston: Beacon Press, 1969.

Badley, Linda. "The Darker Side of Genius: The (Horror) Auteur Meets Freud's Theory." In *Horror Film and Psychoanalysis: Freud's Worst Nightmares*, edited by Steven Jay Schneider, 222–40. New York: Cambridge University Press, 2004.

Baumgartner, Holly Lynn, and Roger Davis. "Hosting the Monster: Introduction." In *Hosting the Monster*, edited by Holly Lynn Baumgartner and Roger Davis, 1–10. New York: Rodopi, 2008.

Bourdieu, Pierre. *Language and Symbolic Power*. Cambridge, UK: Polity Press, 1991.

Flint, Colin. "Introduction: Geography of War and Peace." In *The Geography of War and Peace: From Death Camps to Diplomats*, edited by Colin Flint, 3–16. New York: Oxford University Press, 2005.

Foucault, Michel. "Nietzsche, Freud, Marx." In *Transforming the Hermeneutic Context: From Nietzsche to Nancy*, edited by Gayle Ormiston and Alan Schrift, 59–68. Albany: State University of New York Press, 1990.

Lathrop, Gordon. "O Taste and See: The Geography of Liturgical Ethics." In *Liturgy and the Moral Self: Humanity at Full Stretch before God*, edited by Byron Anderson and Bruce Morrill, 41–54. Collegeville, MN: Liturgical Press, 1998.

Masterton, Graham. *The Devils of D-Day*. Los Angeles: Pinnacle, 1978.

Matheson, Donald. *Media Discourses: Analysing Media Texts*. Berkshire, UK: Open University Press, 2005.

Matloff, Maurice. *American Military History. Volume 2: 1902–1996*. Cambridge, MA: Da Capo Press, 1996.

Willis, Connie. "Jack." In *The Mammoth Book of Vampire Stories by Women*, edited by Stephen Jones, 571–621. Philadelphia: Running Press, 2001.

Wilson, F. Paul. *The Keep*. New York: Jove Books, 1986.

CHAPTER 12

Horror under the Radar

MEMORY, REVELATION, AND THE GHOSTS OF *BELOW*

Christina V. Cedillo

> "A submarine isn't a good place to keep secrets. Is it?"
>
> —Claire Page to Lt. Brice, *Below*

In *Below* (2002),[1] a fictional film about a World War II submarine perchance haunted by spirits of the dead, the crew of the USS *Tiger Shark* experiences a series of mysterious tragedies after rescuing the survivors of the HMS *Fort James*, a British hospital ship reportedly sunk by a German U-boat. When strange noises ringing throughout the sub threaten to reveal the *Tiger Shark*'s location to a pursuing enemy warship, one of the survivors from the *Fort James* is revealed to be a German prisoner of war. The crew suspects that the POW is deliberately attempting to give away their position, but the noises persist even after he is shot by the submarine's commanding officer, Lieutenant Brice. Eerie apparitions and mechanical malfunctions continue to haunt the crew and rescued survivors alike, leading to the revelation of two dark, interlocking secrets: that the *Tiger Shark* torpedoed the *Fort James*, having mistaken her for a German warship, and that the *Tiger Shark*'s officers abandoned the survivors and murdered their own captain, Lieutenant Commander Winters, to protect the secret of their deadly error.

Below uses the unsettling possibility of a supernatural presence to provide a counternarrative to the nostalgic myth of wholly virtuous warfare. The nostalgia surrounding World War II is particularly intense, with the Nazis' genocidal acts and imperial ambitions lending a sense of nobility to the Allied cause. Even noble wars, however, entail death and destruction, which often falls on civilians whose deaths are then glossed over as "collateral damage." *Below* suggests that World War II is no exception to this pattern, and uses the dark secrets hidden by the *Tiger Shark*'s crew to undermine the myth of "the Good War." The ghosts in *Below*—an unruly, ambiguous presence—deliberately disrupt the formation

187

of nostalgic nationalistic memories enabled by the general public's ignorance of the deadly horrors of war.

Rewriting the Story

In contemporary history writing, questions remain over how to reconcile the "the possibility of 'objectivity' in the writing of history" with a subjective "politics of memory" that accounts for situated recollection of the past.[2] This problem necessarily underscores the importance of rhetorical framing in the construction of narratives, that is, how narratives are constructed, by whom, and to what ends. Nations at war routinely create narratives that frame their aims as noble and their warriors as virtuous and brave. Glorification of "the American fighting man" was deemed crucial to building morale during World War II, for example, and witnesses to the fighting, such as reporters and filmmakers, self-censored their work in order to preserve the pristine image of the US armed forces.[3] Subsequent counternarratives demand a deliberate revision of these simplistic heroic master narratives, replacing mono-dimensional depictions of reality with grittier, complex representations that expose uncomplicated good-evil dichotomies and uniformly positive portrayals of armed forces (and especially their commanders) as manufactured illusions.[4] *Below* participates in a revisionist undertaking by presenting a kind of meta-narrative about the construction and subsequent disproving of false accounts intended to cover up wartime atrocities. In so doing, the film highlights the ugly side of war often obscured by popular accounts—even those that acknowledge violence and suffering—by suggesting that we may not really know everything that transpires away from civilian eyes. In this manner, the film subtly asks viewers to consider the extent to which our own national myths are deliberate constructions.

The film begins in August 1943. The officers of the *Tiger Shark* receive instructions to recover survivors from the *Fort James*, a British hospital ship sunk near their location in the Atlantic. There is no indication whether the survivors are enemy troops or "friendlies," a point that frustrates Lieutenant Loomis, who mentions to the acting captain, Lieutenant Brice, that their location is a whole day's journey back. Loomis's reluctance seems understandable given that the crew, we will later be told, encountered and sank a Nazi U-boat in the area to which they must now return. When Brice notes that the directive is an order, not a suggestion, Loomis responds by saying, "What the hell? Might get a Silver Star out of this patrol yet." The moment sheds light on a notion at the heart of the film: that reputation is a carefully constructed façade. Loomis is willing to abandon survivors in the middle of the ocean, but is determined to create the impression of honorable action, even if it means murdering his commander. The scene serves as a synecdochical analogy for the entire film, and its consideration of what lies beneath national myths of honor and integrity.

That the film engages in this process of revision is evident from the outset. The name USS *Tiger Shark* appears in older films such as *Submarine Command* (1951) and *The Atomic Submarine* (1959), situating *Below* in an already established cinematic tradition. Its plot also mirrors that of the well-known *Torpedo Run* (1958). In the latter film, submarine commander Barney Doyle of the USS *Grayfish* attempts to torpedo the Japanese aircraft carrier *Shinaru*, but instead sinks a transport ship loaded with Allied prisoners of war and his own captured wife and children. The Japanese make no attempt to rescue the survivors, hoping that their plight will draw *Grayfish* to the surface where it can be attacked and sunk, but Doyle refuses to take the bait. Dedicating himself to atoning for his error, Doyle—accompanied by his loyal executive officer Sloan, who counseled against the attack—tracks down and sinks the *Shinaru*.

Below rewrites *Torpedo Run*'s patriotic narrative of redemption and sacrifice as one of cowardice, dishonor, and ruin. Having accidentally torpedoed a friendly ship, the officers of the *Tiger Shark* leave the survivors to drown in order to save their reputations. Instead of loyally supporting their captain, they mutiny against him and ultimately murder him outright in order to hide their secret. *Below* thus subverts the Hollywood myth of warfare in which "American heroism and patriotism" are indisputable and enemy forces are monolithically "cruel, devious, and unprincipled."[5] It evokes the ethical codes that ostensibly bind the armed forces only to show how the *Tiger Shark*'s officers flout those codes and the crew pays the ultimate price for their leaders' sins. The heroes of the film—and the only characters spared the supernatural justice meted out—are those who sense that the "official" story told by the officers obscures some very troubling facts.

Revealing Violence, Exhuming Trauma

The haunting of the *Tiger Shark* begins when the three survivors of the *Fort James*—nurse Claire James, a merchant seaman named Kingsley, and an unnamed, badly injured man—are brought aboard. As soon as they are recovered, the boat submerges to avoid detection by an approaching enemy ship. Suddenly, the sonar pings unusually loudly and, as everyone waits with bated breath, a phonograph suddenly begins to play Benny Goodman's "Sing, Sing, Sing (with a Swing)" at full volume. Ensign Odell, the youngest and least-experienced officer aboard the sub, locates and silences the player, but he is too late. The German warship pinpoints the sub's location and drops depth charges, which the *Tiger Shark* barely survives.

Brice blames the attack on the unnamed, wounded survivor, who is found to be wearing clothing made in Berlin, and threatens to execute him. Claire, in an attempt to protect her patient, first appeals to the Geneva Convention and then to Brice's sense of decency. "He had no cause to do those things," she says of the German POW. "He has a family, children. . . . He wants to get home just like the rest of us." Neither sways the lieutenant, however, and when the POW grabs a nearby scalpel Brice shoots him dead.

Later, strange noises continue to plague the *Tiger Shark*, with the record player coming to life once more and stopping on its own when Brice enters the room. Given that the German is dead, the only possibility appears to be that a member of the American crew, or one of the two British survivors, is trying to betray the ship's location. Viewers, who know that *Below* is a horror movie, are invited to consider other possibilities. Are there genuine ghosts aboard, or are the sounds a manifestation of something else? In the end, the film subverts generic expectations by rendering the answer a moot point. What matters is how the potential for ghosts illuminates the characters' and the audience's understanding of the trauma obscured by the officers' cover-up and their/our reactions to the dangers posed by a homegrown enemy. The sinister atmosphere that develops in response to a possible ghostly presence reveals that matters of good and evil are not cast in black and white, and recognition of that fact demands that we engage the shadows of our national(istic) consciousness.

After Brice murders the German POW, seamen Stumbo and Hoag leave the body in the bunk underneath Claire's as a cruel joke in retaliation for her hiding her patient's identity. She realizes it is there when she hears someone say, "Down here." Brice orders Stumbo to stow the corpse for good until they can cast it over-board, but then Stumbo hears it speak: "You need to turn around. . . . So many left behind." When he tells a group of others what he's heard, they laugh at his fear, inquiring whether the dead man spoke to him in German or English. Stumbo admits that the ghost spoke to him in English, but his fears are not assuaged. This small detail proves significant because much later, when Odell and Claire compare the accounts they have heard of Winters's death and the *Fort James*'s sinking, Odell tries to argue that the attack was an accident, but Claire points out that leaving the survivors to die was not. "Not when he heard the cries for help in English," she emphasizes.

Writing about the influence of South African apartheid history on J. M. Coetzee's *Disgrace*, Kimberly Wedeven Segall discusses the "traumatic sublime," a process through which experienced trauma is transformed into "images of oppressed subjects and ghosts." Because the troubling experiences cannot be completely sorted and integrated as aspects of identity, they threaten constantly to escape into the realm of consciousness, rendering sublimation a painful and inadequate process that endangers the ego. "Images of victimized persons create startling symbols of remembrance," she asserts, "and these reminders of someone (or some event) suggest an unresolved issue or past injustice, which is now being re-visited."[6] We see a similar process at work throughout *Below* as the guilty (Brice, Loomis, and their accomplice Lieutenant Coors) and the innocent (Claire, Odell, and seamen Stumbo and Wally) alike witness what appears to be Captain Winters's undead spirit growing progressively more substantial, driving them to acknowledge their culpability or piece together what happened. Brice, Loomis, and Coors must contend with the concealed truth that threatens constantly to become damning public knowledge. Claire must realize that she has sought help from the very men who murdered her patients and fellow crewmembers, and who would endanger her life to protect their secret. Odell, Stumbo, and Wally must unravel the mystery of their commander's death and acknowledge that not everyone aboard the *Tiger Shark* is on the same side. That all parties claim to observe the same phenomena regardless of their respective innocence or guilt confirms that the "ghost" is not simply vengeful or provocative, but symbolic of a trauma that unites them—and us—in a collective experience.

I suggest that this trauma stems from forced recognition of the darkness that lies just beneath the surface of the wholly honorable patriotic fantasy. In one scene, for example, Claire finds the captain's log open on Brice's desk and reads that at the time of the disaster "[the] men [were] getting itchy to come home." A disembodied voice adds, "With at least one kill." A blank page follows, along with sketches of a cross and a ship. Much later, Claire realizes that the design of the German U-boat purportedly sunk by the *Tiger Shark* a few days prior matches exactly that of the torpedoed *Fort James*. If the ghostly voice speaks the truth, then the men actively desired to take enemy lives, equating "real" service with carnage. Their fervor led them to mistakenly kill Allied sailors, prisoners, and civilians, and then deliberately kill their captain. Such physical and ethical betrayal results in trauma, for trauma occurs when "the community of which we considered ourselves members turn[s] against us,"[7] and that is precisely what the *Tiger Shark*'s officers have done to Winters, the *Fort James* survivors, and by extension their nation.

The slippage between sanctioned killing and shameful brutality reflects the history of World War II, in which atrocities were committed by Allied and Axis forces alike. American troops frequently turned on their own fellow soldiers: enlisted women risked rape, and African American soldiers, who often had fewer rights than German POWs, were regularly beaten or killed in highly disproportionate numbers.[8] Allied air forces deliberately targeted civilian areas to break German and Japanese morale, using incendiary bombs that sparked firestorms so intense that people "scorched and boiled and baked to death."[9] They shot POWs and "machine-gunned defenseless enemies in the water or in parachutes," a crime that Coors will later attribute to Winters in an attempt to justify his demise.[10]

Wartime is a quintessential moral gray area, and war crimes especially entail a turning away from those ethics that are thought to define a society and through which, in turn, people identify as members of a collective. Group identity depends on shared values, so when a member violates those values *in the name of the group*, the betrayal results in a complex anxiety that signifies "a wholeness and a closure that is not possible."[11] Even when the cruelty of combat is obscured by fabricated reports and tickertape parades, as it deliberately was during World War II, the grim realities of war persist in haunting us.

The Submarine as Liminal Space

The *Tiger Shark* is a fitting site for the irruption of psychic disturbances, since its diving and surfacing mimics the symbolic descent into and subsequent return from the subconscious that an uncovering of trauma entails. Its mechanical body creates a temporary safe space that nonetheless reminds its inhabitants that both human and environmental dangers lurk just beyond its metal frame. According to Anthony Vidler, "space is assumed to hide, in its darkest recesses and forgotten margins, all the objects of fear and phobia that have returned with such consistency to haunt the imaginations of those who have tried to stake out spaces to protect their health and happiness."[12] Those "darkest recesses and forgotten margins" are highlighted in the boundary-transcending, threshold space encapsulated by the *Tiger Shark*. Dreadful repressed memories of its officers' maritime atrocities are foregrounded, all in a paradoxical recovery of truth and honor.

The sub's space is mapped out, early on, in an extended shot that follows various crewmembers as news spreads that one of the survivors of the *Fort James* is a woman. The sub appears as a progressively artificial space—one filled with machinery, pipes, and gauges—but one punctuated by places transformed by the presence of everyday human activities such as sleeping, eating, and listening to music. It manifests liminality: a mechanical beast that contains both motorized and living components, exists above and below the ocean's surface, and is at once a protective enclosure and deadly threat. The *Tiger Shark*'s very walls help generate a strange locale "that might subsequently be invaded by the apparently excluded abject and disruptive."[13] This enigmatic space will soon be inhabited by ghosts that may or may not exist and thus reflect the sub's quintessential ambiguity.

The division between truth and lies proves equally indistinct aboard the *Tiger Shark*. Narratives that ride the line between reality and fiction abound on the sub, as the three murderers attempt to suppress the truth of their crimes. In the same scene when Claire examines the captain's log, she reads the entry documenting that the *Tiger Shark* has picked up three survivors from the *Fort James*, "reportedly victims of a German U-boat." She notes that the handwriting differs from that of the previous entries. Brice, whom we assume penned the later report, has chosen an indicative expression; "reportedly" suggests the survivors' confusion as to who sunk their ship, but the word also intimates the falsity of the captain's account. When Coors, seeking Brice's sextant, finds her, he says she shouldn't be in the skipper's cabin. She replies that she'll gladly ask him, inquiring pointedly whether Brice is the skipper. Coors states that Brice is the current commanding officer. Like Brice's log entry, he neither lies nor tells the truth. Brice *is* now in charge of the sub but only as a result of treachery against its rightful commander. He is indeed the "C.O." but not the "skipper," whose cabin it rightly is. Even if Brice has moved into Winters's quarters, the respectful and affectionate term that indicates a well-earned post does not befit Brice.

The theme of equivocation persists, becoming more overt as Brice and the other lieutenants realize their scheme is being uncovered, and it is accompanied by increased paranormal activity. After Coors finds Claire in Brice's quarters, Brice "confesses" to Claire that Winters died after hitting his head while topside in search of a souvenir from the sunken U-boat. When he assumes authority in giving her permission to move freely about the boat, he starts to see the specter of Winters. Afterward, Loomis asks him what he told her. Brice replies, "The story," once again using a loaded expression; "story" appears to mean "account" but is revealed to mean "lie." Just then the *Tiger Shark* is attacked by a German ship using dragging hooks, causing a severe leak. When they manage to escape, Loomis assures Brice that he'll "do better at the board of inquiry," only then noting that Odell has overheard them. As Brice, inside the ship, fills in the empty journal page with the "official" version of events, Odell and Coors go outside to repair an oil leak in the space between the inner and outer layers of the hull. When Odell asks how Winters hit his head, the noises return. Coors stares at Odell—hammer in hand, meaning to kill him—and explains that Winters ordered them to machine-gun the survivors of the torpedoed U-boat, causing an argument during which Winters fell. Climbing up into the sub's metal structure, he says: "Slippery metal. Bad footing. Accidents happen, right?" He intends to drop the hammer on Odell's head, but is startled by a flashback of Winters's face and falls to his death, hit by his own hammer on the way down. The story spun by Coors proves true, although not quite right, since the details have shifted to render justice.

As things grow progressively worse, Wally and Hoag ponder—in a scene at once humorous and evocative—whether they and the remaining members of the crew are even alive. They contemplate the possibility that the sub was sunk and that the noises they hear are rescue divers having found them too late. They intend their conversation to be facetious, but it has serious undertones. Their talk highlights the degree to which the line between reality and fiction has begun to blur on both the narrative and rhetorical levels.

The Ghost as Category Disruption

Upholding the logic of ambiguity, *Below* never quite establishes whether the ghosts that appear to haunt the *Tiger Shark* are real beings or shared delusions, the spirits of those killed by friendly fire or fantasies conjured by the confined crew's stressed imaginations. Instead, the film negates the significance of the ghosts' indeterminate realness because, in the end, it doesn't matter whether they are real in a concrete or a psychological sense. What does matter is the revelation of truth. At the very end, once they have been rescued, Odell asks Claire her thoughts on everything they have experienced. Referring to the possibility that the boat was indeed haunted, Claire responds by saying, "Does seem rather unlikely now, doesn't it?" Odell wonders if maybe, when Winters died, he simply died "and that was it." Yet he admits, "And the rest . . . the rest . . . I don't know." Despite the implausibility of a submarine infested by phantoms, Claire answers by saying that, no matter what he says, she will always believe that they were brought back to the site of the *Fort James*'s sinking for a reason.

The film's deliberate refusal to determine the ghosts' ontological status affirms how, as metaphors, they manifest in contexts where inconsistencies are prevalent and the certainties of an apparently seamless reality are revealed to be illusions. The haunting in the film reveals the incongruity between the facts of the *Fort James* sinking and what Brice and the others hope to establish as the "of-

Claire and Odell speculate whether ghosts really haunted the USS *Tiger Shark*.

ficial truth" about them, and suggests our status as the "good guys" may likewise be fabricated. According to film theorist Robin Wood, "the true subject of the horror genre is all that our civilization represses or oppresses."[14] In *Below*, the repressed subject matter includes the shadowy aspect of our national ethos, that which must be denied in order to maintain the impression of absolute morality even in times of war.

As a cultural symbol, "[the] ghost is less an image than a process: immaterial and invisible, it manifests itself only in spatial and temporal distortions."[15] It signifies those disconcerting instances when stabilizing categories cannot be clearly delineated, and causes us to question whether life and death are entirely discrete states, revealing oppositional absolutes as metonymic rather than contrasting notions. Its materialization causes the past and the present to coincide, in the form of one, once fully alive, who now exists solely via perception by the living. Perhaps it is this latter capacity for temporal disruption that proves most troubling, for in demonstrating that the past itself refuses to remain passé, but instead remains embedded in the present, the ghost marks an inability to escape what came before.

The dread this temporal conflation causes is best illustrated in a scene where Loomis comes across a mirror where his likeness is out of sync, replicating his movements with a second's delay. Loomis is both fascinated and repulsed by the delayed reflection. When he turns away, his mirror image continues to stare back at him, at last revealed as a ghost that frightens him so deeply that it leads to his death. Telling Brice, "He's here!" Loomis manages to escape out a hatch; he attempts to swim to the surface but is impaled on damaged periscope structures and pulled back down into the deep. Even in death he cannot evade the consequences of his past actions.

The past and the ghost alike threaten constantly to return, and this tendency toward resurgence proves one of the markers of their shared monstrous nature. Jeffrey Jerome Cohen notes that as a figure of cultural anxiety monsters always come back, often in a slightly different guise that suits their social context: "We see the damage that the monster wreaks . . . but the monster itself turns immaterial and vanishes to reappear someplace else."[16] For this reason the horror wrought by their (re)appearance is always "historically and culturally contingent."[17] In the case of *Below*, this recurrence reveals that the crises of the past are still very much with us. Whether Winters's ghost actually appears before the living or their imaginations are simply running wild out of fear, his lingering influence reveals that an "urge to seek out the ghosts of places is bound up with the politics of remembering the past."[18] Even if the film's spirits are not real, they signify how, as a culture, we instinctively know that the suppressed ghosts of wartime transgressions refuse to be contained by heroic master narratives.

When Secrets Resurface

Because they always come back, ghosts typically signify unsettled matters that must be resolved. As a rule, their existence necessitates the disclosure of dreadful yet crucial knowledge some would prefer to bury, literally and/or figuratively. *Below* emphasizes this point repeatedly through direct references to burial, returning, and going below. Once Brice admits that he murdered Winters, he refuses to allow the others to send a distress call to a passing British ship, going so far as to shoot out the radio. When he realizes that Claire has gone topside to flag down the vessel, he follows her and accosts her at gunpoint, yelling, "We're going below now!" She yells back, "Bury everybody and bury the truth—is that it, Brice?" He refuses to shoot her, turning the gun on himself, instead. Declaring that Winters's ghost did not kill him as it did Coors and Loomis because it didn't have to, he pulls the trigger. Like the ghost of King Hamlet, who may or may not exist but nonetheless demands that his son expose and avenge his murder, the spirits in *Below* instigate the discovery of vital secrets that, in turn, demand retributive action in both the material and psychological realms.

In Shakespeare's play, "revenging and remembering are presented by the Ghost as completely intertwined," to the point that "the degree of eagerness and diligence in revenging is the same as the degree of intensity and devotedness in remembering."[19] Action must be taken in order to allow the spirit to rest, promising not only an end to the haunting but the fulfillment of moral obligations to the dead. With the fulfillment of that obligation comes an understanding that true remembrance entails bringing to light evidence of a painful past and a search for atonement. As Avery F. Gordon observes, "*When the living take the dead or the past back to a symbolic place, it is connected to the labor aimed at creating in the present a something that must be done*" (italics in original).[20] What earlier seemed a charge for Stumbo to turn and face the dead body now appears a directive from Winters, dislocated in space and time, asking his officers to turn back and rescue the survivors of the British ship—and demanding that they return to the scene of their crime so their wrongdoing may be uncovered. Even after his death his noble intentions designate his version of events as the bona fide account, one that will be realized when the survivors of the *Tiger Shark* are themselves saved from the sea by the passing ship searching for any potential survivors of the *Fort James*.

In order to ensure proper action is taken, the *Tiger Shark*—or the ghost at its helm—forces the crew to gaze upon the bitter fruits of their misdeeds. A rash of broken equipment and uncontrollable motions set the boat on a course back to the site of the tragedy. The sub's bizarre performance exemplifies physically the ghost's inclination to "recall that which has been forgotten, whether through deliberate political strategies or because the horrors of the recent past are too painful to confront," forcing a "reconsideration of forgotten events or places."[21] It returns to the site of the *Fort James*'s sinking, hindering the crew's attempts to return to their Connecticut base where the three lieutenants planned to report their concocted story. Yet after most of the crew has perished, and even though most of its equipment has malfunctioned or been destroyed, the *Tiger Shark* rises from the sea of its own accord so that the survivors, those few who have sought out the truth and/or believed in the ghosts' veracity, will be saved by the passing ship. As Odell watches its floating ruin from aboard the HMS *Archimedes*, the British captain remarks of the *Tiger Shark*: "Dead but not buried, I see." With that, the sub finally sinks, coming to rest beside the sunken *Fort James*, perhaps somehow "knowing" that the true story of her flawed-but-honorable captain's demise will now be told. Whether or not the ghost existed, its influence has proven the impetus for revelation and resolution, marking their lack in a violent manner that reflects the violence that might have otherwise remained secret.

It is no coincidence that an entity that refuses to stay dead represents a need for vengeance, for traditionally, ghosts manifest when the ritualistic conditions required to ensure the safe passage of the dead into the next world have gone unmet, conditions that include a "proper burial" and "revenge on [the deceased's] murderer."[22] Both of these requirements highlight appropriate honor for the dead and a respect for their memory, neither of which can be demonstrated until scores have been settled and the dishonor of those causing the death has been

At last, the *Tiger Shark* comes to rest beside the HMS *Fort James*.

revealed. Winters is murdered because he wished to save the survivors of the *Fort James* and take responsibility for a tragedy caused by his own erroneous decision. In attempting to pass it off as a Nazi act and leave the survivors to perish, his lieutenants transform an unfortunate accident into murder, compounding the evil by killing the one person whose voice might ensure justice for the dead.

Stories that illustrate the granting of peace to restless souls point up the moral responsibilities of the living; they instruct popular audiences regarding cultural norms related to right and wrong, injury and justice. They challenge us to face, and lay to rest, those ghosts that haunt our own collective past. This call is echoed in *Below*, a film in which retributive spirits may (or may not) be seeking revenge on those responsible for their deaths. Something is not quite right and the established status quo narrative does not cohere, forcing those directly affected by the alleged ghosts to consider where and why the carefully woven tale threatens to unravel. This order requires that the truth be revealed and scores be settled before the haunting will stop, whether it stems from real ghosts or from externalized mass guilt. The glossy veneer of patriotic glory superimposed on a tale of destruction and trauma via a cover-up must be stripped away so that the unjustly slain can be avenged and memorialized, and viewers are surreptitiously directed to seek the same kind of revelatory justice in their own "real" history.

Conclusion

Ghosts are essentially creatures of memory, made manifest by a failure to remember one's social obligations to the dead or the truth behind past events, and the connection between ghosts and memory underscores the nebulous nature of the latter. Like the ghost, memory, too, proves an ambiguous entity, a biased proxy that cannot encapsulate the fullness of lived experience but must serve nonetheless as the basis for understanding the past. Due to its selective disposition, memory, like the ghost, requires a recovery of facts if the "whole story" is to be recovered despite the mental, emotional, and ideological factors that influence recollection. Narratives, including those enshrined as history, prove highly subjective, but there are facts that should never be forgotten. Fittingly, phantoms are spirits of the dead who refuse to be ignored, the souls of those whose stories must be told even when, and especially if, those stories prove dreadful. They are potent metaphors for the muddled convergence of all these factors, and indicators of circumstances that must be exposed, righted, and incorporated into memory in a just manner.

"Citizens of a nation at war cannot but be affected psychologically by the stresses of war,"[23] but all too often, the hard-learned lessons gleaned through the process of coping with this trauma become muted over time. Memory fades or becomes altered, leaving nostalgia in its stead, and nostalgia permits collective memory to foster nationalistic notions of patriotism, honor, and justified cruelty. *Below* accomplishes its revisionist task by drawing on a twofold evocation of the past, or meta-nostalgia: for the "good old days" of the 1940s and for the films of the wartime and immediate postwar eras that concretized the period's significance in the civilian collective consciousness.[24] *Below* uses themes and images familiar to popular audiences via classic war films to subvert the traditional narrative of the heroic, unified Allies emerging triumphant against the evil Nazis, presenting instead a thought-provoking tale that transcends its supernatural elements and interrogates American identity itself.

Notes

1. *Below*, directed by David Twohy (2002).
2. Nytagodien and Neal, "Collective Trauma," 467.
3. Fussell, *Wartime*, 285–86.
4. Adams, *Best War Ever*, 10.
5. Ibid. 11.
6. Segall, "Pursuing Ghosts," 42.
7. Edkins, *Memory of Politics*, 4.
8. Adams, *Best War Ever*, 9.
9. Dower, *War without Mercy*, 40–41.
10. Adams, *Best War Ever*, 7, 110.
11. Edkins, *Memory of Politics*, 11.
12. Vidler, *The Architectural Uncanny*, 167.
13. Edensor, "Ghosts of Industrial Ruins," 835.
14. Quoted in Schneider, "Monsters as (Uncanny) Metaphors."
15. Gomel, *Narrative Space and Time*, 71.
16. Cohen, "Monster Culture (Seven Theses)," 4.
17. Schneider, "Monsters as (Uncanny) Metaphors."
18. Ibid., 829.
19. Curran, *Hamlet, Protestantism, and the Mourning of Contingency*, 81.
20. Gordon, *Ghostly Matters*, 173, 175. To be precise, the character of Beloved, whom Gordon deems the "fleshy return of the repressed," assumes a corporeal body, making her more of a revenant than a ghost. However, her materialization in the flesh occurs only after her mother and sister attempt to move on after years of enduring a more typical haunting of their home.
21. Edensor, "Ghosts of Industrial Ruins," 835.
22. Edmonds, *Myths of the Underworld Journey*, 187.
23. Tuttle, *"Daddy's Gone to War,"* 31.
24. Doherty, *Projections of War*, 272.

Bibliography

Adams, Michael C. C. *The Best War Ever: America and World War II*. Baltimore: Johns Hopkins University Press, 1994.

Below. Directed by David Twohy. 2002. La Crosse, WI: Echo Bridge Home Entertainment, 2011. DVD.

Cohen, Jeffrey Jerome. "Monster Culture (Seven Theses)." In *Monster Theory: Reading Culture*, edited by Jeffrey Jerome Cohen, 3–25. Minneapolis: University of Minnesota Press, 1996.

Curran, John E., Jr. *Hamlet, Protestantism, and the Mourning of Contingency: Not to Be*. Burlington, VT: Ashgate, 2006.

Doherty, Thomas Patrick. *Projections of War: Hollywood, American Culture, and World War II*. New York: Columbia University Press, 1993.

Dower, John W. *War without Mercy: Race and Power in the Pacific War*. New York: Pantheon Books, 1987.

Edensor, Tim. "The Ghosts of Industrial Ruins: Ordering and Disordering Memory in Excessive Space." *Environment and Planning D: Society and Space* (2005): 829–49.

Edkins, Jenny. *Trauma and the Memory of Politics*. Cambridge: Cambridge University Press, 2003.

Edmonds, Radcliffe G. *Myths of the Underworld Journey: Plato, Aristophanes, and the "Orphic" Gold Tablets*. Cambridge: Cambridge University Press, 2004.

Fussell, Paul. *Wartime: Understanding and Behavior in the Second World War*. New York: Oxford University Press, 1989.

Gomel, Elana. *Narrative Space and Time: Representing Impossible Topologies in Literature*. New York: Routledge, 2014.

Gordon, Avery F. *Ghostly Matters: Haunting and the Sociological Imagination*. Minneapolis: University of Minnesota Press, 2008.

Nytagodien, Ridwan Laher, and Arthur G. Neal. "Collective Trauma, Apologies, and the Politics of Memory." *Journal of Human Rights* 3, no. 4 (2004): 465–75.

Schneider, Steven. "Monsters as (Uncanny) Metaphors: Freud, Lakoff, and the Representation of Monstrosity in Cinematic Horror." *Other Voices: The (e)Journal of Cultural Criticism* 1, no. 3 (1999): n.p.

Segall, Kimberly Wedeven. "Pursuing Ghosts: The Traumatic Sublime in J. M. Coetzee's *Disgrace*." *Research in African Literatures* 36, no. 4 (2005): 40–54.

Tuttle, William M. *"Daddy's Gone to War": The Second World War in the Lives of America's Children*. New York: Oxford University Press, 1993.

Vidler, Anthony. *The Architectural Uncanny: Essays in the Modern Unhomely*. Cambridge, MA: MIT Press, 1992.

CHAPTER 13

The Supernatural, Nazi Zombies, and the Play Instinct

THE GAMIFICATION OF WAR AND THE REALITY OF THE MILITARY INDUSTRIAL COMPLEX

Steve Webley

That zombies have evolved across cultural and media boundaries is beyond doubt. They have undergone a Darwinian journey that parallels humanity's journey from mere primate to *Homo sapiens*. The predominance of the zombie in a vast array of popular media raises questions about whether they resemble our own prehistoric past, act as a mirror reflecting our own social anxieties regarding unfettered capitalism and an errant military industrial complex, or provide insight into our own evolutionary future.[1] A constant in both our own evolutionary tale and that of the zombie, however, is the unending and irrepressible act that is both harbinger and signifier of human evolution: war. It appears that the zombie, like war, is here to stay—a totem that cannot be killed off and simply relegated to the mausoleum of cultures past. Like many manifestations of the fantastic, the zombie has diversified into multiple varieties: fast zombies, slow zombies, dumb zombies, thinking zombies, slapstick zombies, slave zombies, and even romantic zombies. One in particular, however, has become increasingly popular in video games: the Nazi zombie.

The modern zombie has its roots in the work of filmmaker George A. Romero, along with our anxieties regarding late twentieth-century society. Romero's genius lay in simultaneously reinventing the zombie and politicizing it, re-creating horror as social critique.[2] Beginning with *Night of the Living Dead* (1968), Romero created a series of films set in ideologically charged spaces such as shopping malls and fortified neighborhoods. A recurring motif in Romero's films is the survivors glimpsing the tabula rasa of a new society—free of repressive injunctions that are causing the old one to collapse in the face of the undead hordes—only to have their own group implode from hubris, desire, and internecine ideological frictions. Even as Romero's survivors are destroying themselves, however, they are being slowly displaced by the zombie Others who are apparently able to live quite peacefully in the absence of humans.

Romero's greatest achievement was his portrayal of the tension between subjectivity and otherness, which addressed one of the key fantasies of the Atomic Age.[3] Nuclear anxiety is evident in many of the science fiction films of the 1950s, such as the *Godzilla* series from Japan and "big bug" movies like *Them!* from the United States. By the end of the decade, movies portrayed everything from giant arachnids to monstrous alien war machines and weapons capable of extinguishing all human life on Earth. These films relied on a consistent motif—Otherness so huge, so terrifying, that it seemed impossible for it to occupy the same physical and conceptual space on-screen as its human victims.[4] The period from 1957 to 1962 saw a peak in Cold War tensions, fueling hysteria that was intensified by constant civil defense drills, anxieties over home fallout shelters, and new threats in the form of land- and sea-based ballistic missiles. These changes augured a new psychosocial reality for US citizens, one increasingly connected to images of their own imminent death.[5] Indeed, few societies have prepared for collective destruction as did the United States, and this period can be considered a foundational moment when the technology, strategy, politics, and motivations supporting a US security state coalesced, raising questions as to how a society that pursues war as a normalized condition should pause and reflect on its own intellectual and psychosocial processes.[6] The release of *Night of the Living Dead* in 1968 reflected the growing, questioning resistance to this reality. The film was a watershed moment for the horror genre, as Romero's zombies embodied the monstrous Other and Subject together in a single cannibalistic entity. Fantasy cinema became a space within which to explore the tension between America's *Weltschmerz*[7] regarding war—suppressed in mainstream media—and its veneration of the heroic and sacrificial calling of patriotism. Zombies, meanwhile, became the modern projection of an ancient and primordial anxiety over humanity's dualistic identity and unconscious desires.

War, Fantasy and Ideology

> "In man, there's already a crack, a profound perturbation
> of the regulation of life."[8]

The modern study of war emerged from a similar *ur*-moment in our collective history. It was born, along with the modern nation-state, during the French Revolution, and the two evolved in parallel. Its founding fathers—and most prolific early commentators—were Carl von Clausewitz (1780–1831) and Antoine-Henri Jomini (1779–1869).[9] Jomini's understanding was shaped by the Enlightenment: War, he believed, could be studied as a science, and doctrines for waging it formulated through the rational observation of events. Clausewitz, in contrast, was a Romantic, who focused on the nonlinear and irrational realm of human emotion and identified war as a continuation of *politik*.[10] Despite these differences, both theorists agreed that waging war successfully was more art than science, and that combining war-gaming with the study of history was essential to understanding it. The immediate, wide-ranging influence of their ideas ensured that the study of war would have a long affinity with games.

Analysis of the role of play in war has, however, been unable to bridge the gap between Clausewitzian philosophy and Jominian doctrine. That gap leads, in turn, to an inability to differentiate the capacity for war from the actual act of war, and to an inability to analyze the logics of war from within war itself.[11] It obscures attempts to evaluate the irrational motivations and unconscious desires that support our understandings of the reality of war. The gap, synonymous with the irrational human need for fantasy, can be bridged, however, by juxtaposing Clausewitzian study of war with psychoanalysis. The two schools of thought are linked by a shared concern with the irrational, and examining them together allows us to analyze the significance of the evolution of the zombie from mundane ghoul to supernatural Nazi in the modality of play.

The most common psychoanalytic concept applied to the supernatural is Sigmund Freud's idea of the uncanny.[12] However, it is Jacques Lacan's use of Freud's work that proves most useful here. In Lacan's model of the Subject and his creation of the Symbolic realm of human existence, he returned to Freud, suggesting a linguistic reading that considered subjective reality to be an unconscious construct of language.[13] Lacan suggests that the irrational drives experienced by human beings exist in a different psychic realm than language in the Real—a realm beyond that of speech—and that those drives contain knowledge that cannot be realized or signified by language. For Lacan, fantasy underpins the individual's conception of reality, acting as a screen onto which he or she projects fantasy and desire, thus constructing reality. However, the symbolic reality of language, law, and order is inconsistent and ruptured, containing holes and gaps into which particulars of the Real can leak; it is the job of fantasy to paper over these ruptures, administering psychically acceptable dosages of the Real to the individual.

These drives are fueled by the desire not to fulfill a goal, but rather to endlessly reproduce themselves in a cyclical fashion. They result in *jouissance*—a surplus of enjoyment that compels the individual to transgress social prohibitions placed on enjoyment—creating a form of pleasure that can be at once exhilarating and excruciating, orgasmic and unbearable, sublime and terrifying. The desire caused by this is not to obtain a goal—since proximity to "the prohibited" causes horror and anxiety—but to endlessly dance around it.[14]

It is important to note that for Lacan, the "object cause" of desire is not an object in the real sense, but a lack or gap in the construct of the human subject (created by the split between the conscious imaginary and unconscious colonizing power of human language).[15] Thus, for Lacan, fantasy sutures the individual to both enjoyment and reality, dictating not what to desire, but *how* to desire, making fantasy the lodestone of ideology that dictates what, where, how, and how much, he or she can enjoy. The role of fantasy here is both ambivalent and ambiguous: Any object when juxtaposed against the impulse of these drives can take on powerful significance and impose ideological imperatives upon us.[16] That is why, in Lacanian analysis, it is vital to *"traverse the fantasy"*—to recognize that fantasy exists simply to mask inconsistencies and give them purpose.[17] Popular culture abounds with objects that play with fantasies of death, creating figures that merge drives of aggression with play (*jouissance*) and as a result of cycles of violence and pleasure, become suspended in an undead state, existing *between two deaths*, creating horrifically sublime bodies exempted from normal mortality.[18]

Nazism, Horror, and Zombies

> "Let's be honest: People don't play *Call of Duty: World at War* to play *Call of Duty: World at War*; they play it to play Nazi Zombies."[19]

Call of Duty: Nazi Zombies enables players to simulate Real war while enjoying a fantasy world in which Nazi victory is inevitable. *Courtesy of devijavi. http:// devijavi.deviantart.com/art/Nazi-Zombies-Origins-Queen-396839585.*

Academic speculation over the link between the supernatural and Nazism began shortly after World War II, spurred by fascination with Nazism and the suggestion that the Third Reich represented an uncanny lapse into paganism.[20] Overt links between Nazism and paganism included the swastika, a symbol found in Paleolithic art, Egyptian hieroglyphics, and Asian religions, as well as the Germanic mythology that the Nazis mobilized for ideological ends. Hitler reveled in his re-creation of the swastika. "A symbol it really is!" he exclaimed in *Mein Kampf.* "In the swastika . . . [we see] . . . the mission of the struggle for the victory of the Aryan man." The standard of the Third Reich, designed by Hitler himself and influenced by old Roman designs, included a swastika surrounded by a wreath of oak leaves and surmounted by a stylized eagle, along with a swastika-emblazoned banner bearing the slogan "Germany Awake."[21] The manipulation of social meaning through the creation of these sublime icons of Nazi aesthetics has a long, carefully planned, and privileged history.[22] It is, however, a history not without irony, for it entangled the symbols and supernaturalism of a pre-civilized world with the fascist ideology of capitalist revolution.[23]

Following the Great Depression, Germans grappled with social breakdown and the perception that their laws and institutions had failed them. As a result, they sought answers not provided by the establishment and mainstream newspapers. Nazism flourished because it offered revolution and meaning, mobilizing the solidarity and collectivity of social democracy while paying lip service to socialism. What the Nazis offered, however, was a curiously conservative revolution—one rooted in modern science, and aimed at a future defined by technology and industry, but invested with a feudal hierarchical social structure, devoid of class struggle and the social antagonisms inherent in modern capitalism. Nazi ideologues saw the new order as irreconcilable with Christianity, and sought instead to substitute old Germanic tribal gods and the paganism of Nazi fundamentalism.[24]

This unity of premodern mythology and modern capitalism both required and enabled the creation of an ideological narrative of the *Untermenschen:* an Other that functioned as a focal point for universal fears and inconstancies in the new social order. The existence of such an Other rendered ethically acceptable the mobilization of industry, science, technology, and medicine in order to ensure its destruction. Before the outbreak of the war, Carl Jung spoke of dark portents—not because Hitler was leader of Germany, but because he had *become* Germany. Hitler, Jung argued, had ceased to be a man and instead had become myth: a loudspeaker that broadcast all the previously unutterable murmurings of the German unconscious.[25] Fantasy was fundamental to the social policy of *Volksgemeinschaft,* and the goal of creating national ideological unity by cleansing society of anything un-German. The mythological foundations were set for the horrors of the Nazi regime; the precursor of the Holocaust was the euthanasia

(*Aktion T4 programme*) of the handicapped in asylums, and Nazification of the sciences saw the start of sadistic medical experimentation.[26]

Films featuring Nazi zombies—a small but significant subgenre since the mid-twentieth century—draw on this association of Nazi ideology with the morally unfettered use of science and technology, as well as on the visual appeal of Nazi aesthetics. More recent iterations of the Nazi zombie film have become amalgams of horror, humor, and the sexual escapades of teen movies. They position Nazi zombies in the pantheon of contemporary popular culture as ghastly characters void of their original ideological power but still rich in social meaning.[27] A similar alignment of horror, humor, and Nazi aesthetics is also present in games, where Nazi zombie adventures have been a popular subgenre since the release of *Wolfenstein 3D* in 1992. Indeed, the *Wolfenstein* franchise has been somewhat ahead of trends in Nazi zombie cinema, overtly playing with amalgamations of the undead, horrific ideology, sexual repression, and Nazi aesthetics since the release of *Return to Castle Wolfenstein* in 2001.

Questions of what Nazi Zombies signify and what it means to play with them have, however, been largely neglected in game studies. On a purely practical level, they make ideal enemies because they are relentless, already dead, and easy for game designers to develop artificial intelligence routines to animate. The Nazi zombies in *Call of Duty*—the most prolific game franchise to date to use them—have thus been dismissed as mere "re-contextualized shooting gallery props," and the use of low-brow humor and simplistic game mechanics discourages interpretations of them as anything more sophisticated than "oddball" and "harmless fun."[28] The popularity of the *Call of Duty* franchise, however, is evident on the Internet, where fan-made game modifications, fan art, and fan fiction abound, and debate has even spilled over into the dialogue of the AMC drama series *Breaking Bad*.

> *Badger*: "That's a fair point, I guess. OK, OK, OK, *Call of Duty: World at War* zombie mode. Now that's the bomb, man. Think on it, bro. They're not just zombies: they're Nazi zombies."
>
> *Skinny Pete*: "Nazi zombies . . ."
>
> *Badger*: "Yeah, man! SS Waffen troopers, too, which are like the baddest ass Nazis of the whole Nazi family!"
>
> *Skinny Pete*: "Zombies are dead, man! What difference does it make what their job was when they was living?"
>
> *Badger*: "Dude, you are so historically retarded! Nazi zombies don't wanna eat ya just 'cause they're craving the protein. They do it 'cause they hate Americans, man. Talibans. They're the Talibans of the zombie world."[29]

The proliferation and success of the *Call of Duty* franchise and its Nazi zombies thus beg deeper interpretation than they have thus far been given.

Zombies in horror and action games are typically seen as allegorical vehicles for interpretations of otherness. There is something particularly appealing, however, about Nazi zombies: They hate. They are not the mindless, shambling horde of Romero's films—creatures that crave protein for which they have no biological need—and they are not the virus-infected sprinting corpses of post 9/11 popularity.[30] Nazi zombies are motivated by a force that was supposed to have expired with the Cold War: ideology. Like the Taliban they are motivated by a violent determinism that we presume is easily identified in the Other, but absent in ourselves.

The current outbreak of Nazi zombies in the gaming world began in 2008 with the release of *Call of Duty: World at War*, a sequel to the already popular *Call of Duty*. The game featured a last-minute addition by the developer: a scenario in which players struggled together to defend a World War II bunker against hordes of what the game manual described as "Nazi zombies."[31] The addition proved hugely popular. Additional downloadable scenarios using the theme were developed for *Call of Duty: World at War*, and it is now an established part of the franchise. The Nazi zombie scenarios currently available enable players to battle ideologically driven supernatural entities across a total of seventeen locations, including the trenches of World War I, a Nazi occult

The appeal of Nazi zombies lies in the fact that, unlike other undead enemies, they are motivated by ideology. *Courtesy of Carter Reid, thezombienation.com.*

research station and mental asylum, Cold War–era Soviet rocket silos, the halls of the Pentagon, modern Asia, and the nuclear wasteland of a post-apocalyptic United States.

The original scenario, *Nacht der Untoten* (Night of the Undead), was the smallest and most accessible. The premise was simple: Defend the bunker, and survive as long as possible. Players control soldier avatars, and zombies spawn outside and break in through the windows, while players earn points by killing zombies and boarding up open windows. Players can "spend" points to buy more powerful weapons or open doors and access-ways in order to explore the bunker further. The zombies attack in waves, starting as slow shambling zombies and gradually becoming the quicker, sprinting variety, as well as more numerous and harder to kill. There is no narrative other than of the players' struggle for survival, and no possible outcome but ultimate failure. Players strive to stay alive for as many waves as possible, with results logged on high-score tables, but ultimately the zombies are always victorious.

Later downloadable Nazi-zombie scenarios for *Call of Duty* have grown increasingly complex, introducing additional different playable characters and buildings containing hidden objectives and traps. Several of the maps are based on real-world locales, including the Wittenau Sanatorium Berlin, which played a role in the T4 program, and a giant, unfinished underground complex in Lower Silesia, built by the Nazi-run Todt construction company using concentration camp slave labor. A narrative was also retroactively imposed on all the scenarios in the series, requiring players to solve rebuslike puzzles that reveal the origins of the Nazi zombies and the raison d'être of the players' involvement. This meta-narrative accounts for the fact that—even when fighting GI zombies in the Pentagon, native zombies in Shangri-La, or cosmonaut zombies on the Moon—they are still battling undead enemies motivated by Nazism in a universe where Nazi ideologues have been able to cross time, space, and the boundaries of parallel realities. *Origins*, the final installment, unfolds in the trenches of World War I, establishing the origins of the narrative and linking them to the origins of Nazism, total war, and the military-industrial complex.[32]

Traversing the Battlefield of Post-Ideology— Play, War, and Fantasy

> "All wars are things of the same nature. . . . War is the continuation of *politik* by other means."[33]

In 1938, Johan Huizinga posited that play, rather than work, was the formative element in human culture. For Huizinga, humankind's most important activity belonged to the realm of fantasy; play was the structuring element of all culture, the function by which man created his sense of self and identity.[34] In Huizinga's understanding, the need for the mind to impose a symbolic order on the chaos of reality resulted in the birth of mythology, ritual, sports, games, drama, philosophy, and warfare. At the time Huizinga's thesis was controversial; most conventional notions held that that the capacity to make tools rewarded man with the ability to tame the natural world.[35] Most contentious was Huizinga's assertion that war and play were inextricably linked—that play created the myths and rituals that enabled war to become self-renewing, a cycle of ritual violence justifying the creation of cultural institutions. War, he argued, is the game of the highest order governed by rules and institutions. When cultures are at war, and are seen to share common rituals, limiting rules are understood as they are in a game; when one side can perceive the other as Other, they can justify genocidal brutality.[36] Writing during Nazism's ascendancy, Huizinga saw ominous developments in the cycle of the play instinct and war—total war, with its emphasis on mass mobilization and airpower, was expunging the play instinct from the ritual of warfare.[37]

The ideologically driven European politics of the 1930s were, for Huizinga, equally ominous. He warned that ideologies are "unholy. . . . Whenever there is a catch word ending in –ism we are hot on the tracks of a play community." Such play communities bring about an unrivaled rise in aesthetic enjoyment, becoming the substitute for religion, and the play form of myth is utilized to conceal ideological design. Participants in political rallies display behaviors of the lowest order of play: Hails, yells, signals of mythical greetings, and insignia combine with ritual marching and chanting to form a rigmarole of "collective voodoo and mumbo-jumbo."[38]

A generation later, Lewis Mumford also stressed the role of play in human development. He held that man's true evolutionary achievement was utilizing his own mental resources and expressing his latent potential to fulfill his subjective desires. He held that the creation of symbolic networks of meaning in the service of the play instinct far outweighed the creation of tools. Tools were an important corrective for man, however, as he tended to utilize his mastery of the symbolic to substitute magical formulas for efficacious work.[39] Mumford considered man primarily not a nature-mastering animal but a self-mastering animal, whose ultimate creation of technics were mega-machines—huge hierarchical organizations with humans as components—that reached their zenith in the military-industrial complex of the Cold War. Mumford raises a pertinent point. Nonhuman species practice warfare, but man adds another critical element: the play instinct and the stimulant of irrational fantasy, which enable total war and genocide on an apocalyptic scale.

The analyses offered by Huizinga and Mumford in the years bracketing World War II echo ideas advanced by Clausewitz a century earlier. Clausewitz sought to identify the nature of war, and in so doing, introduced the dialectical concepts of "Absolute" and "Real" war. Absolute war is mythic war: war in its Platonic ideal, distilled to its pure essence of overkill and the drive to destroy. Absolute war never occurs, Clausewitz argues, because it is consistently repressed by Real war and its web of human affects, rituals, and rules—the constant presence of *politik*. In this dialectic, Real war exists chimerically, dynamically shifting. It is shaped by three distinct groups: the People, representing primordial violence, passion, and desire; the State, representing reason, order, and political control; and the Army, representing chance, uncertainty, and creativity. Seen in Clausewitzian terms, therefore, even World War II—the paradigmatic "total war" of the twentieth century—is an extreme form of Real war.

Clausewitz, Huizinga, and Mumford all identify an underlying determinism in the symbolic network of rituals and institutions that govern warfare. They thus stray into the realm of Lacan's Symbolic order.[40]

> If man comes to think about the Symbolic order, it is because he is first caught in it in his being. The illusion that he has formed this order through his consciousness stems from the fact that it is through the pathway of a specific gap in his imaginary relationship with his semblance that he has been able to enter into this order as a subject. But he has only been able to make this entrance by passing through the radical defile of speech, a genetic moment of which we have seen in a child's game.[41]

Lacan considered that passing through "the radical defile of speech," as in a game, into the symbolic order of language forever split the Subject from the unconscious, but the unconscious itself functions as a game, forming rebuslike meanings that become inscribed in our symbolic reality through play instinct or fantasy.

He considered war to be an indomitable fissure in the Symbolic, where language ends the game that "violence begins, and that violence reigns there already without us even provoking it. . . . Thus, if you bring war into it, you should at least be aware of its principles and realize that we misrecognize its limits when we do not understand it . . . as a particular form of human commerce."[42] War has always escaped the conscious control of man, and through play, has unconsciously structured our symbolic reality, accounting for the animal-hunt turned man-hunt, the dualism of religion and civilization, and the ultimate tool of total war: the monolith of the military-industrial complex.

We are, however, no longer in the epoch of total war. War has changed in form, and in our post–Cold War conflicts precision-guided weapons and advanced communication technologies have been used to plan for, simulate, and carry out what has been called "Nintendo Warfare." The technology created by the military-industrial complex—which made possible the nuclear brinks-manship of the Cold War (and subsequently cemented the military-industrial complex's place in the symbolic order)—also led directly to video games and the Internet. It is used to control the battlefields, structure news, and create propaganda; it links the horror and reality of war to the mass production that enables war fighting, and entertainment technology to the enjoyment of the commercial products of the military-industrial complex. The images of Real war on our television screens and the images of war-themed computer games and films are nearly indistinguishable—created by the same logics, technics, and technology. Moreover, the same logics and technologies have been utilized as part of war's wider ideological context, to mobilize public support for the declaration and escalation of a new form of war: "Virtuous War."[43] From bomb and missile strikes designed to induce "shock and awe," through counterinsurgency drone warfare, to commercial off-the-shelf games, game logics and technology are now employed as simulators and means of kinetic delivery. Together, they underpin a new understanding of "just war" in which high technology is used to train a new breed of soldiers who can fight war virtually, delivering necessary violence in a virtuous manner. This virtuous war of "smart technology" and precision weapons appears to the public as a war without the need for warriors or ideology: a war on behalf of the just and a panacea to the conundrums of warfare since September 11, 2001.[44]

Playing with Nazi zombies reflects our impulse to enjoy the technology of late-modernity, including the video game—itself a product of the nuclear arms race and perhaps the ultimate consumer product of the military-industrial complex.[45] Conjured by our desire to be free, and our instinct to play, the Nazi zombie is the revenant of our unconscious need to shed ideology and revel in

The convergence of real war and video-game war: footage from the gun cameras of an AC-130 gunship (left) and a scene from *Call of Duty: Modern Warfare* (right).

the *jouissance* of destruction. The message of these "war games" may be found in both the medium and the unconscious structure of the modality of play. The game itself is allegorical: Its survival space is the fantasy screen of our symbolic reality, repeatedly invaded by the ideological monstrous Other. The more Nazi zombies you kill, the more horrific they become—increasingly motivated and increasingly dangerous—until the game ends one way: with the self-replicating Nazi zombies reaching a zenith of frenetic action and the players inevitably destroyed. Narrative consistency must be drawn from the game through the completion of complex and irrational dreamlike puzzles. To traverse the battle-field of Nazi zombies is to indulge in the fantasy that we exist outside of Real war and the reality of the military-industrial complex, while at the same time investing psychologically in the nullity of their play.

Games featuring Nazi zombies reveal anxiety over virtuous war in a post-ideological age—war without ideology to conquer ideology—but they also reveal the surplus of enjoyment drawn from horrific proximity to the object of Freud's and Lacan's unconscious desire. They permit players to transgress ideology, and enjoy the duality of human nature. Playing *Nazi Zombies* is symptomatic of Subjects formed in the world of the game. We have simply come full circle as Huizinga thought: What started as the play instinct now defines our existence, and the Nazi zombies are just the messengers able to cross time, space, and realities. They allow players to enjoy the fantastical pre-ideological elements of Nazism, to enjoy the Real of the death drive, to destroy ideology from inside ideology itself, and to enjoy the unconscious structuring of war in the formation of the individual while keeping an ironic distance from its reality. The Nazi zombies themselves are itera-tive of the true Real war: that to defeat Nazism is to enjoy its fantasy. World War II ended in 1945, but fantasy is the war the Nazis will always win.

Alternatively, the appeal of playing *Nazi Zombies* may also be seen as an embodiment of mass psychosis: a refusal to address the authority of the Other as absolute, a refusal to be objectified or duped. It is an appeal symptomatic of the refusal to accept a reality that demands political responsibility—a reflection of a society addled by an ideology of free will driven by a ceaseless injunction to enjoy the sublime—knowingly subscribing to a fantasy that promises absolution. Nazi zombies continually breathe life into a fantasy that tenuously papers over our knowledge of the Real killing of innocents. When we transgress contempo-rary prohibitions on enjoying ideology, war is the thing that always returns to promote it; to play with Nazi zombies is to enjoy the surplus pro-fascist meaning hidden in the form and texture of the game—fantasy and the play instinct are the battlefield of ideology, and fantasy is a battle that Nazism will always win.

Reading Clausewitz through Lacan allows us to understand the "virtuous war" of the military-industrial complex as an extension of *politik* in our con-temporary context: an inchoate aggregate of the conscious and the unconscious, the rational and irrational, and a sublime, chimerical admixture of politics and policy that will always be in command of human nature. Such a reading also reveals that our anxieties over the ethics of virtuous war are inscribed in the play instinct and the fetishistic disavowal of the military-industrial complex's organization of enjoyment. It reveals insights into beliefs and practices underpinning society that we cynically refuse to acknowledge, but that organize our values and actions. This reading—linking warfare to fantasy, play, and the ideological supernatural—consolidates an interpretation that also underpins previous socioeconomic analysis of the Romeroesque zombie films, with their ideologically charged survival spaces and critiques of consumerism. Seen in this light, the popularity of Nazi zombies is a sign that the game of war has evolved and total war has been sublimated into something much more horrifying.

Notes

1. Lauro and Christie, "Introduction."
2. Loudermilk, "Eating 'Dawn' in the Dark."
3. Russell, *Book of the Dead*, 71–92.
4. Brougher, "Art and Nuclear Culture."
5. Masco, "Terror as Normality."
6. Ibid.
7. Literally, "world hurt"; figuratively, feelings of sadness and despair born of contemplating the gulf between the real world and an imagined ideal world.
8. Lacan, Seminar II (1954–1955).
9. The Clausewitz Homepage (http://clausewitz.com) is an extensive academic source on the writings of the military theorists and the surrounding debates.
10. Clausewitz, *On War. Politik* is a German conceptual term that defies translation and metaphor, and is a term that is usually simply translated as meaning "politics." However, it can be considered as a concept that contains both the meanings of politics and policy. Politics can be read as how power is delineated and distributed among a society and policy defined as the means by which power is maintained, gained, and sustained by members of that society.
11. Masco, "Terror as Normality."
12. Freud's concept involves the standard German negation of the word *heimlich*—homely, cozy, intimate, secure—and is thus suggested to infer its opposite. Implied within *heimlich* is also the concept of hidden away, concealed from the outside world, secretive, and by extension, what is hidden may be threatening, fearful, occult, dismal, ghastly—uncanny. However, the concept of the trauma and anxiety of the *unheimlich* is exactly at the point that the two terms come together, at the point of negation. What is homely and restful can in a sublime instant exist in its true guise of the uncanny that negates any barriers between subject/object, mind/body, spirit/matter, psychic/real, and so on (Dollar, "I Shall Be with You").

13. Lacan was an intellectual magpie. Utilizing the central tenets and concepts inherited from Freud, Lacan constructed a formidable, and notoriously complex, construct of anthropological and psychoanalytical concepts and paradigms to explore the subject's wants and mores. Of importance is both Lacan's and Clausewitz's reliance on topology in their constructs. Lacan constructed a paradigm of three registers, or orders—the Imaginary, the Symbolic, and the Real (ISR)—to explain the subject's relation to, and existence within, the human society and functions. Whereas Freud's model of the mind envisioned it as an interior space, Lacan's subject is far more abstract—it exists "out there" akin to a force field within a universal matrix (Bailly, *Lacan*, 80). The ISR registers are properties of this matrix and provide us with a framework that can be applied to our understandings of the functioning of all human creations and institutions (ibid.). Each register in the ISR paradigm is distinct but conjoined, creating a holistic conceptualization of the human psyche—if one register is removed or damaged, psychosis results (Bailly, *Lacan*, 89–90). In forming a sense of subjectivity the being enters the Imaginary order, the realm of the senses, in which our first false sense of identity is formed by the images of ourselves we see mirrored in others. The Imaginary is the register of the ego, with its obliviousness, alienation, love, and aggressiveness in the dual relationship with the other (ibid.). The Symbolic is the realm beyond language containing all that cannot be signified. It is the realm of human psyche before it becomes colonized by language and slips into the unconscious symbolic ordering of society. The Real is experienced as traumatic gaps in the symbolic. The drives, laughter, and abject terror all belong in the Real, as does the *thing* that always returns and the compulsion to repeat (Bailly, *Lacan*, 92–97).

14. The workings of this paradoxical libidinal economy can be witnessed in Nazi ideology and the Holocaust—the more Jews were exterminated and the fewer their numbers that remained, the more of a threat they were perceived to be to equilibrium of the Nazi state, their threat growing in proportion to their declining numbers (Žižek, *Looking Awry*, 5–6).

15. Žižek, *Looking Awry*, 5–6.

16. Kay, *Žižek*, 54.

17. Ibid.

18. Ibid.

19. Nervous Nick, tvtropes.org.

20. Goodrick-Clarke, *Black Sun*, 107–28.

21. Shirer, *Rise and Fall*, 41–43.

22. Miller, "UnDead of Winter."

23. Ironically, in German pagan mythology the gods themselves were overthrown by the forces of darkness (Shirer, *Rise and Fall*, 41–43).

24. Forster, "Motivation and Indoctrination," 239–41.

25. Van der Post, *Jung and the Story of Our Time*, 22–24.

26. Shirer, *Rise and Fall*, 979–91.

27. Miller, "UnDead of Winter."

28. Aarseth and Backe, "Ludic Zombies."

29. "Thirty-Eight Snub." *Breaking Bad*, season 4, episode 2. Written by George Mastras, directed by Michelle MacLaren. First broadcast July 24, 2011.

30. Bishop, "Dead Man Still Walking."

31. "Survive the Zombie hordes alone or cooperatively. Repel wave after wave of increasingly deadly Zombies in a number of locales. But be warned: there are more than just Zombies lurking these dark hallways . . ." (*Call of Duty: Black Ops* manual).

32. World War I and World War II led historian Arthur Marwick to coin the phrase "total war" to account for what he saw as arrival of a new age of destructive capacity for conflict that required nation-states to mobilize all components of their societies to secure victory. Marwick considered that war could be deemed "total" when it was envisioned as an ideological and cultural conflict between fully mobilized nations whose war aims were national-racial survival through the defeat and subjugation of their enemies. Marwick's principle examined the effects and affects of total war as it pertained to four dimensions of societal change and upheaval. The first dimension was the new "destructive and disruptive" capacity of war that necessitates rebuilding and reconstruction of society—sometimes creating a better society than the previous incarnation. The second dimension explores the "test" of conflict directly on military institutions and their related elements of society such as the economy and politics regarding their suitability and survivability. The third is the "participation dimension"; war creates conditions that require or allow previously excluded members of society to finally participate in previously prohibited activities. The fourth and final dimension implements a deep "psychological impact" that leads to the members of a society acting on the trauma and anxiety caused by the conflict to stimulate the creation of something new (Marwick, "Impact of the First World War"; Ishizu, "Total War and Social Changes"). In Marwick's terms, by the end of World War II, war was indeed total in size and scope.

33. Clausewitz, *On War*.

34. Huizinga, *Homo Ludens*.

35. The notion *Homo faber*—"man the maker"—had been so dominant that when the first Paleolithic cave paintings had been discovered in 1879 they were dismissed out of hand as a hoax. Mumford, *Myth of the Machine*, 7–9.

36. These concepts and rituals colonize our language, as ever since words have existed for fighting and playing, war has been referred to as a game—the two concepts seemingly blending absolutely in the history of civilizations. This blending goes beyond metaphor; both war and play escape absolute definition—both are concepts language struggles to define.

37. Huizinga, *Homo Ludens*, 90.

38. Ibid., 197–203.

39. Mumford, *Myth of the Machine*, 8–9.

40. Bailly, *Lacan*, 93–97.

41. Lacan, *Ecrits*, 40.

42. Ibid., 313.

43. Der Derian, *Virtuous War*.

44. Singer, *Wired for War*.

45. The military-industrial complex is undergoing something of an involuntary revolution. The very technology that powers computers and the software that creates computer games were developed as part of the nuclear weapons programs of the 1960s. These technologies then trickled down into the entertainment industries. However, since the 1990s, the technology and intellectual output of the entertainment sector has far

outstripped that of the military sector, and a reverse process is now in operation. Products and technics from the games industry are being weaponized, and fuel a new epoch of war fighting and a new era of "smart weapons." For a comprehensive breakdown on the relationship between entertainment and the military-industrial complex, see Chaplin and Ruby, *Smart Bomb*; Halter, *From Sun Tzu to XBox*; Turse, *The Complex*; Der Derian, *Virtuous War*.

Bibliography

Aarseth, Espen, and Hans-Joachim Backe. "Ludic Zombies: An Examination of Zombieism in Games." *The Digital Games Research Association 2013: DeFragging Games Studies*. DiGRA, 2013.

Bailly, Lionel. *Lacan: A Beginners Guide*. London: One World Publications, 2009.

Bishop, Kyle. "Dead Man Still Walking: Explaining the Zombie Renaissance." *Journal of Popular Film and Television* 37, no. 1 (2009): 16–25.

Brougher, Kerry. "Art and Nuclear Culture." *Bulletin of the Atomic Scientists* 69, no. 6 (2013): 11–18.

Chaplin, Heather, and Aaron Ruby. *Smart Bomb: The Quest for Art, Entertainment, and Big Bucks in the Video Game Revolution*. Chapel Hill, NC: Algonquin Books, 2005.

Clausewitz, Carl von. *On War*. Edited by Micheal Howard and Peter Paret. Translated by Micheal Howard and Peter Paret. 1832. Reprint London: Everyman's Library, 1993.

Der Derian, James. *Virtuous War*. 2nd edition. London: Routledge, 2009.

Dollar, Mladen. "'I Shall Be with You on Your Wedding-Night': Lacan and the Uncanny." *Rendering the Real* 58 (Autumn 1991): 5–23.

Fink, Bruce. *Lacan to the Letter: Reading Ecrits Closely*. London: University of Minnesota Press, 2004.

Forster, Jurgen. "Motivation and Indoctrination in the Wehrmacht, 1939–1945." In *Time to Kill: The Soldier's Experience of War in the West 1939–1945*, edited by Paul Addison and Angus Calder, 263–73. London: Pimlico, 1997.

Freud, Sigmund. *The Uncanny*. 1919. Reprint London: Hogarth Press, 1955.

Goodrick-Clarke, Nicholas. *Black Sun: Ayran Cults, Esoteric Nazism and the Politics of Identity*. London: New York University Press, 2003.

Halter, Ed. *From Sun Tzu to XBox: War and Video Games*. New York: Thunder's Mouth Press, 2006.

Huizinga, Johan. *Homo Ludens: A Study of the Play-Element in Culture*. London: Routledge & Kegan Paul, 1949.

Ishizu, Tomoyuki. "Total War and Social Changes: With a Focus on Arthur Marwick's Perspective on War." *The National Institute for Defence Studies*. 2014. http://www.nids.go.jp/english/event/forum/pdf/2011/09.pdf.

Kay, Sarah. *Žižek: A Critical Introduction*. Cambridge: Polity Press, 2003.

Lacan, Jacques. *Ecrits*. Edited and translated by Bruce Fink. London: Norton, 2006.

———. *The Seminar of Jacques Lacan: Book 2: The Ego in Freud's Theory and in the Technique of Psychoanalysis 1954–1955*. New York: Cambridge University Press, 1988.

Lauro, Sarah Juliet, and Deborah Christie. "Introduction." In *Better Off Dead: The Evolution of the Zombie as Post-Human*, edited by Deborah Christie and Sarah Juliet Lauro, 1–4. New York: Fordham University Press, 2011.

Loudermilk, A. "Eating 'Dawn' in the Dark: Zombie Desire and Commodified Identity in George A. Romero's '*Dawn of the Dead*.'" *Journal of Consumer Culture* 3, no. 1 (2003): 83–108.

Marwick, Arthur. "The Impact of the First World War on British Society." *Journal of Contemporary History* 3, no. 1 (1968): 51–63.

Masco, Joseph P. "Terror as Normality." *Bulletin of the Atomic Scientists* 69, no. 6 (2013): 26–32.

Miller, Cynthia J. "In the UnDead of Winter: Humor and the Horrific in *Dead Snow*." In *Welcome to the Slaughterhouse*, edited by Johnson Cheu and John Dowell. Lanham, MD: Rowman & Littlefield, forthcoming.

Mumford, Lewis. *The Myth of the Machine: Technics and Human Development*. New York: Harcourt Brace Jovanovich, 1967.

Nervous Nick. "Nazi Zombies." tvtropes.org. http://tvtropes.org/pmwiki/pmwiki.php/VideoGame/NaziZombies?from=Main.NaziZombies.

Russell, Jamie. *Book of the Dead: The Complete History of Zombie Cinema*. Surrey, UK: FAB Press, 2007.

Shirer, William L. *The Rise and Fall of the Third Reich*. New York: Simon & Schuster, 1960.

Singer, P. W. *Wired for War: The Robotics Revolution and Conflict in the 21st Century*. London: Penguin, 2010.

Turse, Nick. *The Complex: How the Military Invades Our Everyday Lives*. London: Faber & Faber, 2008.

Van der Post, Laurens. *Jung and the Story of Our Time*. London: Penguin, 1988.

Žižek, Slavoj. *Looking Awry: An Introduction to Jacques Lacan through Popular Culture*. London: MIT Press, 1991.

Part IV

LEGACIES
AND MEMORIES

CHAPTER 14

"Strange Things Happen in a War-Torn Land"

CAT DEMONS, SAMURAI, VICTIMS' VENGEANCE, AND THE SOCIAL COSTS OF WAR IN KANETO SHINDO'S *KURONEKO* (1968)

Thomas Prasch

Not a word is spoken for over ten minutes at the start of Kaneto Shindo's *Kuroneko*,[1] and yet by the time a samurai breaks the spell by speaking, the story's whole setup has been established. After an already eerie opening credit sequence—savage drumbeats, and then a brief wisp of Hitchcockian violin, accompany brushstroked characters superimposed over images of a dark, fog-ridden bamboo grove, rendered all the more eerie by being filmed (like the rest of the movie) in high-contrast black and white—the film opens on a deceptively tranquil scene: a thatched-roof hut set by a small creek beside a grove of tall trees, the only sound the chirping of crickets. Sixteen samurai silently emerge from the grove, falling upon the creek to drink water—their loud slurping supplants the cricket chirps on the sound track—before entering the hut. There, two women—a mother and her daughter-in-law, we later learn, Yone and Shige, the son/husband absent because conscripted for the war—sit over the meal they have prepared. The samurai ruthlessly set upon the food first, and then the women, in a savage scene of gang rape and animalistic eating, loud chewing as dominant on the sound track as the women's cries, much of the sequence focusing on close-ups of the samurais' faces as they watch the lurid attacks before them while continuing crudely to shovel food into their mouths. The camera retreats to the outside view, the crickets' chirps again the only sound, as the samurai exit the hut, and then retreat into the grove as smoke billows from the doorway (open, since on their way out one of the samurai tears the door off). The next scene shows the charred remains of the hut, the two women's dead bodies—badly burned in places, but surprisingly intact—in the middle of the still smoldering square of the hut's foundations. A black cat, meowing, approaches the bodies and licks at the blood on their necks.

Then it is night, at Rajoman Gate; a black cat meows from atop the wooden structure. A lone samurai approaches, nodding off in the saddle as his horse trots

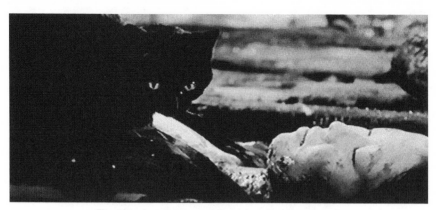

The black cat laps up the blood of the dead.

through the darkness. He does not see a woman, ghost-white as a wisp of smog, somersault over his horse, but she then appears on the road before him. It is Yone, looking rather pale but alive, dressed and made up like an aristocratic woman. He speaks the film's first words: "Who are you? You must be a ghost to be wandering alone so late at night."[2] Good instincts do not prevent him from being enticed to take the mystery woman through the grove to her home, and to his doom.

Shindo's haunting eroticized horror film weaves together a tragic love story, a demon tale drawn from Japanese folklore, and film techniques lifted from both popular horror/action film genres and Kabuki/Noh theater traditions to create a powerful antiwar saga. The antiwar messages resonate with multiple histories: first, with a distant Japanese past, that of the film's actual historical setting, when the nation stood on the verge of the collapse of Heian imperial rule and the descent into warrior-dominated Japanese feudalism; second, certainly for Japanese audiences, at least, with more recent national history, that earlier imperial collapse echoing with the demotion of the emperor at the end of World War II (and echoing as well sentiments expressed elsewhere in Shindo's oeuvre about the human costs of that war); and third, the then-current antiwar spirit of the Vietnam era, with issues in the contemporary world displaced into the past (working, in that sense, much like Anglo-American films of the period such as *M*A*S*H* [1970], *Oh! What a Lovely War* [1969], *Johnny Got His Gun* [1971], *How I Won the War* [1967], or *The Long Day's Dying* [1968], in which opposition to the Vietnam war plays out against treatments of earlier conflicts). Central to the film's antiwar message are, first, a fundamental inversion of conventions for depicting the samurai, reversing their traditionally heroic representation to turn them into animalistic marauders, and, second, the deployment of the demon-cat motif of Japanese folklore to enable the common people (and, significantly, women commoners at that) to take their vengeance on the upper classes for the depredations they suffer in war. *Kuroneko*'s historical setting has, however, been widely misunderstood, and the film's worldwide distribution was significantly delayed and limited. Critical reception at the time of its release reflected these limitations,[3] and was lukewarm at best.[4] The timing of the distribution connects in clear ways to the limited appreciation of the film's antiwar message, but that message is also undermined by the failure to appreciate the significance of the historical setting and the way it echoes forward through time.

Origins and Influences

Kuroneko draws on both high and low culture for its sources. On the low side, it follows on an established subgenre of Japanese horror films with folkloric roots. As Zvika Serper notes: "*Kuroneko* appears at first glance to be merely a good example of *kaibyō eiga*, a very popular genre in the 1950s and 1960s" featuring "monstrous cats," either as a being returned in cat form to take vengeance or as a "monstrous cat that can transform itself into a demonic human being—a vampire, a Western-imported extreme manifestation of a real demonic creature that was mixed with Japanese ghost-story elements."[5] Maitland McDonagh notes the prevalence of cat spirits in Japanese folklore, dividing them between the benevolent *manekineko* and the more sinister *bakeneko*. Though "a kissing cousin to the shape-shifting fox (*kitsune*) and the sly, mischievous *tanuki*," McDonagh notes that "the fact that *bakeneko* often eat the person whose form they've taken suggests they're less amusing and more alarming than their fellow shape-shifters."[6] At least ten different Japanese "ghost cat movies" (*kaibyo*) were released between 1937 and 1960, and these in turn drew upon earlier silent versions and the Kabuki sources for the tales.[7]

But higher culture figures into the mix as well. Serper notes that *Kuroneko* also "is taken from traditional literary sources. One is an episode from *Heike monogatari* (early thirteenth to late fourteenth century), which tells the story of Watanabe-no-Tsuna who meets a beautiful woman on a bridge and accompanies her on her way. While crossing the river she transforms into a demon, which he fights, using a famous sword, and slashes off one of its arms. . . . The other source is a story from *Konjaku monogatari* (compiled by about 1120) about a demon that inhabits the Rashōman Gate. . . . Shindo himself mentions these two traditional literary sources in his production notes."[8] Even here, Shindo mixes his cultural levels: The former source deals with the adventures of samurai warriors, while the latter collects a more diverse range of popular stories (both Buddhist and secular).[9]

These tales, in turn, found their way into Noh and Kabuki theater as well as into Japanese visual arts. Serper, for example, mentions Kanze Kojirō Nobumitsu's Noh play *Rashōman* (fifteenth to sixteenth century) and Kawatake

Mokuami's Kabuki sequel to it, *Ibaraki* (1883).[10] C. Andrew Gerstle also discusses the translation of tales of Raiko into Kabuki traditions, focusing in particular on the career of Chikamatus Monzaemon (1653–1725).[11] One tale incorporated into the film, samurai Raiko's battle with the demon Shuten Doji (or "Drunken Demon"), has had, Noriko T. Reider notes, multiple incarnations as oral tale, literary story, and picture scroll, with extant versions dating back to the Muramachi Period (1392–1573).[12] Haruo Shirane points out that the popularity of the tale ensured its adaptation across a range of genres, from printed scrolls and picture books to Noh, puppet, and Kabuki staged versions.[13] Raiko's exploits even figured into later Tokugawa political cartoons, as Peter Duus has shown.[14] Such tales worked across a range of forms, from high to popular culture. Masako Nakagawa Graham, for example, analyzes the transmission of medieval tales about Raiko and his quartet of servants translated into puppet plays in the 1660s; indeed, Graham notes, "Only a puppet can convincingly execute the scenes of Yank Kuei-fei's spirit soaring from her body in the form of a bird and Kin Shōtan's severed head flying through the air with a message in its mouth."[15] Those sixteenth-century audiences, clearly, had not seen movies yet. But Japanese filmmakers other than Shindo had read, or seen, variations of the tales; Jay Novak notes, for example, that Akira Kurosawa's *Rashoman* (1950) has roots in *Heike monagatari* as well.[16]

The film's limited release outside Japan necessitates a brief summary of the story. After the lone samurai's opening lines, Yone explains that she had been "at Lord Fujiwara's mansion"—a story that reaffirms the (false) aristocratic marker of her dress—"but I'm afraid of that grove ahead" given the bandits that frequent the night. To the samurai's query, "So what if I'm a bandit myself?" Yone responds with coquettish compliments: "Such a fine samurai could not be a bandit. I assumed you were one of the renowned vassals of the illustrious warrior Raiko." Flattery works its magic; the samurai accompanies her across the grove. Following the woman to her house—a strikingly theatrical setting: a series of wooden platforms, unwalled, but divided by sheer fabric and by the surrounding shoots of bamboo,[17] spot lighting bringing up key areas, following Kabuki conventions[18]—the samurai is invited in, meets the mother, and is plied with sake. The conversation develops the backstory (as the mother tells of her son taken off to the war, the samurai assures her: "I'm sure he's a fine samurai somewhere by now"), speaks to the conditions in the nation ("Even cats are starving these days," the samurai notes), and develops the mood of eeriness ("Strange things happen in a war-torn land," the samurai tells the women: "Hail fell this summer. Then it suddenly grew so hot that birds fell from the sky," and yet he does not quite process the mystery right before him: a woman whose black hair flicks like a cat's tail, whose arm momentarily seems furred). In the end, the mother leaves the two alone, as fog rolls over the platforms. She performs a dance drawn from Noh theater in an adjacent part of the house—Serper notes: "Shindo's diary refers to [the dance] as *koroshi no mai* (the [Noh] dance of murder)"[19]—as the daughter leads the warrior to her bed, kissing him several times before biting into his neck. In the morning, his throat-slashed body lies in the charred ruins of the old hut.

The samurai killings are ritually repeated over subsequent nights, following largely the same pattern, presented in more compressed form: woman at the gate, trip across the grove, seduction and death in the house on the other side. Only the fourth samurai victim suspects something amiss, cued in by the demonic reflection of Yone in a puddle; he draws his sword to kill her, but she leaps high into the bamboo trees[20] and then drops onto him to make her kill. In the later sequences, conversation becomes minimal; the killings are accompanied by a haunted soft drumbeat, with an occasional cat's meow. The murders lead the emperor to summon his chief samurai, Raiko Minamoto, and order him to deal with the problem: "Only one who takes pride in his martial prowess may be called 'leader of the samurais.' As things stand, this ghost could appear in the palace at any moment. I cannot sleep peacefully at night." Although Raiko is contemptuous of the emperor's fears later among his samurai—"He says to me in that exalted voice, 'I cannot sleep peacefully at night.' Shit. Who's running all over the country fighting his wars? Me, Raiko Minamoto. The courtiers kick balls around and play board games"—when in the presence of the emperor, Raiko's sweat puddles the ground as he bows.

The scene shifts to a savage battle fought amid muddy reeds between a young man (the conscripted son, we will learn) and a larger, ferocious, club-wielding foe whom he succeeds in killing before riding back to the imperial court (at one point riding against a huge sun that recalls the imperial flag). Ragged, covered in mud—the court women giggle at his appearance—he stands before Raiko bearing his enemy's head. "You took Sunehiko the Bear's head?" He did. "And my 2,000 men?" Raiko asks. "They all died. And all the enemy," the warrior explains. Facing his final foe, he recounts: "He asked me to identify myself, but I don't have a battle name yet. . . . I was born in a house in a grove, so I said 'Gintoki of the Grove.'" Raiko elevates him to the rank of samurai, making him the fifth of his "trusted retainers," and—ritually bathed and clad in samurai finery—he is sent off to carry out a new mission: to deal with the "monster that's been feasting of the necks of my samurai and exterminate it." The order sets up the conflict that will carry the movie's final movement, a matter of divided loyalties shaping a tragic love story.

Both Zvika Serper and Colette Balmain define the conflict at the heart of the movie's final movement as a "*giri-ninjo* conflict," although they define the terms somewhat differently. Serper sees *giri* as "the obligation to act according to reciprocal relations with particular people with whom the individual has certain

Gintoki delivers the head of the enemy to Raiko.

social relations," and *ninjo* as "natural inclination."[21] Balmain says of *giri* that it "requires obedience to one's superiors, necessitating that he defeat the women," while *ninjo* is "compassion, emotion and love."[22] While these interpretations frame the film in terms of traditional Japanese categories, the conflict can also be viewed more simply and universally: both Gintoki and the women have conflicting demands placed on them once he takes Raiko's orders. For Gintoki, perhaps most simply, the orders given by his commander (and the man responsible for his social advancement) conflict with his love for his wife and mother (ameliorated somewhat, perhaps, by the fact that the two are dead). The women share familial bonds with the son/husband, but for them his elevation to the rank of samurai complicates things. As Shige explains to him: "I am bound by a vow and cannot tell you who or what we are. We promised the god of evil, the god of those who return from the netherworld to right past wrongs. We promised to get revenge by drinking blood. . . . To drink the blood of samurai. To drink the blood of every last samurai in the world. You too are samurai." Who they are is not very complicated: They may not be able to tell him, but he recognizes them. The vow is another matter.

As Gintoki returns night after night to the haunted house at the edge of the grove, each of the three characters deals with the conflict differently. Yone chooses self-sacrifice, as Shige explains when, on the eighth night, Gintoki returns to find her gone: "She was given seven days to see you and make love to you. Please count the days for yourself. Last night was the seventh. She shortened her life to seven days so that she could pledge her love to you. . . . Instead of drinking the blood of hateful samurai, she chose to love you and be banished to hell." In Gintoki's case, while Yone awaits him—or perhaps while he makes love to her nightly, declaring on their last night together, "Shige I want to devour you! I want to chew you up and consume you"—he finds himself unable to act. With her gone, and under more direct orders from Raiko ("If you let this one get away as well, I'll kill you. On my honor as a man, I will kill you"), he returns to the grove, apparently ready to face the remaining demon, his mother. She entices him with a promise of her own sacrifice: "My plan was to see you once more and then follow her to hell. . . . Please come to my abode. You can read a sutra to me. Then I can rest in peace. Please. I have chosen a sacred sutra. If you read it to me, my hatred will be extinguished." But when he sees her demon reflection in a puddle, he draws his sword and, although failing to kill her—she can leap as high as her ghost daughter—he slices off her arm. When she demands its return—because "My arm is my weapon. Without it I cannot drink the blood of samurai"—he demands to know: "Mother, will you wander as a vengeful ghost forever?" She assures him she will, "because of my hatred for samurai, for all warring samurai."

He brings the arm, one more trophy, to Raiko, and he and it are taken to a temple for a period of ritual cleansing. His mother, in the guise of a seer and claiming the authority of the emperor, convinces him to let her in, reclaiming her arm in one final battle. He chases her back to the house and dies striking at the empty air with his sword. In the film's closing scene, his body, in the charred hut's ruins, is blanketed by a new fall of snow.

The demon mother gets her severed arm back.

Locating the Story:
Understanding Time and Place

For Shindo, *Kuroneko* might seem familiar territory; he had explored a similar story four years before, in *Onibaba* (1964). There, as in *Kuroneko*, two peasant women, a mother and her widowed daughter-in-law (living, however, not ghosts), prey on samurai, using sex and sake as enticement. *Onibaba* similarly combines eroticism with social critique, portraying a nation devastated by war (the women's violence seems, in the context of the film, justified as a necessity to which they are driven by wartime impoverishment). It also has a similar setting, an isolated house (surrounded, however, by reeds rather than bamboo), and it similarly makes use of Kabuki and Noh conventions in its style (with a particularly heavy use, in the earlier film, of Noh masks). Like the later film, *Onibaba* also features a supernatural element, although it only comes into play at the film's end: When the mother seeks to end an affair the daughter-in-law is having with a neighboring farmer, she dons a Noh demon mask to scare her, but the mask sticks; when it is finally hammered off, the mother has the leprous face of the demon. As one reviewer of *Kuroneko* has insisted, however: "Make no mistake, though, this is no *Onibaba* appendage or patchwork melding."[23] The court politics and family crisis at the center of *Kuroneko*'s story distinguish it from its predecessor.[24] *Onibaba* differs from the later film in another respect as well: It was more widely distributed and reviewed at the time of its release, and has received broader critical attention since then.

The key to interpreting *Kuroneko*'s story and Shindo's methods in relating it lies above all else in its historical location, and yet that has presented a significant difficulty for critics. Most commentators, it must be noted, do not bother fixing the date; the film takes place in some undesignated samurai-era war-torn past. But when they try to get more specific, critics have been strikingly off base. "The Mark of the Cat," Maitland McDonagh's essay in the brochure accompanying the Criterion DVD release (2011), simply gets it wrong, asserting that the film is "set during Japan's Sengoku (or Warring States) period, some 150 years—from roughly the mid-fifteenth century to the early seventeenth century—of bloody conflict among regional oligarchs."[25] Balmain similarly claims: "*Kuroneko* is set during the Sengoku Period, also known as the 'Warring States Period,' which lasted from the Ōnin War (1467–1477) until the unification of the country by the Shogun Tokugawa Ieyasu in 1615."[26] But that is off by about five centuries.

That historical setting is belied by the leading samurai figure named in the film. Raiko Minamoto, also known as Yorimitsu, thrived much earlier, living from 948–1021. Raiko served the Fujiwara, the dominant military family of the era, and held multiple governorships. He is most famous in lore, as noted above, for his defeat of the monster Shuten Doji, or "Drunken Boy," on Mount Oe, and for being served by four retainers (the records neglect Gintoki), dubbed the Four Golden Kings, who garnered their own legendary tales.[27] The earlier period matters in part because it was the samurai of this era that became the focus of the legendary tales—with all their supernaturalism and magic, and their rich mix of Shinto and Buddhist elements—of the late Heian and Kamekura era, those sources upon which first Noh and Kabuki theater, and then Shindo (and other Japanese directors), drew. The later era was more fixed in traditional historiography, with far fewer legends accruing.

The earlier setting matters most, however, precisely because of what was at stake in the closing years of the Heian period: the collapse of effective imperial rule. The rise of the samurai warrior class undermined the authority of a central state, with two principal warrior clans, the Minamoto and the Taira, coming to dominate the military picture, as rebelliond begun.[28] The rise of the samurai coincided, over the course of a century or so,s against central authority became increasingly prevalent by the tenth century. Tensions would eventually precipitate full-scale war between the two clans in the twelfth-century Gempei War; by that time, the warriors had supplanted the effective political power of the emperor, and the era of Japanese feudalism ha with the demolition of a unified Japan, increased levels of endemic warfare and other violence (bandits benefiting from the weakening of central authority, for example), and the descent into fractured warlord states.

This understanding of the negative dynamics of the transition from Heian to feudal Japan deeply informs Shindo's work, and most dramatically marks its difference from the traditional forms he used as sources. As Japanese critic Tadao Sato notes: "Long ago there was a samurai named Raiko Minamoto. This was when the samurai class system was newly established in Japan. . . . Among Japanese legends, they're extraordinary, like Kabuki heroes, amazing heroes from another time. But in Shindo's films, they're depicted as a bunch of boorish oafs. That was typical of his representation of samurai."[29] This was consistent with Shindo's political position. As he told Joan Mellen: "My mind was always on the commoners, not on the lords, politicians, or anyone of name and fame. I wanted to convey the lives of down-to-earth people. . . . My eyes, or rather the camera's eye, is fixed to view the world from the very lowest level of society. . . . If you have to look at society through the eyes of those placed on its bottom level, you cannot escape the fact that you must experience and perceive everything with a sense of the political struggle between classes. This sets the general political background of the film."[30] When Mellen asked, "Does any character in *Kuroneko* represent the director?" Shindo

Seducing samurai with sake.

answered: "My sympathies are expressed through the peasant mother."[31] Shindo places himself on the side of the demons drinking samurai blood.

Interestingly, it is the samurai themselves who provide the fullest account of their depredations, bragging about their glorious wars. In the sake-fueled scene with the first samurai victim, the mother does note their own privations: "In this age of war, we must sow crops ourselves to keep from starving," but their son "was taken away, plow still in his hand." But the samurai's response is more revealing: "He was lucky to be taken off to war. It's a samurai's world now. The court nobles are incapable of warfare, so samurai are poised to rule the land. Even the emperor will answer to our master Raiko one day."

Raiko, not surprisingly, shares this view. When Gintoki dares to suggest to Raiko a more negative view of war—"Noblemen may benefit, but the farmers are forced to flee and often starve and die," Raiko's answer embodies a sort of medieval social Darwinism: "The weak ones do. The weak always starve." The ethos of the warrior informs his self-image. Meanwhile, the lower orders feel the brunt of the wars. When Gintoki goes searching for his mother and wife only to find the burned shell that was once his home, the peasant Jimbei tells him: "It was last summer. Kyoto burned for three days and three nights. Conquerors and conquered alike set homes on fire. War sends everything up in flames." Among the poor, it can be noted, women suffer most.

In Raiko's own case, it can also be noted, triumphs over supernatural foes played no part in his rise to power. Raiko debunks his own most popular legend, that of his conquest of the Shuten Doji: "They once said there was a demon on Mount Oe, so I went to stop it on the emperor's orders. There are no such things as demons. It turned out to be the bandit Shuten Doji. There's no glory in killing a bandit, so I said it was a demon." Raiko's own legends are unmasked as state propaganda, but nothing in the film mitigates the reality of the demon Gintoki struggles with.

Demons Are Not Only in the Past

Shindo's historical setting echoes forward as well. As he put it to Mellen, explaining his choice of historical material: "We select certain old stories which have sufficient modern application. . . . When I want to dissect a modern problem, I actually find many similar problems in ancient days. In fact, without the many outer layers of so-called modern civilization, the themes I find in old stories are more clear-cut. . . . By using a comprehensible social structure such as we had in the past, it is much easier for me to convey or recreate modern situations." The past informs the present in Shindo's work.

The first range of echoes suggested by such historical understanding is the Japanese experience of World War II. Shindo was a veteran himself, and, Ronald Bergen recalled: "In 1943, during the Second World War, he was drafted into the Japanese army. Of the 100-strong squad with which he was serving, 94 were killed, something that haunted him for the rest of his life."[32] He was also a native of the city of Hiroshima. Early in his career, Shindo had broken boundaries to treat survivors of the atomic bomb in *Children of Hiroshima* (1951) and then to attack the problems produced by American nuclear tests in the Pacific in *Lucky Dragon No. 5* (1959). *Kuroneko*'s setting—a time when samurai become the dominant force, leading to wars that will lead to the downfall of imperial power—clearly echoes this later era as well.

It resonates, too, with the then-contemporary war in Vietnam. Japan officially supported the American war, and provided bases for US naval and air operations; its businesses, too, benefitted enormously from a war-profit-driven boom. At the same time, by the mid-1960s, Japan had developed a strong antiwar movement, New Leftist in its methods and its ideological critique of American imperialism, closely coordinated in interesting ways with emergent feminism, and dovetailing with local sites of political resistance (especially focused on US occupation of Okinawa) and broader antiwar issues (especially embodied, unsurprisingly in Japan, in antinuclear activism).[33] Shindo, a self-declared socialist (if not quite Marxist),[34] engaged with developing history from below, expressing a recurrent antiwar theme throughout his career while siding with the victims of war, and feminist in his sensibilities,[35] can be expected to side with the movement. Jasper Sharp argues that an anti-Vietnam argument was already explicit in *Onibaba*, although the film also demonstrated for Sharp the deepening "mismatch between Japanese filmmakers' intended meanings and the interpretations of overseas audiences": "Kaneto Shindo (one of contemporary Japan's most steadfastly independent filmmakers) intended a critique of Japan's role as passive beneficiary to America's wars against communism in Korea and Vietnam. But, in America, the film was marketed as a straight horror and advertised in *Variety* as 'the most nude, sexiest pic to be unveiled in New York so far.'"[36] Sharp also highlights the antiwar themes in Shindo's 1970 film *Live Today, Die Tomorrow* ("Hadaka no Jukyusai"), a film about a serial killer who uses a gun stolen from a US naval base to slay his victim and that features several sympathetic scenes of antiwar demonstrators.[37] In *Kuroneko*, the highlighting of peasant victims of war, the disequilibrium of power and technology between the ravaging military and the local people, and even the battle fought among the muddy reeds suggest quite deliberate evocations of Vietnam.

What holds together the three levels of historical argument, the simultaneous engagement with deep past, recent history, and current events, is the common thread: the emphatic insistence that we see the deep human cost of war, and the deep sympathy the director holds for its lowliest victims. Shindo's deliberately conceptualized history-from-below, informed by his personal history, brings the multiple levels of historical understanding together, while simultaneously universalizing it: making it the story of all wars in all times. This makes the failure of overseas audiences to understand the message all the more unfortunate.

Why that disconnect? Two reasons suggest themselves, one formal, one purely accidental. The formal reason has to do with Shindo's deep roots in Japanese theater traditions. It was by reading stage plays, he recalls, that he taught himself to write films,[38] and the theater's conventions suffuse his work. Beyond, as noted above, the Noh/Kabuki influences on his staging, lighting, and use of dances and masks, his acting company was, as Tadao Sato notes, largely drawn from Kabuki companies and employed acting styles drawn from the Kabuki repertoire.[39] Such methods make the product more difficult to export outside Japan; where more naturalistic acting is the norm, the tendency will be to see the Japanese style as melodramatic or generic. Thus non-Japanese audiences tend to see only the horror and miss the social comment, and the effect is amplified by the relative ignorance of Japanese history outside of the nation (witness the film's misdating as a case in point). Similarly, by anchoring his critique on a distant Japanese past with which foreign audiences are less familiar, the critical analysis (especially Shindo's debunking of samurai heroics) is far more likely to be lost.

The accidental reason is also an ironic one: The antiwar movement itself derailed Shindo's film, preventing it from being more widely and promptly seen at a time when its antiwar message might better have been received (and when, as noted above, war films often carried strong antiwar inflections, employing past conflicts to resonate with Vietnam). As Maitland McDonagh writes, answering the question about *Kuroneko*'s relative neglect: "The answer is partly sheer bad luck. Like *Kwaidan*, *Kuroneko* went to the Cannes Film Festival, but it arrived in 1968, the year François Truffaut, Jean-Luc Godard, and Louis Malle spearheaded a successful effort to shut the festival down," and *Kuroneko* was not seen as a result. McDonagh argues: "Without that validation, *Kuroneko* opened briefly in New York six years later, sans fanfare, and to withering critical indifference."[40] McDonagh gets the year wrong (again)—the film opened in New York in 1971—but the basic story is right.[41]

In this matter, at least, we should not let Truffaut and Godard have the last word: *Kuroneko* deserves to be seen. Its rich blend of traditional elements, of horror and melodrama and political commentary, of Kabuki and folklore and modern politics, all framed in such deeply haunting scenes, well repays the time taken to understand the sources of its vision. And Shindo's passionate commitment to the commoner and to war-aggrieved women provides a deep universal ground for appreciating the work. Bring on the blood-drinking black cats.

Notes

1. Originally released in Japan in 1968 as *Yabu no naka no kuroneko* ("Black Cat of the Grove"); the shortened title *Kuroneko* (just "Black Cat") came with its American release in 1971.

2. Throughout, this essay draws on the subtitling of the 2011 Criterion DVD release of the film for quotations.

3. Indeed, I have found precisely one review corresponding to its brief 1971 New York opening: A. H. Weiler's four-paragraph (and eight-sentence) summary in the *New York Times*. See "The Screen: 'Kuroneko,' a Mystical Story from Japan," *New York Times*, 28 May 1971, at nytimes.com. Its brief rerelease in 2010, and the subsequent Criterion DVD release in 2011, garnered significantly more critical attention, but by then its specific antiwar message was decidedly less noticed than it might have been four decades before.

4. I know of only two significant at-length critical treatments of the film: Serper, "Shindō Kaneto's Films *Kuroneko* and *Onibaba*" (the logic for Serper's pairing will become clear in time), a close consideration of Shindo's sources and his uses of Kabuki/Noh conventions; and Balmain, *Introduction to Japanese Horror Film*, an analysis primarily focused on the demonic feminine in Shindo's film. The film receives more cursory treatment in, among others: Hand, "Aesthetics of Cruelty," 24, and Richie, *Hundred Years*, 151. Surprisingly, it merits only a passing reference—in a paragraph-long discussion of Shindo's use of his wife Otowa Nobuko as a leading lady—in Desser, *Eros Plus Massacre*, 122.

5. Serper, "Shindō Kaneto's Films," 234.

6. Maitland McDonagh, "The Mark of the Cat," essay accompanying the Criterion DVD release of *Kuroneko* (2011), 10. For more, see Fiona, "'Here Kitty, Kitty...' Obake Series: Bakeneko" at http://www.tofugu.com/2012/07/19/obake-series-bakeneko/ (*obake* being, the site notes, the "blanket term for the shapeshifters of Japanese folklore").

7. "Ghost Cat Movies," *Weird Wild Realm*, http://www.weirdwildrealm.com/f-kaibyo.html; see also the site's discussion of *Kuroneko* at http://www.weirdwildrealm.com/f-kuroneko.html.

8. Serper, "Shindō Kaneto's Films," 235.

9. Although both collections feature supernatural tales, there are more, and creepier ones in the more popular collection. Algernon Bertram Redesdale's translation of sixty-two tales (from over one thousand in the anthology) includes one clear example of a *bakeneko* tale (although not one directly employed as a source by Shindo): "The Vampire Cat of Nabeshima."

10. Serper, "Shindō Kaneto's Films," 235.

11. Gerstle, "Heroic Honor," esp. 335–36.

12. Reider, "*Shuten Dōji*," 146–47. Other tales of Raiko not included in the film have similarly broad ranges of textual and theatric reincarnations, notably the "Earth Spider" shape-shifting demon the samurai faced. See Takeuchi, "Kuniyoshi's 'Minamoto Raiko and the Earth Spider.'"

13. Shriane, ed., *Traditional Japanese Literature*, 1123.

14. Duus, "Presidential Address," 972.

15. Graham, "The Consort and the Warrior," 5.

16. Novak, *Warriors of Legend*, 71.

17. The stage set recalls the standard Noh theater, albeit with more trees. On Noh staging, see Nakamura, *Noh*, 218–19, and illustrations 75, 76, 120, 121. See also Serper, "Shindō Kaneto's Films," 240–41.

18. On the spot lighting techniques developed in Kabuki, see Leiter, "From the London Patents to the Edo *Sanza*," 33–34; Miyao, *Aesthetics of Shadow*, 64. American director Francis Ford Coppola experimented with such lighting techniques in his (commercial failure) *One from the Heart* (1982). See his discussion of the matter in "A Pinewood Dialogue with Francis Ford Coppola" (2003) at http://www.movingimagesource .us/files/dialogues/2/28801_programs_transcript _html_254.htm.

19. Serper, "Shindō Kaneto's Films," 241.

20. Wire-work flying, most associated today with kung-fu films, had its origins in Kabuki practice; see Toshio, *Kabuki*, 68–69.

21. Serper, "Shindō Kaneto's Films," 236.

22. Balmain, *Introduction*, 77. This coincides, in Balmain's reading, with a Freudian psychoanalytic (or post-Freudian Lacan-informed feminist literary-critical) reading of the "monstrous feminine," in which "the ghost cats of *Kuroneko* might well be symbols of male desire and projections of male anxiety, but at the same time they offer a mode of empowerment outside traditional binaries" (74). This corresponds to Shindo's own view, at least when prodded in that direction. To Joan Mellen's query, "Is there a Freudian aspect to the relationship between the mother and son in *Kuroneko*?" the director responds: "Yes, there is. There is a strong Freudian influence throughout all my work." Mellen, *Voices from the Japanese Cinema*, 90.

23. Starek, "The Cat Came Back," www.cineoutsider.com/reviews/dvd/k/kuroneko .html.

24. For a fuller treatment of *Onibaba*, especially rich for its analysis of the way the film draws on traditional Noh/Kabuki character roles, see Serper, "Shindō Kaneto's Films," 244–51.

25. McDonagh, "The Mark of the Cat," 9.

26. Balmain, *Introduction*, 74.

27. Sato, *Legends of the Samurai*, 60–64. See also the Minamoto genealogical table in Rizō, "Rise of the Warriors," 651 (although Raiko does not appear in the actual text).

28. For a fuller—much fuller—account of the transition, see Rizō, "Rise of the Warriors." For a less full version, see Friday, *Samurai, Warfare and the State*, 7–10.

29. Sato, "*Kuroneko*," bonus feature accompanying the Criterion DVD release, 2011.

30. Mellen, *Voices from the Japanese Cinema*, 80.

31. Ibid., 81.

32. Bergen, "Kaneto Shindo Obituary."

33. The fullest account of Japan's conflicted response to the Vietnam War is Havens, *Fire across the Sea*. See also Avenill, *Making Japanese Citizens*, 106–48; Masayuki, "The Model of an Economic Power, 93–95; and, for the feminist connection with the antiwar movement, Shigematsu, *Scream from the Shadows*, 38–42.

34. Mellen records her question and his answer on the subject: "Mellen: Do you consider yourself a Marxist? Shindo: Ah, Marxist! I am a believer in socialism. I can say that I am a socialist." *Voices from the Japanese Cinema*, 80.

35. Indeed, David Desser notes that Shindo is a director that Tadeo Sato "puts forward as an exemplary *feminisuto*" (*Eros Plus Massacre*, 120). In his discussion of *Kuroneko*, Sato notes: "The strength of women is what Shindo puts on clear display in *Kuroneko*."

36. Sharp, "Ozu vs Godzilla." Donald Richie dismisses *Onibaba* and *Kuroneko* in strikingly similar terms: "Both films might have been read as antigovernment allegories, but so filled were they with naked flesh and sex (a subject hitherto alien to the Shindo oeuvre) that no one did" (*Hundred Years*, 151).

37. Sharp, "Live Today, Die Tomorrow."

38. Kaneto Shindo, interview for the Directors Guild of Japan, 1992, included as a bonus feature on the Criterion DVD release of *Kuroneko*.

39. Sato, "*Kuroneko*."

40. McDonagh, "Mark of the Cat," 7.

41. Dates might not be McDonagh's strong point, but in this case McDonagh comes closer than Michael Atkinson, who was convinced that the film's 2010 showing was its "New York premiere." See "Women Are Out for Bloody Revenge."

Bibliography

Atkinson, Michael. "The Women Are Out for Bloody Revenge in Japanese Gothic Horror *Kuroneko*." *Village Voice*, October 20, 2010. http://www.villagevoice.com/2010 -10-20/film/the-women-are-out-for-bloody-revenge-in-japanese-gothic-horror -kuroneko/.

Avenill, Simon Andrew. *Making Japanese Citizens: Civil Society and the Mythology of the Shimin in Postwar Japan*. Berkeley: University of California Press, 2010.

Balmain, Colette. *Introduction to Japanese Horror Film*. Edinburgh: Edinburgh University Press, 2008.

Bergen, Peter. "Kaneto Shindo Obituary." *The Guardian*. May 30, 2012. http://archive .today /MQyh8.

Desser, David. *Eros Plus Massacre: An Introduction to the Japanese New Wave Cinema.* Bloomington: Indiana University Press, 1988.

Duus, Peter. "Presidential Address: Weapons of the Weak, Weapons of the Strong—the Development of the Japanese Political Cartoon." *Journal of Asian Studies* 60, no. 4 (2001): 965–97.

Friday, Karl F. *Samurai, Warfare and the State in Early Medieval Japan.* New York: Routledge, 2004.

Gerstle, C. Andrew. "Heroic Honor: Chikamatsu and the Samurai Ideal." *Harvard Journal of Asiatic Studies* 57, no. 2 (1997): 307–81.

Graham, Masako Nakagawa. "The Consort and the Warrior: *Yokihi Monogatari.*" *Monumenta Nipponica* 45, no. 1 (1990): 1–26.

Hand, Richard J. "Aesthetics of Cruelty: Traditional Japanese Theatre and the Horror Film." In *Japanese Horror Cinema,* edited by Jay McRoy, 18–28. Honolulu: University of Hawaii Press, 2005.

Havens, Thomas R. H. *Fire across the Sea: The Vietnam War and Japan, 1965–1975.* Princeton, NJ: Princeton University Press, 1987.

Leiter, Samuel. "From the London Patents to the Edo *Sanza*: A Partial Comparison of the British Stage and Kabuki, ca. 1650–1800." In "Crosscurrents in the Drama: East and West, edited by Stephen Vincent Longman, 19–37. Tuscaloosa: University of Alabama Press, 1998.

Masayuki, Tadokoro. "The Model of an Economic Power: Japanese Diplomacy in the 1960s." In *Diplomatic History of Modern Japan,* edited by Makoto Iokibe, 81–107. New York: Routledge, 2011.

McDonagh, Maitland. "The Mark of the Cat." *Kuroneko.* New York: Criterion DVD Collection, 2011.

Mellen, Joan. *Voices from the Japanese Cinema.* New York: Liveright, 1975.

Miyao, Daisuke. *The Aesthetics of Shadow: Lighting and Japanese Cinema.* Durham, NC: Duke University Press, 2013.

Nakamura, Yasu. *Noh: The Classical Theatre,* 4th edition. Translated by Don Kenny. New York: Walker Weatherhill, 1971.

Novak, Jay. *Warriors of Legend: Reflections of Japan in Sailor Moon.* North Charleston, SC: Booksurge, 2008.

Redesdale, Algernon Bertram, translator. "The Vampire Cat of Nabeshima." In *Tales of Old Japan,* 245–54. London: Macmillan and Co., 1908.

Reider, Noriko T. "Shuten Dōji: 'Drunken Demon.'" *Asian Folklore Studies* 64 (2005): 207–31.

———. "*Tsuchigumo sōshi*: The Emergence of a Shape-Shifting Killer Female Spider." *Asian Ethnology* 72, no. 1 (2013): 55–83.

Richie, Donald. *A Hundred Years of Japanese Film: A Concise History.* Tokyo: Kodansha International, 2001.

Rizō, Takeuchi. "The Rise of the Warriors." In *The Cambridge History of Japan* [Vol. 2, *Heian Japan*], edited by Donald H. Shively and William H. McCullough. Cambridge: Cambridge University Press, 1999.

Sato, Hiroaki. *Legends of the Samurai*. Woodstock, NY: Overlook Press, 1995.

Serper, Zvika. "Shindō Kaneto's Films *Kuroneko* and *Onibaba*: Traditional and Innovative Manifestations of Demonic Embodiments." *Japan Forum* 17, no. 2 (2005): 231–56.

Sharp, Jasper. "Live Today, Die Tomorrow." *Midnight Eye: Visions of Japanese Cinema*. www.midnighteye.com/reviews/live-today-die-tomorrow.

———. "Ozu vs Godzilla." *BFI Film Forever*. http://www.bfi.org.uk/news-opinion/news -bfi/features/ozu-vs-godzilla.

Shigematsu, Setsu. *Scream from the Shadows: The Women's Liberation Movement in Japan*. St. Paul: University of Minnesota Press, 2012.

Shriane, Haruo, ed. *Traditional Japanese Literature: An Anthology, Beginnings to 1600*. New York: Columbia University Press, 2007.

Smith, Evans Lansing, and Nathan Robert Brown. *The Complete Idiot's Guide to World Mythology*. Hammondworth: Penguin, 2007.

Takeuchi, Melinda. "Kuniyoshi's 'Minamoto Raiko and the Earth Spider': Demons and Protest in Late Tokugawa Japan." *Ars Orientalis* 17 (1987): 5–38.

Toshio, Kawatake. *Kabuki: Baroque Fusion of the Arts*. Translated by Frank and Jean Connel Hoff. Tokyo: I-House Press, 2006.

CHAPTER 15

Public Memory and Supernatural Presence

THE MYSTERY AND MADNESS OF WEIRD WAR TALES

Terence Check

Intent on thwarting a Nazi plot to clone the world's leaders, a top-secret team of American soldiers parachutes behind enemy lines during World War II. Nazi soldiers confront the miscreant group and a battle ensues, "with one of the most incredible, sense-stunning displays of pure power ever recorded in the annals of war."[1] When the smoke clears, the Germans lay dead from the violent exchange, some with their blood drained from their bodies. The Nazi soldiers have succumbed to the Creature Commandos, a team of supernatural warriors consisting of a werewolf, a vampire, and a version of the Frankenstein monster.

This scene and others like it were depicted in the pages of *Weird War Tales*, an anthology series that DC Comics published from 1971 to 1983. Well known for its war and mystery titles, DC blended these genres to create a comic book series that endured for over a decade. While the stories in *Weird War Tales* were not the pinnacle of comics literature, they nevertheless promoted attitudes about the supernatural and the battlefield that were instructive for young readers growing up in an era marked by uncertainty over America's military prowess. With stories set on various battlefields, *Weird War Tales* offered moral fables of military conflict with ghostly intervention. Given that the series started in the Vietnam War era and ended during the Reagan years, just months before the American invasion of Grenada, it is an important text through which to assess popular memories about war and the way publics utilize them to make sense of contemporary problems.

In the past several years, there has been extensive interest in public memory studies. John Bodnar describes public memory as the "body of beliefs and ideas about the past that help a public or society understand both its past and present, and by implication its future."[2] Public memories of war can help guide societies in determining the proper moral choices for the current conflicts they face. For years, comic books have invoked memories of war as they told tales of valor in the battlefield, but they have garnered less critical attention than other prominent memory texts, in part due to their perceived insignificance. Yet comics scholars have long recognized the importance of these texts in reinforcing or contesting political ideology.[3] Given their ability to marshal discursive narratives and visual imagery, as well as their use of characters that transcend human limitations, comics have the ability to disrupt culturally held assumptions about morality and virtue.

In particular, supernatural characters in comic book stories have the ability to "disrupt the taken-for-granted realm of the uncontested and commonplace," since they are not bound by earthly conventions and mandates.[4] The presence of ghosts and other supernatural beings on the battlefield can unsettle assumptions generated by public memories of war. After all, a ghost is "an afterimage, a specter that should disappear but refuses to go away, and whose very presence troubles the modern present and its logic of linear time."[5] However, as this essay demonstrates, the specters and undead beings of *Weird War Tales* squandered this opportunity. Although the series debuted during the Vietnam War, it failed to even mention the war in its early issues. In *Weird War Tales*, the dominant framework for understanding conflict is World War II, with its corresponding assumptions of American exceptionalism in contrast to Nazi despotism. The ghosts and demons intrude into these stories in ways that naturalize dominant war narratives, rather than challenge them. This chapter describes the developments in the comics industry that preceded *Weird War Tales*, and uses rhetorical concepts of public memory and presence to analyze the narratives featured in this series.

War Comics and the Supernatural

Prior to the publication of *Weird War Tales* in 1971, comics publishers offered numerous titles in the war and horror genres, but rarely had blended them. After comic books emerged in the late 1930s and early 1940s, they quickly became part of the overall war propaganda effort to rally Americans to unify against foreign foes. Patriotic heroes such as Captain America and Uncle Sam came on the comics scene just prior to America's involvement in World War II, and their adventures were soon followed by the war-themed exploits of established superheroes such as Superman, Batman, and Wonder Woman.[6] Shortly after the war ended, however, readers were weary of superheroes and publishers replaced these titles with comics that had war, crime, horror, and science fiction themes. Even Timely Comics' flagship title changed its name from *Captain America Comics* to *Captain America's Weird Tales* to adjust to the changing tastes of its readers.

EC Comics, a prominent publisher during the postwar period, developed several horror titles, such as *Tales from the Crypt* and *Haunt of Horror*, with grisly and macabre themes. In addition, under the direction of editors Harvey Kurtzmann and Al Feldstein, EC published two innovative war titles, *Frontline Combat* and *Two-Fisted Tales*. The writers and artists of these books, many of whom had combat experience themselves, attempted to depict war realistically, with stories about the brutal conditions soldiers faced, the difficult moral choices they encountered, and the incompetent superiors who managed them. In contrast, the majority of war stories from the mainstream comics publishers, such as DC Comics' *G. I. Combat*, *All-American Men of War*, and *Our Fighting Forces*, typically featured stories with heroic male soldiers fighting morally unambiguous battles.[7]

Comic books came under criticism in the early 1950s for their portrayals of crime and horror, leading to an investigation in the US Senate over the potential link between comic books and juvenile delinquency. The industry responded with the Comics Code Authority (CCA), which placed significant restrictions on the content of comics. One of the stipulations of the CCA forbade comics publishers from depicting police officers, judges, government officials, and other representatives of "respected institutions" in ways that might generate "disrespect for established authority."[8] While the authors of this provision intended to target the crime comics that were the focus of the congressional hearings, the language also created a chilling effect on war comics, as writers and artists were now reluctant to depict realistic imagery or tell stories that questioned America's motives or purpose in wartime conflicts.

The horror comics fared even worse after the establishment of the Code. The new rules expressly prohibited the words "horror" or "terror" in comic book titles, and also forbade any scenes dealing with the "walking dead, torture, vampires and vampirism, ghouls, cannibalism, and werewolfism." In response to the new guidelines, EC stopped publishing comics and focused instead on magazines such as *Mad*, which were free of these restrictions. The horror and mystery comics that survived, such as DC Comics' *House of Mystery* and *House of Secrets*, turned to science fiction and superhero themes. Horror comics had disappeared from the comics landscape while the war genre was populated with titles such as *Fight the Enemy* that promoted patriotic themes and depicted American protagonists with resolve and courage. The most prominent comics archetype of the patriotic soldier was Sgt. Rock, which DC Comics debuted in the pages of *Our Army at War* in 1958. Rock was a plain-speaking fighter who exemplified "the fantasy of the American soldier, superior to any other on the planet."[9]

DC Comics did publish two notable titles in the 1960s that would inspire the stories later found in *Weird War Tales*. In 1960, it introduced the ongoing stories of "The War That Time Forgot" in the pages of *Star Spangled War Stories*.

The series featured stories of American soldiers fighting prehistoric beasts—as well as Japanese military forces—on a South Pacific island during World War II.[10] In 1961, DC introduced the Haunted Tank in the war comic *G. I. Combat*. The series told the story of the apparition of Civil War–era Confederate general J. E. B. "Jeb" Stuart, sent by the spirit of Alexander the Great to offer ghostly advice and protection to his heir and namesake Jeb Stuart in World War II, as he commands a tank in conflicts from Africa to Europe. Lasting until 1987, these stories constituted the second-longest-running DC war series behind Sgt. Rock, and likely gave DC confidence that it could explore war and supernatural themes with commercial success.

As the readership of comics matured and the dominance of the major publishers was challenged by "underground" comics in the late 1960s and early 1970s, the industry modified the rules of the Comics Code in 1971 to allow for the return of horror-themed books. Marvel Comics responded by adapting some of the Universal Studios horror monsters with new features, resulting in titles such as *Tomb of Dracula*, *Werewolf by Night*, and *Frankenstein* in the early 1970s. DC Comics had experimented with changes prior to the new rules, converting *House of Mystery* and *House of Secrets* back to horror books, as well as adding titles such as *The Unexpected* and *The Witching Hour* in the late 1960s. Once the new rules were in place, DC went further by adding titles such as *Ghosts*, *Weird War Tales*, and *Weird Mystery Tales* to its lineup.

Although the relaxation of the Code led to the publication of numerous horror and mystery titles, *Weird War Tales* was distinctive because it fused the horror and war genres. In particular, the hybrid war/supernatural title allowed DC to exploit interest in battlefield ghosts. By the early 1970s there was a growing literature about ghosts and battlefields, although the phenomenon was a relatively new one in the popular imagination. As Owen Davies notes, "Battlefields were another location in the landscape where the dead lay without a proper Christian burial. Somewhat surprisingly, though, prior to the twentieth century there was not a great deal of evidence regarding the presence of ghosts on such sites."[11] But the growing popular fascination with the battles of the Civil War and both world wars led to the belief that the ghosts of the war dead might haunt these sites and be contacted.[12] The writers of *Weird War Tales* were able to tap into these assumptions about the presence and purpose of the undead in battlefield settings.

Weird War Tales debuted during a period of intense social and political unrest over the Vietnam War. Prior to the publication of the first issue in September–October 1971, major events had led to public scrutiny over the war and its purpose. In 1968, enemy forces launched the Tet Offensive, a series of surprise attacks against civilian and military targets in South Vietnam, which "convinced many that the war could not be won, thus strengthening the anti-war movement which was becoming so widespread it could not be ignored."[13] In March 1969, President Richard Nixon authorized the secret bombing of Cambodia, leading to enormous public outcry when the *New York Times* exposed it two months later. In the spring of 1969, student protestors at Harvard seized administration buildings and had to be forcibly removed by law enforcement officers. In a June 1969 issue, *Life* magazine published photographs of all 242 American soldiers who had perished in Vietnam during the previous week, raising significant doubts about the purpose and cost of the war. On May 4, 1970, National Guardsmen fired into a crowd of protesters at Kent State University, killing four students and wounding several others, further catalyzing public opposition and uncertainty over the war. In addition, during the spring of 1971, some Vietnam veterans organized themselves into a group that began protesting the war.[14] The rhetorical context was established for oppositional argument that "unsettles the appropriateness of social conventions, draws attention to the taken-for-granted means of communication, and provokes discussion."[15] The undead characters appearing in *Weird War Tales* were in a unique position to question established norms and enthymematic assumptions about the war. An array of ghostly narrators told the tales in the early issues, but the signature "host" for the series was Death itself, who appeared in every issue starting with #8 in November 1972. A skeletal figure dressed in the military uniform of a character from one of the stories, Death would become the prominent voice of the tales of the weird war.

Constructing a Useable Past in *Weird War Tales*

Scholars in a wide range of disciplines have examined the importance of public memory as a way for communities to utilize notions of the past as a guide for present and future behavior. Kendall Phillips argues that public memories are "multiple, diverse, mutable, and competing accounts of past events," that are also remembrances that come with assumptions about how to interpret contemporary situations.[16] Thomas R. Dunn observes, "Within the frame of public memory, the past operates not as historical *fact* but as historical *interpretation* for the purposes of making public argument. Through framing the past, we serve a present need."[17] Similarly, Janice Hume contends that public memories are the "collective beliefs about the past that inform a social group, community, region, or nation's present and future."[18] Public memories are ways of thinking about the past that are rhetorical, since they generate understanding and meaning, as well as urge people to action.[19]

The debut issue of DC Comics' war and supernatural anthology series. Pictured: *Weird War Tales* #1, published by DC Comics in September–October 1971. Cover art by Joe Kubert. *Author's private research collection and © DC Comics.*

What type of memories are present in public discourse, and how they are recalled by audiences to serve contemporary needs, depends in part on their "presence" in the public sphere. Presence is "the importance accorded to an argument"[20] that "fixes the audience's attention while altering its perceptions and perspectives" so that it will "initiate action" or be disposed "toward an action or a judgment."[21] The selection of a historic event as a rhetorical touchstone, combined with an audience's desire to utilize the lessons constructed by its use, gives presence to memories of historical analogies in the public sphere. Presence can also be achieved with the insertion of characters into scenes that draw attention to some of its properties. Ghosts and other liminal beings have such potential, given their ability to both shock and inspire people.

One of the key features of the ghostly hosts and other undead characters from *Weird War Tales* is the sense of ethos generated by their presence in the stories, a characteristic central in the telling of public memories. Bradford Vivian writes, "the ethos of authenticity plays a vital role in the production of public memory."[22] In *Weird War Tales*, the ghostly narrators occupy a position of authority, in part based on their incorporeal qualities. Owen Davies contends that the righteousness of ghosts is "enhanced by their heavenly residence,"[23] and the beings of *Weird War Tales* occupy a space outside of mortal limits that infuse them with power. An integral feature of the undead's moral authority is their ability to bear witness to the acts of humanity. Since they are ageless and timeless, the ghostly characters of *Weird War Tales* watch war unfold over time. Their knowledge of war and the pain it inflicts imbue them with "the authority of direct experience," giving them "special standing . . . with a terrible tale to tell, people whose very lives are defined by that story."[24] As Robert Hariman and John Louis Lucaites contend, a ghost is "an unbidden presence who functions as a witness to other relationships and who makes the familiar strange."[25]

Ghosts serve as the evidence of death, and some of them seek vengeance by haunting those who have committed wrongs against them. "The concept of the vengeful ghost was so engrained in popular belief," writes Owen Davies, "that it was thought that the living could determine to haunt someone after death as an act of malice and retribution. Such ghosts were, in effect, a curse."[26] Ghosts are reminders of "unfinished business"[27] that have power to "come back as agents of social control to haunt the living who have done them wrong either before or after their death."[28] One of the recurring themes in *Weird War Tales* is the notion of the purposeful dead who seek retribution. For example, in the story, "The Room That Remembered," a Nazi commander at a concentration camp instructs his soldiers to steal jewelry and other valuables from the prisoners, with the intent of burying them so that he may collect them at a later time. Years after the war, he returns in search of his treasure, only to be confronted by the ghosts of the dead. As ethereal mists, the ghosts cannot physically prevent the former commander from digging for the riches, but their taunting drives him mad in the end.

Jack Oleck's story, "The Die-Hards," also employs themes of retribution and justice. Nazi soldiers have taken over a village in Eastern Europe, but some of the German soldiers have mysteriously fallen to unknown assailants, causing the Nazi colonel in charge to confront the mayor for answers. The mayor insists the deaths are the result of vampires, which infuriates the colonel, who then orders executions of random citizens to extract a confession. When the towns-people stick to their story, the Nazi colonel orders all of the residents killed, only to discover later that they are vampires. In the last page of the story, the vampires take their revenge on the hapless Nazi soldiers. In these stories, mere mortals cannot impede the vengeance of the undead. Given their superior powers, the undead are "avengers of unmatched tenacity and ferocity."[29]

According to Death, the host of the series, no side is spared the ravages of war ("All men are equal—equal prey for me, Death, the reaver of souls!"). But throughout the series, the victims of the undead are typically enemy combatants, while American soldiers are either spared, aided by spirits, or prevail as a result of their ingenuity. As in survival narratives, those who elude the clutches of the undead "are not only presented as the most fit to live another day but also serve as the embodiment of what counts as an ideal citizen."[30] The stories in *Weird War Tales* emphasize the resourcefulness of American soldiers. For example, in "Goliath of the Western Front," a robot behemoth dressed in full Nazi uniform attacks a group of American soldiers. The mechanical menace appears unstoppable, but a diminutive soldier musters his courage and finds the robot's weak spot, shooting it underneath its foot to destroy its mechanical apparatus. Another story, "I Can't See," by writer Marv Wolfman, follows the story of an American GI named "Charlie," whose company is attacked by a German fighter pilot. With his buddies gravely wounded, Charlie leaves them to seek reinforcements, only to come across a group of German soldiers. Fearing the soldiers will discover his wounded friends, Charlie attacks them single-handedly and prevails. At the end of the story, readers discover that Charlie was blinded by the original attack and has miraculously defeated the enemy, possibly with the assistance of supernatural forces.

In contrast to the narrative of American exceptionalism, *Weird War Tales* depicts enemies as corrupt, vile, and unworthy of redemption. This is especially the case with portrayals of Nazis, who are the most frequently depicted villains in the series and often shown as sadistic and bloodless, but who suffer a miserable fate at story's end. In "Death of a Dictator," Adolf Hitler faces his final moments at the end of the war, and with the help of German scientists, is transported into the future. He hopes to resume his despotic ways, but instead is killed by a future

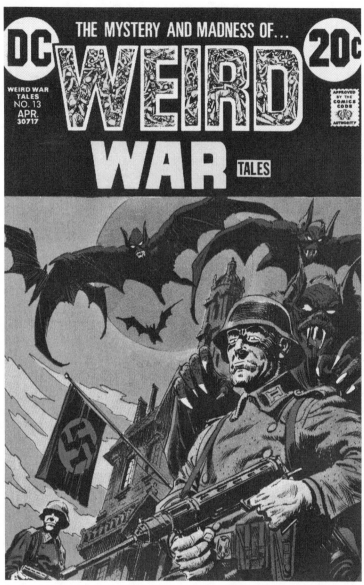

In the series, the undead often sought the blood of Nazi victims. Pictured: *Weird War Tales* #13, published by DC Comics in April 1973. Cover art by Luis Dominguez. *Author's private research collection and © DC Comics.*

version of himself, who also intends to escape in a time machine from a similar fate. Hitler thus becomes a victim of his own ruthlessness, doomed to die many deaths throughout time.[31] "The Elements of Death" portrays a similar case of just deserts, in its story of a Nazi camp commandant who tortures an American to death, only to be confronted by the soldier's ghost, who arranges for the German to die by inhaling the gas he has used to poison others.

Occasionally, ghosts return to forewarn soldiers of imminent dangers, or to assist them as they struggle on the battlefield. The opposite of the ghostly curse is the supernatural being that returns "at the other's time of need to forewarn of imminent danger."[32] The writers of *Weird War Tales* used this plotline frequently. In "Dream of Disaster," a ghostly sergeant confronts two soldiers and urges them against taking a tunnel through the jungle. When the confused soldiers resist, the spectral sergeant shoves them aside and walks into the tunnel, only to detonate a bomb and presumably die again. In the tale "The Unknown Sentinel," two American soldiers get separated from their unit and consider thoughts of desertion, until they discover, to their amazement, a fire and a kettle of soup waiting for them in the wilderness. Their benefactor reveals himself as the ghost of a Revolutionary War soldier, and the humbled GIs realize they have been taught a valuable lesson about loyalty. In "The Attack of the Undead," a young female vampire kills Nazi soldiers, who become vampires themselves. Realizing she has loyalties to her native France despite being undead, the female vampire alerts Allied forces, who subdue the Nazi vampires with crosses and kill them with wooden stakes.

Besides the host, Death, the first recurring characters in the series were the Creature Commandos, a product of a top-secret American scientific experiment called "Project M." The goal of the project was to scientifically re-create physical manifestations of horrific monster archetypes to assist the Allies in World War II. The "team" consisted of three monsters: Warren Griffith, a school boy who became a talking werewolf; Vincent Velcro, a former army sergeant gone bad who received a second chance by agreeing to let scientists transform him into a vampire; and "Lucky" Taylor, a soldier who was badly injured by a land mine and reconstructed to resemble the Frankenstein monster. Lieutenant Matthew Shrieve of the Army Intelligence Corps led the monstrous trio, guiding them on dangerous missions inside Nazi territory. Although initially repulsed by the macabre team, American military leaders realized they were nevertheless "the most effective secret weapons this country has ever seen," and were needed to "teach those damnable Nazis the true meaning of the word fear!"[33]

Unlike the previous adventures in *Weird War Tales*, the Creature Commandos resembled typical superhero fare, but there were brief moments of critical reflection in these stories. In "The Children's Crusade," the Creature Commandos are sent to thwart a plot by Hitler to brainwash children into becoming

The Creature Commandos make their comic book debut. Pictured: *Weird War Tales* #93, published by DC Comics in November 1980. Cover art by Joe Kubert. *Author's private research collection and* © *DC Comics.*

unthinking fascist zombies. The team sympathizes with the afflicted children, as the vampire Velcro observes, "These kids aren't so different from us . . . guinea pigs for a government war machine that doesn't give a damn about human life!" In another story, "In the Kingdom of the Damned," the Creature Commandos invade a Nazi concentration camp, and compare their own plight to that of the hapless inmates. And in all of the stories featuring the Creature Commandos, the team's human leader, Shrieve, is portrayed as an archetypal headstrong fighter who cares little about the well-being of the horrific secret operatives he commands. Yet these moments are fleeting in the series, and they are contextualized by comparisons to Nazism, which functions as a signifier of ultimate evil. When the Creature Commandos attack the concentration camp, Velcro muses: "No matter how much we despise what we are and loathe the government war machine that made us this way, we can't deny the fact that places like this make our loonies look like heroes!"[34] Readers are left to assume that the government has experimented on the commandos only as a last resort, in order to prevent a greater evil.

The Good War and the Weird War

Because individuals hold different ideological commitments, public memory—which serves as the basis for communal and national identity—is often contested space. This is especially true when communities recall great conflicts of the past as exemplars to guide moral and political behavior in the present. In her analysis of World War II memory texts, Barbara A. Biesecker argues that the resurgence of films and memorials about the "Good War" may be understood as a conservative response to the crisis of national identity over what it means to be a "good American." Biesecker explains, "what we remember and how we remember it can tell us something significant about who we are as a people now, about the contemporary social and political issues that divide us, and about who we may become."[35]

In *Weird War Tales*, the presence of the undead is significant. Given that ghosts occupy an intermediary position between the soldiers' mortal state and the afterworld, their intrusion into battlefield stories can disrupt the taken-for-granted assumptions of the war narratives. Their experiences with war make the undead privy to knowledge that the living must heed. Some are witnesses to war, others are its victims, but all of the undead are in positions of authority to render judgments and act as "supernatural agents of social control."[36] They are paradoxically evil and loathsome, yet they seek retribution and justice for the acts of evil men. They are feared but they are also respected for their power and otherworldly wisdom. They are aberrations of nature but part of nature itself. Most important, through hauntings they have the power to change perceptions and alter consciousness. Avery F. Gordon writes that hauntings "draw us affectively, sometimes against our will and always a bit magically, into the structure of feeling of a reality we come to experience, not as cold knowledge, but as transformative recognition."[37] The "chaotic categories" generated by the presence of the supernatural in otherwise stable narratives has transformational possibilities.[38]

The potential for the supernatural characters of *Weird War Tales* to examine assumptions about war is largely squandered, however, by the series' focus on memories of World War II, an exemplar that valorizes the American experience. As Mary E. Stuckey argues, "World War II has been emptied of potentially controversial content and moral ambiguity; it stands as a national symbol of a 'good' war, when all the villains were on the other side, and Americans fought a clearly delineated foreign enemy, not one another . . . and ensured the triumph of freedom and justice."[39] The ability of ghosts and demons to "provide an escape from the amnesia of the present" is nullified when these otherworldly characters fight Nazis and save American soldiers, affirming a dualism that limits choices offered to readers.[40]

Given the political context when the series debuted, it is noteworthy that this series about war failed to even address Vietnam in any of its early stories. In the 124-issue run of the series, there were only five stories set in Vietnam, the first of which was published in October 1974, close to the war's end and well after the American withdrawal. "Homecoming" tells the tale of a self-centered American who deserts his patrol and kills one of his fellow soldiers. Eventually he returns home at the conclusion of the war, only to discover his life is an illusion: He died in Vietnam and has gone to hell as punishment for his transgressions, as revealed by the devil in the story's last panel.

Weird War Tales' next Vietnam stories did not appear for another five years. In "Dead Image," a journalist pursues a scoop rather than using the information he possesses to save American lives, and is confronted by the undead soldiers who died as a result of his decision. Like its predecessor, it added a fundamentally conservative message to the emerging national discourse over the Vietnam War, equating self-interest and less-than-complete support for the war with disloyalty. "Know Your Enemy," the second Vietnam story published in 1979, took a more nuanced view. Indeed, it was the only story published during the series' run to raise some of the antiwar arguments prominent during the Vietnam War. It begins with a mystic confronting two citizens with divergent opinions about the war, and transporting each of them to the battlefields of Vietnam, where they are forced to experience the war from the perspective of the other side. They return humbled by the experience, each of them now realizing it is important to listen to the viewpoints of others. However, by using the synecdoche of the student radical to represent the antiwar perspective, the story reinforces a dualism that lumps the varied objections to the war into one voice, diminishing the visibility—and the rhetorical force—of antiwar arguments based on other concerns such as race and class. Presence can make "certain elements stand out while simultaneously obscuring or diverting attention from others."[41] Raymie McKerrow argues, "absence is as important as presence in understanding and evaluating symbolic action."[42] Kristen Hoerl uses the term "selective amnesia" to describe instances when rhetors forget or exclude aspects of historical memory, and as such it can be "a particularly insidious form of forgetting that undermines social justice and collective empowerment."[43] While it was common for mainstream popular culture to avoid serious discussions of the war until after its conclusion, the omission of the Vietnam conflict from the pages of *Weird War Tales*, as well as the stereotypical representations that were featured in the few stories that did mention the war, seriously limited the series' oppositional force.

In the early issues of *Weird War Tales*, as with all of the war titles that DC published during this period, editor Joe Kubert directed the typesetter to place a bulletin in the last panel of each story with the coda, "Make War No More." Kubert later explained the slogan was his attempt to inform readers that DC "wasn't doing war books for the purpose of glorifying war or killing," but to identify with ordinary soldiers who found themselves in difficult situations during wartime.[44] One of DC's prominent artists, Kubert also drew many of the covers and some of the early stories for *Weird War Tales* and other DC war titles, yet thought of himself more as an antiwar artist.[45] Despite these intentions, the "Make War No More" tag appeared in DC combat titles that were "full of gleeful mayhem and Nazi-smiting," diluting the pacifist message amid images and narratives that sanctified American military actions.[46] The "Make War No More" motto was dropped after appearing in only the first seven issues of the series.

The ghostly apparitions of *Weird War Tales* were imbued with an ethos that placed them in a unique position to render a critique of war. Even the cartoonish monsters of the Creature Commandos had the ability to raise moral awareness about the contradictions inherent in waging war. Instead, these characters succumbed to familiar tropes affirming American valor and individualism. Perhaps now that mainstream comics have matured, with realistic portrayals of war more common, the series may someday return to offer critiques befitting the "mystery and madness of weird war tales."

Notes

1. DeMatteis, Kanigher, and Carrillo, *The Creature Commandos*, 16.
2. Bodnar, *Remaking America*, 7.

3. See: Berger, "Comics and Culture"; Faust, "Comics and How to Read Them"; McClelland-Nugent, "Wonder Woman against the Nazis"; and Schmitt, "Deconstructive Comics."

4. Olson and Goodnight, "Entanglements of Consumption," 250.

5. Hariman and Lucaites, "Public Identity and Collective Memory," 60.

6. For a description of the content of comics during World War II, see: Benton, *The Comic Book in America*; and Thompson, "OK, Axis, Here We Come!"

7. For summaries of the war comics genre, see: Clarkson, "Virtual Heroes"; Scott, "Comics and Conflict," 112; Willson, "The Comic Book Soldier," 114–16; and Witek, "The Dream of Total War."

8. The text of the CCA is reprinted in Scott, "Comics and Conflict," 275–78. For the history of the Code, see: Nyberg, *Seal of Approval*.

9. Scott, "Comics and Conflict," 112.

10. In fact, after a run that lasted into the late 1960s, the "War That Time Forgot" story lines would be reintroduced to readers in the 1980s in *Weird War Tales*.

11. Davies, *The Haunted*, 54.

12. Kutz, "Chief of a Nation of Ghosts."

13. Paris, "American Film Industry and Vietnam," 21.

14. For a summary of events during the Vietnam War, see: Maclear, *Vietnam*.

15. Olson and Goodnight, "Entanglements of Consumption," 250.

16. Phillips, "Introduction," 2.

17. Dunn, "Remembering 'A Great Fag,'" 439.

18. Hume, "Memory Matters," 181.

19. Numerous scholars have examined the rhetorical significance of public memory. For examples, see: Blair, "Communication as Collective Memory"; Hasain, "Authenticity"; Jorgensen-Earp and Lanzilotti, "Public Memory and Private Grief"; and Mandziuk, "Commemorating Sojourner Truth."

20. Murphy, "Presence, Analogy, and *Earth in the Balance*," 1.

21. Karon, "Presence in *The New Rhetoric*," 97.

22. Vivian, "Jefferson's Other," 299.

23. Davies, *The Haunted*, 4.

24. Winter, *Remembering War*, 239.

25. Hariman and Lucaites, "Public Identity and Collective Memory," 60.

26. Davies, *The Haunted*, 6.

27. Hariman and Lucaites, "Public Identity and Collective Memory," 60.

28. Emmons, "Ghosts," 89.

29. Miller and Van Riper, "Introduction," xvii.

30. Baldwin and McCarthy, "Same as It Ever Was," 75.

31. For a discussion of the ways Nazism is depicted in popular culture, see: Buttsworth and Abbenhuis, *Monsters in the Mirror*.

32. Davies, *The Haunted*, 6.

33. DeMatteis, Kanigher, and Carrillo, *The Creature Commandos*, 12.

34. Ibid., 70.

35. Biesecker, "Remembering World War II," 406. Other communication scholars have discussed the importance of public memories of war. See: Kretsinger-Harries, "Commemoration Controversy"; and Fried, "The Personalization of Collective Memory."

36. Emmons, "Ghosts," 91.
37. Gordon, *Ghostly Matters*, 8.
38. Miller, "So This Zombie Walks into a Bar . . . "
39. Stuckey, "Remembering the Future," 246.
40. Hariman and Lucaites, "Public Identity and Collective Memory," 60.
41. Jenkins, "The Presence of Perelman," 407.
42. McKerrow, "Critical Rhetoric," 107.
43. Hoerl, "Selective Amnesia," 181.
44. "The Joe Kubert Interview."
45. Fox, "Joe Kubert Dies at 85: Influential Comic-Book Artist."
46. "Comic Book PSA: Make War No More," *Lady, That's My Skull*, August 7, 2005, http://thatsmyskull.blogspot.com.

Bibliography

Abbenhuis, Maartje, and Sara Buttsworth. "The Mundanity of Evil: Everyday Nazism in Post-War Popular Culture." In *Monsters in the Mirror: Representations of Nazism in Post-War Popular Culture*, edited by Sara Buttsworth and Maartje Abbenhuis, xiii–xl. Santa Barbara, CA: Praeger, 2010.

Baldwin, Martina, and Mark McCarthy. "Same as It Ever Was: Savior Narratives and the Logics of Survival in *The Walking Dead*." In *Thinking Dead: What the Zombie Apocalypse Means*, edited by Murali Balaji, 75–87. Lanham, MD: Lexington Books, 2013.

Benton, Mike. *The Comic Book in America: An Illustrated History*. Dallas: Taylor Publishing, 1989.

Berger, Arthur. "Comics and Culture." *Journal of Popular Culture* 5, no. 1 (1971): 164–77.

Biesecker, Barbara A. "Remembering World War II: The Rhetoric and Politics of National Commemoration at the Turn of the 21st Century." *Quarterly Journal of Speech* 88, no. 4 (2002): 393–409.

Blair, Carole. "Communication as Collective Memory." In *Communication as . . . Perspectives on Theory*, edited by Gregory J. Shepherd, Jeffrey St. John, and Ted Striphas, 51–59. Thousand Oaks, CA: Sage, 2005.

Bodnar, John. *Remaking America: Public Memory, Commemoration, and Patriotism in the Twentieth Century*. Princeton, NJ: Princeton University Press, 1992.

Clarkson, Alexander. "Virtual Heroes: Boys, Masculinity and Historical Memory in War Comics 1945–1995." *Thymos: Journal of Boyhood Studies* 2, no. 2 (2008): 175–85.

Costello, Matthew J. *Secret Identity Crisis: Comic Books and the Unmasking of Cold War America*. New York: Continuum, 2009.

Davies, Owen. *The Haunted: A Social History of Ghosts*. New York: Palgrave Macmillan, 2007.

DeMatteis, J. M., Robert Kanigher, and Fred Carrillo. *The Creature Commandos*. New York: DC Comics, 2014.

Dunn, Thomas R. "Remembering 'A Great Fag': Visualizing Public Memory and the Construction of Queer Space," *Quarterly Journal of Speech* 97, no. 4 (2011): 435–60.

Emmons, Charles F. "Ghosts: The Dead among Us." In *Handbook of Death and Dying*, edited by Clifton D. Bryant, 87–95. Thousand Oaks, CA: Sage, 2003.

Faust, Wolfgang Max. "Comics and How to Read Them." *Journal of Popular Culture* 5, no. 1 (1971): 194–202.

Fox, Margalit. "Joe Kubert Dies at 85: Influential Comic-Book Artist." *New York Times*, August 13, 2012.

Fried, Amy. "The Personalization of Collective Memory: The Smithsonian's September 11 Exhibit." *Political Communication* 23 (2006): 387–405.

Gilbert, James. *A Cycle of Outrage: America's Reaction to the Juvenile Delinquent in the 1950s*. New York: Oxford University Press, 1986.

Godfrey, Richard, and Simon Lilley, "Visual Consumption, Collective Memory and the Representation of War." *Consumption, Markets & Culture* 12, no. 4 (2009): 275–300.

Gong, Jie. "Re-Imaging an Ancient, Emergent Superpower: 2008 Beijing Olympic Games, Public Memory, and National Identity." *Communication and Critical/Cultural Studies* 9, no. 2 (2012): 191–214.

Gordon, Avery F. *Ghostly Matters: Haunting and the Sociological Imagination*. Minneapolis: University of Minnesota Press, 1997.

Hariman, Robert, and John Louis Lucaites. "Public Identity and Collective Memory in US Iconic Photography: The Image of 'Accidental Napalm.'" *Critical Studies in Media Communication* 20, no. 1 (2003): 35–66.

Hasain, Marouf Jr. "Authenticity, Public Memories, and the Problematics of Post-Holocaust Remembrances: A Rhetorical Analysis of the *Wilomirski* Affair." *Quarterly Journal of Speech* 91, no. 3 (2005): 231–63.

Hoerl, Kristen. "Selective Amnesia and Racial Transcendence in News Coverage of President Obama's Inauguration." *Quarterly Journal of Speech* 98 no. 2 (2012): 178–202.

Hume, Janice. "Memory Matters: The Evolution of Scholarship in Collective Memory and Mass Communication." *Review of Communication* 10, no. 3 (2010): 181–96.

Huxley, David. "Naked Aggression: American Comic Books and the Vietnam War." *Comics Journal: The Magazine of News and Criticism* 136 (1990): 105–12.

Inuzuka, Ako. "Remembering Japanese Militarism through the Fusosha Textbook: The Collective Memory of the Asian-Pacific War in Japan." *Communication Quarterly* 61, no. 2 (2013): 131–50.

Jenkins, Eric. "The Presence of Perelman: Selection and Attention in a Noisy World." In *Concerning Argument*, edited by Scott Jacobs, 404–13. Washington: National Communication Association, 2007.

"The Joe Kubert Interview." *The Comics Journal*, November 1994. www.tcj.com/the-joe-kubert-interview.

Jorgensen-Earp, Cheryl R., and Lori A. Lanzilotti. "Public Memory and Private Grief: The Construction of Shrines at the Sites of Public Tragedy." *Quarterly Journal of Speech* 84 (1998): 150–70.

Karon, Louise A. "Presence in *The New Rhetoric*." *Philosophy & Rhetoric* 9, no. 2 (1976): 96–111.

Kingsepp, Eva. "Hitler as Our Devil? Nazi Germany in Mainstream Media." In *Monsters in the Mirror: Representations of Nazism in Post-War Popular Culture*, edited by Sara Buttsworth and Maartje Abbenhuis, 29–52. Santa Barbara, CA: Praeger, 2010.

Kodosky, Robert J. "Holy Tet Westy! Graphic Novels and the Vietnam War." *Journal of Popular Culture* 44, no. 5 (2011): 1047–66.

Kretsinger-Harries, Anne C. "Commemoration Controversy: The Harpers Ferry Raid Centennial as a Challenge to Dominant Public Memories of the US Civil War." *Rhetoric & Public Affairs* 17, no. 1 (2014): 67–104.

Kukkonen, Karin. "Popular Cultural Memory: Comics, Communities and Context Knowledge." *Nordicom Review* 29, no. 2 (2008): 261–73.

Kutz, Kimberly N. "Chief of a Nation of Ghosts: Images of Abraham Lincoln's Spirit in the Immediate Post–Civil War Period." *Journal of American Culture* 36, no. 2 (2013): 111–23.

Maclear, Michael. *Vietnam: The Ten Thousand Day War*. York, UK: Thames/Methuen, 1981.

Mandziuk, Roseann M. "Commemorating Sojourner Truth: Negotiating the Politics of Race and Gender in Spaces of Public Memory." *Western Journal of Communication* 67 (2003): 271–91.

McClelland-Nugent, Ruth. "Wonder Woman against the Nazis: Gendering Villainy in DC Comics." In *Monsters in the Mirror: Representations of Nazism in Post-War Popular Culture*, edited by Sara Buttsworth and Maartje Abbenhuis, 131–53. Santa Barbara, CA: Praeger, 2010.

McKerrow, Raymie E. "Critical Rhetoric: Theory and Practice." *Communication Monographs* 56, no. 2 (1989): 91–111.

Miller, Cynthia J., and A. Bowdoin Van Riper. "Introduction." In *Undead in the West: Vampires, Zombies, Mummies, and Ghosts on the Cinematic Frontier*, edited by Cynthia J. Miller and A. Bowdoin Van Riper, xi–xxvi. Lanham, MD: Scarecrow Press, 2012.

Miller, Cynthia J. "'So This Zombie Walks into a Bar . . . ': The Living, the Undead, and the Western Saloon." In *Undead in the West: Vampires, Zombies, Mummies, and Ghosts on the Cinematic Frontier*, edited by Cynthia J. Miller and A. Bowdoin Van Riper, 3–18. Lanham, MD: Scarecrow Press, 2012.

Murphy, John M. "Presence, Analogy, and *Earth in the Balance*." *Argumentation & Advocacy* 31, no. 1 (1994): 1–16.

Nyberg, Amy Kiste. *Seal of Approval: The History of the Comics Code*. Jackson: University Press of Mississippi, 1998.

Olson, Kathryn M., and G. Thomas Goodnight. "Entanglements of Consumption, Cruelty, Privacy, and Fashion: The Social Controversy over Fur." *Quarterly Journal of Speech* 80, no. 3 (1994): 249–76.

Paris, Michael. "The American Film Industry and Vietnam." *History Today* 37, no. 4 (1987): 19–26.

Phillips, Kendall R. "Introduction." In *Framing Public Memory*, edited by Kendall R. Phillips, 1–14. Tuscaloosa: University of Alabama Press, 2004.

Pividori, Cristina. "Of Heroes, Ghosts, and Witnesses: The Construction of Masculine Identity in the War Poets' Narratives." *Journal of War & Culture Studies* 7, no. 2 (2014): 162–78.

Schmitt, Ronald. "Deconstructive Comics." *Journal of Popular Culture* 25, no. 4 (1992): 153–61.

Scott, Cord A. "Comics and Conflict: War and Patriotically Themed Comics in American Cultural History from World War II through the Iraq War." Dissertations, Paper 74. 2011. http://ecommons.luc.edu/luc_diss/74.

Showcase Presents: Weird War Tales Volume 1. New York: DC Comics, 2012.

Stuckey, Mary E. "Remembering the Future: Rhetorical Echoes of World War II and Vietnam in George Bush's Public Speech on the Gulf War." *Communication Studies* 43 (1992): 246–56.

Thompson, Don. "OK, Axis, Here We Come!" In *All in Color for a Dime*, edited by Dick Lupoff and Don Thompson, 121–42. New York: Ace Books, 1970.

Vivian, Bradford. "Jefferson's Other." *Quarterly Journal of Speech* 88, no. 3 (2002): 284–302.

Willson, David A. "The Comic Book Soldier: Vietnam War Comics of the 1960s and 1970s." *Comics Journal: The Magazine of News and Criticism* 136 (July 1990): 114–16.

Winter, Jay. *Remembering War: The Great War between Memory and History in the Twentieth Century.* New Haven, CT: Yale University Press, 2006.

Witek, Joseph. "The Dream of Total War: The Limits of a Genre." *Journal of Popular Culture* 30, no. 2 (1996): 37–46.

Wright, Bradford W. *Comic Book Nation: The Transformation of Youth Culture in America.* Baltimore: Johns Hopkins University Press, 2001.

CHAPTER 16

War in *The Twilight Zone*

ROD SERLING'S HAUNTED VISIONS OF WORLD WAR II

Vincent Casaregola

In Francis Ford Coppola's *Apocalypse Now* (1979), the dying Colonel Kurtz utters a phrase that hangs in the air, long after the film has ended: "The Horror . . ." Open to endless interpretation, the line captures a dying man's sense of guilt, fear, and awe at his own and his fellow humans' capacity for ruthlessness. Certainly, any combat veteran can understand the power surging beneath the surface of this simple phrase, along with the nightmarish visions it can evoke. That war has always been a source of real and imagined horrors is undeniable, and all who have participated in the violence of combat and killing are haunted by its memories.

Twilight Zone creator Rod Serling was one such combat veteran, having served during World War II in the 11th Airborne Division, fighting in the Philippines in 1944 and 1945.[1] Wounded himself, he saw many—soldiers and civilians alike—killed or severely injured. His combat experience thus provided ample inspiration for scripts that explored both the literal horrors of the war and the shadowy ghosts that haunted the minds of the war's traumatized survivors. Indeed, the tone and tenor of the series—particularly its sense of pervasive and often bitter irony—grew from an imagination shaped by such trauma.

Serling constructed the show as a series of moral exempla, exploring the psychological conflicts and moral dilemmas that might manifest themselves as horrors of the soul. As a result, over the show's five seasons, characters were more often menaced by monsters of their own minds than by paranormal beings. Though few in number,[2] the *Twilight Zone*'s war episodes can be seen as central to the vision behind the whole series—the desire to remind the audience that the greatest horrors are those that human beings inflict upon one another and upon themselves.

The Second World War haunted the postwar lives of many of those who survived it, and for Serling and his generation, it cast three very deep shadows across their cultural space.[3] The first of these was the shadow of the fighting itself, in which millions of soldiers and civilians were killed, and millions more deeply wounded in body or mind. The second shadow grew from the unprecedented horror of the Holocaust, which revealed unsuspected depths in humans' capacity for violence and cruelty. The war's third and final shadow was cast by the atomic bombs that supposedly ended it, but which grew in power and number in the postwar era until they threatened the survival of the human race. As a combat veteran, a Jew, and a member of a unit stationed in occupied Japan after the war's end, Serling was personally touched by all three. Their effects merged in his *Twilight Zone* episodes about World War II, which explore the haunting of postwar culture by wartime experiences of previously unimagined horrors. Even those episodes not dealing with war were shaped, at least in part, by an artistic vision emerging from the experiences of the war, along with the horrible costs and consequences that lingered throughout the Cold War era.

Soldiers' Stories—Wounds That Will Not Heal

The traumatized war veteran became a commonplace figure in American literature, film, and television during the second half of the twentieth century, and remains so today. Though most closely associated with World War I and the Vietnam War, the character began to appear in narratives of World War II, as published memoirs revealed the depths of its veterans' traumas.[4] Literary works exploring the psychological and moral costs of the war emerged, however, almost as soon as it ended. They included the war novels of James Jones and Norman Mailer, the nonfiction narratives of John Hersey, and much of the poetry of Randall Jarrell, Howard Nemerov, and others. Films of the immediate postwar period—notably *The Best Years of Our Lives* (1946) and *Twelve O'Clock High* (1949)—also confronted issues of combat trauma and its effects (what would currently be labeled PTSD) even as they endorsed the mainstream "good war" narrative.[5] Television programs from the 1950s and the early 1960s made considerable use of this material as well, and *The Twilight Zone* was at the forefront of this trend.

Among the earliest of Serling's explorations of this material was the first-season episode "The Purple Testament."[6] The story takes place during the latter stages of the war on the island of Luzon in the Philippines—a campaign in which Serling himself fought—where US Army units faced stiff resistance from Japanese forces holding out in rural areas.[7] The story focuses on Lieutenant "Fitz" Fitzgerald (William Reynolds), an experienced and highly capable platoon leader in a beleaguered infantry company. Returning from yet another assault, he begins to develop an uncanny sixth sense: the ability to see a purplish light in the faces of those about to die. He tries to shake off this experience as a figment of his imagination, but soon realizes that the "purple testament" cannot be ignored. His sympathetic-but-skeptical commanding officer, Captain Riker (Dick York) tries to get medical help for him, without success, and before the next attack Fitz sees the ominous light in Riker's face.

After Riker's death, headquarters finally decides to relieve Fitz. As he is gathering his things, he catches sight of his face in his shaving mirror, his features now suffused with the purple glow. The glow also covers the features of the jovial driver assigned to drive him to safety. When the driver comments on the long trip ahead of them, Fitz, resigned to his fate, responds that it will not be so long. As they leave, they are warned about mines on the road, and moments after they drive off, an explosion testifies to the death of both men. The prophecy of the purple testament has once more been fulfilled.

In this episode, Serling dramatizes long-term combat veterans' realization that, no matter what they do, the odds are good that they will die in the war. Infantry veteran and novelist James Jones refers to the growth of this realization as the "Evolution of the Soldier"—a trajectory along which men in combat pass, as they move from denial of death to its acceptance. Initially, most believe that they are too good, or too clever, or too lucky to be killed or severely injured, but those who survive long enough evolve to the point that they know that death awaits them.[8] Resigned to their fate, combat veterans gain a sense of peace that comes with knowing the future and accepting it. For them, Jones argues, each moment of life then becomes more intense and powerful. The "evolved" soldier, knowing that he is "already among the dead," can go about his dangerous work with a calm resolve that men who still hope to survive cannot match. Knowing that his fellow soldiers also belong to the dead, he develops a strange combination of closeness and distance in his relationships with them. Their shared awareness of the presence of death links these men in a unique brotherhood, but buffers the shock of loss when one is killed.

Serling uses an expressionistic trope—the purple light—to represent this presence of death among the living. Fitzgerald's unique gift makes explicit to the audience what every combat soldier knows implicitly: that the hand of death may reach out and leave its fingerprints on any one of them, at any time. Serling's treatment of combat in "The Purple Testament" is a testament of its own—one that points to the intensity of his own combat experience and the extent of the memories that must have haunted him.[9]

The seeming inevitability of death in combat also means that fortunate but unexpected survival has psychological consequences. Among the most painful is "survivor guilt": the survivor's belief that he should have died with his lost comrades, that he failed to save them, or even that in some way, directly or indirectly, he actually helped to cause the events that led to their deaths. Survivor guilt is common among the veterans of intense and prolonged combat, who have witnessed the deaths of numerous comrades. It often manifests itself in the survivor's inability to understand why he lived when other men, as good as or better than he, perished. Serling explored survivor guilt in two episodes about military branches other than his own: the Air Force in "King Nine Will Not Return" and the Navy in "The Thirty-Fathom Grave." In both, events in the show's present (the early 1960s) propel the protagonist into a confrontation with his wartime past, when his comrades died but he, by happenstance, survived.

"King Nine Will Not Return" is based, in part, on the true story of the *Lady Be Good*, a B-24 bomber lost during a 1943 mission over the Mediterranean. The plane was assumed to have crashed into the sea until the late 1950s, when oil exploration crews discovered the wreckage deep in the Libyan desert.[10] The bodies of all but one of the crew were found in the surrounding area, having died of thirst and exposure in their futile efforts to cross the 400 miles of nearly impassable desert that lay between them and their base. Lost and disoriented because sandstorms obscured the coastline, the inexperienced crew had taken the plane far into the desert and, thinking they were still over water, bailed out when their fuel was exhausted. The plane itself glided to a "pancake" landing in the sand miles farther south, leaving most of its fuselage intact. Ironically, in bailing out, the crew lost access to the plane's supplies of food and water that might have sustained them longer, perhaps even long enough to be rescued.

Serling's fictionalized version of the story begins with the main character, Captain James Embry (Robert Cummings), awakening beside his B-25 bomber, known as *King Nine*, which has crash-landed in the desert.[11] The scene appears to be taking place during World War II, but as the disoriented pilot becomes increasingly panicked during his futile search for the crewmembers, it becomes clear that things are not what they seem. Embry has not only been separated from his crew, but apparently, separated from his *reality*. At one point, he sees jet aircraft flying above the crash site: something he apparently recognizes but cannot understand in this context. Finally, he collapses and loses consciousness again—overwhelmed by what appears to be heat exhaustion—and awakens in a present-day (1960) hospital.

Exposition is provided by the doctors, who explain that Embry collapsed on the street after seeing the story of *King Nine*'s discovery in the headlines. Embry, who missed that mission because he had been ill, has been haunted for years by his guilt over having not been with his men on their final mission; seeing the picture in the paper triggered a flashback to the war. The doctors leave the room—confident in the rationality of their explanation despite Embry's feeling that he had been "back there"—discussing the case and assuring each other that his condition will improve. When a nurse brings the pilot his clothes, however, one of the shoes tips over, and out pours a pile of sand—something that, as Serling would assert, could only be explained in the Twilight Zone.

Serling's merging of the paranormal with real psychological phenomena—survivor guilt and combat neurosis—creates a form of "haunting" for the former pilot, illustrating that, while much about the psychology of combat veterans can be explained and understood by others, only veterans themselves grasp the true horror of the experience of carrying such memories in their minds and hearts and reliving them in dreams. The sand functions as a manifestation of the intimate knowledge of that horror, which can never be fully explained.

Another aspect of survivor guilt is explored in "The Thirty-Fathom Grave," which begins with a present-day (1963) US Navy destroyer on patrol in an area of the South Pacific that was the site of many World War II naval battles against the Japanese. Chief Bell (Michael Kellin), a veteran member of the crew, is a survivor of one of those battles, in which his submarine was sunk with the loss of all hands, except him. The destroyer's sonar detects the wreckage of a submarine on the ocean floor, and onboard hydrophones record the sound of metal banging rhythmically on metal, as if someone aboard the wreck is striking a bulkhead with a hammer. A sailor asks, rhetorically, "Who could be inside that sub?" and the destroyer's captain responds: "Somebody who dies damn hard!" Ordered to investigate, the ship's diver confirms that the wreck is, in fact, Chief Bell's old sub, sunk twenty-one years before.

The revelation, and his shipmates' half-serious speculations that the sub is haunted, leaves Chief Bell increasingly disturbed. He is haunted by guilt over his survival, compounded by the fear that, on the night of the sinking, his own error doomed the sub. Preoccupied with memories of the war, he begins to have hallucinations of his dead shipmates, dripping wet and draped with seaweed, motioning for him to join them. The ship's doctor, recognizing the signs of survivor guilt, tries to counsel him, but Bell insists that the hammering is the sub's ghostly crew "calling muster" and summoning him to the deep. The chief grows more distraught, and his hallucinations grow more frequent, until he finally throws himself overboard to drown. The destroyer's crew is puzzled to find puddles of seawater and strands of seaweed belowdecks at the site of one of the chief's hallucinations, and the diver, sent to search for the chief's body, discovers a further mystery. The sub's broken periscope, moved by underwater currents, provides a wholly rational explanation for the banging sounds picked up by the destroyer, but when the diver enters the sub, he finds the bodies of eight sailors who survived the sinking in a partly flooded compartment, only to die of asphyxiation. One holds a hammer clutched in his hand.

Once again, Serling juxtaposes the well-understood pain and guilt of survivor psychology with images that cannot be explained. Audiences are left to ponder the physical horrors of war—the slow, terrified deaths of the eight survivors aboard the sub as the oxygen in their compartment was exhausted—and, through Chief Bell, the cost that is exacted well after the guns have been silenced and the last casualties buried and forgotten. Serling also, however, presents the audience with glimpses of the uncanny: the vividness of Bell's hallucinations, the seaweed and water found aboard the destroyer, and the dead man with the hammer. As in "King Nine will not Return," Serling leaves the story open-ended. When the diver reports his dis-covery, the destroyer captain merely responds that the story is "something to tell your grandchildren." The unexplained and perhaps unexplainable horror of com-bat is the permanent possession of those who must live with its indelible memories, and for Serling such lives must be lived out, at least in part, in the mental state he calls the Twilight Zone.

Holocaust Horror

The violence and suffering caused by the Second World War reached its apex with Nazi Germany's systematic program of genocide directed at European Jews, Gypsies, homosexuals, and others deemed racially or ethnically undesirable. The program of extermination—dubbed the "final solution" by its perpetrators, and known to history as "The Holocaust" (or "The Shoah")—ultimately killed almost twelve million people and enslaved, tortured, starved, and brutalized mil-lions more who, by some miracle, survived. When the liberation of the Nazi-run death camps by Allied armies revealed the full scope and monstrous brutality of the Holocaust, that knowledge reshaped peoples' awareness of their own vulner-ability to, and potential for, extreme evil. After the war, the arts—including film and television—kept alive memories of the Holocaust, and of the sense of horror it evoked, even as firsthand memories of it began to fade.

Serling was proud of his ethnic heritage and painfully aware that, had he lived in Europe, it would have qualified him and his loved ones for the fate meted out to millions of others.[12] His revulsion at the Holocaust manifested itself, however, not as a hatred of Nazi Germany specifically, but of racism and prejudice in all its forms. On one hand, while he detested all that the Nazis stood for, Serling did not equate them with all Germans.[13] His *Playhouse 90* teleplay "In the Presence of Mine Enemies" (1960), in fact, presents a sympa-thetic characterization of a young German soldier who is horrified at the Nazis' treatment of the Jews, and in love with a young Jewish woman.[14] On the other hand, Serling consistently used his talents as a writer to oppose and warn against prejudice in all times and places, emphatically including his own. He saw rac-ism and discrimination in America, especially against African Americans, as a particular affront.[15] His scripts for *The Twilight Zone* and his other teleplays consistently attacked it while promoting civil rights, and his most famous battle with network censors involved his attempt to write a teleplay about the 1955 lynching of Emmett Till in Mississippi.[16]

Serling's loathing for racism and other forms of bias is most apparent in the *Twilight Zone* episode "Death's Head Revisited," which deals directly with the Holocaust. Set long after the war has ended and the camps have been emptied, the episode focuses on SS captain Gunther Lutze, a former concentration camp commandant who escaped capture and now is living under an assumed name. In an act that reflects his boundless arrogance, he travels back to the site of his former camp, preserved as a memorial, both to savor his personal triumph at having escaped justice, and to relive the memories of his own perverse pleasure at torturing and killing his fellow human beings. A driver deposits Lutze at the camp gates, and he asks to be picked up there a short time later.

Once alone at the site, he begins his stroll through the camp and reminisces about the power he once held over his victims, but those victims refuse to remain silent or unavenged. A man emerges, clad in the ragged costume of the camp inmates, who seems to be a caretaker for the place. He is Alfred Becker (Joseph Schildkraut), and we discover that he was, himself, one of the camp's residents. At first Lutze is merely confused by Becker's presence, but eventually it dawns on him that he had killed Becker and that the figure confronting him must be either a hallucination or a ghost. He is too arrogant to succumb to horror, however, and only as the pair engage in dialogue does it become evident to Lutze that his journey back to the camp is intended to serve as a form of cosmic justice, meted out by Becker and the other ghostly victims who subsequently appear. Succumbing to terror and panic, Lutze tries to flee, but to no avail. In the episode's final scene, the driver who took him to the site has returned, and is explaining to a physician and other authorities what he found: Lutze in a state of physical agony—constant, horrific pain—without any apparent physical cause or possibility of relief. The authorities can neither account for nor alleviate his condition, but Serling, in his final commentary, offers an explanation already obvious to the audience: that horrific justice will come to those who enact horrors upon others, and that the Twilight Zone is just the place where such justice can be exacted.

Western knowledge of the Holocaust deepened in the immediate postwar years, as its perpetrators were tried at Nuremberg for the "crimes against humanity" that their actions had come to define. The last major Nazi war criminal, Adolf Eichmann, was apprehended by Israeli agents in 1960, the year after *The Twilight Zone* premiered. Coming to terms with the horrors of World War II was complicated, however, by the growing tensions of the Cold War. The threat of nuclear armageddon, for many, dwarfed even the worst memories of wartime destruction, and the realignment of international politics made America an enemy of its former allies China and the Soviet Union, and a friend of former enemies Japan and Germany.

This realignment brought about a conscious effort, in both Washington and Hollywood, to rehabilitate and sanitize the image of the former Axis powers, and film and television productions about World War II began to offer more nuanced characterizations of Japanese and German soldiers.[17] To some extent, this effort was salutary, overcoming the simple stereotypes found in the earlier propagandistic portrayals during the war itself (especially the typically racist depictions of the Japanese). Serling himself participated in this process, scripting the *Twilight Zone* episodes "A Quality of Mercy" and "The Encounter," as well as his *Playhouse 90*'s "In the Presence of Mine Enemies," already noted. The effort to distinguish between "good Germans" and evil Nazis tended, however, to obscure the scale of the Holocaust and the pervasiveness of anti-Semitism and racism in wartime Germany.

The early sixties, however, witnessed a gradual reversal of the trend, leading to a more complete sense of the magnitude of the crimes committed in wartime Germany. For many artists and writers, Serling among them, the effort to remember and represent these horrors was linked to the need to confront racism and discrimination in the contemporary United States. Support for the Civil Rights movement was interwoven with the awareness that one cannot decry the racism of Nazi Germany while continuing to replicate it, in a different form, at home. For Serling, as for others, this was a passionate commitment, and whenever he could, he tried to produce scripts that addressed such issues.[18] The episode "Death's Head" treats this commitment specifically in the context of the Holocaust, but it is—structurally and philosophically—of a piece with other episodes that focus on human injustice without invoking war. A striking example of the latter is "I Am the Night—Color Me Black," in which an unjust execution causes one small American town to remain in a state of literal darkness as a result. The episode ends with a radio announcer reporting similar outbreaks elsewhere, and Serling's on-camera plea to the audience to keep darkness from overwhelming the world. "I Am the Night," though set in peacetime, embodies a worldview forged amid the horrors of World War II. Men of good will saved the world from darkness once, Serling argues. It is in all our hands and upon all our consciences to keep the light alive in a world where the horrors of the Holocaust persist in many new forms.

Things That Go "Boom" in the Night

Like many World War II combat veterans, especially those who were continuing to fight against protracted Japanese resistance during the summer of 1945, Serling was relieved to hear about the atomic bombings of Hiroshima and Nagasaki and the announcements of Japan's impending surrender that soon followed.[19] Few veterans thought, initially, about the lingering consequences of "the bomb," or the possibility that the next major war might bring about total human destruction—that came later. By the 1950s, however, with Cold War tensions increasing and the nuclear arms race accelerating, many veterans—even those who thought that the bomb had saved their lives—began to question the wisdom, and even the sanity, of continuing to build and deploy such weapons.[20]

Serling was among those who raised such questions, and almost a decade and a half after the destruction of Hiroshima and Nagasaki, he would explore the issues of nuclear war across the five seasons of *The Twilight Zone*. Several episodes deal with the possibility of nuclear war or with its consequences. At least two of these—"Third from the Sun" and "Probe 7, Over and Out"—end with the revelation that the armageddon took place on another planet, and the survivors are trying to find a new peaceful life on what turns out to be Earth. "Probe 7," the latter of the two, deals with two characters from different worlds. Adam Cook (Richard Basehart) appears to be from Earth, while Eve Norda (Antoinette Bower) seems to be from another world, but is humanoid. Both are explorers, brought together because they have crash-landed on the same planet. In Adam's case, we learn that during the course of his mission, hostilities on his home world have spiraled into a global thermonuclear war that has destroyed all civilization. It is up to the pair to overcome their mutual suspicion of one another and to begin life again on this new planet. In the end, however, we discover that the Adam and Eve of this story have, indeed, landed on a place called Earth (Adam's planet, seeming so Earth-like in its horrors, was only an earlier shadow of our world). So the old story continues: one where conflict grows out of prior harmony but the survivors symbolize a new hope for the peace that had been lost.

Serling's focus, in these and other episodes, is less on the danger of nuclear war—things that go "boom" in the night—and the mass destruction that would follow, than on the motives that lead human beings into such levels of fear, mistrust, and anger that total war seems the only solution. These were the conditions of the Cold War era in which Serling lived and wrote, and which shaped his consciousness and political views. Moreover, having seen the consequences of a war in which nuclear weapons were used at the very end, he was all too well aware of the human capacity for indiscriminate slaughter once war began.[21] He explores these motives in episodes that do not deal so much with nuclear conflict but with human conflict, both during World War II and in its aftermath.

"The Encounter," which aired in May 1964 near the end of the series' final season, concerns two men in an attic who recall and reenact the fear, pain, anger, and guilt that drive nations to war. One of the pair is Fenton (Neville Brand), a middle-aged veteran who fought the Japanese in the Pacific; the other is a young Japanese-American, Taro Takamuri (George Takei), who runs a lawn-and-garden service. When Taro comes to Fenton's home to offer his services and finds him cleaning out his attic, Fenton hires him on the spot to help with the cleaning. They are initially cordial to one another, but Fenton harbors unresolved anger toward the Japanese, evident in an earlier scene where he finds a samurai sword in the attic and throws it aside with fear and hostility. The two men soon fall to arguing about the war, and when Taro tries to leave, the door to the attic will not open, trapping them in the hot, cramped space.

The dialogue-driven episode quickly reveals how the men's memories of the war entrap the two far more than the physical space of the attic. Fenton reveals that the sword, which he originally claimed to have taken as a prize of war after a battle, was actually taken from a Japanese officer whom he murdered in the act of surrendering. For his part, Taro reveals that his father, whom he originally claimed to have been a hero who saved sailors' lives while working at Pearl Harbor, was actually a traitor who helped the Japanese bombers to find and sink American ships. Both men are obviously doubly haunted by anger and guilt, and in the end, they fight over the sword, which carries the inscription: "This sword will avenge my death." Taro ultimately uses it to kill Fenton, but then, overwhelmed with intense emotion, shouts "banzai" and jumps to his death from the attic window, sword in hand. The episode reveals Serling's pessimistic side, suggesting that the scars left by old conflicts beget new ones, and human beings are trapped in a cycle of "mutual assured destruction" that will end only when all are dead.

In contrast, "A Quality of Mercy"—an earlier episode set in the Pacific Theater of World War II—takes a more optimistic view, suggesting that human beings might see their enemies as flawed human beings like themselves. Like "The Purple Testament," it takes place during the waning days of the war in the Philippines. Lieutenant Katell (Dean Stockwell) is a gung-ho but green officer who has yet to experience combat, but has just taken command of the remnants of a small platoon. Japanese troops are holding out in a cave near their position, but they are sick and starving, posing little threat. Katell's own men, among them the veteran Sergeant Causarano (Albert Salmi), suggest that the cave be left alone, but Katell is hell-bent on seeing combat before he loses his chance to do so, and he orders his men to prepare to assault the cave. When the lieutenant accidentally drops his binoculars, breaking them, he finds himself a different person in a different time—but in the same place. It is now 1942; he is Japanese Lieutenant Yamuri, and the soldiers in the cave are sick and starving Americans, desperately clinging to life. Katell, as Yamuri, pleads with his Japanese commanding officer to allow the Americans to live, but the officer angrily denounces him, relieving him of his duties and promising further punishment after the assault.

Suddenly, Katell is back in his own body and his own time, and shocked by what he has just experienced in this momentary but powerful vision. As he reconsiders his plan to attack the cave, the platoon's radio relays orders to pull back—reporting that some kind of big bomb has been dropped on Japan and all units are ordered to return to their bivouacs and await orders. Katell's vision has saved him from committing a horrific act of unnecessary violence, leaving him chastened, and Causarano notes that there will always be more wars in the future, ensuring the lieutenant a chance to experience the horror of combat firsthand. The audience, however, knows that Katell's "mercy" was made possible by the atomic bomb. Mercy at the cost of hundreds of thousands of lives is ironic indeed, and Serling leaves the audience to ponder whether humans, as a species, have the strength and courage to overcome their penchant for slaughtering one another.

Even when it is not the specific focus of an episode, the shadow of potential nuclear war provides a grim background for the whole *Twilight Zone* series, making each episode a kind of chiaroscuro painting against a somber field of the unknown and knowable possibilities of darkness and evil. In the end, what captivated Serling as a writer and an individual were not monsters of fantasy or science fiction but the problem of human evil and the question of whether the meek and the innocent might be able, by some miracle of courage, to transcend those inner monsters that would destroy them and others. He explores the question again and again, always within the lengthening shadows cast by World War II. At times, the meek do, indeed, prevail, but other episodes suggest that even places that seem idyllically innocent and peaceful harbor the dark seeds of fear and distrust. "The Monsters Are Due on Maple Street," for example, takes place on a quiet suburban street whose residents—after all electrical devices suddenly and inexplicably stop working—turn on one another in a downward spiral of suspicion, distrust, and violence. The final scene reveals that "monsters" (conquest-minded aliens) are responsible for the mysterious power outage, but as in "I Am the Night," Serling's closing paints the residents of Maple Street as the real monsters. We are all too willing to destroy one another, he argues, completing the work of conquest for those who wish to destroy us. The episode can be read as an analog of the self-destructive frenzy of the postwar Red Scare that so appalled Serling,[22] but it also makes a larger, more general—and thus more chilling—point about human nature.

For Serling, the problem of human choice in the face of what is sometimes called "the glamour of evil" was central. In *The Twilight Zone,* he returned multiple times to a single unanswered question: Can a life-affirming spirit of forgiveness and brotherhood be powerful enough to enable humankind to overcome its worst impulses? The horrors of war, so powerfully rooted in Serling's own memories, provided a context and a motive for his continuing exploration of human evil. What his considerations of war in *The Twilight Zone* reveal, in no uncertain terms, is that there is no monster more horrific than the human being who has allowed fear, anger, and bloodlust to take charge of his soul. To paraphrase Cassius in Shakespeare's *Julius Caesar*, it is not in the stars but in our-selves that we find the horrible monsters, and it is there that we must confront and overcome them. Serling's speculative teleplays reveal him as a concerned and committed moralist who often used *The Twilight Zone* as his laboratory for examining the most fundamental questions of human morality in conditions of conflict and violence. For him, we are always at war in the "twilight zones" of our own psyches.

Notes

1. Serling, *As I Knew Him*, 34–64; Sandler, *Serling*, 34–50.
2. Only about one-sixth of the episodes (24 of 156) deal directly or indirectly with war.
3. Biographical facts about Rod Serling in this passage come from Anne Serling, chapters 6 and 7 (34–64) and Sandler, chapter 3 (34–50).
4. Notable examples include: Manchester, *Goodbye Darkness*; Fussell, *The Boys' Cru-sade*; and Sledge, *With the Old Breed*. Also, I discuss these kinds of memoirs at length in my book *Theaters of War: America's Perceptions of World War II* (see chapter 8, "Now It Can Be Told: Reopening Old Wounds," 185–211).
5. Casaregola, *Theaters of War*, 122–28, 186–87, and 253n.
6. The title "The Purple Testament" comes from the phrase "the purple testament of bleeding war" in Shakespeare's *Richard II*, Act III, Scene 3.
7. Serling, *As I Knew Him*, 52–53.
8. Jones, *WW II*, 54.
9. Serling, *As I Knew Him*, 52–53.
10. On the history of the *Lady Be Good*, see: "Factsheet: *Lady Be Good*."
11. "King Nine" was likely intended to be the bomber's radio call-sign, with "King" indicating the squadron and "Nine" the individual aircraft.
12. Serling, *As I Knew Him*, 30–34, 94–99, and 134–36.
13. Ibid., 97–99.
14. Ibid.
15. Ibid., 94–97, 167–69, and 210–12.
16. Serling, 94–97; Sandler, 116–17.
17. Casaregola, *Theaters of War*, 143–44.
18. Serling, *As I Knew Him*, 70–71, 94–97, 167–69, and 210–12. Also, concerning Serling's struggle to confront the Emmet Till murder, specifically see 94–97.
19. Serling, *As I Knew Him*, 58.
20. For an example of this ambivalence about the bomb, see the epilogue to Robert Leckie's 1957 war memoir, *Helmet for My Pillow*, where he acknowledges relief at the ending of war but also expresses his wariness about the weapons that were used to end it.
21. Rod Serling's unit was sent to serve as part of the occupying force in Japan after the bombs had been dropped and Japan had surrendered. This experience and his am-bivalence about the bomb are recounted in Serling, 58, and Sandler, 50.

22. On Rod Serling's reaction to McCarthyism and the attendant aspects of the 1950s Red Scare and the Blacklisting, see Sandler, *Serling*, 94–96.

Bibliography

Casaregola, Vincent. *Theaters of War: America's Perceptions of World War II*. NY: Palgrave Macmillan, 2009.

"Factsheet: *Lady Be Good*," National Museum of the US Air Force, 7 February 2001. http://www.nationalmuseum.af.mil /factsheets/factsheet.asp?id=2475.

Jones, James. *WW II*. New York: Grosset & Dunlap, 1975.

Leckie, Robert. *Helmet for My Pillow*. 1957. Reprint. New York: ibooks, 2001.

Sandler, Gordon F. *Serling: The Rise and Twilight of Television's Last Angry Man*. New York: Dutton, 1992.

Serling, Anne. *As I Knew Him: My Dad, Rod Serling*. New York: Citadel Press, 2013.

CHAPTER 17

Specters of Media

JACQUES TARDI'S GRAPHIC REANIMATION OF THE *WAR OF THE TRENCHES*

Katherine Kelp-Stebbins

Private Huet cannot escape the young woman he shot. Night after night she appears to him in the trenches holding on to the two children who fall with her, again and again. In order to flee the specters of these civilians he murdered in the line of duty, Huet leaves the trenches of the French army and crosses no-man's-land toward the German lines. Having been shot by a German sniper rifle, "he saw the girl and the kids one final time . . . then he saw no more."[1] One of more than twenty soldiers' stories recounted in Jacques Tardi's *It Was the War of the Trenches* (1993/2010), Huet's story is the most explicitly haunted of all those depicted in the graphic narrative. Or is it? While Huet's might be a traditional ghost story, I argue in this essay that Tardi's book, set on the European battlefields of World War I, exhibits haunting at the narrative, pictorial, and material levels. Just as comics interweave verbal and visual codes, the three analytical approaches that I use in this essay—diegetic, iconologic, and media specific—are necessarily interwoven, as are the words and images that assemble this graphic work. In the following sections I explore the interplay among these registers.

Author/artist Tardi has produced numerous graphic narratives set during the First World War. Most recently, 2013 saw the English translation of *Goddamn This War!* Tardi's work on this subject is especially well known for posing "*la question du réel*": interrogating the boundaries between the real and the imaginary.[2] The historical accuracy of his depictions of World War I is supported by copious archival research, yet historicity within the books is belied by stories like that of Huet, and images of skeletons with bulging eyeballs. Both *Goddamn* and *Trenches* feature back matter listing the historical sources used. *Trenches* includes an extra-diegetic account of Tardi's reliance on historians to help him decipher some of the photographic documentation that he used for the work. However, Tardi's works also function as a trenchant critique of reality as it is presented in official, jingoistic reports and in histories that rarely document wartime activities as they were suffered by soldiers and civilians.

It Was the War of the Trenches was originally published as a complete album in France as *C'était la guerre des tranchées* (1993). The book is comprised of vignettes in which World War I soldiers frequently face the ghosts of their victims (and themselves) while traversing a black-and-white Franco-Belgian no-man's-land. The circular, interwoven stories suggest both the inevitable conclusion of war as well as its inevitable continuation throughout the twentieth century. The final pages of the book depict soldiers from the Algerian and Vietnamese colonial forces while foretelling their future combat against colonial "masters of war."

At a visual level, Tardi's work pictorially cites numerous documentary photos and makes allusions to Abel Gance's film *J'accuse* (1919), reanimating these spectral images within the comics storyscape of *Trenches*. The referents of these images—men long dead despite their continuation in filmic and photographic form—attain new afterlives through their recirculation as comic book figures. Additionally, Tardi's black and white palette alludes to erstwhile mediation of the battlefield while ironically commenting on the moral ambiguity of the war.

Trenches provides an ideal example of how the formal properties of comics may be used to underscore narrative, pictorial, and thematic elements. Belgian theorist Thierry Groensteen has described the one fundamental aspect of comics as being "iconic solidarity": interdependent images that are at once separated and "plastically and semantically over-determined by [their] coexistence *in praesentia*."[3] Separation between images is the basis for comics narrative. The material substrate of the book compels a reader to order panels into narrative sequence while simultaneously navigating the two-page tableau of assembled images. As *Trenches* demonstrates, comics operate as fragmentary wholes, creating a formal display of how traumatic memory structures experience. Over the course of a work like *Trenches*, panels aesthetically and representationally recall other panels, while the necessary disjuncture between panels (the gutter or "trench" in this case) is both imperative for the progression of story, and symbolic of that which gets left out, forgotten, or buried.

Tardi's work takes the disjunctive resonances of comics even further, using symbolic panel design and page layout. Many pages feature panels whose composite shape forms the Arc de Triomphe in Paris, a monument-cum-burial marker for the unknown soldier entombed underneath. By utilizing this motif, Tardi suggests the proleptic situation of the working-class soldiers in his book, sent to the battlefield to die unknown. The very layout becomes its own spectral presence, creating a situation in which the unburied men drawn beneath the arc-shaped panels appear in tension with their burial by the page's design. Further tensions between page layout and life and death implicate the reader bodily in the outcome of war. As I explore in more detail below, the book's opening recto and verso pages feature weapons and infantry, respectively, so that the reader's turning of the page brings these forces together physically, and results narratively in a two-page spread of dead soldiers strewn across a battlefield. The material involvement of the reader in the narrative act of ghost-making adds another layer of spectrality to the work. Resonances between the dead and the living extend beyond the plane of representation to the relationship between media and user. Tardi's graphic design in *Trenches* suggests that media may be the most haunted field of all.

Narrative Haunting

At a diegetic level, *Trenches* is organized by the simultaneous inevitability and unexpectedness of death in battle. Oftentimes, but not always, the stories in the book result in the death of the focalizing character. "Focalization" is a term used by Gérard Genette to describe the orientation of narrative perspective. In a graphic narrative, as in a film, focalization is often implied by the visual as well as the verbal presence of a specific character. When a specific character comes to visually dominate or seems to orient the panels or frames, the reader is cued to that character's role in determining the narrative perspective on the story. Tardi's work plays on the possibly uncanny disjuncture between visual and verbal focalization. As in the film *Sunset Boulevard*, *Trenches* is consistently narrated by voices from beyond the grave. The reader is sometimes only made aware of the narrator's death through images that convey the nonliving state of the narrator, or by the incursion of other narrators who describe the demise of the previous narrator before launching into a different story. The deaths of many focalizing characters are verbally and/or visually depicted, yet because some do not die within the course of the narration, the reader is plagued by the inconsistency of battle: Will this character die? Is he already dead?

As if directly referring to the narrative structure of *Trenches*, Jan Mieszkowski describes the experiential conception of World War I as a "series of ironic vignettes."[4] He details the radical discontinuity in space, time, and pacing that characterized life at the front. In Mieszkowski's analysis, one of the implications for such a structure of experience was the lack of a "coherent battle narrative." The modern industrialized battlefield shifted the scale of warfare so radically that soldiers were denied the sequential unfolding of experience. Mechanized, repetitive destruction removed every conflict from a human scale of comprehension. Machine gun fire punctuated the battlefield with a rhythm beyond human capacity in the act of creating decidedly human casualties. Tardi's work models the discontinuous time of the battlefield. After an introductory section set in 1917, the remaining vignettes proceed chronologically in terms of dates noted and specific battles depicted. However, the duration of and connection between these events lacks a discernible pattern or scheme. The twenty-odd narratives—which span the period from the 1914 outbreak of the war to the 1918 Armistice—often commingle, so that it is difficult to discern where one story ends and another begins. Some stories are narrated using first-person pronouns and speech balloons emanating directly from characters, while others are told seemingly in third person or in an unattributed third-person plural voice. A story may begin with one narrator or focalizer, but end with another, once the first has been dispatched by a grenade or a sniper. The only certainty throughout the book is the unceasing progression of the war itself.

Narratively, *Trenches* enacts the dislocation of the place of death as Sigmund Freud describes it in his 1915 response to World War I, *Reflections on War and Death*. Freud details the realization of the reality of death that the war has necessitated. Previously, he states, each individual believed that death was ultimately something that happened to others. While one might associate with the death of a literary hero or even a loved one, the very fact that one survived this association allowed one to preserve a sort of imagined immortality. However, due to the characteristics of the First World War, Freud avows:

> It is obvious that the war must brush aside this conventional treatment of death. Death is no longer to be denied; we are compelled to believe in it. People really die and no longer one by one, but in large numbers, often ten thousand in one day.[5]

To directly tie this point—which Mieszkowski also cites—to the loss of coherent narrative, we must relinquish the concept of death as the assured end of every story. Instead, as both theorists posit, World War I temporally and spatially resituated death, by launching an all-out assault on the human subject as the center of experience and military praxis. The human story, with its trajectory from birth to death, was replaced by the rhythm and disjuncture of machine gun fire and artillery bombardment.

Trenches' narrative structure dislocates death from the end of every individual's story. The proliferation of stories also dislocates the human individual as the scalar model for war narrative. Instead we find stories like the first vignette in the book, which opens by describing, both textually and visually, "No Man's Land." At the bottom of the fourth page a drawing of a man clutching his abdomen is accompanied by the text "In this image, in the foreground, you can see a dead soldier: Private BINET."[6] In the next panel we see Binet *alive* and manning a parapet, and the text describes his position when the Captain directs another soldier, Faucheux, to go on reconnaissance. Binet's sudden diegetic revivification defines the following panels as a ghost story. A reader knows that Binet is dead already, but now sees him alive, an image and focalizing voice from beyond the grave. The other soldiers similarly inhabit quasi-alive states both verbally and visually.

Visually, Faucheux is depicted in four out of five panels on page 5, and then he disappears for the next eleven pages. Textually, Faucheux continues to reappear as an indication of the amount of time Binet spends thinking of him and wondering after his life-or-death status. On the tenth page a panel shows Binet having come across "FAUCHEUX's little booklet. There were addresses, notes, a photograph. He was surely dead, FAUCHEUX, and his booklet was a bother to BINET."[7] At this point, Faucheux's death is indeterminate, realized only by the textual assertion focalized through Binet's thoughts. Finally, on page 14, Binet has a dream in which a skeleton in soldier's uniform is reciting from (what is presumably) Faucheux's book, above a trench in which Binet cowers in fear before a giant rat atop a skeleton with eyeballs and brains protruding from its skull. This event leads Binet to relieve another soldier, Charroi, of his post and go running through no-man's-land in search of Faucheux, whose corpse he discovers, just in time to be shot by a German sniper himself. The irony of Binet's death is structurally facilitated by comics' verbal/visual media technology. A reader's visual realization of Faucheux's death coincides with the death of the textual narrator. A reader can now *see* that which Binet has been verbally imagining, at the precise moment that the verbal imagination as a focalizing medium cedes to visual imaging.

The final pages of the vignette feature two panels depicting Binet as he first appeared on page 4. In one he is surrounded by the ghosts of the neighbors he left behind in his apartment building in France, creating an inversion of life and death, whereby the dead man is haunted by the living. Finally another soldier, face hidden by a gas mask, describes coming upon Binet and Faucheux, "I saw: the ruins, the German with his machine gun, the shell-hole with FAUCHEUX at the bottom of it, the downed Fokker, and BINET . . . I was in the front row . . . like in the theatre . . . There was gas, too . . . So I headed home." As a sort of epigraph, the following page shows two German soldiers, who—after shooting a child who has dressed up in Binet's clothing—discover Faucheux's book and ponder whether Faucheux is alive or dead while a circular panel in the center of the page shows a skeleton with eyeballs staring out at the reader. Although the preceding may sound like a long and complex weave of soldiers' stories, the entire section is only sixteen pages in a 118-page work. The proliferation of characters and deaths produce repetition at a narrative level. However, not every character is guaranteed death, nor do the narrative strands allow a reader to anticipate which characters may be proleptically dead at the time that a vignette begins. Narrative conventions only serve to disorient the reader further. Some characters are named without any indication of what befalls them, while others are never named, yet drawn repeatedly or specifically shown dying in battle. Just as Freud and Mieszkowski demonstrate the incoherence of human narrative in the battlefields of World War I, so do the disjunctures, repetitions, and narrative asymmetry of *Trenches* induce the reader into a diegetic space where death is both guaranteed and shocking, due to its uneven distribution and the fragmentation of plotlines. This fragmentation, or the situation of death among the procession of lives, is further exhibited in the pictorial aspect of the work.

Visual Haunting

Tardi's drawings are stylized enough to generate ambiguity in terms of representations. The use of an entirely black and white palette entails a lack of distinction between, say, a soldier's spilled entrails and the mud lining the trenches. Tardi plays on such ambiguity in order to depict soldiers who have been mortally wounded before the audience is made aware of their condition. Similarly, fantasy and reality are conflated through the insertion of many grotesque elements such as the aforementioned eyeballs in the sockets of human skulls. A reader is left to determine the precise relation of these elements to the diegetic world. Are the battlefields of *Trenches* actually populated by the living dead? Are these merely fantastical projections of dreaming or dying characters? Or do these images demonstrate the radical discontinuity that World War I produces in terms of visual experience? Further complicating this fantasy/reality divide is Tardi's inclusion of numerous images taken directly from famous photographs of World War I. In this section I focus on how the use of photography engenders layers of visual spectrality in *Trenches*.

Tardi creates an ironic and haunting framework for the photographic record. Ernst Friedrich, in his photobook, *War against War!* (1924), sought to galvanize pacifist sentiment by juxtaposing horrifying photographs from World War I with militaristic rhetoric and propaganda from the period. Tardi similarly remediates war photographs in order to redirect their medial effects. Using photographs as the basis for numerous panels in *Trenches*, Tardi inserts these images created by another inscription technique into a graphic narrative, shifting their medial character as well as their relation to the story of war. The light-writing, or photography, that originally inscribed these soldiers on a two-dimensional surface is replaced by the hand-writing of the graphic narrative. The photographs are denatured from their existence as photograph, while their inclusion recalls photography as a documentary mode of pictorial inscription. Thus the "reality" of *Trenches* is bolstered by the inclusion of redrawn photographs, attesting to the verity of the images depicted, and yet also lessened by their very re-presentation as drawings within a comic book's diegetic world.

Roland Barthes famously claimed that photography is "tormented by the ghost of Painting."[8] *Trenches* is then doubly haunted, tormented by the ghost of photography, which is in turn tormented by the ghost of painting. Let us tease out the implications of such reduplicated ghosts. Barthes asserts that a photograph is tied to painting through pictorial and technical means. Pictorially, photography develops in reference to the iconographic codes influencing perspective and composition in painting. Technologically, Barthes states, the development of photography is linked to the "painters' *camera obscura.*" This is not to contend that photography is inescapably similar to painting; if anything, the ghostly torment is rooted in the displacement of the one by the other. In a passage where she directly describes one of the photographs that Tardi redraws, Susan Sontag specifies that war photography develops according to standards that separate it from art. If a photograph of suffering appears too "aesthetic" it is criticized for compromising its "authenticity."[9] Thus war photographs are haunted by the comparison to painting, a comparison that they must eschew through their reality.

Sontag also asserts that "in a world ruled by photographic images, all borders ('framing') seem arbitrary."[10] She contends that photographs make reality discrete and deny interconnectedness. For Sontag, the knowledge that photographs give of the world is inferior to a narrative: "Narratives can make us understand. Photographs do something else: they haunt us."[11] Working directly from Sontag's distinction between, on the one hand, photography and art, and on the other, photography and narrative, allows us to see the significance of Tardi's remediation of photographic images. By re-presenting well-known photographs as drawn images, Tardi draws upon the hauntedness of photography and gives it a new life in graphic narrative. The "authenticity" of the photographs, or their clear position as "not art," is ironically and paradoxically overturned. The documentary impetus that dictated the specific perspectival and iconographic production of these images inheres in, or haunts, what Tardi has now reimagined as drawn images assembled into narrative. The succession of medial ghosts finds its way from painting, to photography, to the graphic narrative, which situates the images in sequence, denaturing their position as discrete elements and overwriting their authenticity with hand-drawn lines.

However, the uncanny trace of the photograph persists in the very recognizability of the images that Tardi redraws. Because a reader can recognize a drawing in *Trenches* as a photograph, she is confronted with the presence of doubled and conflicting afterlives. There is the medial afterlife of the photograph as drawing, as well as the representational afterlife of the image's subject. The soldier whose life or death was once inscribed on the photograph is given new existence within Tardi's narrative. This second afterlife, that of the representational subject, is especially freighted with photography's relationship to death. A number of theorists of photography—including Walter Benjamin, Barthes, and Sontag—have written on the uncanny nature of photographs. In describing how the photograph functions as a specter, Barthes writes:

> In Photography, the presence of the thing (at a certain past moment)
> is never metaphoric; and in the case of animated beings, their life as
> well, except in the case of photographing corpses; and even so: if the
> photograph then becomes horrible it is because it certifies, so to speak,
> that the corpse is alive, as corpse: it is the living image of a dead thing.[12]

The economy of the photograph, as Barthes describes it, brokers in life and
death. Giving life to the dead subject and life after death for the living subject,
photographs mediate a relation between their subjects and their viewers that is
always a form of a "living image." Recast as a comic book panel, these photographs are divested of their "living" quality, creating further ambiguity between
the image and its referent. Once again, the boundaries governing the sovereignty
of the real and the sanctity of life are blurred in photography, and then further
confounded by Tardi's recycling of photographic images. If we know that a soldier was once alive, then photographed, and now appears as a character in Tardi's
work, what ghostly visions does his double mediation produce? Does the graphic
narrative bestow more life upon a referent who is now long gone, or does the erasure of his photographic trace reproduce his image as an even more ghostly presence? The interplay between photographic and graphic narrative images produces
a powerful visual hauntology. The media technology of comics is determined by
tensions like those discussed above: between the presentational and the representational, the verbal and visual, as well as the narrative and the pictorial. A similar
tension exists between the graphic and narrative aspects of *Trenches*.

Haunted Media

In *Alternative Comics: An Emerging Literature*, Charles Hatfield enumerates four
tensions that produce "the otherness of comics reading."[13] In addition to the
tensions between image and text or that of the relation of each image to those
surrounding it, Hatfield lists two other tensions specific to comics that I explore
in this section. The first is the tension between tabular and linear reading modes
and the second is the tension between narrative and materiality. *Trenches* demonstrates the haunting implications that each of these tensions might offer.

Originally described by French scholar Pierre Fresnault-Deruelle, the tension between linear and tabular reading consists in:

> on the one hand creating a page, building a two-dimensional spread,
> with all that entails in terms of formatting, on the other hand, telling
> a story, i.e., creating a divided, perspectival space-time. This tension
> could equally be formulated as follows: how, starting from a diversi-
> fied fragmentation, does one come to manage the diverse points of
> view within a unifying construction? Or again, one might say, how
> does one reconcile surface and space?[14]

As Fresnault-Deruelle asserts, at any point in a comic book, two alternate reading modalities simultaneously coexist in the same space. While a reader may follow the linear sequence of panels, she is also confronted with the page, as a composition unified by its tabular dimension. The perspectival dimension of any singular panel—as a discrete representation of space—operates concurrently to the reader's apprehension of the page as its own perspectival assemblage. Tardi orchestrates ironic and macabre effects through the deployment of these two registers in the pages of *Trenches*.

As mentioned above, panels are often arranged into the shape of the Arc de Triomphe. While this symbol first appears in upright formation, Tardi goes so far as to indict the nationalist symbol by flipping it, literally. The shape of the Arc—upright on pages 7 and 10—is inverted through the placement of the panels on page 19. This inversion at a tabular level also coincides at a linear or narrative level with the death of the soldier whose story is being told. On page 19 linear and tabular reading modes intersect so that the narrative and the national icon work against each other to challenge the meanings of each. The inversion of the Arc serves as a trenchant critique of the Tomb of the Unknown Soldier, especially as this soldier—and every other in the book— has been explicitly named. Tardi's attack on nationalist ideology operates on multiple levels, prompting attention to the framing of the war, as much as the content. By turning the shape of the monumental marker upside down in the space of the page, the symbolic grave is also representationally emptied of its contents in the panel that shows the soldier Binet succumbing to his bullet wounds. The shape of the monument and the narrative ironically comment upon each other, shifting meanings and creating ghostly resonance. On the page, Binet is the soldier ensconced visually beneath the inverted symbolic shape, yet his literal naming forecloses the possibility of his situation in the anonymous grave. Through tensions between linear and tabular readings, Tardi forces the audience to question how war memorials bury the individual narratives that enable such spectacles.

Furthermore, the materiality of the book creates a ghostly apparatus physically implicating the reader in the process of death making. As Pascal Lefèvre has noted of comics: "The material aspects of the format will determine the page lay-out, the choice between monochrome or colour, the type of story, the way in which it will be told, etc."[15] Although it may seem to go without saying, Lefèvre alerts us to the importance of print platforms and the difference between a comic strip drawn for inclusion in a newspaper and a book-length work like *Trenches*. Tardi utilizes the traditional *album* format, the standard book form for Francophone comics. As the glossary in *History and Politics in French-Language Comics and Graphic Novels* explains, an album is "oftentimes hardbound and almost always in the European A-4 paper format . . . paper is often of good quality and glossy."[16] Drawing directly

Jacques Tardi, *It Was the War of the Trenches*, 19. *Reprinted courtesy of Fantagraphics.*

from the above discussion on tabular and linear reading modes, we can understand the possibilities that the album format creates for meaningful design and panel placement. *Trenches* mobilizes the reader's page-turning to highlight the process of modern military death production.

Throughout the opening pages, the text invokes the similarity between the French and German sides: "These men have dug trenches, built shelters in the earth, and learned how to live in the mud like rats. Here we see the French." // "On the other side, it's more or less the same. But the trenches are better organized, because they're German."[17] The verbal is emphasized and enhanced through the page layouts. Pages 2 and 3 feature pictorial content showing the French and German tanks and trenches, respectively. Because the weapons and soldiers from each side are drawn side by side on the page, we understand their opposition in war and the thin lines that separate them. This separation engenders a tension that is banished by the fourth page where the sides have spilled out into the no-man's-land, littered with bodies and skulls. According to this linear reading, war is depicted as a symbolically empty parallelism ultimately leading only to death.

At the level of tableau, pages 2 and 3 both demonstrate bilateral symmetry at once uniting the sides of the page through composition and style, while dividing them into opposing sides, mirrored in the layout of gutters and panels. This mirror effect is doubled at the level of the two-page spread, where verso (page 2) and recto (page 3) parallel and comment on each other. In page 2 the double-panel unit that forms the middle of the page opposes German tanks on the left side and French on the right. On page 3 this opposition is reversed so that the trenches of the French are on the left, with the Germans on the right. This mirroring entails the overlaying, when the page is turned, of the French tank on the French soldiers, and the German tank on the German soldiers. Structurally this format suggests that the sides, while formally opposed, are ultimately self-destructive. Page 4 depicts the narrative and formal consequence of the war's opposition. The reader is implicated in this consequence, by bringing pages 2 and 3 together physically (when the pages are pressed together). Once the tanks and troops collide, literally by the turning of the page and figuratively by the course of narration, the devastation of life ensues. Tardi's pages demonstrate the many fields that coexist along the planes of the battlefield and the gutters.

The subject of depiction, the battlefield, is in Tardi's work always an already haunted space, merely awaiting the turn of a page before it is littered with the bodies that were always marked for death in the calculus that war necessitates. The battlefield is itself the subject of numerous media fields, which Tardi imbricates in meaningful association. The graphic narrative is haunted by the field of photography, itself always already haunted by the trace of light that functions

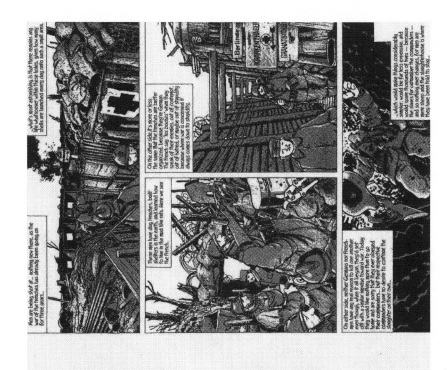

Tardi, *Trenches*, 2–3. Reprinted courtesy of Fantagraphics.

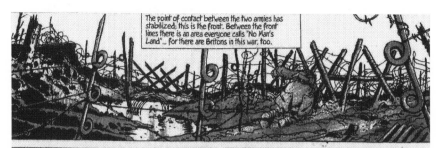

The point of contact between the two armies has stabilized; this is the front. Between the front lines there is an area everyone calls "No Man's Land"... for there are Britons in this war, too.

On a fairly regular basis, the soldiers are forced to emerge from the trenches and horrific hand-to-hand combat erupts in the No Man's Land. This is how the game is played: The French try to overrun the Germans' front line, and the Germans try to overrun the front lines of the French.

In the No Man's Land the following are to be found: barbed wire, placed there to fend off surprise attacks; dead men from the previous night's offensives; the dying wounded; and all manner of debris, as well as shell-holes filled with rainwater.

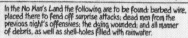

The place is hopping at night. Men are sent to observe the doings on the other side; to perform upkeep on the network of barbed wire; and to hit the enemy with the goal of bringing back prisoners, recovering wounded men, or burying dead men who are too visible and too much of a drain on morale, like a buddy's corpse hanging, rotting, from the barbed wire.

In this image, in the foreground, you can see a dead soldier: Private BINET.

Tardi, *Trenches*, 4. Reprinted courtesy of Fantagraphics.

in Barthes' word, as a form of ectoplasm, relating the moribund subject of the photograph with the viewer who encounters the image as a past-ness. In *Trenches* this particular media technology is further mediated so that the spectral photographs of the battlefield are given a second life. Reanimated within the graphic narrative, these images haunt the pages by creating further disjuncture between real and imagined, as well as between dead and alive. Finally it is in the media specificity of graphic narrative that Tardi involves and thus implicates the reader in the ghost making of war. World War I, by most estimates, is the last major armed conflict in which combatant casualties outnumbered those of civilians. By directly tying the actions of the reader to the mounting death toll depicted through the pages, the media technology foregrounds the unexpectedness of the events of war, and indicates the connectedness between those who can view its atrocities at a remove, and those who experience its horror directly in and between the trenches.

Notes

1. Tardi, *War of the Trenches.*
2. See Screech, *Masters of the Ninth Art*, 131–37.
3. Groensteen, *System of Comics*, 18.
4. Mieszkowski, *Watching War*, 152.
5. Freud, *Reflections on War and Death*, 47.
6. Tardi, *War of the Trenches*, 4, all proper names appear in capital letters in the original.
7. Ibid., 10.
8. Barthes, *Camera Lucida*, 30.
9. Sontag, *Regarding the Pain of Others*, 76.
10. Sontag, *On Photography*, 22.
11. Sontag, *Regarding the Pain of Others*, 89.
12. Barthes, *Camera Lucida*, 78–79.
13. Hatfield, *Alternative Comics*, 32–67.
14. In the original French: *"d'un côté réaliser une planche, construire un ensemble à deux dimensions, avec tout ce que cela suppose comme mise en forme, de l'autre, raconter une histoire, i.e susciter un espace-temps fractionné et perspectif. Cette tension pourrait également se formuler de la façon suivante: comment, en partant d'une fragmentation diversifiée, arriver à maîtriser la disparité des points de vue dans une construction unifiante? Autrement dit, encore, comment concilier surface et espace?"* Fresnault-Deruelle, "Du linéaire au tabulaire," 17.
15. Lefèvre, "The Importance of Being 'Published.'"
16. "French-Language Comics Terminology and Referencing," in McKinney, *History and Politics*, xiii.
17. Tardi, *War of the Trenches*, 3.

Bibliography

Barthes, Roland. *Camera Lucida: Reflections on Photography.* Translated by Richard Howard. New York: Farrar, Straus and Giroux, 1981.

Fresnault-Deruelle, Pierre. "Du linéaire au tabulaire." *Communications* 24 (1976): 7–23.

Freud, Sigmund. *Reflections on War and Death.* Translated by A. A. Brill and Alfred B. Kuttner. New York: Moffat, Yard & Co., 1918.

Friedrich, Ernst. *Krieg dem Kriege! Guerre à la guerre! War against war! Oorlog aan den Oorlog!* Berlin: Freie Jugend, 1924.

Groensteen, Thierry. *The System of Comics.* Translated by Nick Nguyen and Bart Beaty. Jackson: University Press of Mississippi, 2007.

Hatfield, Charles. *Alternative Comics: An Emerging Literature.* Jackson: University Press of Mississippi, 2005.

Lefèvre, Pascal. "The Importance of Being 'Published': A Comparative Study of Different Comics Formats." In *Comics and Culture: Analytical and Theoretical Approaches to Comics,* edited by Anne Magnussen and Hans-Christian Christiansen, 91–105. Copenhagen: Museum Tusculanum Press, 2000.

McKinney, Mark, ed. *History and Politics in French-Language Comics and Graphic Novels.* Jackson: University Press of Mississippi, 2008.

Mieszkowski, Jan. *Watching War.* Stanford, CA: Stanford University Press, 2012.

Screech, Matthew. *Masters of the Ninth Art: Bandes dessinées and Franco-Belgian Identity.* Liverpool: Liverpool University Press, 2005.

Sontag, Susan. *On Photography.* New York: Farrar, Straus and Giroux, 1973.

———. *Regarding the Pain of Others.* New York: Farrar, Straus and Giroux, 2003.

Tardi, Jacques. *C'était la guerre des tranchées.* Paris: Casterman, 1993.

———. *It Was the War of the Trenches.* Translated by Kim Thompson. Seattle: Fantagraphics Books, 2010.

CHAPTER 18

R-Point as Postcolonial Palimpsest

GENERIC COMPLEXITY AND THE GHOST IN THE WAR/HORROR FILM

Amanda Landa

> On 07 January, the South Korean base in Nah-Trang, Vietnam, receives a radio transmission from a missing platoon presumed dead. The high-command assigns the veteran and decorated Lieutenant Choi Tae-in to lead a squad with eight other soldiers and rescue the missing soldiers from R-Point.[1]

And so begins the nightmarish tale of *R-Point* (Su-chang Kong, 2004), a South Korean film set in 1972 during the Vietnam War. The introductory scenes possess a mise-en-scène and dialogue reminiscent of American Vietnam War films as Choi's ragtag squad heads there to search for the lost unit. But once they begin exploring the area around "Romeo Point," the film converges with the horror genre: a ghostly specter inhabits their radio and recording equipment, appears in various human guises, and eventually possesses their bodies, exacting vengeance for Vietnam's long, bloody colonial history. The mass hysteria and violence spiral out of control, until only one battered and blinded soldier is left alive.

This chapter will explore how, through both generic complexity and the politics of ghost narratives, Romeo Point represents a site of trauma that continually repeats the violent acts that have been committed there, from Chinese to French colonialism, to an American and Korean military presence during the Vietnam War.[2] Generically, *R-Point* merges the war and the ghost/horror genres, using the narrative unpredictability thus created to barrage the spectator with multiple possible readings and creating an open generic discourse. The convergence of the war film (as a historically and politically charged text) and the ghost film, in particular, brings *R-Point* into the milieu of postcolonial and palimpsestic readings of regional cinemas. The film not only comments on Vietnam's colonial past and Korea's own relationship with its status as postcolonial nation, but also the current filmic and political environment in East Asia. Ultimately, *R-Point* allows us to think about the state of South Korea's postcolonial/postmodernist film industry, as it critiques historical narratives by rewriting the image of the ghost girl, which the popularity of Japanese horror films has made into an internationally recognized trope at the turn of the millennium.

R-Point: The Film

The film opens at a South Korean military headquarters in Nah Trang, Vietnam, as the radio operator receives a distress call from a platoon with the call sign "Donkey-3"—a unit missing for six months, whose members are presumed to be dead. Soon afterward, a single survivor from the platoon appears: bloodied, disfigured, and carrying his fallen comrades' dog tags. Donkey-3 is the latest in a series of units sent to Romeo Point—a "noncombat" zone located deep in South Vietnamese territory, on an island 150 kilometers south of Saigon—and never heard from again. Senior officers summon Lieutenant Choi to headquarters and assign him to investigate. He is placed in command of eight soldiers from the base hospital who are awaiting discharge from the army—Sergeant Jin and Privates Oh, Joh, Lee, Byun, Cook, Park, and Jang—and sent to R-Point to solve the mystery and rescue any remaining survivors of Donkey-3. Upon reaching the island, however, Choi's unit (code-named "Mole-3") finds not lost soldiers, but malevolent spirits. Over a period of three days, the soldiers experience a series of hauntings and, one by one, they become casualties of an unnatural war.

The ghosts begin to appear as soon as Choi's squad arrives on the island, becoming bolder and more numerous as the soldiers move inland. They manifest themselves as phantom voices on the radio, units of soldiers that appear where they should not be, and humanlike apparitions—notably a dark-haired young woman in a white *áo dài* (a long tunic). The hauntings begin in earnest after Mole-3 encounters a gravestone with a cryptic, foreboding message written in Chinese, prompting a member of the squad to recount part of the area's long, bloody history. The abandoned, decaying mansion that Choi selects as their base on the island prompts the retelling of another episode from that history. A relic of the French colonial era, the mansion was used as a field hospital by the French army in the First Indochina War (1946–1954), where hundreds of French troops were massacred on New Year's Eve, 1952. Later, as he follows the ghostly apparition of the woman in white, Choi stumbles onto a mass graveyard where the victims were buried.

Surrounded by the dead and continually haunted by their ghosts, the members of Choi's squad begin to break down. Private Joh mistakes a ghostly squad of Donkey-3 troops for his own comrades and attempts to engage with them, but they soon disappear into the tall grass. Private Oh, guilt-ridden over his theft

The squad cautiously approaches the abandoned mansion that will serve as their headquarters on the island.

of a camera from one of the soldiers in Donkey-3, gradually loses his mind and dies when he stumbles into a booby trap. Private Byun, the radio operator for Mole-3, insists that he has received a transmission from French troops, although the French left the area a generation ago. Separated from the group, Sergeant Jin discovers the radio that sent the phantom signal to headquarters, along with the corpse of Donkey-3's radio operator, and returns to the mansion carrying the corpse's head.

The members of Choi's squad—strangers to one another before the mission began—become increasingly paranoid as their secrets and lies are revealed. Their trust in each other erodes, and the mission begins to unravel. Private Cook, despite his claim of having killed many men, is revealed to be merely a cook, and dies when Joh, driven mad with fear, mistakes him for the enemy and shoots him. Realizing that he is losing control, Lieutenant Choi regroups his men at the mansion-hospital and radios for help. As they wait for a response, however, Jin becomes possessed by a ghost and—under its influence—initiates a gruesome bloodbath. The ghost jumps from one member of the squad to another, possessing each of them in turn and causing them to turn on and kill one another. Soon the only two left are Jang—the youngest and most innocent member of the squad—and Lieutenant Choi, who sacrifices his own life in an effort to save Jang's. The final scene of the film shows a new phantom signal being received at the South Korean headquarters in Nah Trang, this time from Mole-3, calling for help and suggesting that the cycle of violence at R-Point is about to begin anew.

R-Point and the Vietnam War Film

Generically, *R-Point* merges the war film and the ghost/horror film. In his writing on the Hollywood war film, Stephen Neale discusses the generic structures of these films, drawing particular attention to the "primary situation," the reality of the film or the logic of the narrative world, and the "initial event," an occurrence within the narrative that sets the plot in motion. True to its compound nature, *R-Point* demonstrates dual primary situations and initial events, one set each for the war and the ghost/horror film. Initially the film is marked by "the absence of monsters and monstrosity,"[3] but it progresses into a reality where ghosts/monsters become present.

Initially, the film is situated squarely within the Vietnam War genre. The radio distress call in the opening scene, and the arrival of the bandaged and bloody sole survivor of Donkey-3, do not yet signal a world governed by the logic of ghost stories. The post-traumatic stress of the remaining soldier and his extensive injuries are unremarkable to those familiar with Vietnam War film tropes. The scenes that introduce the lead character, Lieutenant Choi also employ familiar Vietnam War film elements. Choi, along with his last survivor from his old squad, visits a brothel in a town whose appearance speaks of US influence. The sign on the brothel reveals that it is called "Texas," and employs Vietnamese prostitutes who speak English. The brothel scenes themselves draw from a long tradition of Hollywood Vietnam War films, recalling iconic scenes from *Hearts and Minds* (1974), *Full Metal Jacket* (1987), and *Off Limits* (1988), among others. As Choi attempts to sleep in a prostitute's bed, he hears gunshots. In the hallway, he confronts a young cleaning woman whom he suspects of being Viet Cong. In English, she asks him to not shoot, and despite his warnings, continues to approach. As she reaches for something hidden in her cleaning supplies, he shoots her down and uncovers a large rifle.[4] The woman serves as an easily recognizable symbol of Vietnam War film protagonists' inner conflicts about the potential danger posed by innocent-seeming civilians, and ultimate vindication when they act on those suspicions.

After Choi's fatal shootout at the brothel, he is sent to military headquarters. Within the office, the first shot is of a portrait of Park Chung Hee, the authoritarian and militaristic prime minister of South Korea during the Vietnam War. Choi is offered Ho Chi Minh's favorite tea by his commander, which Choi refuses. His commander recounts Choi's military exploits, noting his heroic record, and the death of all but one member of his squad on his last mission. The general, in a scene that echoes the opening of *Apocalypse Now* (1979), shows Choi a confidential folder containing a photograph of the lieutenant in command of Donkey-3, and orders him to take a squad, travel by water to R-Point, and determine the fate of the now-missing lieutenant and his men.

Choi, determined to redeem himself in combat, tries to refuse the assignment, but he is given direct orders.

His squad consists of volunteers from the infirmary, all syphilis victims except Jang, a young untested cadet who sold his medical pass for 50 *won*. The men get acquainted as they await the ship to take them to R-Point, gossiping among themselves and sizing each other up, part of the process of "demythologization" of war that characterizes so many Vietnam-era war films.[5] The heroic and sacrificing "noble band of brothers" featured in World War II narratives, gives way, in Vietnam films, to unflattering portrayals that expose in-group fighting and the ambiguous or amoral choices of the protagonists. Following this pattern, *R-Point* presents Choi and his second-in-command, Sergeant Jin, as battle-tested leaders, but their men as foulmouthed, and selfish either prone to bragging about their exploits of extreme violence or completely apathetic.

As soon as the squad reaches the island and wades onto the shore, one soldier suggests a souvenir photograph. Another soldier appears with them on the beach, and eventually offers to take the photograph of the eight men in Choi's unit. Though it is not yet apparent, this ninth soldier is the ghost of Jung, a member of the lost Donkey-3 unit they have been sent to find. After the camera clicks, the image stills and fades to black and white. The intertitle "R-Point Day 1" appears at the bottom of the screen, and low, moaning sound effects are heard, foreshadowing the ghostly influence but not yet revealing itself to the audience or the characters.

Soon after this, the men are caught in a firefight with a Viet Cong guerilla, a young woman whom Choi injures with a grenade. They discover her, dying, in a foxhole. As they lift her head and reveal her face, there is a close-up of Choi. The men stand over her, inspecting the body, and Sergeant Jin handles a bracelet on her wrist, causing the bells attached to it to ring. Joh asserts that touching a dead person's things will bring a curse, and Jin retracts in horror. The men argue over who should kill her and as Sergeant Jin commits to doing it, Choi orders the rest to move out. The woman's gasping face, covered in blood, watches them go. The entire mise-en-scène recalls Vietnam War combat films—the overgrown jungle, the men's uniforms, and the girl's Viet Cong black "pajamas" are all familiar. As the squad continues farther inland, the next scene shows them coming across the beginning of R-Point proper, which is marked by a gravestone with a foreboding message.

The appearance of the gravestone is the initial event of the ghost narrative. The war film genre has been dominant up until this point, with the action revolving around military procedures, the inter-workings of rank and power through dialogue, and the two separate conflicts with the Viet Cong. Once the squad encounters the gravestone, however, a world without the possibility of ghosts is changed to one with such possibilities. The gravestone's eerie epitaph alerts the spectator to the shift in generic categories, a shift reinforced by the presence of fog, close-ups of tense faces, and slow moaning music. The characters do not yet know it, as the "monster" has yet to be revealed, but it is clear to the audience that the ghost genre has now converged with the Vietnam War genre.

Corporal Joh is an undertaker's son and can read Chinese as a result of his occupational training. Asked to translate the gravestone for the others, he reads: "Hundreds of years ago, the Chinese killed Vietnamese and dumped them into the lake. After that, they filled the lake and built a temple on it. Wherever you go, I'll be there. If you have blood on your hands . . ." Joh stops at this point, unable to see the rest. Choi confirms Joh's translation, and the men seem slightly unsettled at the revelation. The sole exception is Corporal Lee, who urinates on the gravestone in defiance. The act of urinating on the stone reveals the final Chinese character that Joh could not see, and the crucial last phrase of the translation appears on the screen: "If you have blood on your hands, you can't go back."[6] The soldiers, however, have already moved on and this revelation is only evident to the viewer. As the camera cranes upward as they enter R-Point in the distance, they remain ignorant of the true nature of the stone's warning. The viewer has seen the gravestone's final warning, but the soldiers have not.

From this point on, like the soldiers, all the narrative action stays within R-Point, the outside world appears only distantly, through radio transmissions. The contextual war conflict has shrunk down to a more specific ghostly one. In addition, the layers of knowledge will become increasingly complicated, as the viewer will have access to characters' private memories, revealing their backstories in cutaway scenes so as to explain their personal traumas in relation to how the ghost will manifest itself to them.

As the members of the squad increasingly lose confidence in Choi, they begin to distrust the chain of command, as well as their comrades-in-arms, often withholding details from each other as a result. Their questions and doubts grow when they realize that their seemingly harmless errant mission is something far more sinister. *R-Point* highlights the ignorance of the military command to the evil that resides in Romeo Point. The fact that headquarters personnel will not heed Lieutenant Choi's urgent request for extraction means that R-Point will continuously call new units to their doom.

R-Point and the Ghost Film

The narrative formula for the war genre film is clear,[7] but the convergence of these two particular forms, war and horror, is particularly resonant and makes available new possibilities. As Hantke notes, the use of gratuitous violence and gore is a key point in the compatibility between the war and the horror film genre,[8] and this is particularly true of *R-Point*, in which violence is inflicted on the soldiers by each other, through the ghost's manipulation of their bodies, rather than by the ghost itself. It is important to note, however, that this convergence of the war film (as a decidedly historically and politically charged text) and the ghost film in particular, enters into the milieu of postcolonialism and palimpsestic readings of regional cinemas. Bliss Cua Lim writes, "Ghosts call our calendars into question. The temporality of haunting—the return of the dead, the recurrence of events—refuses the linear progression of modern time consciousness, flouting the limits of mortality and historical time."[9] The film's violence and gore is closer to the war genre than to horror, but it is the appearance of the ghost/haunting itself that creates readings of the overlapping colonial violence of Vietnam. It is the particularity of place that is the foundation of *R-Point*, made most significant through the various levels of knowledge available to the Mole-3 unit and the audience.

On the first morning, as the sun rises, the fog lifts to reveal the French colonial mansion-turned-hospital, and the squad establishes their headquarters. The layers of occupation and violence that characterize modern Vietnamese history are thus distilled, in the film, into a single location. R-Point represents multiple layers of colonial violence, concentrated in one isolated place, from Chinese occupation signified by the gravestone, to French colonialism as represented by the mansion, to the existence of South Korean soldiers fighting on behalf of the United States during the Vietnam War.

The first acknowledgment of the possibility of ghosts materializes after the squad's discovery of the French mansion: a scene made all the more striking because it takes place during the day. The men have regrouped and begun to patrol R-Point. One group of the men cuts through the tall grass. It is sunny and there is a strong wind. The camera shows a medium close-up of Corporal Joh, with his back turned to the camera.

The camera follows Joh as he tries to find his companions, and then pulls back and lowers to the ground. This is the first time this kind of camera movement is used, and illustrates that the camera is no longer an "omnipresent" eye but instead the perspective of diegetic subjectivity. Later in the film it becomes more explicit that it is a ghost's subjectivity by adding digital effect filters over the image when it is watching the men through the windows. The sense of place that the film creates around R-Point is central to the film's transition from a Vietnam War story to a ghost/horror story. Ian Conrich writes:

> The power of the Gothic can exist within a dark truth revealed, the uncovering of a troubling past moment or experience that has refused to remain hidden, or the startling revelation that a secure environment has been transformed into one of threat. . . . It exists at the point where "controls" such as doors and windows, which

when closed are designed to maintain boundaries, have been unable to prevent the external and the nocturnal from invading those sites associated with the domestic, comfort and the self. Moreover, it is where the tame or the innocent has become wild and malevolent; and the living and the dead have merged.[10]

The ghost's subjectivity, represented with digital filter and distorted sound, freely moves in and out of the mansion through the windows and the doors. Just as the audience was privy to the gravestone warning, they also witness the change in viewpoint that signals a shift to the ghost's perspective. In addition, the landscape continues to change as the malevolent presence exposes itself. During the Vietnam War, guerilla warfare always made the jungle a dangerous place, but the second half of the film takes this process further. The actual landscapes of R-Point will vary according to the time of day and to whoever is traveling through them. It is the violent colonial past that cannot remain hidden, and the layers of colonization are written on this land.

As Lim notes, "the return of the dead, the recurrence of events—refuses the linear progression of modern time consciousness," and as a film *R-Point* often becomes confusing with the various time frames and chronologies written into the narrative. There are flashbacks—a different kind of haunting—which take place at times when Choi and the men are reflecting on their past sins. R-Point is a place where all histories are written atop each other, existing coterminously, and cyclical violence is relived over and over again. At the end of their first day at R-Point, Choi and his men are visited at the mansion by a small US Army unit. The American lieutenant in charge of the unit tells Choi that his own men are betting that, when they return in four days, Choi and his men will be dead. Two days later, however, Choi finds the wreckage of a crashed American helicopter containing the corpses of the very men he just met, who have been dead and decaying for weeks. In a parallel occurrence, Corporal Byun, who mans Mole-3's radio set, reports receiving a message from a French corporal who informs him that he and his brother are coming to visit. The French soldiers, however, are also long dead. Later in the film, both Choi and Jin will independently stumble upon the graveyard where their bodies lie, surrounded by the other French victims of the New Year's Eve massacre.

R-Point and the Ghost Girl

Prior to the film's climax, Choi sees the ghost of the dead Viet Cong agent walking in a white áo dài, in the rain. He decides to follow her, hoping to get answers to the haunting of R-Point. Through Choi, the audience will learn how she in particular represents the history of colonial violence at R-Point, and the key to unlocking the real truth behind the ghost girl is gradually revealed at the end of the film.

On the second night, after it is revealed that Private Jung—the soldier who appeared on the beach—was a ghost, the men contemplate their transgressions: Oh remembers his sin of stealing the camera, and Jin remembers his orders to close the case. Intertitles appear at the bottom of the screen, "R-Point Day Three" beneath a shot of Lieutenant Choi. The camera is positioned outside the mansion so that he is framed by a window. The screen is digitally filtered to imply the specter's subjectivity, watching Choi. Choi turns away from the window and the bracelet bells are heard as thunder crashes. Choi stops and looks over his left shoulder, out the window. The image filter is gone, and the film cuts to a medium close-up of Choi, still framed in the window, as he looks out. A reverse shot shows the ghost, manifested as the dead Viet Cong, in a white áo dài, in the same perspective: shown as if in a mirror image. The bells are heard again, and the specter is shown wearing the same bracelet that Jin had considered stealing off the dying girl. She turns and walks off screen right, and Choi exits the mansion to follow her. She eventually leads him to an open field with an ancient stone statue and disappears into the distance. The lighting flashes over the face of the statue. As Choi turns around, the previously empty field becomes filled with white crosses. All of the graves have French names and the same death date: December 30th, 1952, during the First Indochina War. The American lieutenant's voice is heard in a voice-over, repeating his previous story: "a retreat for French soldiers. Yeah, a retreat for French soldiers. Fuck, a lot French soldiers were exterminated here. It all happened so fast. Sure as hell can tell you it wasn't VC that did it. Hell, during that time the VCs didn't exist. There's nothing alive here in R-point. Neither ROK soldiers nor VCs can survive here."[11] Choi recognizes the names Paul and Jacques from Byun's radio transmission, and, kneeling in front of their grave marker, finds the girl's bracelet.

R-Point's double genres use several nationally marked bodies to represent conflicting national histories, and this "dislocated vision of two [or more] moments provides access to the prior conflict through the lens of the current one."[12] When the film first layers the horror genre onto the war film, it "creates "parallels . . . [that are] conspicuous and insightful."[13] *R-Point*'s setting and use of complicated temporalities illustrates the layering of historical conflict in Vietnam, one in which Romeo Point represents violent pasts from Chinese and French colonialism, to the American and Korean military presence during the Vietnam War. I borrow the term "palimpsest,"—the ancient practice of scraping animal hides used for writing, and then reinscribing them with new words or pictures, creating several layers of text atop each other—from Andreas Huyssen, who writes, "My focus on reading palimpsests is . . . the conviction that literary

The field of the dead. White crosses mark the graves of French soldiers killed during the First Indochina War.

techniques of reading historically, intertextually, constructively, and deconstructively at the same time can be woven into our understanding of urban spaces as lived spaces that shape collective imaginaries."[14] Whereas Huyssen's project is concerned with lived historical traumas in real spaces, *R-Point* distills the project of collective imaginaries and historical traumas into a generic device, one that not only accomplishes the desired effect on the spectator, but also draws from real historical conflicts in Vietnam.

After Choi recovers the bracelet adorned with bells from Paul and Jacques's grave, he insists on revisiting the corpse of the Viet Cong guerilla they killed before entering R-Point, but is unable to pass the gravestone. He and his squad helplessly go in circles as they realize that the stone's prophecy has come true, and they are unable to leave R-Point. Jin and his squad, meanwhile, revisit the area where Choi saw the graveyard, which is now without crosses. Jin buries dog tags from the soldiers of Donkey-3, but then falls into a cave. His men, unable to find him, encounter Choi's own lost, disoriented squad, and the two groups—mistaking one another for the enemy—get into a firefight, leading to another casualty. Once order is restored, they return to the mansion. The climax of the film occurs in its main room, as the ghost (represented, again, by the camera's deliberately distorted view) circles the terrified and confused men as it turns them against one another. Choi tries desperately to save his unit—ordering them to recite their names and official ranks as a way to focus their minds and call them back to reality[15]—but his plan fails and they cut one another down.

The camera, still representing the perspective of the ghost, now circles Choi as he kneels down to reassure Jang that they will both make it home. Seeing a photograph in Jang's shirt pocket, he inspects it. The picture shows a group of French soldiers in front of the mansion and, with them, scowling, is the girl in the white áo dài whom he has seen in the field. Hearing the bells again, Choi turns and finds them in the middle of the floor. He now grasps that the ghost girl is in the room with them, that she is the malevolent force controlling them. The ghost girl appears behind him, the bells (now also shown on her wrist) ringing as she approaches. Choi instructs the blind Jang to raise his rifle and instructs him where to aim: toward Choi. As the girl nears Choi, blood begins to drip from her eyes. She smiles and her long black hair shifts from being pulled back, as in the picture with the French soldiers, to hanging loosely around her face. Other images of the ghost girl flash into the screen: her in the photograph, her in the rain, and her as the Viet Cong dead in the foxhole. Choi's eyes turn bloody red. Knowing that she is starting to possess him—and determined not to be forced to kill the last survivor of his unit—he orders Jang to pull the trigger and kill him.

Mole 3's sole survivor, the blinded and battered Jang Young-Soo (Tae-kyung Oh).

In this way, the ghost girl's origins are revealed to be directly tied to colonialism, and specifically the First Indochina War. The mansion has been described as a retreat, but the girl's role is never elaborated. She was clearly under the employ of the French soldiers, most likely as a prostitute. The "extermination," described earlier, is a reference to the Vietnamese rebellion against French colonial presence. Though *R-Point* builds on historical violence at the national level, it is a colonial and sexual violence as written onto the feminine national body, represented by the ghost girl. Portrayed by the same actress, the girl's identity is collapsed across two conflicts, first in the photograph and second as the Viet Cong in the foxhole. The fact that the film portrays the final ghost as the ghost girl does not necessitate that this is the ghost's true form but does represent a national construct. It speaks to the specific sins in which Choi has participated, and which specifically tie him to the French, US, and South Korean presences in Vietnam: sexual exploitation of the female population of occupied countries. The Korean soldiers are, themselves, also exploited, but the ghost's final appearance as a dead Vietnamese woman returns the focus to the gendered violence that has been made evident throughout the film. That members of Mole-3—except for Jang—are also guilty of sexual exploitation is underscored by the fact that they have all been diagnosed with venereal diseases, most likely contracted from brothels near their base camps. "In these films the repressed from the past can return via the repressed of the present."[16]

Conclusion

R-Point not only opens up the discourse of Vietnamese colonialism and postcolonialism, but, as a Korean film in 2004, also comments upon the contemporary transnational film industry in East Asia. Its use of the horror film trope of the "ghost girl," is a conscious quotation within the East Asian film industry, specifically drawn from Japanese films of the 1990s:

> Given the international success of [Japan] with films such as the *Ringu* trilogy (*The Ring*, Hideo Nakata; Hideo Nakata; Norio Tsuruta, 1998–2000), *Ju-on: The Grudge* (Takashi Shimizu; four films, 2000–2003), and *Honogurai mizu no soko kara* (*Dark Water*, Hideo Nakata, 2002), it was perhaps inevitable that elements would seep into the Korean horror film seeking commercial recognition.[17]

The ghosts in these films are typically victims of domestic violence: the spirits of children and women abused by the men around them. The avenging spirit is one that fights back against patriarchal repression, and though the ghost must be stopped, it is often done so by a living woman, reaching out to let the troubled soul rest in peace. This is true of *Ringu* and *Dark Water*, though not as clear in *The Grudge*, as the ongoing nature of the franchise does not allow for any definitive ending. As such, the international popularity of these film series has given rise to several other Asian and Southeast Asian iterations of the ghost girl/woman phenomena, most specifically with *R-Point*, Thailand's *Shutter* (2004), Singapore's *The Maid* (2005), and Philippines' *The White Lady* (2006) among many others. Though each national context places its own folkloric history on their ghostly women, the long black hair and white attire are fairly similar throughout. In particular, South Korean ghost films often use the image of a young girl "crying" blood, as in the film posters for *Whispering Corridors 4: Voice* (2005) and *Someone Behind You* (2007). I hesitate to strictly identify the image as "crying" as it may be meant to be something more horrific. The ghost in *R-Point* has a sinister smile, and clearly uses eye contact as a way to possess Choi.

Despite being one of many films to use the popularized image of the ghost girl, however, *R-Point* goes a step further by commenting on South Korea's particular global position. First, of course, it addresses South Korea's past as the country with the second-largest military presence in Vietnam during the Vietnam War, a step it took in order to secure financial ties with the United States. Secondly, it underscores the ways in which the Korean film industry made use of the breakout popularity and recognizability of the ghost girl from Japan, advancing it from a domestic to a national level of allegory. Despite South Korea's and Japan's mutual interest in each other's domestic products, the two nations have historically fraught relationship, and a competitive attitude toward soft power, expressed (in part) through the international popularity of popular cultural products. Although *R-Point* did not have the same cultural impact as *Ringu*, it represents an entry into a long line of historically complicated, high-budget genre films—one that represents the growing success of the South Korean film industry.

Notes

1. Opening narrative, *R-Point*.
2. Much thanks to Professor Lalitha Gopalan for her instruction and guidance. Her Asian Horror film course in spring 2010 introduced me to *R-Point*, Lim's book, and Neale's article.
3. Neale, "Aspects of Ideology," 36.
4. It should be noted that as he shoots her, she falls to her death in slow motion, the director filmically underscoring the significance of her death.
5. Williams, "Concealment and Disclosure," 37.
6. DVD subtitles.
7. Neale, "Aspects of Ideology."

8. Hantke, "Military Horror Film."

9. Lim, *Translating Time*, 149.

10. Conrich, "Gothic Bodies," 111.

11. DVD subtitles, but this soldier actually speaks in English. ROK stands for Republic of Korea.

12. Lim, *Translating Time*, 168.

13. Ibid.

14. Huyssen, *Present Pasts*, 7.

15. This scene can be read as a reference to the climax of *The Thing* (1982), directed by John Carpenter.

16. Conrich, "Gothic Bodies," 114.

17. Ibid., 108.

Bibliography

Conrich, Ian. "Gothic Bodies and the Return of the Repressed: The Korean Horror Film of Ahn Byeong-ki." *Gothic Studies* 12, no. 1 (2010): 106–15.

Hantke, Steffan. "The Military Horror Film: Speculations on a Hybrid Genre," *Journal of Popular Culture* 43, no. 4 (2010): 701–19.

Huyssen, Andreas. *Present Pasts: Urban Palimpsests and the Politics of Memory*. San Jose, CA: Stanford University Press, 2003.

Lim, Bliss Cua. *Translating Time: Cinema, the Fantastic, and Temporal Critique*. Durham, NC: Duke University Press, 2009.

Neale, Steve. "Aspects of Ideology and Narrative Form in the American War Film." *Screen* 32, no. 1 (1991): 35–57.

R-Point. Directed by Su-chang Kong. 2004. New York: Tartan Video, 2006. DVD.

Williams, Doug. "Concealment and Disclosure: From 'Birth of a Nation' to the Vietnam War Film." *International Political Science Review* 12, no. 1 (1991): 29–47.

Index

truth, 15, 99, 101; impossibility of
discovering, 173–74, 178–180;
searches for, xviii, 76, 83–86, 99, 101,
187–200, 291; wartime revelations
of, xxi, 122, 129–30, 187–200,
291–92. *See also* censorship; cover-ups;
memory, historical
Twelve (novel, 2010), xvii, 24–37
The Twilight Zone (television series,
1959–1964), xxi, 136, 145, 151,
257–269

the uncanny, xiii, 14, 137, 139, 142,
175–78, 182, 213n12, 259, 262, 272,
276
United Nations, 136–149
Unknown Soldier, 129–130, 133n67,
135, 271, 278
Uryupin (village), 24, 33, 35
USS *Tiger Shark* (fictional ship). *See* ships

vampires, xvii–xviii, 3–23, 24–37, 38–52,
59, 157, 169n20, 175, 179, 238,
240, 245–47; as allies, 24–27, 238,
249; brutality of, 7, 34–35, 42–43,
45, 47; created by science, 42–45;
embodiments of evil, 27–28, 29, 36,
44, 46, 47; as enemies, 3–23, 27, 42–
45; Old World associations, 4, 11, 39,
179; in Slavic folklore, 27–29, 36, 179
*Vampires, Burial, and Death: Folklore and
Reality*, 131
Van Riper, A. Bowdoin, xi–xxii, 38–52,
252n29, 255, 299
the Vanished Battalion, 121
vengeance, xx, 9, 35, 59, 75, 87, 160,
168, 176, 196–98, 221–37, 244–45,
263–66, 285–298
veterans, 114, 257, 258–62, 264–65;
Franco-Prussian War, 111; Vietnam
War, xvii–xix, 91–106, 155–172,
170n26, 242; World War I, 40, 108–
109, 130–131; World War II, 107,
140, 161, 231, 257–61
Vidler, Anthony, 192, 199n12, 200

Viet Cong. *See* guerillas
Vietnam War, 45, 50n26; and American
culture, xxi, 114, 116, 147, 158,
167–69, 241–42, 258; and Asian
culture, 231–32, 235n33, 296–97;
media images, 158, 160–62, 166–67,
171n42, 222, 238–39, 250–51,
288–90; undead narratives of, xix–xxi,
91–106, 155–172, 250–51, 285–298.
See also First Indochina War; veterans
violence, interrogation of, xxi, 33–35, 36,
79, 83–84, 86–88, 211, 228, 267. *See
also* brutality
Vivian, Bradford, 244, 252n22, 256
von Richthofen, Manfred ("The Red
Baron"), xviii, 39–41, 49n4
voordalak(i), 26–36

war: effect on women, 34, 57, 143, 161,
183, 191, 221–37, 286, 288, 289,
296–97; language and, 173–86; play
instinct and, 208–213; psychological
effects of, 88, 122, 126–127, 138–39,
215n32, 257–261; theories of, xx,
202–203, 208–216, 215n34n37, 303
War against War! (1924), 275, 284
war crimes, xvi, 75–76, 183, 188–92. *See
also* brutality in war; death camps; the
Holocaust
war economy, 54
war film (genre), 81, 88, 93, 114, 118–19,
155–56, 158, 162 166–68, 288–92
War of the Dead (2011), 56, 71
"The War That Time Forgot," 108, 240,
252n10
Ward, James J. xviii, 53–71, 303
Webley, Steve, xx, 201–216, 303
Wehrmacht, 53, 55, 59, 65n2, 68, 216
Weird War Tales (comic book), xxi,
238–256
werewolf, 28, 55, 57–58, 238, 241, 247
Western Front, 40, 118–122, 127–130,
245
Westfront 1918 (film, 1930), 119
Wilson, F. Paul, xix, 173–186

About the Editors
and Contributors

Cynthia J. Miller is a cultural anthropologist specializing in popular culture and visual media. Her writing has appeared in a wide range of journals and anthologies across the disciplines. She is the editor of *Too Bold for the Box Office: The Mockumentary, from Big Screen to Small* (2012), and coeditor of *Undead in the West: Vampires, Zombies, Mummies, and Ghosts on the Cinematic Frontier* and *Undead in the West II: They Just Keep Coming* (both with A. Bowdoin Van Riper, 2012, 2013), *1950s "Rocketman" TV Series and Their Fans: Cadets, Rangers, and Junior Space Men* (with A. Bowdoin Van Riper, 2012), *Steaming into a Victorian Future* (with Julie Anne Taddeo, 2012), *Border Visions: Identity and Diaspora in Film* (with Jakub Kazecki and Karen A. Ritzenhoff, 2013), and *International Westerns: Re-Locating the Frontier* (with A. Bowdoin Van Riper, 2013). She is also Film Review Editor for the journal *Film & History*, and series editor for Rowman & Littlefield's *Film and History* book series.

A. Bowdoin Van Riper is a historian who specializes in depictions of science and technology in popular culture. His publications include *Science in Popular Culture: A Reference Guide* (2002); *Imagining Flight: Aviation and the Popular Culture* (2003); *Rockets and Missiles: The Life Story of a Technology* (2004; rpt. 2007); and *A Biographical Encyclopedia of Scientists and Inventors in American Film and Television* (2011). He was guest-editor, with Cynthia J. Miller, of a special two-issue themed volume (Spring/Fall 2010) of *Film & History* ("Images of Science and Technology in Film,") and the editor of *Learning from Mickey, Donald, and Walt: Essays on Disney's Edutainment Films* (2011). He is also coeditor, with Cynthia J. Miller, of *Undead in the West: Vampires, Zombies, Mummies, and Ghosts on the Cinematic Frontier* and *Undead in the West II: They Just Keep Coming* (2012, 2013), *1950s "Rocketman" TV Series and their Fans: Cadets,*

Rangers, and Junior Space Men (2012), and *International Westerns: Re-Locating the Frontier* (2013).

* * *

Thomas Robert Argiro is an associate professor of English in the Department of Foreign Languages and Literature at Tunghai University, Taichung, Taiwan. His specializations include American literature, ethnic literature, postmodernism, literary theory, and cultural studies. His publications include an article in the *Mississippi Quarterly*, "Miss Emily after Dark," and an article in the *Journal for Cultural Research* treating the mysterious figure Saint Germain. Other pieces include an article in *MELUS* on William Faulkner's representations of Italian Americans, and a book chapter comparing Thomas Pynchon's novel *Vineland* and the television series the *X Files* in *The X Files and Literature: Unweaving the Story, Unraveling the Lie to Find the Truth*. His book chapter on Mark Twain's "To the Person Sitting in Darkness" appears in the collection *Guerre et race dans l'aire anglophone*.

Vincent Casaregola is a professor of English and the director of film studies at Saint Louis University. His areas of interest include film and media studies, rhetorical studies, and American literature from 1900 to the present. His book *Theaters of War* (2009) examines the American representation of World War II, in literature and on film, from the war itself up to the twenty-first century. He has published numerous academic articles and book chapters, along with poetry and creative nonfiction, and he has won several awards for creative writing. He also serves on the boards of directors of the Media Ecology Association and the St. Louis Poetry Center.

Christina V. Cedillo is currently assistant professor of English in the Languages and Literature Department at Northeastern State University in Broken Arrow, Oklahoma, where she teaches classes in modern rhetorical theory, women's studies, and creative writing. She received her PhD in 2011 from Texas A&M University, where she concentrated in histories of rhetoric, with minor fields in women's and gender studies and medieval studies. Her research focuses on the intersections of race and gender in the construction of embodied rhetorics. In her spare time, she plays video games, obsesses over *Doctor Who*, and dotes on her Sheltie pup, Cilantro.

Terence Check, who received his PhD from the University of Pittsburgh, is professor of communication and chair of the Communication Department at the College of St. Benedict and St. John's University in Minnesota, where he also serves as chair of the Joint Faculty Assembly. His research and teaching interests are in the areas of rhetoric and public address, environmental communication and advocacy, and popular culture studies. He has published work in *Environmental Communication: A Journal of Nature & Culture*, as well as anthologies.

Katherine Kelp-Stebbins is an assistant professor of English at Palomar College, San Marcos, California. She received her PhD in comparative literature in 2014 from UC Santa Barbara. Her work examines comics and visual media as tools for rethinking world literature and remapping transnational media flows. She is interested in decolonial and feminist methodologies for research and teaching. She has published articles in *Studies in Comics* and *Media Fields*.

Christina M. Knopf is an associate professor of communication at SUNY, Potsdam, where she teaches courses in rhetoric and communication theory. She holds a PhD in sociology and communication from the University at Albany. Her research explores representations of war and the military, and her articles have appeared in *nano, Political and Military Sociology: An Annual Review, The Air and Space Power Journal-Africa & Francophonie*, and several edited books. She is the author of the forthcoming book *The Comic Art of War: A Critical Study of Military Cartoons, 1805–2014, with a Guide to Artists*.

Amanda Landa is a PhD candidate at the University of Texas–Austin in the Department of Radio-Television-Film, writing her dissertation "No Regrets for our Youth: Contemporary Japanese Genre Film." In addition, her research focuses on Japanese anime and transnational East Asian film, most specifically on Japanese and South Korean television, film, and popular culture.

Paul O'Connor is a hands-on pop culture veteran, designing video games and writing comic books for better than thirty years. He is presently design director for Machine Zone San Diego, a mobile games development studio. Paul's latest comic project is *4 Seconds*, an original noir thriller for Thrillbent.com, a premiere site pioneering new techniques in digital comics storytelling. Since 2011, Paul has published *Longbox Graveyard* (www.longboxgraveyard.com) a weekly pop culture blog examining the Bronze and Silver Ages of comics.

Fernando Gabriel Pagnoni Berns currently works at Universidad de Buenos Aires (UBA), Facultad de Filosofía y Letras (Argentina), as graduate teaching assistant of "Literatura de las Artes Combinadas II." He teaches seminars on American Horror Cinema and Euro Horror. He is director of the research group on horror cinema "Grite" and has published essays in *Undead in the West*, edited by Cynthia Miller and A. Bowdoin Van Riper, *To See the Saw Movies: Essays on Torture Porn and Post 9/11 Horror*, edited by John Wallis, and *Reading Richard Matheson: A Critical Survey*, edited by Cheyenne Mathews, among others.

Thomas Prasch is professor and chair of the Department of History, Washburn University. He served as film-review editor for the *American Historical Review* from 1995 to 2004, and since 2001 he has edited a biannual selection of film reviews for *Kansas History*. Recent publications include "Blood on the Border: The Mexican Frontier in *Vampires*" (1998) and "*Vampires: Los Muertos*" (2002), in Cynthia Miller and A. Bowdoin Van Riper, eds., *Undead in the West: Vampires, Zombies, Mummies and Ghosts on the Cinematic Frontier* (2012); "Between What Is and What If: Kevin Willmott's CSA" in Cynthia Miller, ed., *Too Bold for the Box Office: The Mockumentary from Big Screen to Small* (2012); and entries on *Born on the Fourth of July*, *Alexander*, and "Appendix A: *JFK* and the Critics," in James Welsh and Donald Whaley, eds., *The Oliver Stone Encyclopedia* (2013).

Michael C. Reiff has taught at University at Buffalo, Buffalo State College Cayuga Community College, and Onondaga Community College. He is currently a teacher of Film, Media Production and Broadcasting and World Literature at Ithaca High School in Ithaca, New York. He is also the instructor and creator of the Auburn Film Seminar through Cayuga Community College, a noncredit course open to the public, which is in partnership with the Cayuga Museum of History and Art in Auburn, New York. He has also curated the "Making Movies" film series, featuring independent New York State filmmakers, and presented by the Schweinfurth Memorial Art Center in Auburn. Michael has been published in *Film & History* as well as the academic anthologies *Undead in the West* and *International Westerns*. Michael is currently developing media literacy curricula and programs for high schools, community colleges, and library programs.

Robert A. Saunders is a professor in the Department of History and Political Science at Farmingdale State College–SUNY, where he teaches courses on comparative religions, global politics, and world history. His research explores the impact of popular culture on geopolitics, nationalism, and religious identity. Dr. Saunders is author of three books, including *The Many Faces of Sacha Baron Cohen: Politics, Parody, and the Battle over Borat* (2008) and *Ethnopolitics in Cyberspace: The Internet, Minority Nationalism, and the Web of Identity* (2010). His research has appeared in the journals *Progress in Human Geography*, *Geopolitics*, *Slavic Review*, and *Nations and Nationalism*, among others.

Marzena Sokołowska-Paryż is an associate professor at the Institute of English Studies, University of Warsaw, Poland, where she teaches courses on contemporary British and Commonwealth literature, with specific emphasis on war fiction and film in relation to history, memory, and national identity. She is the author of *Reimagining the War Memorial, Reinterpreting the Great War: The Formats of*

British Commemorative Fiction (2012) and *The Myth of War in British and Polish Poetry, 1939–1945* (2002). Her most recent project is *The Great War in Post-Memory Literature and Film*, coedited with Martin Löschnigg (2014).

Christopher D. Stone is an assistant professor of history at University of Wisconsin–Manitowoc. He has presented at conferences organized by the Organization of American Historians, Popular Culture Association, Midwest Popular Culture Association, *Film & History*, and Queens University. He has been published in the *OAH Magazine of History; Historical Journal of Film, Radio and Television; Southwest Historical Quarterly; Indiana Magazine of History;* and *Film & History*. His most recent publication, "Comin' Back to the Sixties: Mobilizing Music and Performing Politics, 1988–1990," appears in *Anxiety Muted: American Film Music in a Suburban Age* (2014). His current research focuses on depictions and invocations of the sixties in American cinema.

James J. Ward is professor of history at Cedar Crest College in Allentown, Pennsylvania, where he teaches courses in European and German history, urban history, and film and history. His articles have appeared in *The Journal of Contemporary History, Central European History, The Journal of Popular Culture,* and *Film & History*, among others. He has published a number of essays on representations of the Nazis in film, including in the science fiction and horror genres. He attributes his interest in the latter both to their relevance to some of the courses he teaches and to his exposure to such classic examples as *She Demons* (1958) and *They Saved Hitler's Brain* (1963) at an impressionable age. His most recent research focuses on the nexus of zombies and pornography, in which the Nazis, so far, have yet to make an appearance.

Steve Webley is a lecturer at Staffordshire University, UK. He currently runs MINISTRY—the military and civil simulation technology research and enterprise institute—in the Games Technology Department. His research has three interlinked spheres: the Clausewitzian study of war, psychoanalysis, and our enjoyment of the products of the military-industrial sector. Reading war studies through the lens of Lacanian psychoanalysis is key to his work, as it allows for the correct situating of Clausewitz as a post-Kantian and post-Hegelian philosopher, and places the marxisant critique of ideology as essential to understanding the role of entertainment and commerce in late-modern warfare. Along with war and game studies, he specializes in consultancy for war game and military simulation design and interactive narratology.